THE BRITISH WAY IN
COUNTER-INSURGENCY, 1945–1967

The British Way in Counter-Insurgency, 1945–1967

DAVID FRENCH

OXFORD
UNIVERSITY PRESS

OXFORD
UNIVERSITY PRESS

Great Clarendon Street, Oxford OX2 6DP

Oxford University Press is a department of the University of Oxford.
It furthers the University's objective of excellence in research, scholarship,
and education by publishing worldwide in

Oxford New York

Auckland Cape Town Dar es Salaam Hong Kong Karachi
Kuala Lumpur Madrid Melbourne Mexico City Nairobi
New Delhi Shanghai Taipei Toronto

With offices in

Argentina Austria Brazil Chile Czech Republic France Greece
Guatemala Hungary Italy Japan Poland Portugal Singapore
South Korea Switzerland Thailand Turkey Ukraine Vietnam

Oxford is a registered trade mark of Oxford University Press
in the UK and in certain other countries

Published in the United States
by Oxford University Press Inc., New York

British Library Cataloguing in Publication Data
Data available

Library of Congress Cataloging in Publication Data
Data available

Typeset by SPI Publisher Services, Pondicherry, India
Printed in Great Britain
on acid-free paper by
MPG Books Group, Bodmin and King's Lynn

ISBN 978-0-19-958796-4

1 3 5 7 9 10 8 6 4 2

Acknowledgements

Many friends and colleagues gave me help and encouragement above and beyond the call of duty while I was writing this book. I would especially like to thank Keith Neilson, who once again read my entire manuscript, and whose suggestions improved it in countless ways. Professor Richard Vinen, Drs Jim Beach, Huw Bennett, and Matthew Hughes, and Major-General John Sutherell offered me their knowledge and insights with unstinting generosity. Derek Page shared with me reminiscences of his time in Palestine, and Mrs Helen Matthews kindly sent me a copy of her father's recollections of his time there. Members of seminars at the universities of Kent, Hull, Oxford, and the Institute of Historical Research of the University of London, provided me with much needed constructive criticism, advice, and encouragement. None of the above is responsible for what appears here, but I am grateful to all of them. I alone am responsible for any errors of fact or interpretation.

The staffs of the following institutions have once again placed me in their debt by giving me every possible assistance: Essex Public Library inter-library loan system, the Imperial War Museum (Departments of Documents and the Sound Archive), the Liddell Hart Centre for Military Archives, King's College London, the National Army Museum, the National Archives at Kew, the Senate House Library and the Institute of Historical Research of the University of London, the Suffolk Record Office, Bury St Edmunds Branch, and University College London library.

Crown copyright material is reproduced under class Licence Number C2006 0000011 of OPSI and the Queen's Printer for Scotland. The following institutions and individuals have kindly given me permission to quote from material to which they own the copyright: the Department of Documents and the Sound Archives of the Imperial War Museum; the Trustees of the Liddell Hart Centre for Military Archives, King's College London; the Trustees of the National Army Museum; Colonel D. J. Lear, Mrs Isabel Oliphant, Mr James Paul; Lt.-Col. J. A. Rymer-Jones. Despite my best efforts I was unable to contact the holders of the copyrights to the papers of Brigadier D. F. A. T. Baines, Mr N. J. Baptiste, Major C. R. Butt, General Sir Kenneth Darling, Mr T. L. Hewitson, Mr Michael McConville, and Mrs J. M. Somerville. I hope that they will accept my apologies. All reasonable effort has been made to contact the holders of copyright materials reproduced in this book. Any omissions will be rectified in future printings if notice is given to the publisher.

This book is dedicated to my friends Alan and Caroline Russell, because it's time they had one.

David French

Contents

List of Abbreviations

BDCC	British Defence Co-ordinating Committee
BFAP	British Forces Arabian Peninsula
BGS	Brigadier General Staff
BTE	British Troops Egypt
CAB	Cabinet
CAF	Central African Federation
CCO	Clandestine Communist Organizations
CDS	Chief of the Defence Staff
CID	Criminal Investigation Department
CIGS	Chief of the Imperial General Staff
C-in-C	Commander-in-Chief
CO	Colonial Office
COIN	Counter-insurgency
Col.	Colonel
COMBRITBOR	Commander British Forces Borneo
COS	Chief of Staff
CT	Communist Terrorist
DCIGS	Deputy Chief of the Imperial General Staff
DDO	Deputy Director of Operations
DGMT	Director-General of Military Training
DJAG	Deputy Judge Advocate General
DMI	Director of Military Intelligence
DMO	Director of Military Operations
DO	Dominions Office
DPS	Director of Personal Services
DSO	Defence Security Officer
ECAC	Executive Committee of the Army Council
ECHR	European Convention on Human Rights
EHR	*English Historical Review*
EOKA	Ethniki Organosis Kyprion Agoniston (National Organization of Cypriot Fighters)
FARELF	Far Eastern Land Forces
FLOSY	Front for the Liberation of Occupied South Yemen
FM	Field Manual

FO	Foreign Office
FSA	Federation of South Arabia
Gen.	General
GOC	General Officer Commanding
GOC-in-C	General Officer Commanding-in-Chief
GSO	General Staff Officer
HQ	Headquarters
IBTs	Indonesian Border Terrorists
ICRC	International Committee of the Red Cross
ILO	International Labour Organization
INS	*Intelligence and National Security*
Intsum	Intelligence summary
IWMDoD	Imperial War Museum Department of Documents
IWMSA	Imperial War Museum Sound Archive
IZL	Irgun Zvai Leumi (National Military Organization)
JIC	Joint Intelligence Committee
JSS	*Journal of Strategic Studies*
JICH	*Journal of Imperial and Commonwealth History*
JRUSI	*Journal of the Royal United Services Institute*
KAR	King's African Rifles
KAU	Kenya African Union
KCA	Kikuyu Central Association
KEM	Kikuyu, Embu, and Meru
Lt.-Gen.	Lieutenant-General
LHCMA	Liddell Hart Centre for Military Archives, King's College London.
LIC	Local Intelligence Committee
Lt.-Col.	Lieutenant-Colonel
Maj.	Major
Maj.-Gen.	Major-General
MCP	Malayan Communist Party
MELF	Middle East Land Forces
MIO	Military Intelligence Officers
MI5	The UK Security Service
MML	*Manual of Military Law*
MOD	Ministry of Defence
MRLA	Malayan Races Liberation Army
NAC	Nyasaland African Congress
NAM	National Army Museum

NLF	National Liberation Front
OAG	Officer Administering the Government
OC	Officer Commanding
OCPD	Office Commanding Police District
Perintrep.	Periodical intelligence report
PKI	Partai Komunis Indonesia (Indonesian Communist Party)
PPP	Progressive People's Party
PRB	Partai Rakyat Brunei
PREM	Prime Minister's Office
PUS	Permanent Under Secretary
RWAFF	Royal West African Frontier Force
SAF	South Arabian Federation
SAS	Special Air Service
SIFE	Security Intelligence Far East
SIME	Security Intelligence Middle East
SW&I	*Small Wars and Insurgencies*
TNA	The National Archives
TNKU	Tentera Nasional Kalimantan Utara (National Army of North Kalimantan)
UN	United Nations
VAG	Vice Adjutant-General
VCDS	Vice Chief of the Defence Staff
VCIGS	Vice Chief of the Imperial General Staff
WO	War Office
YAR	Yemen Arab Republic

Introduction

In mid-1952 Michael McConville, a young District Officer in Malaya, met the new High Commissioner and Director of Operations, Lt.-Gen. Sir Gerald Templer. Templer was

> lithe, athletic, well-briefed and incisive. His dress was an elegant jungle-green tropical uniform splashed with a colourful display of medal ribbons. His voice rasped. In conversation, he pushed his red-banded cap to the back of his head, shifted his glasses to the end of his nose and peered disconcertingly over the top, the meanwhile making gestures with the swagger cane he carried. He looked a dangerous sort of general. His interrogation of me started with a jab in the navel from the cane, a move I found unendearing. The exchanges were crisp, he providing the crispness.
>
> 'How long have you been here?'
>
> 'Six weeks, Sir.'
>
> 'Where were you before?'
>
> 'Tapah.'
>
> 'For how long?'
>
> 'Eighteen months.'
>
> 'Before that?'
>
> 'Trinity,' I said. I should have added 'Dublin', but decided against it. The poke in the stomach still rankled.
>
> 'Oxford or Cambridge?'
>
> 'Trinity,' I repeated stubbornly.
>
> 'TCD?'
>
> 'Yes, Sir.'
>
> This biographical fragment seemed to cheer him up markedly. He pushed his cap even further back, beamed and thumped me on the shoulder.
>
> 'Arraboy,' he said approvingly, 'We'll show these English bastards how to run a war.'[1]

They, that is Templer and the Malayan campaign, have been doing so ever since, and not just the English. The Americans, too, have seen Templer as the personification of a successful counter-insurgency leader, and the Malayan campaign as the epitome of how to fight such a campaign.[2] Today British and

---

[1] M. McConville, 'General Templer's capitol idea'. Downloaded 30 March 2009 at http://www. themightyorgan.com/features_geese.html.

[2] D. Branch, 'Footprints in the sand: British colonial counterinsurgency and the war in Iraq', *Politics & Society*, vol. 38 (2010), 15–34; M. Moyar, *A Question of Command. Counterinsurgency from the Civil War to Iraq* (New Haven & London: Yale University Press, 2009), 109–32; W. Chin, 'Examining the Application of British counterinsurgency doctrine by the American Army in Iraq', *SW&I*, vol. 18 (2007), 1–26; R. W. Komer, *The Malayan Emergency in Retrospect: Organization of a*

American official field manuals still cite aspects of the campaign as examples of best practice.[3]

One reason for this is that the 'lessons' of the campaign were codified in a classic textbook of counter-insurgency, Sir Robert Thompson's *Defeating Communist Insurgency*. Published in 1966, it has remained in print ever since, both because it was written in plain language, and because it remains a text for our times.[4] Until the First World War it was acceptable for western governments to use brute force to stamp out insurgencies. But thereafter Wilsonian concepts of legitimacy and self-determination came to dominate thinking about the proper use of force. Templer himself recognized this shortly after arriving in Malaya, when he announced that victory would come not from pouring more troops into the jungle, 'but in the hearts and minds of the people'.[5]

What Thompson showed was how such a strategy could work.[6] Insurgents wished either to take over, or secede from, the colonial state. They employed guerrilla and/or terrorist tactics against the state's security forces, tried to rob the colonial authorities of their legitimacy, and to persuade or coerce the mass of the people into supporting them rather than the established government. If the counter-insurgents wanted to prevent this they had to isolate the active insurgents from the mass of the civil population who provided them with food, supplies, intelligence, recruits, and money. An insurgency was, therefore, a contest between the insurgents and the colonial state to win political legitimacy in the eyes of the civil population. The colonial state needed policemen and soldiers to prevent the insurgents from intimidating or coercing the civil population, but these forces should never, as laid down by law, employ more than the minimum necessary force to do so. While artillery and aircraft might kill some insurgents, they would also kill innocent bystanders, and a government that was willing to kill its own people was not likely to retain or regain their loyalty. The colonial government also had to resist calls by the security forces to ignore the law because it was too cumbersome to allow them to deal effectively with the insurgents. If the security forces broke the law by summarily executing or torturing prisoners, the government would undermine its own claims to legitimacy. To ensure that force was used with discrimination, the police, as the lead intelligence agency, had to create an efficient intelligence service in the guise of its Special Branch, able to distinguish the (guilty) insurgents from the mass of (innocent) bystanders. To ensure that they operated in harmony with all of the other agents of the colonial state, the policy framework

Successful Counterinsurgency Effort (Santa Monica, CA: Rand Corporation, 1972), (iii); D. H. Ucko, 'The Malayan Emergency: the legacy and relevance of a counter-insurgency success story', *Defence Studies*, vol. 10 (2010), 13–39.

[3] FM 3-24. Headquarters of the Army, *Counterinsurgency* (December 2006), 6-21–6-22, E2; MOD, *Joint Doctrine Publication 3–40. Security and Stabilization: The Military Contribution* (London: MOD, 2009), xx, 2–8, 4–34, 6–14, 8–16, 10–15.

[4] A. Mumford, 'Sir Robert Thompson's lessons for Iraq: bringing the "basic principles of counter-insurgency" into the 21st century', *Defence Studies*, vol. 10 (2010), 177–94.

[5] *Times*, 20 November 1952; J. Cloake, *Templer. Tiger of Malaya* (London: Harap, 1985), 1, 477.

[6] Sir R. Thompson, *Defeating Communist Insurgency. The Lessons of Malaya and Vietnam* (St Petersburg, FL: Hailer Publishing, 2005; originally published 1966).

within which soldiers, policemen and civil servants worked should be determined by a series of interlocking committees that brought them together to maintain the primacy of the civil power.

Thompson also recognized that an insurgency sprang from the civil population's legitimate grievances, and it was therefore incumbent upon the government to address them through socio-political reforms. These could include the concentration of scattered rural populations into 'New Villages'. These allowed the government not only to protect the people from being intimidated by the insurgents, but also to provide them with better health, education and social services. If the insurgents wanted access to the food and intelligence that the population had previously provided, they would have to fight for it on ground of the security forces own choosing. Population resettlement could, therefore, undermine the insurgents' political appeal, create a psychological barrier between them and the civil population, enable the government to rally the people behind it, and lead to the physical destruction of the insurgents' armed forces.

Thompson's analysis was seductive. He seemed to show that western liberal notions of what was right and wrong could be made compatible with the imperatives of waging war amongst the people, that force could be used effectively but with discrimination, and that a more just and prosperous society could emerge from the struggle. His ideas have provided the intellectual underpinning of numerous studies, not just of the Malayan campaign, but also of other campaigns fought in the 'classical' age of counter-insurgency during the era of decolonization.[7] For the British that period ran from the outbreak of the Zionist insurgency in Palestine in 1945 until their final withdrawal from Aden in 1967. The legacy of his work has endured. Other practitioners, such as Julian Paget and Frank Kitson, elaborated upon his basic thesis, and his principles are still cited in modern British and American doctrinal publications.[8] In 2009 the Ministry of Defence codified them as being:

The government must have a clear political aim: to establish and maintain a free, independent and united country which is politically and economically stable and viable.

- The government must function in accordance with the law.
- The government must have an overall plan.

[7] D. Kilcullen, 'Counterinsurgency *redux*', *Survival: Global Politics and Strategy*, vol. 48 (2006), 111–30.

[8] J. Paget, *Counter-Insurgency Campaigning* (London: Faber & Faber, 1967); F. Kitson, *Low Intensity Operations. Subversion, Insurgency, Peace-Keeping* (London: Faber & Faber, 1971); US Army and Marine Corps's Field Manual, *FM 3-24/*MCWP 3-33.5, Counterinsurgency*, published in December 2006, contains two approving references to Thompson's book. MOD, *Army Doctrine Publication. Vol. 1 Operations* (London: DGD&D/18/34/46, 1994), 142–5; MOD, *Joint Warfare Publication (JW3-50). Military Contribution to Peace Support Operations* (London: MOD: 2nd edn, 2004), 120. They still form the basis of teaching about counter-insurgency at the MOD's Joint Services Command and Staff College. See Joint Services Command and Staff College, 'Library Bibliography: Research Guide Series. Counterinsurgency (COIN)', downloaded 12 July 2009 at http://www.da.mod.uk/colleges/jscsc/jscsc-library/bibliographies/research-guides.

- The government must give priority to defeating the political subversion, not the guerrillas.

- In the guerrilla phase of an emergency, a government must secure its base areas first.[9]

Some of those who have followed in Thompson's footsteps have also pointed to ways in which they believed British practice was exceptional compared to that of other colonial powers. The first was the insistence that the security forces had to operate within a legal framework severely constricting the degree of force they could employ. Although conceding that there was some evidence that the security forces did occasionally misbehave, they have contended that this was the exception, not the rule, and that those responsible were usually members of locally raised militias, not regular soldiers.[10] They have also claimed that the British learned from their mistakes, and by gathering, analysing and disseminating the lessons of their campaigns, created a virtuous counter-insurgency learning cycle.[11] The fragmented structure of the British army, based on the regimental system, created a military culture which made it easy for the army to dispense with conventional tactics and to adopt a highly decentralized approach based on small units and what later analysts have called 'distributed operations'.[12] Finally, although their record was occasionally chequered, on balance they won more campaigns that they lost.[13] 'The withdrawal from Empire', according to Sir William Jackson, a former Quartermaster-General, 'although precipitate in historical perspective, never became a rout; nor did it cost as much blood and treasure as the French, Dutch, Belgian and Portuguese withdrawals, or as the humiliating American fiasco in Vietnam.'[14] It was that, according to John Pimlott, who taught generations of British officer cadets at the Royal Military Academy Sandhurst, that 'makes a study of British techniques essential to any assessment of counter-insurgency in the modern age, particularly when it is borne in mind that other Western powers have spent the same period facing humiliation and defeat at the hands of similar insurgent groups.'[15]

This mode of analysis has become so dominant that some writers have claimed that they constitute an ' "Ideal Type" of British counterinsurgency' which is distinguished by the implementation of six 'benchmarks'—'The importance of

---

[9] MOD, *Joint Doctrine Publication 3-40. Security and Stabilization: The Military Contribution* (London: MOD, 2009), 2–8.

[10] T. R. Mockaitis, *British Counterinsurgency, 1919–60* (London: Macmillan, 1990).

[11] J. A. Nagl, *Learning to Eat Soup with a Knife. Counterinsurgency Lessons from Malaya and Vietnam* (Chicago: University of Chicago Press, 2002/2005), 79–80, 95–8, 105–7; R. Gregorian, ' "Jungle bashing" in Malaya: towards a formal tactical doctrine', *SW&I*, vol. 5 (1994), 338–59.

[12] Lt.-Col. R. M. Cassidy, 'The British army and counter-insurgency: the salience of military culture', *Military Review*, May–June 2005, 55; D. Ucko, 'Countering insurgents through distributed operations: insights from Malaya 1948–1960', *JSS*, vol. 30 (2007), 48–72.

[13] Lt.-Col. M. Dewar, *Brush Fire Wars. Minor Campaigns of the British Army since 1945* (London: Robert Hale, 1984), 180.

[14] Gen. Sir W. Jackson, *Withdrawal From Empire. A Military View* (London: Batsford: 1986), 248.

[15] J. Pimlott, 'The British Army: the Dhofar campaign, 1970–1975', in I. F. W. Beckett and J. Pimlott (eds), *Armed Forces and Modern Counter-insurgency* (New York: St Martin's Press, 1985), 16.

coordinated government machinery; Defeat insurgent subversion not the insurgent per se; Use minimum force; Adhere to the law; "Clear and hold" not "search and destroy"; Operations should be intelligence-led; and, Success is obtained by political settlement.' However, some analysts are also quick to enter two caveats. They accept that 'There will be disagreements as to the finer points of this model and as to the degree to which it has been applied with any real consistency,' and, 'The degree to which the standard historical narrative of British counter-insurgency theory in the post-war period is reflective of actual practice is a matter of some dispute, but must remain beyond the scope of this particular article.'[16] It is not, however, beyond the scope of this book. It will focus on precisely that question. To what extent did British soldiers, policemen, colonial civil servants, and politicians in London between 1945 and 1967 put into practise the 'Ideal Type' of British counter-insurgency as identified by Thompson and those who have elaborated on his principles?

Such an investigation is timely because the received wisdom of the applicability of this 'dominant paradigm' has increasingly been called into question.[17] In the early 1990s John Newsinger insisted that much of the existing literature minimized the degree of force the British were willing to employ. He contended that outright brutality was often a hallmark of their operations, and that the only reason the British did not embark upon the same policy of large-scale violence that characterized the French in Algeria, the Americans in Vietnam, the Portuguese in Angola, and the Soviets in Afghanistan was because their politicians decided to withdraw rather than confront full-scale rebellions in large and heavily populated colonies.[18] More recently other writers, notably Ashley Jackson, Hew Strachan, Paul Dixon, and Alex Marshall, have echoed Newsinger's insistence that the Thompson-inspired discourse represents a serious misreading of what really happened. Strachan has argued that winning hearts and minds was not 'about being nice to the natives, but about giving them the firm smack of government. "Hearts and minds" denoted authority, not appeasement.'[19] The British usually not only deployed their army, but they also employed an array of other security organizations, who were not always committed to fighting with kid gloves. Far from being determined to use only minimum force, they readily committed the maximum possible force they could deploy and had no hesitation in employing what Jackson called 'methods of dubious legality' to intimidate the civil population. Winning hearts and minds was 'as much about creating fear as winning the socio-economic battle for the support of the general population'.[20]

[16] D. Betz and A. Cormack, 'Iraq, Afghanistan and British strategy', *Orbis* (Spring 2009), 321–2.

[17] Kilcullen, 'Counterinsurgency *redux*', 111.

[18] J. Newsinger, Review of T. R. Mockaitis, *British counterinsurgency 1919–1960*, *Race and Class*, vol. 34 (1992), 96–8; J. Newsinger, *British Counterinsurgency from Palestine to Northern Ireland* (London: Palgrave, 2002).

[19] H. Strachan, 'British counter-insurgency from Malaya to Iraq', *JRUSI*, vol. 152 (2007), 8.

[20] A. Jackson, 'British counter-insurgency in history: a useful historical precedent?' *British Army Review*, no. 139 (2006), 12; P. Dixon, '"Hearts and minds"? British counter-insurgency from Malaya to Iraq', *JSS*, vol. 32 (2009), 353–81; A. Marshall, 'Imperial nostalgia, the liberal lie, and the perils of postmodern counterinsurgency', *SW&I*, vol. 21 (2010), 233–58.

Several of the issues raised by Newsinger and others have been the subject of detailed historical research. Some commentators have pointed to the fact that almost invariably, at the start of each insurgency, and operating without adequate intelligence, the security forces fell back on large-scale drives and clumsy cordon and search operations in an effort to locate their enemies. This suggested that the British did not have an institutional memory and that lessons learnt in one campaign were not transmitted to those who were conducting the next one.[21] Others have suggested that on occasion the British were willing to act with considerable ruthlessness. In Malaya they began the campaign by mounting wide-spread search and destroy operations, which were both ineffective and conducted with considerable brutality. These subsequently gave way to a harsh but highly effective regime of population control that was the real foundation of their success and which had swung the campaign in their favour even before Templer arrived.[22]

In the case of Kenya, David Anderson has demonstrated the manifold ways the colonial authorities manipulated the legal system to mete out rough justice to Mau Mau suspects.[23] Caroline Elkins, claiming to have uncovered evidence that was deliberately hidden from public scrutiny at the time, argued that the colonial authorities created a system of detention and rehabilitation camps for Mau Mau detainees that bore a striking resemblance to Stalin's gulag. Over a million people were subject to state surveillance in barbed-wire surrounded villages.[24] Huw Bennett has shown that the army did engage in the violent coercion of the civilian population.[25] Daniel Branch has examined the role of the home guard in coercing their neighbours into submitting to the colonial state.[26] The statistical foundations underpinning Elkins's charge that the British practised genocide against the Kikuyu

---

[21] C. McInnes, *Hot War, Cold War. The British Army's Way in Warfare 1945–95* (London: Brassey's, 1996), 146–7; Betz and Cormack, 'Iraq, Afghanistan and British strategy', 323; J. Kizley, 'Learning about counter-insurgency', *JRUSI*, vol. 151 (2006), 16–17.

[22] R. Stubbs, *Hearts and Minds in Guerrilla Warfare. The Malayan Emergency 1948–60* (Oxford: OUP, 1989); K. Hack, 'British intelligence and counter-insurgency in the era of decolonisation: the example of Malaya,' *INS*, vol. 14 (1999), 124–55; *idem*, 'Corpses, prisoners of war and captured documents: British and Communist narratives of the Malayan Emergency, and the dynamics of intelligence transformation', *INS*, vol. 14 (1999), 211–41. For attempts to rebut Hack's thesis see K. Ramakrishna, 'Anatomy of a Collapse: Explaining the Malayan Communist Mass Surrenders of 1958', *War And Society*, vol. 21 (2003), 109–33; S. C. Smith, 'General Templer and counter-insurgency in Malaya: hearts and minds, intelligence, and propaganda,' *INS*, vol. 16 (2001), 60–78.

[23] D. Anderson, *Histories of the Hanged. Britain's Dirty War in Kenya and the End of Empire* (London: Weidenfeld & Nicolson, 2005).

[24] C. Elkins, *Britain's Gulag. The Brutal End of Empire in Kenya* (London: Jonathan Cape, 2005).

[25] H. C. Bennett, 'British Army counterinsurgency and the use of force in Kenya, 1952–56' (Ph.D. dissertation, University of Wales, Aberystwyth, 2007). Charges such as these have produced sometimes impassioned rebuttals. See, for example, R. Thornton, '"Minimum force": a reply to Huw Bennett', *SW&I*, vol. 20 (2009), 215–26. A story published in *Scotland on Sunday* in December 2003 about an alleged massacre in Malaya perpetrated by a battalion of the Scots Guards in 1948 brought forth a series of old soldiers (none of whom were present or serving with the battalion at the time of the events surrounding the allegations) ready to defend the reputation of the regiment. (See K. Bayer and G. Ogilvy, 'Veterans' fury at "Malay massacre" claim', *Scotland on Sunday*, 14 December 2003, accessed 17 November 2006 at http://scotlandonsunday.scotsman.com/index.cfm?id=1371332003.)

[26] D. Branch, *Defeating Mau Mau, Creating Kenya. Counterinsurgency, Civil War, and Decolonization* (Cambridge: Cambridge University Press, 2009).

have been questioned.[27] But as one of Elkins' critics noted, the conclusion that she and Anderson reached, that wholesale repression could be an effective counter-insurgency doctrine, still stands.[28] A brief comparative study of the campaigns in Malaya and Kenya points to the same conclusion. In both campaigns the security forces resorted to housing the civil population behind barbed-wire fences. But only in Malaya did they do much to try to improve the conditions of life of their captive population. Yet in both cases the security forces won. This suggests that efforts to win the 'hearts and minds' of the population through political reforms or economic development were of little account. The key to a successful counter-insurgency campaign was not winning the hearts and minds of the population, but establishing physical control over them.[29]

These issues are of more than just historical interest. They are important because much contemporary British counter-insurgency doctrine is based upon historical arguments that are at best ill-informed, and at worst almost the opposite of what actually happened.[30] Before they moved into Helmand in Afghanistan in 2006 British troops studied 'how we dealt with the Malaya insurgency of the 1950s and how we were going to use the same strategy of first creating these secure zones or ink-spots around the main locations of Lashkar Gah and Gereshk and then move out.'[31] But in 2007, 'Young officers returning from Afghanistan and Iraq are saying with some asperity that global insurgency will not be overcome by a doctrine that resembles a "stretched version of the Malaya campaign".'[32]

There are two weaknesses in much of the literature on how the British conducted counter-insurgency operations between 1945 and 1967. Historians have written studies in which they have drawn upon considerable bodies of primary sources, but have usually focused on just a single campaign. This makes it impossible to determine how and to what extent doctrine and practice developed over time. Political scientists have adopted a broader approach and made such comparisons. But they have sometimes done so on the basis of an inadequate grasp of the contingent circumstances of the case studies they have examined. This book will attempt to be both historical—in that its conclusions will be based upon a

[27] J. Blacker, 'The demography of Mau Mau: fertility and mortality in Kenya in the 1950s: a demographer's viewpoint', *African Affairs*, vol. 106 (2007), 205–27; P. Murphy, review of Elkins and Anderson, *History*, July 2006, 427–8; T. Parsons, review of Anderson and Elkins, *American Historical Review*, vol. 110 (2005), 913–14; D. Elstein, 'Tell me where I'm wrong', *London Review of Books*, vol. 27, no. 11, 2 June 2005; J. Darwin, 'No tea and farewell, just brutal repression', *Times Higher Education Supplement*, 30 September 2005, 25; B. A. Ogot, 'Review Article', *Journal of African History*, vol. 46 (2005), 493–505.
[28] S. Carruthers, 'Being beastly to the Mau Mau', *Twentieth Century British History*, vol. 16 (2005), 489–96.
[29] W. Markel, 'Draining the Swamp: The British strategy of population control', *Parameters*, Spring 2006, 35–48. Karl Hack has come to a similar conclusion from a different starting point, arguing that the MCP was effectively on the defensive even before Templer arrived in Malaya thanks to the strict policies of population control already put in place by his predecessors. See Hack, 'British intelligence and counter-insurgency,' 124–55.
[30] A. Jackson, 'British counter-insurgency in history: a useful historical precedent?' *British Army Review*, no. 139 (2006), 12–22; Dixon, '"Hearts and minds"?', 353–81.
[31] C. Lamb, 'What a bloody hopeless war; Interview', *Sunday Times*, 10 September 2006.
[32] J. Mackinlay, 'Is UK doctrine relevant to global insurgency', *JRUSI*, vol. 152 (2007), 34.

considerable body of archival material—and comparative. It draws its evidence from ten major counter-insurgency campaigns that the British mounted between 1945 and 1967: Palestine, Malaya, the Canal Zone, Kenya, British Guiana, Cyprus, Oman, Nyasaland, Borneo, and Aden, as well as making passing references to other smaller but significant operations, such as the Gold Coast riots of 1948. But here it is appropriate to enter a warning. Anyone who hopes that this book will provide easy answers about how to conduct counter-insurgency operations in the early twenty-first century should stop reading now. This is not a 'how-to-do-it' manual. It is not an attempt to serve up pre-digested answers based upon historical precedents for those whose task it is to grapple with modern insurgencies. History cannot serve that purpose. The past and the present are different, for, as one recent commentator has noted, 'it is rare for the prevailing strategic, political and cultural conditions of one era to be replicated in another.'[33] Nor does it try to use the past as a body of examples that observers can plunder to support whatever theories they want to espouse. What it will try to do is to bring some historical rigour to the study of an area of the recent past that has sometimes lacked it. I agree with Tim Benbow that 'the past contains much potential wisdom that can, suitably modified, be of great benefit, if not providing a standard model or a checklist of points to guarantee success.'[34]

This book is divided into eight chapters. The first analyses the bureaucratic and military structures and ideologies that underpinned the British empire after 1945. Colonial governments declared states of emergency not because they were strong, but because they were weak. Modern counter-insurgents are wrong to claim that they have to work with failed or failing states, whereas their grandfathers in the colonies could work within more robust and 'effective state institutions'.[35] Insurgencies are not likely to happen if a state has robust and effective institutions. The next chapter examines the aims, organizations, and strategies of those groups trying to subvert the colonial state and how the British understood, or more usually misunderstood, their opponents' objectives. Chapter 3 explores the legal framework that colonial administrators evolved to combat insurgencies, and determines to what extent it is meaningful to argue that the British operated within clearly defined legal frameworks. It also suggests that, by refusing for political and practical reasons to impose martial law on rebellious colonies, the British had to find other means to harmonize the efforts of the various government agencies involved in counter-insurgency operations. Chapter 4 examines the wide variety of coercive methods that British security forces employed to terrorize civil populations into withdrawing their support from the insurgents, and Chapter 5 tries to determine whether they waged 'dirty wars' in their colonies. Chapter 6 examines the meaning and limitations of the British commitment to 'hearts and minds' by exploring how

---

[33] C. Tripodi, 'British policy on the North-West Frontier of India 1877–1947: a suitable precedent for the modern day?' Downloaded at: http://www.rusi.org/research/militarysciences/history/commentary/ref:C4AB377DACA5CF/, 28 September 2009.

[34] T. Benbow, 'Introduction', in T. Benbow and R. Thornton (eds), *Dimensions of Counter-insurgency. Applying Experience to Practice* (London: Routledge, 2008), xv.

[35] MOD, *Joint Doctrine Publication 3–40. Security and Stabilization*, 2–15, 2–17.

it was practised on the ground. Chapter 7 shows that claims that the British moved along a virtuous learning curve that enabled them to transfer 'lessons' from one campaign to another need to be heavily qualified. Finally, success (and failure) in counter-insurgency usually took years, not months, to become apparent, and Chapter 8 will consider how the British confronted the problem of sustaining their efforts over the long haul, and point to some of the reasons for their successes and failures.

A NOTE ON TERMINOLOGY

An insurgency was more than simply an armed rebellion. Insurgents commonly employed not only different kinds of force, ranging from guerrilla warfare to urban terrorism, but also different kinds of political tools to subvert the colonial state. Similarly, counter-insurgents did not just use force to crush their opponents, although I will argue that coercion in a variety of guises was a mainstay of British policy. They also employed political, economic, and social programmes to make support for the state more attractive than fighting against it.

Anyone writing about insurgency and counter-insurgency is confronted by two problems: what generic title to give to the state's opponents, and how to define the concepts of 'terrorism' and 'counter-terrorism'. The ways in which the British employed language such as 'thugs', 'bandits', and 'gangsters' to deny political legitimacy to their enemies is discussed in Chapter 2. To employ the same language would be to commit the same error. I have preferred to use the more neutral term 'insurgent' to describe those people who fought against British rule.

'Terrorism' is an elusive concept. It is trite, but true, that one side's terrorist is another side's freedom fighter. Here it will be defined as an attempt by actors, either insurgents or members of the security forces, to coerce a population through violent actions intended to induce extreme fear. In the case of the insurgents, this might include attacks on economic targets and public utilities, and the assassination of soldiers, policemen, civil servants, or civilians suspected of collaborating with the state. In the context of terrorism employed by the agents of the state, it is necessary to draw a distinction between 'counter-terrorism' and certain other measures, best labelled 'exemplary force', that were designed to have a lesser impact on the civil population. Measures that fell into this second category ranged from the establishment of road blocks to control the movement of goods and people, censorship to control the dissemination of ideas, through cordon and search operations, to the imposition of collective fines. Ostensibly their function was to allow the state to function effectively despite the efforts of the insurgents, to dislocate the insurgents' organization, and perhaps to enable the security forces to arrest their enemies. But they also had a second and even more important purpose, to demonstrate to the civil population the latent power of the government to control their lives. They entailed, as one soldier recognized, 'an element of embuggerance'.[36]

---

[36] IWMSA Accession No. 20320. Gen. Sir D. Thorne, reel 5.

Counter-terrorist measures were also intended to demonstrate the power of the state, but their impact on both the civil population and the active insurgents was qualitatively different. They went beyond disrupting and dislocating people's everyday existence, for they might deprive them of their liberty or even their lives. They involved the application of physical force leading to mass arrests, wholesale detention without trial, deportations, forcible population resettlement, and, at their extreme, the creation of free fire zones. From this it should be apparent that 'terrorism' and 'counter-terrorism' are not moral categories. They are tactics, and as such can be used for good or bad purposes.[37]

[37] M. L. R. Smith, 'William of Ockham, where are you when we need you? Reviewing modern terrorism studies', *Journal of Contemporary History*, vol. 44 (2009), 320–4.

1

The Colonial State

In 1960 the Colonial Secretary, Iain Macleod, recognized that 'that the process of disturbances in public order in the Colonial territories is rarely a sudden transformation from normal peaceable conditions to a state of great disorder, followed by an equally rapid return to normal. There is rather an initial phase of gradual development of conditions of unrest, intimidation, lawlessness and erosion of authority which, if not checked, leads to actual physical disorder and violence.'[1] That such a process had taken place not once, but many times in the preceding fifteen years, suggests that there were certain systemic weaknesses in the structure of the British colonial empire.

From the perspective of the early twenty-first century, and with the experience of conducting counter-insurgency operations in Iraq and Afghanistan, it is all too easy to draw a sharp distinction between the problems of government power that faced the British fifty years earlier and those they confront today. 'In classical COIN, the UK buttressed an existing colonial political order with effective state security, governance and political structures' and in such a situation 'UK forces and agencies controlled all levers of government.' Today, what is supposed to be different is that 'Recent operations, however, have been conducted within the context of state fragility and state failure.'[2] This distinction can be overdrawn. Because the British were the sovereign or the 'protecting' power in most of the territories where they operated (the Canal Zone was an exception), they did control the levers of state power. However, those levers were often fragile and inadequate. British colonies were never administered by strong and powerful governments, and the men on the ground knew it. In April 1959, Sir Richard Armitage lamented that 'the Government has always been extremely thin on the ground as regards the Provincial and District Administration and the Police. . . . We have never had any money here to build up extensive establishments and the problem now is what to do about the future?'[3] Armitage was writing about his own colony, Nyasaland. But he could have been writing about almost any colony.

---

[1] TNA CO 1055/207. I. Macleod to Sir E. Hone, 8 January 1960.
[2] MOD, *Security and Stabilization*, 2–15; See also A. Roberts, 'Doctrine and reality in Afghanistan', *Survival*, vol. 51 (2009), 33–4, 38.
[3] TNA CO 1015/1839. Armitage to Morgan, 18 April 1959.

THE STRUCTURE OF THE COLONIAL STATE

British colonial administrations were of two kinds, crown colonies and protect-orates. In the former the government was headed by the governor, a British civil servant answerable to a Cabinet Minister in London, the Colonial Secretary. The governor was assisted by civil servants and appointed Ministers, and in most cases by a legislative council. Their composition varied. Colonies that were close to or had reached internal self-government, like British Guiana in 1952, had legislative councils composed entirely of elected members. Colonies that were further from internal self-government had legislative councils that consisted of varying propor-tions of elected and nominated members. At the local level administration was controlled by a small number of British colonial civil servants serving as Provincial and District Commissioners and District Officers.[4]

There were exceptions to this model. British Guiana enjoyed the most 'advanced' constitution of any Crown Colony discussed in this book. Although the governor retained extensive reserve powers, day-to-day governance was in the hands of a bicameral legislature. The lower house, the Legislative Council, was elected on the basis of universal suffrage, but the members of the upper house, the State Council, were nominated by the Governor.[5] This was a system that left power dangerously divided. Elected representatives had effective control of the Legislature Council, and had a majority on the Executive Council (effectively the Cabinet), but the colony's dominant economic interest groups, particularly the Sugar Producers Association (SPA), still exerted power through the State Council and un-elected officials held the three key ministerial portfolios, those of the Chief Secretary, the Financial Secretary and the Attorney-General, and were responsible for defence, police, and law and order.[6] In Cyprus, the Legislative Council had been suspended following serious riots in 1931. Since then the island had been governed by a Governor assisted by an Executive Council of four official and three unofficial nominees. Palestine, although a territory that had been mandated to the British by the League of Nations, was run on similar lines to a Crown Colony. The governor was formally called the High Commissioner, there was no legislative council, but, as in Cyprus, he had the assistance of an appointed Advisory Council. In practice, however, the colonial administration in Jerusalem shared power, at least as far as its authority was concerned over the Yishuv, that is the Jewish community, with their spokesmen in the Jewish Agency.

British authority in the Federation of Malaya, Oman, and the SAF was even more diluted because they were protectorates. The indigenous rulers had handed control of their foreign and defence policy to the British, but continued to enjoy a

---

[4] TNA CAB 129/98/C(59)124. Colonial Secretary, Report of the Nyasaland Commission of Inquiry, 17 July 1959.

[5] TNA CO 859/772. [Cmd 8980]. *British Guiana. Suspension of the Constitution*, 20 October 1953.

[6] J. G. Rose, 'British colonial policy and the transfer of power in British Guiana, 1945–1964' (Ph.D. dissertation, University of London, 1992), 133–9.

considerable degree of domestic autonomy, although they were required to accept the 'recommendations' of a British 'adviser'. What that meant was explained by Julian Amery, then serving as a junior minister at the War Office in Harold Macmillan's government, when he described relations between Britain and the Sultan of Oman. The Sultanate was an independent state ruled by its own sultan, but it was linked to Britain by a treaty of friendship. '"In other words", explained Amery, "we give him help; we sometimes give him advice. But"—he gave me a knowing smile—"we do not give him orders."'[7]

A further layer of complexity was created by the fact that Malaya/Malaysia and South Arabia were Federations. The Federation of Malaya consisted of two British Crown Colonies, Malacca and Penang, and nine Malay States, each of which was a British protectorate, governed by its own sultan. In January 1946, the British had tried to reduce the sultans to figureheads, to extend citizenship rights to the Chinese and Indian immigrant populations, who made up nearly half of the population, and to centralize administrative and financial control in the hands of a British governor. But the majority Malay population were outraged both by the way their sultans were to be treated, and by the promise of political rights to the Chinese community. The British accepted that the new constitution was unworkable and came to a new compromise in the shape of the Federation. Established in February 1948, the Malay States remained protectorates governed by their own sultans, and as James Griffiths, the Colonial Secretary, explained in July 1950, 'the British Government has no jurisdiction in the States other than in matters of defence and foreign affairs; British advisers are attached to each Sultan and under the terms of the treaty the Sultan is obliged to follow any formal advice that may be tendered to him, but this power device has not in practice been exercised since the reoccupation.'[8] The British thus found themselves with the worst of two worlds. By offering and then withdrawing political concessions to the Chinese community they had alienated them from the government and predisposed them to support the Communist insurgents. Furthermore, the new constitution deprived the British of the kind of powerful, centralized government that might have been able to act decisively to coordinate the counter-insurgency campaign from the outset. When Malaysia was established in 1963 by the joining together of the Federation of Malaya with Singapore, Sabah (North Borneo) and Sarawak it, too, adhered to the Federal model.

Aden also consisted of separate entities that were only loosely connected. Aden proper was a Crown Colony governed by a British-appointed governor. To the north and east of the colony were the two dozen separate states of the East and West Aden Protectorates. This was an inhospitable and undeveloped region of 112,000 square miles, inhabited by 800,000 people. They were of no economic value to the British but they provided a kind of insulation for the colony. They were ruled by their own emirs and sheiks, although the real law in the region was administered by

---

[7] D. Smiley, *Arabian Assignment* (London: Leo Cooper, 1975), 5.
[8] TNA CAB 21/1681/MAL.C(50)27. Colonial Secretary, Cabinet Malaya Committee: General Background, 14 July 1950.

the rifle and the blood feud. Writing in 1959, a British intelligence officer concluded that 'The States themselves are headed by Rulers who do not have absolute power over their subjects. They are "first among equals" rather than despots, and nearly every male would like to carry a rifle and would be ready to use it. The Rulers are backed by treaties with HMG and helped with advice and funds, but in each State and in each tribe there is an opposition.'[9] Tribal warfare remained endemic through-out the protectorates. The British contained its worst effects by providing subsidies to tribal gendarmeries, by raising their own gendarmerie (the Aden Protectorate Levies), by dispatching RAF aircraft on occasional punitive air raids, and by paying stipends to rulers to buy their loyalty.[10] They created the SAF because they wanted to retain access both to the economically and strategically important port of Aden and to Khormaksar airfield, but without continuing to rule Aden directly themselves. They hoped that a Federation, dominated by the conservative rulers of the interior, not the radical nationalist politicians of Aden colony, would enable them to do so. In 1959 they began by creating the Federation of Arab Emirates of the South. It consisted of six states, later increased to twelve, of the Western Arabian Protectorates. In January 1963, London brought the project to completion by adding Aden colony to form the SAF.[11] That may have brought the British a step nearer to their political goal. But it also left responsibility for internal security dangerously divided between the Federal, State, and British authorities.[12]

The Canal Zone was neither a Crown Colony nor a protectorate. The legal foundation of the British position was the Anglo-Egyptian treaty of 1936. The treaty, which was due to expire in 1956, permitted the British to maintain a garrison of 10,000 troops and 400 pilots in the Canal Zone.[13] During the Second World War the garrison had swollen to many times that size, and, as it never returned to the treaty limits after 1945, the British remained in technical breach of the treaty. The garrison lived in an uneasy relationship with the Egyptian civil population and government. The base employed 44,000 Egyptians. The Egyptian state railway carried 30,000 tons of War Department stores and 85,000 personnel each month, and Port Said cleared 30,000 tons of British cargoes each month. There were supplies of fresh food in the Canal Zone sufficient for only between 40 and 60 days. If either Egyptian labour were withdrawn or the British were denied the use of these facilities, the base would become untenable.[14] A further cause for

[9] TNA WO 32/18518. Captain P. G. Boxhall to Col. J. H. S. Bowring, 29 June 1959.

[10] TNA CAB 129/92/C(58)79. Minister of State for Colonial Affairs, The Yemen, 14 April 1958; TNA DEFE 13/570. Draft Report on the Ministry and Force HQ Organization of the security forces of the Federation of South Arabia, 17 June 1964; S. C. Smith, 'Rulers and residents: British relations with the Aden Protectorate, 1937–1959', *Middle Eastern Studies*, vol. 31 (1995), 509–14.

[11] S. Mawby, *British Policy in Aden and the Protectorates 1955 to 1967. Last Outpost of a Middle East Empire* (London: Routledge, 2005), 183–5.

[12] TNA CO 1055/198. W. H. Formoy, Responsibility for Internal Security in Aden and the Federation of South Arabia, 8 January 1964; TNA DEFE 13/570. Draft Report on the Ministry and Force HQ Organization of the security forces of the Federation of South Arabia, 17 June 1964.

[13] L. Morsy, 'The military clauses of the Anglo-Egyptian Treaty of Friendship and Alliance, 1936', *International Journal of Middle East Studies*, vol. 16 (1984), 67–97.

[14] LHCMA. Gen. Sir H. E. Pyman mss 7/1/9. C-in-Cs Middle East to COS, London, 25 September 1947.

concern was the safety of British nationals and their property in Cairo and Alexandria, who had been left unprotected following the withdrawal of British forces from the cities of the Nile delta in 1947.[15]

But no matter what forms colonial government took, three features were common to all of them. The British authorities retained the right to exercise a wide range of special powers in an emergency. The nature of those powers will be examined in Chapter 3. Second, the Colonial Office could advise, and make recommendations to the governor on the spot, but, mindful of the lessons of 1776, officials and ministers in Whitehall were usually reluctant to override him, lest they made a difficult situation even worse. As one former colonial governor noted, 'One is reminded, firmly and correctly that Governors exist to govern, that the Colonial Office does not run Colonial territories, and that their job is to advise; if necessary, to exhort; but rarely, if ever, to command.'[16] For their part colonial administrators were jealous of their quasi-independence and usually resisted attempts by Whitehall to reduce their autonomy.[17] Third, the British administrative cadre were spread very thinly across the empire. The membership of the Colonial Administrative Service expanded after 1945, but even so in 1957 there were only 2,362 members of the Colonial Administrative Service in the whole of British Africa.[18]

British colonial government was a confidence trick. In normal times it worked because, although the British cadre was small, its members were generally competent, and because they could enlist the support of large numbers of local collaborators to do much of the work on the ground. But this approach meant that, if government was to function at all, Europeans had to work with the grain of local society and through local elites, each member of which became 'in effect a salaried government servant allowed, to a limited extent, to go his own way.'[19] That way could be difficult. The authority and legitimacy of local collaborators rested on their ability to preserve the well-being of their own people. But it also rested on their ability to exploit those same people on behalf of the colonial regime. For the British this was a cheap way to govern their empire, but it also placed limitations on what the colonial authorities could do. If they placed too many demands on their collaborators, the latters' legitimacy in the eyes of the people they helped to

[15] LHCMA. Gen. Sir H. E. Pyman mss 7/1/7. Diary entry, 12 July 1947; LHCMA. Gen. Sir H. E. Pyman mss 7/1/7. Pyman to CIGS, 13 July 1947; LHCMA. Gen. Sir H. E. Pyman mss 7/2/2. Notes for conference between CIGS and C-in-C MELF, 6 August 1947.

[16] TNA CAB 129/76/CP(54)89. Sir Gerald Templer, Report on Colonial Security, 23 April 1955; B. J. Berman, 'Bureaucracy and incumbent violence: colonial administration and the origins of the Mau Mau emergency', *British Journal of Political Science*, vol. 6 (1976), 143–75.

[17] IWMDoD. Field Marshal Lord Harding mss AFH5. George Sinclair to Harding, 12 November 1956.

[18] A. H. M. Kirk-Greene, 'The Thin White Line: the size of the British Colonial Service in Africa', *African Affairs*, vol. 79 (1980), 25–44; A. H. M. Kirk-Greene, *On Crown Service. A History of HM Colonial and Overseas Civil Service, 1837–1997* (London: I. B. Tauris, 1999), 39–91.

[19] TNA CAB 129/98/C(59)124. Colonial Secretary, Report of the Nyasaland Commission of Inquiry, 17 July 1959.

administer would evaporate.[20] Consequently it was only where local practices were thoroughly repugnant, or where they did not serve British political or economic interests, that British officials intervened.[21] Such interventions had to be carefully managed for the usually small police and military forces that provided the ultimate underpinning of colonial rule were often far away, and isolated officials could not easily summon their assistance. They had to learn not to give orders unless they were reasonably confident they would be obeyed, for to give orders that were not obeyed would reveal the hollowness of their authority.[22]

THE COLONIAL POLICE

Threatened by a breakdown of public order, colonial governments looked first to their own police forces.[23] Most colonial police forces had common weaknesses. Whitehall expected colonial administrations to pay for their own governments, including the police. Colonies were poor, and most governors were reluctant to impose heavy taxes lest in doing so they provoked unrest. In 1956 the Governor of Sarawak responded to suggestions from the Colonial Office that he should increase his police force by noting that taxpayers in the colony were already complaining about the cost of the police, and he was not willing to incur their further wrath without apparent good cause.[24] The result was that colonial police forces were small, under-equipped, and under-trained. In the early 1950s there were more policemen in the United Kingdom (71,392) than there were in the whole of the empire (1,160 gazetted senior European officers and 56,912 locally recruited rank-and-file policemen).[25] 'No one realises more than I do', wrote the governor of Nyasaland in 1952, 'the necessity for a fully trained and adequate Police Force in this territory, and I shall do my utmost to work to this end. The difficulty, of course, is finance and I am very much afraid that the Police, like all the other Departments of this Government, will continue to be short of funds since our financial position at the present moment is very precarious, and I am very much afraid that our revenue for next year will be substantially less than this year.'[26] On the ground that meant that a District Officer in Northern Nyasaland had a single European policeman and fifteen African constables and sergeants to police 100,000

---

[20] T. Spear, 'Neo-traditionalism and the limits of invention in British colonial Africa', *Journal of African History*, vol. 44 (2003), 3–27; R. L. Tignor, 'Colonial chiefs in chiefless societies', *Journal of Modern African Studies*, vol. 9 (1971), 339–59.

[21] D. Killingray, 'The maintenance of law and order in British colonial Africa', *African Affairs*, vol. 85 (1986), 411–37.

[22] J. W. Cell, 'Colonial rule', in J. M. Brown and Wm. Roger Louis (eds), *The Oxford History of the British Empire* (Oxford: Oxford University Press, 1999), 232–4.

[23] TNA CO 537/2768. Colonial Secretary, Communist infiltration and the security situation in the colonies, nd but *c.* 20 July 1948.

[24] TNA CO 1035/100. Sir A. Abell to Colonial Secretary, 14 September 1956.

[25] TNA CO 537/5440. Report of the Police Adviser to the Colonial Secretary, 28 December 1949; *Whitaker's Almanac, 1954* (London: John Whitaker, 1954).

[26] TNA CO 968/274. Sir George Colby (Governor Nyasaland) to J. B. Williams (CO), 7 August 1952.

people.[27] Colonial police forces were short of radios, transport, proper training, and in many cases accommodation.[28]

Effective policing also required the police to establish intimate relations with the people they were policing.[29] This rarely happened in the colonies. Colonial policemen were often unable to master the human terrain in which they operated because they were poorly positioned to understand the currents of opinion flowing through the societies they were policing. Unlike policemen in Britain, who were politically independent servants of the people, and whose main function was to prevent and detect crime, the main functions of colonial policemen were protecting the economic and political interests of the colonial state, and ensuring that the government was not overthrown.[30] This emphasis was further intensified after 1945 when many colonial police forces either created or expanded their paramilitary branches. By 1944 the Palestine Police had a 2,000-strong Police Mobile Force equipped with small arms and trained as light infantry. After the Palestine Police Force was disbanded in 1948, former members migrated to other colonies and put their experience to use. The Malayan Police Jungle Squads, created in 1948, the Kenya General Service Unit, and the Police Mobile Reserve division in Cyprus, were all based on the Palestine model.[31] Cheaper than soldiers, paramilitary police units could reduce the need for troops. The dozen police field force companies deployed in Eastern Malaysia by the end of 1965 were the equivalent of about three infantry battalions.[32] But they did so at the cost of placing still more distance between the police and the people.

The police were further distanced from the communities they policed by measures that the British took to maintain their political reliability. They ensured both that indigenous policemen who filled the ranks of the regular police force were not required to police their own ethnicity, and that the senior ranks of the force were filled by European officers.[33] In Palestine the police were kept deliberately aloof from both Arabs and Jews so that neither community could accuse them of favouring the other.[34] Caught between the two, they felt like 'piggy in the middle'.[35] In Malaya the Malay rulers had ensured that few Chinese joined the

---

[27] IWMSA. Accession No. 4716. N. Harvey, Transcript, 16.

[28] TNA CO 537/5421. W. C. Johnson to Sir C. Woolley, 11 April 1950.

[29] IWMSA. Accession No. 10392. R. C. Catling, Transcript, 4.

[30] G. Sinclair, *At the End of the Line. Colonial Policing and the Imperial Endgame, 1945–80* (Manchester: Manchester University Press, 2006); S. Hutchinson, 'The police role in counter-insurgency operations', *JRUSI*, vol. 114, no. 656 (1969), 56.

[31] C. Smith, 'Communal conflict and insurrection in Palestine, 1936–48', in D. M. Anderson and D. Killingray (eds), *Policing and Decolonisation. Politics, Nationalism and the Police, 1917–1965* (Manchester: Manchester University Press, 1992), 67–75; G. Sinclair, '"Get into a crack force and earn £20 a month and all found...": the influence of the Palestine Police upon Colonial Policing, 1922 to 1948', *European Review of History*, vol. 13 (2006), 49–65; TNA CAB 21/1682/COS(50)468. Director of Operations, Malaya, An appreciation of the military and political situation in Malaya as on 25 October 1950, 16 November 1950.

[32] TNA WO 305/3326. The Director of Borneo Operations, Quarterly Operation Report, 1 October 1965 to 31 December 1965, 17 January 1966.

[33] Killingray, 'The maintenance of law and order', 422–8.

[34] IWMSA. Accession No. 12208. J. A. S. Adolph, reels 1–2.

[35] IWMSA. Accession No. 10300. J. Sankey, reel 1.

police before 1948, while in Cyprus the minority Turkish population was over-represented in the force. The wholesale expansion of colonial forces once an emergency began usually meant importing senior British officers who knew little of the people or their culture. In 1948, 400 ex-Palestine police and other Europeans arrived in Malaya, few of whom could speak local languages or knew local customs. The rapid expansion of the Malayan police between 1948 and 1950 meant that the force was inexperienced, inadequately trained, poorly disciplined, and prone to take bribes and extort money. Unsurprisingly the civilian population had little faith in its efficiency or honesty.[36] In Kenya British police inspectors received little training before arriving in the colony, the African rank and file were poorly paid and often illiterate, the Kikuyu were under-represented in the force, and there were so few policemen that some areas, such as the shanty-towns of Nairobi, were practically no-go areas for them.[37] In most African colonies the regular police were supplemented by tribal policemen.[38] Their task was to uphold the principle of indirect rule by imposing customary laws where they were not utterly repugnant to British nostrums of right and wrong. But their venality meant that they were widely detested. In 1949, according to the Colonial Office's Police Adviser they were 'of a very variable standard in every respect and whatever merits there may be in their retention at the present time, it must be recognized that they provide no surety of a fair and impartial policing and would be no safeguard against internal disorder.'[39] Whether tribal police or regulars, they were usually so distrusted by the people they were policing that they were divorced from many sources of information that might have given them forewarning of political disaffection.[40]

The Colonial Office knew of these deficiencies and encouraged colonial governments to remedy them. Following riots in the Gold Coast in February 1948 that had left 26 dead and nearly 230 injured, and the declaration of a State of Emergency in Malay in June, the Colonial Secretary, Arthur Creech Jones, appointed a Colonial Police Adviser, subsequently entitled the Inspector-General of Colonial Police. He and his assistants visited colonies and made periodic

---

[36] TNA CAB 21/1682/COS(50)468. Director of Operations, Malaya, An appreciation of the military and political situation in Malaya as on 25 October 1950, 16 November 1950; TNA CAB 130/65/GEN 345/1. Note by the Secretary, Meeting with the Director of Operations, Federation of Malaya, 27 November 1950; TNA CAB 130/65/GEN 345/3. Colonial Secretary, Meeting with the Director of Operations, Federation of Malaya. Recruitment of Staff for Malaya, 30 November 1950; R. Stubbs, *Hearts and Minds in Guerrilla Warfare. The Malayan Emergency 1948–60* (Oxford: Oxford University Press, 1989), 72–4; A. J. Stockwell, 'Policing during the Malayan emergency, 1948–60: communism, communalism and decolonisation', in D. M. Anderson and D. Killingray (eds), *Policing and Decolonisation. Politics, Nationalism and the Police, 1917–1965* (Manchester: Manchester University Press, 1992), 106–9; IWMSA. Accession No. 10192. Sir R. Thompson, reel 2.

[37] D. Throup, 'Crime, politics and the police in colonial Kenya, 1939–63', in D. M. Anderson and D. Killingray (eds), *Policing and Decolonisation. Politics, Nationalism and the Police, 1917–1965* (Manchester: Manchester University Press, 1992), 133–8; P. Hewitt, *Kenya Cowboy. A Police Officer's Account of the Mau Mau Emergency* (London: Avon Books, 1999), 78–9.

[38] TNA CO 885/119. Record of the Conference of Colonial Police Commissioners at the Police College, Ryton-on-Dunsmore, 3–6 April 1951. Appendix V. Native Administration Police. TNA CAB 129/76/CP(55)89. Sir Gerald Templer, Report on Colonial Security, 23 April 1955.

[39] TNA CO 537/5440. Report of the Police Adviser to the Colonial Secretary, 28 December 1949.
[40] Ibid.

recommendations to governors about how to improve the efficiency of their police.[41] The Colonial Office also began to put its own house in order. In 1955 it established a separate Police Department to ensure that the Inspector-General's recommendations were acted upon, and an Intelligence and Security department to collate the information in the intelligence reports that were produced by each colony. But on the ground little happened. The Inspector-General could advise, and the Colonial Office could exhort. But unless the British Treasury was prepared to find the money, they could not compel a colony to act. In 1959, looking back over a decade of reports, the Inspector-General noted that he and his predecessors regularly made three recommendations: the need for adequate numbers of policeman to ensure the prevention and detection of crime, the need for a striking force for internal security duties, and the provision of satisfactory housing and pay to keep personnel happy and free from nationalist political pressures. But except in the case of a few rich colonies, lack of money had rendered most of their recommendations nugatory.[42] No amount of administrative tinkering in London could overcome the fact that it was often not until an emergency had begun that colonial governments were willing to dip their hands into their coffers and find the money needed to make their police efficient.

INTELLIGENCE MACHINERY

It is easy to assume that security forces fighting counter-insurgency campaigns in the pre-independence era enjoyed the inestimable advantage that, as soon as they arrived in the theatre of operations, they were presented with a comprehensive intelligence briefing based on an extensive knowledge of local events built up by the colony's own intelligence service.[43] They were rarely so fortunate. An effective intelligence system had to be able to perform five functions. Machinery had to be in place to determine which targets should be the focus of intelligence activity. Personnel had to be made available who were able to collect information about those targets. Machinery had to be in place to collate and analyse that information and turn it into intelligence. The intelligence then had to be disseminated to those who needed it quickly enough for them to act upon it. Finally, a parallel organization had to be in place to prevent the enemy from gathering intelligence about British activities. But the outset of most emergencies was characterized by a lack of

---

[41] TNA W0 191/87. Report by headquarters, Gold Coast District, on disturbances in the Gold Coast, 26 February to 31 March 1948; TNA CO 537/2768. Note of meeting of Deputy and Assistant Under Secretaries of State held by Sir T. Lloyd on 16 July 1948 to consider the creation of the post of Inspector-General of Colonial Police or of Police Adviser; TNA CO 537/2768. A meeting was held in the Secretary of State's office at 5.15pm on Friday, 30 July 1948.

[42] TNA CO 968/680. Minute by I. Stourton, 23 April 1959; TNA CAB 129/76/CP(55)89. Sir Gerald Templer, Report on Colonial Security, 23 April 1955.

[43] M. Crawshaw, '"Running a country". The British Colonial experience and its relevance to present-day concerns', *The Shrivenham Papers*, no. 3 (2007), 24.

intelligence, not a superfluity of it, and that lack bedevilled some of them through-out their course.

In August 1948, as part of his efforts to overhaul colonial policing and intelligence following Gold Coast riots and the outbreak of the Malayan emergency, Creech Jones asked every colony to examine its own intelligence machinery.[44] But the tone of his letter was significant. He asked and advised, he did not order. 'It is of course impossible to lay down in general terms a framework to the organisation of these services suitable to all Colonies', he conceded, but

> Experience has shown, however, that, whatever the structure of the particular intelli-gence organisation, it is essential that the central coordination of reports from the various sources shall be in the hands of a political officer of high calibre (not necessarily high rank), who will be in a position to devote the necessary time to this work. Only such an officer, whose business it is to see all reports from all sources, can adequately build up from small and superficially unrelated scraps of information a general picture of conditions as a whole, on the basis of which the importance of individual events and trends and be properly assessed and the central government is suitably advised. In some cases this is no doubt the existing arrangement, but where it is not, I hope that it will be found possible in the very near future to assign a suitable officer to this task which, as you will I feel sure agree, must now be regarded as of the first importance.[45]

Beyond that, the advice sent to colonial governments about the machinery they should establish was vague and contradictory. In May 1949, Sir Henry Gurney, the former Chief Secretary to the Palestine government and the current High Commissioner in Malaya, wrote a lengthy dispatch that was widely circulated to colonial governments recommending that the job should be done by the police Special Branch.[46] But the Joint Intelligence Committee, responsible in London for pre-paring comprehensive intelligence reports for the Cabinet, disagreed. It recom-mended that every colony should have its own LIC, bringing together experts not only from the Special Branch, the three armed services, and the administration, but also from MI5, which was responsible for counter-espionage in both Britain and the empire. Consequently the advice that went to colonies was non-committal, leaving those who wanted to do so ample opportunity to drag their feet.[47] Many did so. Some LICs lacked full-time chairmen or secretaries, although the Colonial Office was not necessarily convinced that was a bad thing. Better to give the job to a senior member of the governor's secretariat who was in contact with other aspects of life in the colony. Anyone who did the job full time was likely, they believed, to acquire a warped view. 'He is bound to see only the subversive side of things and it is essential that the other factors, rains, good budget, etc., etc. should be brought

---

[44] TNA CO 968/727. A. Creech Jones to colonial governors, 5 & 20 August 1948.
[45] Ibid.
[46] TNA DEFE 11/33. Sir H. Gurney to Colonial Secretary, 30 May 1949.
[47] TNA CAB 134/534/ODC(49)43. Guidance to colonial governors on the preservation of internal security. Note by the Colonial Office, 10 August 1949; TNA CAB 134/534/ODC(49)6 meeting Overseas Defence Committee, 25 August 1949; TNA CAB 134/535/ODC(50)14. Note by the Secretary, Guidance to colonial governments on the preservation of internal security, 19 May 1950; TNA CAB 134/535/ODC(50)3 meeting, 1 June 1950.

into the assessment.'[48] Some colonies did not issue regular reports and even when they did so, they often took the form of 'sit[uation] rep[ort]s', summarizing what had already happened, rather than trying to identify future problems.[49] These shortcomings were a reflection of the larger weakness of most colonial administrations already mentioned: they usually had only just enough senior civil servants to deal with normal routine business.[50]

Asked to examine how colonial governments might be better prepared to counter subversion, Templer discovered in 1955 that

> Whereas in the military world 'Intelligence' is a highly specialized field of its own, in the Colonial (and other civilian) services it naturally tends to be regarded as merely one aspect of the political 'knowledge' which permeates the whole business of administration. Nor is this aspect held to be a very important one: 'intelligence' is often considered to be a narrow, if sensational, function of the police. The administration is apt not to concern itself closely with the machinery for its collection and appreciation, nor with its relation to security in the broadest sense. As a result, security intelligence has I think come to be regarded as a kind of spicy condiment added to the Secretariat hot-pot by a supernumerary and possibly superfluous cook, instead of being a carefully planned and expertly served dish of its own.[51]

Consequently it was not until April 1956 that the Colonial Office finally insisted that all colonies must establish a LIC, chaired by a senior officer from the Secretariat, with a full-time secretary, and drawing its members from the administration, police, Special Branch, the armed services, and with the Security Liaison Officer, who was MI5's local representative. Intelligence targeting was also widened to include not just Communist and 'Extreme Nationalism', but also labour and agrarian unrest, racial, religious, and tribal tensions, and frontier incidents.[52]

SPECIAL BRANCH

In most colonies the central government relied on two sources for its information about potentially subversive organizations. Provincial and District Commissioners and their subordinates were supposed to submit regular reports. But they were busy men with a multitude of other tasks and their reports often contained little of real importance. The job of ferreting out subversion on the ground was usually left to the police Special Branch, but they were no better funded or manned than other parts of the colonial police. The Palestine Special Branch had only three senior officers who could speak Hebrew. 'This was disastrous', admitted its deputy head. 'It meant we were limited in our means of interrogation. We were limited in our

[48] TNA CO 1035/28. Governor Nyasaland to Colonial Secretary, 4 June 1956;TNA CO 1035/28. Minute by Juxton Barton, 11 June 1956.
[49] TNA CAB 129/76/CP(55)89. Sir Gerald Templer, Report on Colonial Security, 23 April 1955.
[50] TNA CO 968/680. Minute by I. Stourton, 23 April 1959.
[51] TNA CAB 129/76/CP(55)89. Sir Gerald Templer, Report on Colonial Security, 23 April 1955.
[52] TNA CO 1035/28. Colonial Secretary to all Colonies and Protectorates and High Commission Federation of Malaya, 28 April 1956.

ability to translate confiscated documents in Hebrew and our ability to conduct operations to overhear the conversation of two Jewish suspects put in the same cell for example.'[53] In Malaya domestic intelligence was initially gathered by the Malay Security Service. But the war had badly disrupted its organization and personnel and it had not recovered by the eve of the outbreak of the emergency. By the end of 1948 it had been disbanded and its roles passed to the Special Branch.[54] But most experienced pre-war Special Branch officers had either been killed, or were medically unfit, the branch was only at half its established strength, and although the MCP was predominantly a Chinese-speaking organization, few Special Branch officers could speak Chinese. Furthermore, its most important resource, its records registry listing subversive and potentially subversive people and organizations, had been destroyed during the war.[55] In Kenya on the eve of the emergency in October 1952, Special Branch consisted of just four European officers and a handful of African rank and file, and it activities were focused entirely on Nairobi and Mombasa.[56] Cyprus had only an embryonic Special Branch by 1954 and, according to Field Marshal Harding, who became governor of the colony in October 1955, it relied on what 'I call gossip sources—cafes, coffee houses and so on, which is totally inadequate. And anyway, there was no clear information about EOKA, its strength, its armament, its tactics or anything.'[57] Not only was it undermanned, underfunded, and under-trained, but the system by which information was collated and turned into intelligence was woefully inadequate. Information from the police, the administration, and MI5's Security Liaison Officer, all arrived at the governor's secretariat without any preliminary collation and analysis.[58] Similar shortcomings existed elsewhere. The British Guiana Special Branch was, according to the Inspector-General of Colonial Police in 1953, the most efficient in the West Indies. But it was still too small to do its job effectively, and two years later it lacked an efficient registry to maintain its records, the steel filing cabinets needed to contain them, and sufficient typewriters to produce them.[59] The Nyasaland Special Branch had typewriters, but was so short of funds that in 1952 senior officers had to do their own typing.[60]

The work of collecting information on the ground was usually left to indigenous junior policemen. Dressed in plain clothes, they could mingle with crowds and

---

[53] IWMSA. Accession No. 10392. Sir R. Catling, Transcript, 12–13.

[54] L. Comber, 'The Malayan Security Service (1945–1948)', *INS*, vol. 18 (2003), 128–53. J. Gentry, 'Intelligence learning and adaptation: lessons from counterinsurgency wars', *Intelligence and National Security*, vol. 25 (2010), 50–60, provided an excellent summary of the multifarious weaknesses of domestic intelligence services in the colonies.

[55] TNA CO 537/2647. Sir Percy Sillitoe to Sir Thomas Lloyd, 17 December 1947; TNA CO 537/2647. G. F. Sell to MacDonald, Gent and Gimpson, 22 May 1948; TNA KV 4/408. J. P. Morton, 'The co-ordination of intelligence in the Malayan Emergency', n.d. but *c*.1960.

[56] R. W. Heather, 'Intelligence and counter-insurgency in Kenya, 1952–56', *INS*, vol. 5 (1990), 61; Throup, 'Crime, politics and the police in colonial Kenya', 133–8.

[57] IWMSA. Accession No. 8736. Field Marshal Lord Harding, Transcript, 368.

[58] TNA CO 1035/98. A. M. MacDonald to Governor, Cyprus, 21 August 1954.

[59] TNA CO 1031/103. W. A. Muller to OAG British Guiana, 24 March 1953; TNA CAB 129/76/CP(55)89. Sir Gerald Templer, Report on Colonial Security, 23 April 1955.

[60] TNA CO 968/274. W. A. G. Muller to Governor Nyasaland, 26 May 1952.

attend political meetings without attracting the kind of attention that Europeans were bound to arouse. But anyone taking notes was liable to be suspected of being a government informer. 'He'd have been lynched. The wretched chap had to stand in the crowd and listen, and then come back and give a verbal report. So you would never get the completely accurate account as to what had been said.'[61] Furthermore, as one former British police officer with experience of working in Africa remembered, there was 'a danger of the constables being influenced by two things. The first is a very natural desire to acquire merit in the eyes of his superior officers by producing the kind of information that he thinks they would like. The second is the common human propensity to embroider a report and to accept idle gossip for serious talk.'[62] There was a third danger, the possibility that paid agents might concoct information in order to settle old scores with their personal enemies.[63]

Even before the Gold Coast riots some East African colonies had asked MI5 for help in training their Special Branches.[64] The first training course was held in June and July 1948, and by 1957 about 840 colonial policemen had received some training in this work.[65] They either travelled to London or to a Special Branch training school established at Kuala Lumpur in 1953, where they were introduced to 'the routine methods and techniques employed by officers charged with ensuring civil security: these methods and techniques cover interrogation, the searching of suspects, search of premises, surveillance, the writing of reports, the handling of agents, clandestine meetings and other methods of communication, and protective security.'[66] A lack of trained Special Branch officers remained a problem.[67] By 1965 the COS were at their wits end to find sufficient Special Branch officers to meet the needs of Aden and Borneo.[68]

One reason for this shortage was that Special Branch work was unpopular. As a senior Royal Ulster Constabulary officer sent to examine the Special Branch in Palestine in 1946 explained, policemen were reluctant to volunteer because 'modern scientific aids are of little value—and the consequent inability over long periods to produce spectacular results, the risk involved and the lack of adequate incentive to take up work of this kind, and to persist in it to a successful conclusion.'[69] The risks could be very real, for Special Branch policemen were prime targets for

[61] IWMSA. Accession No. 10224. Sir A. Swann, Transcript, 13.

[62] A. I. Bowman to the editor, *Manchester Guardian*, 28 March 1959.

[63] IWMSA. Accession No. 10224. Sir A. Swann, Transcript, 14.

[64] TNA CO 537/2683. East African High Commission to CO, 9 February 1948; TNA CO 537/2683. Governor Nyasaland to Colonial Secretary, 04/02/1948; TNA CO 537/2683. Logan to T. D. Patterson, 25 February 1948.

[65] TNA CO 537/2683. A. J. Kellar to Sir M. Logan, 16 March 1948; TNA CO 885/124. Records of the Second Conference of Commissioners of Police Forces held at the Police College, Ryton-on-Dunsmore, July 1954; TNA CO 885/124. Records of the Third Conference of Commissioners of Police Forces held at the Police College, Ryton-on-Dunsmore, June 1957; TNA CO 1035/54. Colonial Secretary to all colonies and protectorates, 20 March 1956.

[66] TNA CO 1030/169. Malcolm MacDonald to Eden, 1 & 24 July 1954; TNA CO 1030/169. K. W. Wilford to F. L. Carter, 1 October 1956.

[67] Sinclair, *At the End of the Line*, 202–3.

[68] TNA DEFE 13/710. CDS to Secretary of State Defence, 5 February 1965.

[69] TNA CO 537/2269. Enc: Mr Moffatt, CID, n.d. but *c.*late 1946.

insurgent attacks. In Aden in 1956 'an officer was subject to a form of intimidation as a warning not to be too efficient, by the "kidnapping" of his small son for 1.5 hours.'[70] That officer was lucky. His son was released unharmed. But in Palestine, Cyprus, and in Aden in the mid-1960s, the insurgents, by a carefully targeted campaign of assassinations, inflicted major damage on the local Special Branches. In Palestine they assassinated both the MI5 representative in Jerusalem and the head of Haifa's CID.[71] The result was that the army discovered that 'the supply of intelligence was strictly limited. The police intelligence used to indicate that something was going to happen, but they didn't know what or where. And so we were always taken by surprise!'[72] In June 1955, EOKA began to target Special Branch officers and by the end of the year most ethnic Greek officers had either been assassinated or intimidated into ineffectiveness.[73] Consequently the British were so slow to build up an intelligence picture of their opponents that it was only in November 1955 that they discovered that the leader of EOKA was a Greek army officer, Colonel George Grivas.[74] Although they did eventually understand the structure, strategy and financing of EOKA, Grivas's readiness to assassinate real or suspected informers meant that they were slow to penetrate it with agents who could provide them with real time tactical intelligence.[75] In Aden in January 1964 Radio Cairo began to threaten senior Arab Special Branch officers by name and on Christmas Day 1964 the NLF started to assassinate them.[76] Chief Inspector Fadhle Khalil 'whilst sitting in his car parked near municipal market Crater was killed by fire from automatic weapon from a passing car.'[77] In January 1965 another officer was killed and a third, a Deputy Superintendent who was lightly wounded, decided in February that it was prudent to defect to the Yemen.[78] In September 1965 the body of a Special Branch Arab constable, bound and gagged and shot, was discovered with 'a white turban on the head of the body bearing the words in Arabic "this execution was carried out by the Front."'[79] Special Branch informers were liable to meet the same grisly fate.[80] The result was that in June 1965 the High

---

[70] TNA CO 1035/86. G. R. H. Gribble to Governor Aden, 17 September 1956.

[71] TNA WO 106/3107. CIGS summary No. 33, 18 February 1946; TNA CO 537/1838. Secretary of State to High Commissioner and High Commissioner to Secretary of State, 23 & 24 October 1946; S. Dorril, *MI6. Fifty Years of Special Operations* (London: Fourth Estate, 2001), 544.

[72] Captain A. Gibson-Watt, *Empire Warriors: The Jewish War*, BBC, 2004.

[73] TNA CO 1035/98. Enc: Organisation of intelligence in Cyprus, 22 December 1955; C. Foley (ed.), *The Memoirs of General Grivas* (London: Longman, 1964), 42–3.

[74] Dorrill, *MI6*, 551; TNA T 220/573. Minutes of the first Meeting of the Cyprus Internal Security committee, 11 May 1955.

[75] D. Panagiotis, 'British Intelligence and the Cyprus Insurgency, 1955–1959', *International Journal of Intelligence and Counter Intelligence*, vol. 21 (2008), 375–89; IWMSA. Accession No. 11133. Col. H. J. Sweeney, reel 1; IWMDoD. 86/85/1. Maj. C. R. Butt, 'Cyprus Drafts (I)', 86; IWMSA. Accession No. 11146. Col. M. Gray, reel 3.

[76] TNA CO 1055/199. Trevaskis to CO, 22 January 1964.

[77] TNA CO 1055/202. Acting High Commissioner to CO, 25 December 1964.

[78] TNA CO 1035/178. Turnbull to CO, 9 February 1965.

[79] TNA CO 1055/221. Turnbull to CO, 14 September 1965.

[80] TNA CO 1055/221. Turnbull to CO, 24 November 1965; TNA DEFE 11/505. C-in-C Mideast to CDS, 8 November 1966; FO 371/185233. Turnbull to Foreign Office, 6 & 7 November 1966.

Commissioner reported that 'Aden State Special Branch has now virtually no Arab element and will take a considerable time to re-establish on an Arab basis even if Arabs can be found to serve in it. There is no likelihood of this happening in the foreseeable future.'[81]

British efforts to rebuild the Aden and Cyprus Special Branches by importing expatriate European officers met only limited success. Few of them could speak the local languages, and their dependence on local interpreters erected a sometimes impenetrable barrier between themselves and local informers. The latter might have been willing to give information directly to an Englishman, but doing so through a Greek intermediary was, in view of Grivas's propensity for assassinating informers, too dangerous.[82] In Aden it took expatriates between 6 and 12 months to acquire a working knowledge of Arabic, and they received little help from the ordinary police, who had been thoroughly penetrated by the insurgents.[83]

But even a small and poorly trained Special Branch was better than none at all, which was the situation that faced the military authorities in the Canal Zone. There, the British confronted the problems of conducting a counter-insurgency campaign in a foreign country and against a hostile population and government. During the Second World War, the British had been well informed about the internal security situation in Egypt. The local MI5 representatives had maintained close contacts with the Egyptian police and run their own agent networks.[84] In 1947, following the withdrawal of British troops from the Delta and their concentration in the Canal Zone, they continued this liaison, operating under diplomatic cover from the British embassy in Cairo.[85] But as soon as the Egyptians abrogated the Anglo-Egyptian treaty in October 1951, that liaison stopped.[86] The result, as an officer at the HQ of BTE noted, was that, 'The only real safeguard against terrorism is a good police force and C.I.D. This is where "we are up against it" at the moment because: (a) The Egyptian police will not co-operate fully with out F[ield].S[ecurity].S[ection]. (b) We have no expert C.I.D. officers with real Egyptian experience.'[87] The British were also slow to switch their intelligence organs to target their main enemies. It was only some days after the abrogation that the service commanders in the Middle East told SIME, the organization that co-ordinated the work of MI5 stations throughout the Middle East, 'to take immediate action to

[81] TNA CO 1035/178. T. Oates to C. S. Roberts, 2 January 1965; TNA CO 1035/183. Turnbull to CO, 7 June 1965; TNA CO 1035/178. Maj.-Gen. K. W. D. Strong to Chair, JIC, 1 February 1965.
[82] N. Crawshaw, 'Cyprus and its crisis. Mounting hostility', *Manchester Guardian*, 20 January 1956; Maj. E. A. Cooper-Key, 'Some reflections on Cyprus', *British Army Review*, no. 5 (September 1957), 40.
[83] TNA CO 1035/178. J. P. Morton to MI5, 23 February 1965; TNA CO 1035/179. Extract from Intelligence Brief, Aden, 11 March 1965; TNA CO 1035/179. Turnbull to CO, 20 April 1965; TNA DEFE 11/506. LIC Aden to JIC, London, 12 December 1966.
[84] TNA KV 4/234. Maj. T. A. Roberts, Report on visit to Egypt, 20 Feb. to 17 March 1942, 7 May 1942; TNA KV 4/438. Report on visit to Middle East by Mr J. C. Robertson, 14 April to 14 June 1947.
[85] TNA KV 4/235. Extract from SIME circular, 24 May 1947.
[86] TNA WO 236/8. Problems in the Canal Zone after the abrogation of the 1936 treaty, n.d. but *c.*1952.
[87] TNA WO 236/25. Counter-terrorist measures, 14 November 1951.

identify and locate members of the Ikhwan [the Moslem brotherhood] and other extremist elements in the Canal Zone.'[88] A GSO1(I) was appointed at HQ BTE to improve the handling of such information as was available, Field Security sections recruited their own agent networks in the Canal Zone, and an MI5 officer, working under diplomatic cover in Cairo, was appointed to run an intelligence organization in the Delta.[89] But their success was limited and, as in Palestine, Cyprus and Aden, the British struggled to establish an effective intelligence system inside Egypt and the Canal Zone.[90]

Protective security measures were another significant weakness in several colonies. In Palestine most of the Jewish members of the Palestine Police were also members of the Haganah, the main Zionist underground army, and readily leaked information to the insurgents.[91] It took the British some time to realize how widely both the police and the rest of the government machine had been penetrated, but once they did so the army stopped telling the police about their plans.[92] They faced a similar problem in Cyprus. In the early 1950s the British identified the main threat to their hold over the island as coming from the local Communists, not from Greek nationalists. Consequently they had purged the police of anyone with left-wing sympathies, so that in 1955 they found that the force was dominated by right-wing nationalists who were sympathetic to EOKA, and many of whom were willing to provide the insurgents with information. But the security forces had to continue to use Greek-Cypriot detectives to investigate EOKA because most British and Turkish policemen on the island had an inadequate command of Greek.[93]

The situation in Aden was probably even worse. When John Prendergast, by the early 1960s the most experienced senior colonial Special Branch officer in the empire, visited Aden in 1965, he was appalled at the lack of protective security. 'It seemed to me', he told the governor, 'that the principle [was] that if a person got through the outer ring he therefore had access to any establishment within the particular perimeter—there was rarely a second check', and he warned that 'I would suggest that the white face and smile open too many doors in Aden.'[94] Doors were not the only things that were open in Aden. Arms smuggling was rife. Sixty thousand people, 20,000 vehicles, and 300 camels, passed through check points

[88] TNA WO 236/25. Colonel H. V. Ewbank, Secretary, BDCC(Middle East) to GOC BTE, 29 October 1951.
[89] IWMSA. Accession No. 17650. Sgt. R. Knutsen, reels 1, 3; TNA WO 216/798. Robertson to Lt.-Gen. Sir N. Brownjohn (VCIGS), 17 December 1951.
[90] W. Scott Lucas and A. Morey, 'The hidden "Alliance": the CIA and MI6 before and after Suez', *INS*, vol. 15 (2000), 101–2; TNA WO 236/8. Problems in the Canal Zone after the abrogation of the 1936 treaty, n.d. but c.1952.
[91] Smith, 'Communal conflict and insurrection in Palestine', 75.
[92] Charters, 'Eyes of the Underground', 168–70; R. Aldrich, *The Hidden Hand. Britain, America and Cold War Secret Intelligence* (London: John Murray, 2001), 259; IWMSA. Accession No. 16395. Lt.-Gen Sir, N. Crookenden, reel 1.
[93] TNA WO 33/2736. History of EOKA, 1954–1959, 20 April 1960.
[94] TNA CO 1035/180. Prendergast to Turnbull, Intelligence in Aden. Report by Mr J. V. Prendergast, Director of Special Branch Hong Kong, on his visit to Aden from 17 to 30 October 1965, 18 November 1965.

between Aden State and its hinterland daily. But only 5.5 per cent of people and an even smaller percentage of vehicles were stopped and searched.[95]

INTELLIGENCE AND THE 'MALAYAN MODEL'

Soldiers who were suddenly dumped into an emergency were even less well equipped than the police to understand the culture and language of the people amongst whom they were operating. A trooper with the King's Dragoon Guards who served in Malaya thought that only Chinese policemen could sense if a suspect he had stopped was an insurgent. The ordinary British soldier would have no idea. 'He just would not be able to recognise the tell-tale signs or even have that sort of sixth sense that leads to positive suspicion.'[96] But within days of the start of the Malayan emergency the Commanders-in-Chief of the three armed services had 'complained bitterly of the serious lack of battle intelligence in the Federation, and the lack of coordination between the intelligence staffs of the Army, Air Force, MSS and CID.'[97] How to resolve the conflicting intelligence requirements of the police and the army was a problem common at the start of most emergencies. In 1949 the General Staff recognized that 'Soldiers and police have a fundamentally different approach to the same problems: the former take a short and the latter a long-term view. The soldier has to complete his task specially [speedily] and move on to the next trouble spot. The police, however, stay behind to clear up after operations, prepare and conduct court cases and help people to return to normal conditions.'[98] The police CID wanted to gather evidence to bring prosecutions in court, whereas military intelligence officers wanted contact intelligence so that they could locate and capture or kill insurgents. The needs of the two agencies were clearly in conflict. '"When we catch an EOKA man we want information quickly before the rest of his gang gets away," a British Army officer explained. There is no time to hang around waiting for the CID to take down statements. Thus, evidence vital to the prosecution may be rejected by the courts because rules of procedure have been overlooked. Men known by the police to have committed major crimes go free, it would appear, on a legal technicality.'[99] In fact, the situation was even more complicated, because there was a third interested party, the Special Branch. They wanted information so they could build up a picture of the enemy's order of battle and the personalities and habits of its members, information that they hoped would

---

[95] TNA DEFE 11/527. Gribbon to VCDS, 1 January 1967.

[96] IWMSA. Accession No. 10107.N. J. D. Baptiste, reel 1.

[97] TNA CO 537/2647. Sir R. Hone to G. F. Seel, 26 July 1948; TNA WO 106/5884. Gen. Sir N. Ritchie, Report on operations in Malaya, June 1948 to July 1949, 6 September 1949.

[98] TNA WO 279/398. War Office, *Keeping the Peace. Part 1. Doctrine* (London: War Office, 7 January 1963); TNA CO 968/690. Brigadier G. Baker, A Review of the Cyprus Emergency April 1955–March 1958; K. Jeffery, 'Intelligence and counter-insurgency operations: some reflections on the British experience', *INS*, vol. 2 (1987), 119.

[99] N. Crawshaw, 'Justice in Cyprus. II. The Special Courts', *Manchester Guardian*, 2 July 1957.

enable them to destroy the enemy's organization by 'turning' captured enemy personnel and using them as double-agents.[100]

The different goals of the three organizations bred mistrust. To the Special Branch, for example, the uniformed police were 'lock testers and knob pullers, you know. Like the old copper who used to try shop door knobs at night.'[101] The army and Special Branch understood success in quite different ways. Army officers were slow to realize that the kind of background intelligence that the Special Branch was able to give them could, if they exploited it properly, be turned into contact intelligence.[102] But this took time and, as Tom Hatton, a Malayan Special Branch officer noted, 'it was important to explain to the Military Intelligence officers that short-term results, important for battalion "scores", would sometimes have to give way to more important and productive long-term projects.'[103]

It was in Malaya that a solution of sorts to some of these problems was found.[104] At the very top Templer appointed a single official, Jack Morton, an MI5 official, as the Director of Intelligence. His role was to coordinate the work of all intelligence agencies, to supervise the collation, evaluation, and dissemination of all intelligence, and to advise the Director of Operations on intelligence matters. To assist him he had a Combined Intelligence Staff that included members of the police, civil administration, and all three armed services. The Director also chaired the Federal Intelligence Committee. It included representatives of all three services, the Special Branch, SIFE (the organization that co-ordinated the work of MI5's stations in South East Asia), and those government departments closely concerned with the emergency, and it provided appreciations of the security situation and forecasts of likely developments. 'It was the machine', according to Morton, 'by which the Director of Intelligence, who had no executive authority, was enabled to coordinate.'[105]

At the tactical level, having served as Commissioner of Police in Palestine, Lt.-Col. W.N. Gray, who was Commissioner of Police in Malaya from 1948 to 1952, had seen and understood the tension between the police and army. In Palestine he had suggested that the easiest way to overcome it was to ensure that the army had better access to police intelligence. To achieve that he suggested that the army should post intelligence liaison officers to each level of police headquarters to pass back to the army information of use to them. But the army could not find suitable

---

[100] IWMSA. Accession No. 10232. L. O. Crosland, reel 2; IWMSA. Accession No. 10175. R. J. W. Craig, Transcript, 22.

[101] IWMSA. Accession No. 10232. L. O. Crosland, reel 3; TNA CO 968/690. Brigadier G. Baker, A Review of the Cyprus Emergency April 1955–March 1958.

[102] IWMSA. Accession No. 11162. Anon., reels 1–2; Gen. Sir F. Kitson, *Bunch of Five* (London: Faber & Faber, 1977), 69–151.

[103] T. Hatton, *Tock Tock Birds* (Lewis, Sussex: The Book Guild, 2004), 180; TNA KV 4/408. J. P. Morton, Malayan emergency, n.d. but *c*.1960.

[104] For the development of the Malayan Special Branch see L. Comber, *Malaya's Secret Police 1945–60. The Role of the Special Branch in the Malayan Emergency* (Victoria, Australia: Monash University Press, 2008).

[105] TNA KV 4/408. J. P. Morton, Malayan emergency, n.d. but *c*.1960.

officers and nothing came of it.[106] However, in Malaya, his idea was implemented. Special Branch offices at Federal, Provincial and District levels became joint civil and military intelligence centres, and from 1952, Military Intelligence Officers (MIOs) were posted to them to establish joint operations rooms with the police. The Special Branch was given sole responsibility for the evaluation, collation, and dissemination of intelligence, and the troops were expected to pass to them all the information they gathered.[107] It was the task of the MIO to extract from Special Branch intelligence those items that were of immediate operational importance to their military superiors, clear their release with the senior Special Branch officer present, and then pass the intelligence on to the army.[108] By 1954 the Malayan Special Branch was providing troops on the ground with information, often provided by surrendered insurgents, that enabled them to make increasing numbers of successful ambushes.[109] But the establishment of such a system was a slow and uncertain business. Officers with an aptitude for such work were hard to find, some commanders were reluctant to second good officers to such posts, some colonial governments did not understand that they had to serve two masters, the head of Special Branch and the local army commander, and sometimes officers who had shown a real aptitude for such work were allowed to go elsewhere.[110] Many aspects of the 'Malayan model' were replicated in Borneo during the Confrontation. In January 1963 a Director of Intelligence was appointed to the staff of the Director of Operations, a Joint Territories Intelligence Committee was established to co-ordinate the intelligence systems of the three governments involved, Special Branch became the lead agency in gathering and collating intelligence, and MIOs were integrated into the Special Branch to extract the intelligence the army needed.[111]

But further up the administrative hierarchy, there was sometimes a reluctance to replicate the Malayan committee structure or to override the feelings of officials in situ and appoint a single Director of Intelligence. In both Kenya and Cyprus officials at least initially refused to accept that the Mau Mau and EOKA constituted the same kind of serious threat that the MCP posed in Malaya.[112] In Kenya, following the recommendations of the Director-General of MI5, Sir Percy Sillitoe,

---

[106] TNA KV 4/438. Report on visit to Middle East by J. C. Robertson, 14 April to 14 June 1947.

[107] TNA WO 231/38. Notes of Conference held by GOC Malay District on 11 July 1950; TNA WO 296/23. General Staff, *Keeping the Peace. (Duties in Support of the Civil Power)* (London: War Office, 1957), chapter 9; TNA WO 279/241. Director of Operations, *Malaya, Conduct of Anti-terrorist operations in Malaya* (Malaya: Kuala Lumpur, 3rd edn, 1958), ch. 14.

[108] TNA CO 1035/156. Maj.-Gen. M. St J. Oswald (DMI, WO), to all overseas commanders et al., 23 August 1963.

[109] IWMSA. Accession No. 10106. Col. J. B. Buckmaster, reel 1.

[110] Maj. P. Halliday, 'Employment of the Intelligence Corps', *British Army Review*, No 10 (April 1960), 22; TNA CO 1035/156. Maj.-Gen. M. St J. Oswald to J. N. A. Armitage-Smith, 16 August 1963; IWMDoD. Field Marshal Lord Harding mss AFH5. Sinclair to Harding, 27 February 1958.

[111] TNA WO 305/2519. Director of Operations Borneo, Instruction no. 3, 29 December 1962. Intelligence Structure, 6 January 1963; TNA WO 305/2520. Director of Operations Borneo Instruction number 3 (Revised March 1963) Intelligence Structure, 23 March 1963.

[112] TNA CAB 129/57/C(52)407. Colonial Secretary, Kenya, 14 November 1952; TNA CO 968/690. Sir H. Foot to Sir J. Martin, 22 April 1959.

an MI5 official, A. S. Macdonald, was appointed as Intelligence Adviser to the Governor. He became chairman of the Kenya Intelligence Committee, which had the same functions as the Federal Committee in Malaya, and at Provincial and District levels there were Intelligence Committees with similar functions.[113] However, it was not until 1955 that Kenya followed Malaya in appointing a single Director of Intelligence who reported directly to the Director of Operations. This was done at the insistence of the GOC, Sir Gerald Lathbury. He was 'not entirely happy about the Intelligence organisation. Unlike Malay there is no Director of Intelligence and it has been the rule to retain parallel organisations within the Special Branch to deal with political and military intelligence. There was also a good deal of friction between the Army and Police in this sphere. I have now combined the two Branches under the Director of Intelligence and Security—a policeman—who will virtually become Director of Intelligence.'[114]

Cyprus and Aden were even slower to follow the Malayan model. The efficiency of the intelligence machinery in both emergencies was degraded for too long because too many individuals and agencies were concerned in collecting intelligence, and no single organization or individual was responsible for co-ordinating their work and for collating, analysing, and disseminating their findings.[115] In Cyprus this situation was only righted in the second half of 1958 when John Prendergast, who had served in Kenya as Director of Intelligence and Security, was appointed to the new post of Chief of Intelligence.[116] He made the Cyprus Local Intelligence Committee an effective organization. Prendergast brought together the heads of all service, internal, and external intelligence agencies for regular meetings to decide priorities, prepare assessments, and issue policy directive to its subordinate District Intelligence Committees.[117] The situation was never put to rights in Aden. This was partly because the problem was inherently more complicated due to the existence of a Federal government intelligence system that existed in an uneasy relationship with the British-run system and produced a machine of Byzantine complexity.[118] It was also because the Aden Intelligence Centre was understaffed, overcrowded, and had too few MIOs. Finally it was difficult because there was 'a very bad atmosphere within the intelligence Centre, Aden, involving widespread

---

[113] TNA CO 822/445. H. S. Potter to P. Rogers, 9 March 1953; TNA WO 291/1670. Operational Research Unit (Far East). Report Number 1/57. A comparison of the emergencies in Malaya and Kenya, 6 June 1957; TNA CO 822/445. Notes of a meeting held in the Secretary of State's Room, 15 December 1952.

[114] TNA CO 822/782. Lt.-Gen. G. W. Lathbury to CIGS, 14 June 1955; Heather, 'Intelligence and counter-insurgency in Kenya', 65–8; Maj. G. W. Croker, 'Mau Mau', *JRUSI*, vol. 100 (1955), 47–8; TNA WO 236/20. Lt.-Gen. Sir G. Lathbury, The Kenya Emergency, 3 May 1955 to 17 November 1956.

[115] IWMDoD. Field Marshal Lord Harding mss AFH 10. Note by Maj.-Gen. K. T. Darling, Director of Operations, n.d. but *c*.April 1959.

[116] Dorril, *MI6*, 554.

[117] TNA CO 926/1077. Report on the Cyprus Emergency, 31 July 1959; IWMDoD. Field Marshal Lord Harding mss AFH 10. Sir H. Foot to Sir J. Martin, 22 April 1959.

[118] TNA CO 1035/181. Wallace to Burrows and Hollis, 14 January 1964.

personal rivalries of a lamentable kind.'[119] The Federal government's system was even more poorly resourced.[120] In January 1964, and only after some prodding from London, did the High Commissioner, Sir Kennedy Trevaskis, agree that there was a need to appoint a Security Adviser, in effect, a Director of Intelligence, to oversee the collation, assessment and distribution of military and political intelligence and to make recommendations on action to be taken.[121] But finding an individual with the right qualifications who could also speak Arabic took several months. The Colonial Office, MI5, and MI6 could not find a suitable candidate and eventually had to appoint someone who knew about intelligence, but could not speak Arabic.[122]

The establishment of the Malayan model of intelligence organization did yield positive dividends. Morton's first objective was to achieve the long-term penetration of the MCP. 'It was laid down that the primary targets should be the leadership and higher structures which gave these bodies life and direction. The requirement for short-term tactical intelligence had therefore to be subordinated to the achievement of this major aim.'[123] Special Branch was the only organization permitted to run agents and it became increasingly adept at doing so. Recruitment methods included bribery and threats. The latter took the form either of long prison sentences if potential agents did not cooperate, or exposure to the MCP as 'traitors', with the resulting likelihood of assassination.[124] The Branch could be utterly ruthless.[125] Morton recalled instances where 'several penetration agents had to be sacrificed so that security force action could be taken to relieve guerrilla pressure in sensitive areas. I recall that in one district a succession of successful operations led to a full scale Communist inquisition into the security of the local Party organisation. Unfortunately, the Special Branch agent was among those who were liquidated in the ensuing purge. He was made to dig his own grave and two strong men then slowly strangled him to death. It was, however, some consolation to know that other comrades who were not agents were also executed. The Communists were taking no chances.'[126]

Building on the work of his predecessor, Sir William Jenkin, Morton transformed the intelligence situation in Malaya.[127] Whereas in 1950 the Colonial

[119] TNA CO 1035/182. Extract from JIC(64)40 meeting, 6 August 1964; TNA CO 1035/181. JIC(IO)(M.E.)(WP)3/65. Intelligence Organization, Middle East, Working Party, 14 May 1964.
[120] TNA CO 1035/184/JIC(IAF)(65)3. D. J. McCarthy, Intelligence Organization in Aden, 17 December 1965.
[121] TNA CO 1035/181. Note of a meeting between the Minister of Defence and H. E. the High Commissioner for Aden and the South Arabia Federation, 3 January 1964; TNA CO 1035/178. Sir K. Trevaskis to Secretary of State, 16 January 1964; CO 1035/181. Thorneycroft to Colonial Secretary, 21 January 1964.
[122] TNA CO 1035/182. Higham to Morton, 20 October 1964; TNA CO 1035/182. Roberts to Trevaskis, 23 October 1964.
[123] TNA KV 4/408. J. P. Morton, Malayan emergency, n.d. but *c*.1960.
[124] R. Miers, *Shoot to Kill* (London: Faber & Faber, 1959), 52; Aldrich, *The Hidden Hand*, 508–9.
[125] J. Starling, *Soldier On! The Testament of a Tom* (Tunbridge Wells: Spellmount, 1992), 12–4.
[126] TNA KV 4/408. J. P. Morton, The problem we faced in Malaya and how they were solved, July 1954.
[127] Comber, *Malaya's Secret Police*, 131–218.

Secretary had to admit that 'it was very difficult to find out even the names of the directing members of the Malayan Communist Party, or, if their names were found, to track them down', by 1956 the Special Branch had built up a detailed picture of the insurgents' order of battle, numbers, names, locations, and plans.[128] On the ground good intelligence did matter. In Malaya in the third quarter of 1952 the chance of springing a successful ambush were about 1 in 10 if the security forces had information about the location of the insurgents they were trying to trap, but only 1 in 88 without it.[129] In Kenya by September 1953 the security forces knew the leading personalities in Mau Mau, and the capture in January 1954 of 'General China' provided them with excellent intelligence about the gangs on Mount Kenya.[130] But it was Operation ANVIL, the mass detention and screening of Mau Mau suspects in Nairobi, that gave the security forces real intelligence dominance, and thereafter an increasing number of security forces operations could be mounted on the basis of intelligence provided by informers.[131] In Malaya, as elsewhere, they discovered that success bred success, and that people were more likely to give them information if they believed that the security forces were winning the struggle, and therefore would be able to protect them from retaliation by the insurgents.[132] In Cyprus by early 1959 EOKA had been brought to its knees and the security forces 'stood poised to strike with certainty at the leadership of EOKA.'[133] 'Operation Sunshine' had located Grivas in a house in Nicosia and the security forces wanted to use a snatch squad to arrest him. They only stayed their hand on a direct order from the Prime Minister, Harold Macmillan, who was concerned that his arrest or assassination would cause the collapse of talks then taking place to end the emergency.[134] Even in Aden the intelligence picture improved. In the autumn of 1965 the interrogation of NLF suspects began to yield results. Between September and November the security forces built up a picture of the whole order of battle of NLF in Aden State, the names of the members of each of its cells, and the code names of all active members. They numbered about 100, and half of them were arrested.[135] But multiple weaknesses remained. The Federal government still lacked an effective staff to collate and

---

[128] TNA CAB 21/1682/MAL.C(50)10 meeting, Malaya Committee, 17 October 1950.

[129] TNA WO 291/1724. Lt.-Col. C. R. Nicholls, OC Operational Research Section, Malaya. Memorandum Number 4/52. Ambushes, 6 November 1952.

[130] Croker, 'Mau Mau', 49.

[131] TNA WO 276/457. GSO 3 (Intelligence) GI(K), 6 August 1954; A. Clayton, *Counter-insurgency in Kenya 1952–60. A Study of Military Operations Against Mau Mau* (Nairobi: Transafrica Publishers, 1976), 34.

[132] Miers, *Shoot to Kill*, 105.

[133] TNA CO 926/1077. Report on the Cyprus Emergency, 31 July 1959; IWMDoD. Field Marshal Lord Harding mss AFH 10. Sir Hugh Foot to Sir John Martin, 22 April 1959.

[134] R. Holland, *Britain and the Revolt in Cyprus 1954–1959* (Oxford: Oxford University Press, 1998), 312–14; IWMDoD. Gen. Sir Kenneth Darling mss 01/41/1/file 5. Sir John Prendergast to Gen. Sir K. Darling, 22 May 1983; IWMDoD. Gen. Sir K. Darling mss 01/41/1/file 5. Darling to Lt.-Gen. Sir F. Kitson, 15 September 1981; IWMDoD. Gen. Sir K. Darling mss 01/41/1/file 5. Gen. Sir K. Darling, Cyprus, the final round, October 1958–March 1959, n.d. but *c.*April 1979.

[135] TNA CO 1035/183. Review of current intelligence, 28 September 1965; TNA CO 1035/183. Maj.-Gen. Oswald, Report on visit to Aden by Director of Management and Support, Intelligence, 6 November 1965.

disseminate intelligence, the Aden Intelligence Centre received too little information about events in neighbouring Yemen, and 'the Intelligence machine was greatly hampered by interdepartmental rivalry and jealousies, a state of affairs which seems to be deeply ingrained in Aden.'[136]

The failure of most colonial governments to develop efficient domestic intelligence systems before the outbreak of an emergency, and the failure of some to put matters to rights once one had begun, had important consequences for the ways in which the British conducted their counter-insurgency operations. Sir Hugh Foot, who had served as a senior official in Palestine during the Arab Revolt of the late 1930s before becoming Governor of Cyprus in 1957, recognized that

> action against a subversive or terrorist movement of the kind we had here must be selective and not indiscriminate. That sounds obvious enough, but in Palestine and again in Cyprus there was often a tendency to attempt to make up for lack of Intelligence by using the sledge hammer—mass arrests, mass detentions, big cordons and searches and collective punishments. Such operations can do more harm than good and usually play into the hands of the terrorists by alienating general opinion from the forces of authority. It is not by making the life of ordinary people intolerable that a nationalist movement is destroyed—it is by a selective drive against the terrorist leadership undertaken by small numbers of skilled forces acting intelligently on good information.[137]

As subsequent chapters will show, the sledge-hammer was a favourite British technique.

THE ARMY AND COUNTER-INSURGENCY

Confronted by a serious breakdown of public order and supported by only a small, poorly resourced police force, colonial governments invariably called on the army for assistance. But the post-war British army, designed by the CIGS, Lord Montgomery, and labelled by him with suitably Cromwellian overtones, as his 'New Model Army', was not primarily configured to fight colonial counter-insurgencies. Its main task was to deter Soviet aggression by preparing to conduct conventional operations in Western Europe.[138] It had adopted a forward deployment in West Germany supported by a strong home base in Britain. In March 1951, out of a total of 429,000 soldiers serving in the army, 244,000 were stationed in Britain, and 63,000 in West Germany. There were only 45,000 men in the Canal Zone and

---

[136] TNA CO 1035/183. Report by VCGS on visit to Aden, 31 March 1965; TNA CO 1035/183. Report by Colonel D. J. Willison on a visit to Middle East, 8–14 November. 1965; TNA CO 1035/183. Maj.-Gen. Oswald, Report on visit to Aden by Director of Management and Support, Intelligence, 16 November 1965; TNA CO 1035/180. Prendergast to Turnbull, Intelligence in Aden. Report by J. V. Prendergast, Director of Special Branch Hong Kong, on his visit to Aden from 17 to 30 October 1965, 18 November 1965.

[137] IWMDoD. Field Marshal Lord Harding mss AFH 10. Sir Hugh Foot to Sir John Martin, 22 April 1959.

[138] TNA WO 216/233. Memorandum by the CIGS, The British Army II, 23 September 1947.

35,000 in Malaya.[139] The end of National Service and the establishment of an all-regular army did not fundamentally change this pattern. By September 1963, of the 171,000 regulars then serving, 80,000 men were stationed in Britain and 51,000 were in West Germany. Only 6,000 soldiers were in Aden and 14,000 in the Far East.[140]

It was only in November 1947, and under pressure from the Foreign Secretary, Ernest Bevin, that Montgomery accepted that he would also have to form 'a small, efficient, and properly equipped regular force which could be available to proceed overseas *at short notice* in peace time.'[141] But when Sir William Slim succeeded Montgomery as CIGS in November 1948, he inherited a force in which the regular army was little more than a gigantic training machine for the Territorial Army and National Servicemen. Its priority was to prepare for a hot war in 1957, not to fight a Cold War that had actually begun.[142] For the next decade the War Office improvised a series of reserve brigades, only to see them committed almost as soon as they had been scraped together, to conduct Cold War operations, first in Malaya, then in Hong Kong, Korea, the Canal Zone, Kenya, and Cyprus. Thanks to these improvisations, it was possible for the War Office to bolster garrisons in emergencies. In 1948 there were 13 units in Malaya. By 1953 that number had doubled.[143] The nine units stationed in the Canal Zone in December 1949 had risen to 30 by March 1953.[144] The garrison in Kenya increased from three units in early 1952 to 11 by January 1955, the Cyprus garrison increased from four units in March 1955 to 21 by July 1957, while the number of units stationed in east Malaysia rose from four and a half in March 1963 to 15 by December 1965.[145]

But by 1952, with commitments in three colonial emergencies plus Korea, the War Office's cupboard was bare. If another emergency arose they would have to remove a brigade from West Germany, although fear of the likely political repercussions on their NATO partners meant that they kept that fact secret even from the brigade commander.[146] It was to avoid just such a potential crisis that in 1957, Duncan Sandys, the Minister of Defence, decided that a strategic reserve, located in the United Kingdom and able to move by air and sea to any trouble spot, would be

[139] TNA WO 384/1. Disposition of British troops as at 31 March 1951.

[140] TNA WO 384/50. Active army strength, 31 September 1963.

[141] TNA WO 216/233. Montgomery, The British Army: Post-war. Fundamentals of its structure, 6 November 1947.

[142] TNA WO 216/563. Note by CIGS, Tasks, 29 October 1952.

[143] TNA CO 537/3692. Notes of a meeting at 10.30am on 17 June 1948 to discuss the military situation in Malaya; M. A. Bellis, *The British Army Overseas 1945–1970* (privately published, 2001), 9–10. A 'unit' was a Lieutenant-Colonel's command. It might have been an infantry battalion, a cavalry regiment, or an artillery regiment. These figures ignore sub-units, i.e. infantry companies, armoured car squadrons, artillery batteries, etc.

[144] Bellis, *The British Army Overseas*, 22–3.

[145] Bellis, *The British Army Overseas*, 26–7, 30–1; TNA WO 32/19267. Extract from minutes of COS(63)22 meeting, 29 March 1963; TNA WO 305/3326. The Director of Borneo Operations, Quarterly Operation Report, 1 October 1965 to 31 December 1965, 17 January 1966.

[146] TNA DEFE 11/18/COS(52)10. Note by War Office, Strategic Reserve, 2 January 1952; TNA DEFE 11/18/COS(52)4 meeting, 8 January 1952; TNA DEFE 11/18/COS(52)22 meeting, 7 February 1952; TNA DEFE 11/18/COS(52)185. Note by CIGS, Provision of strategic reserve, 29 March 1952.

one of the centrepieces of the all-regular army he created. A sensible solution in theory, in practice it was less than ideal. Because there were too few soldiers in the all-regular army to provide the support and administrative units for it, the reserve was initially divided into two echelons. The first echelon, consisting of two infantry brigade groups and a parachute brigade group, none of which could be maintained at their full manpower establishment, were designated for immediate deployment overseas for internal security operations. Each brigade group was air transportable, and had its proper complement of administrative units. Equipment that could not be moved by air was held in stockpiles overseas in likely theatres of operations. The second echelon, which was manned at an even lower level, consisted of an armoured and two infantry brigade groups. It was designated to fight limited and global (i.e. nuclear) wars, but because it was bereft of all administrative units, it could not be sent overseas unless regular army reservists were first mobilized.[147]

The experiment of dividing the Strategic Reserve into two echelons, only one of which was specifically designated to conduct internal security operations, was short-lived. In 1958 almost the whole of the Strategic Reserve was committed overseas, to Kenya, Aden, Cyprus, and Jordan, often on the kind of operations for which it was neither prepared nor trained. Units that had expected to be given three months of specialized training before being sent abroad were dispatched at three days' notice. Soldiers were cross-posted between units to bring units up to their proper manpower establishment, and so found themselves amongst strangers. One brigade sent to Cyprus had not done any company training for over a year. Another brigade was broken up and its battalions placed under different brigade commanders, and much of their hurriedly issued mechanical transport broke down.[148] The most important lessons were that the whole Reserve had to come under a single commander, all units had to be trained for both internal security and limited war operations, all had to be made air-transportable, and holding some units at a very low level of manning had made realistic training impossible.[149] Henceforth all brigades were to be trained for both roles.[150] But what the War Office could not do was to overcome shortages of personnel. In the early 1960s the army was trying slowly to build itself up to an all-regular force of 182,000 men, and infantrymen and administrative units were in short supply. The War Office had hoped to create a Strategic Reserve of one parachute and four infantry brigade groups by withdrawing formations from BAOR, but political considerations made that impossible. Consequently, in the early 1960s the Strategic Reserve consisted of only three undermanned brigade

---

[147] TNA WO 32/17428. WO to all GOC-in-Cs United Kingdom, 30 August 1957; TNA DEFE 13/86. Deputy Chief of Staff, The organisation of the strategic reserve, 7 January 1958.
[148] TNA WO 32/17428. Maj.-Gen G. C. Gordon Lennox, GOC 3 division, The Strategic Reserve and its state of readiness for war—both 'hot' and 'cold', n.d. but *c*.11 September 1958; TNA WO 163/630/ECAC/G(58)51. DCIGS, Analysis of the situation resulting from recent emergency moves, 23 October 1958.
[149] TNA WO 32/17428. Lt.-Gen. Sir R. Bower to WO, 12 September 1958.
[150] TNA WO 32/17428. DSD to all GOC-in-Cs home and overseas, 22 October 1958; TNA WO 32/17428. Army Commanders Conference, 30 January 1959; TNA WO 163/653/ECAC/P(59)21. DCIGS, Directive to GOC-in-C Southern Command, 31 March 1959; TNA WO 32/17428. Directive to Commander, 1 Division, for period 1 January to 31 December 1959.

groups, only two of which had their proper complement of administrative units and so could be dispatched overseas quickly.[151]

Unable to deploy more than a small proportion of their own manpower in the counter-insurgency role, the British looked elsewhere for men. Between 1950 and 1957, an average of between 10 and 15 per cent of soldiers in the British army were recruited in the colonies. They served in regular colonial regiments such as the Kings African Rifles (raised in the East African colonies), the Royal West African Frontier Force (recruited in the West African colonies), the Gurkhas (recruited from the independent kingdom of Nepal), or the Malay and Federation Regiments, recruited in Malaya. But the forces that the British deployed in Malaya and Kenya during the emergencies included a disproportionate number of colonial troops. Although the proportion of colonials deployed in East Africa fell from 85.5 per cent of the garrison in 1952 to 57.6 per cent at the end of 1956, throughout the Kenya Emergency, soldiers recruited in Britain were always in a minority in the colony. In Malay the proportion of colonial soldiers remained fairly steady at between 42 and 44 per cent of the garrison between 1950 and 1956, before rising to just below 50 per cent in 1957.[152] During the Borneo Confrontation the British relied even more heavily on colonial troops. Sixty-three per cent of the troops in FARELF in December 1962 were colonials, and even after a build-up of British personnel in the theatre, colonials still accounted for over 53 per cent in June 1966. In Aden the proportion of colonials varied from 46.3 per cent in December 1963 at the start of the emergency, to 39 per cent by June 1966.[153]

Employing colonial regular soldiers to fight counter-insurgency campaigns had two advantages. If they became casualties the British electorate was, on the whole, indifferent, and their fate was not likely to generate the same level of concern in Britain as the deaths of British soldiers. They were also cheaper. In 1949 the DCIGS estimated that two colonial soldiers could be had for the same price as a single British soldier.[154] This raises the question of why, given these advantages, and their determination to employ as many British troops as possible on other tasks, the army did not make even more use of colonials. The Second World War had demonstrated that Britain alone did not have sufficient military manpower to

[151] TNA WO 163/645/P(60)12. DCIGS, Composition of the Strategic Reserve and the provision of administrative support, 29 March 1960; TNA WO 163/645/P(60)18. DCIGS, Pre-proclamation reservists for limited war, 26 May 1960; TNA WO 163/660/AC/P(61)14. DCIGS, Organisation of the Strategic Reserve, 10 March 1961; TNA WO 163/660/AC/M(61)5. Minutes of the 249 meeting of the Army Council, 16 March 1961.
[152] TNA WO 384/20 . Table 13. Strength at home and overseas. Male all ranks, including colonial troops, March 1956; TNA WO 384/30. Table 14. Strength at home and overseas. Male all ranks, including colonial troops, September. 1958; TNA WO 384/50. Table 11. Strength at home and overseas. Male all ranks including the Colonial Troops, 1 December 1963; TNA WO 384/55. Table 11. Strength at home and overseas. Male all ranks including the Colonial Troops, 1 March 1965.
[153] TNA WO 384/50. Table 11. Strength at home and overseas. Male all ranks including the Colonial Troops, 1 December 1963; TNA WO 384/55. Table 11. Strength at home and overseas. Male all ranks including the Colonial Troops, 1 June 1966.
[154] TNA WO 216/322. DCIGS, Army Commanders Conference to be held on 17 November 1949. Brief for item 1. Overall size and shape and problems of organisation in the army, 8 November 1949.

be a great power unless it could also mobilize the resources of its empire.[155] But Indian independence in August 1947 meant that the British lost control of their single most powerful imperial military asset, the Indian army. However, they retained a considerable empire in Africa and South East Asia, and the Labour government and its advisers believed they could make good the shortfall in military manpower caused by Indian independence by raising extra troops from there. Thus they took care when negotiating Indian independence to reach an agreement with the governments of India and Nepal that they would be permitted to raise a force of 10,400 Gurkhas, sufficient to man part of an Anglo-Gurkha division to garrison Malaya.[156] After touring the African empire in 1947 Montgomery returned home full of ideas for a large African army.[157] However, colonial military manpower was never the panacea that it might at first sight seem to have been. Someone had to pay for it, someone had to lead it, and there were a variety of political obstacles that restricted the places where it could be employed.

The doctrine governing expenditure on the defence of the colonies was established in 1899. Each colony was expected to pay for its own locally raised forces from its own revenues. A colony that paid nothing towards the cost of the Royal Navy was expected to bear the full cost of any British garrison, provided that such a charge did not absorb an undue proportion of its revenues. It was also expected to pay in proportion to its means towards the cost of the general defence of the Empire.[158] In 1939 most colonial regular forces passed from the control of their own governments and came under the direct control of the War Office. After 1945 the War Office wanted this state of affairs to continue.[159] As Montgomery explained in December 1947 'the solution to aim at was that the War Office should retain control whilst the Colonies paid and he thought that a solution on these lines might well be achieved.'[160]

It could not be, for colonial governments were unwilling to write a blank cheque which the War Office could cash. In December 1948 ministers agreed in principle

---

[155] TNA WO 163/94/ECAC/P(44)52. Joint Secretaries, Plans for the transition period: reversion of colonial forces to Colonial Office control, 13 June 1944; TNA CAB 131/2/DO(46)29. Secretary of State War, The use of colonial and foreign manpower, 1 March 1946.

[156] TNA CAB 131/4/DO(47)22. Secretary of State India, The future of the Gurkhas, 7 March 1947; TNA CAB 131/4/DO(47)30. Note by the Joint Secretaries, The future of the Gurkhas, 28 March 1947; TNA WO 163/634/AC/P(57)46. VCIGS, Progress of negotiations with Nepal over the use of Gurkhas, 3 July 1957; TNA WO 163/108/ECAC/M(49)2. Minutes of the 386 meeting of the ECAC, 28 January 1948.

[157] IWMDoD Field Marshal Viscount Montgomery of Alamein mss. BLM 183/1. Diary part 10, 13 Nov. to 15 February 1948.

[158] TNA WO 163/94/ECAC/P(44)52. Joint Secretaries, Plans for the transition period: reversion of colonial forces to Colonial Office control, 13 June 1944.

[159] TNA WO 163/94/ECAC/P(44)52. Joint Secretaries, Plans for the transition period: reversion of colonial forces to Colonial Office control, 13 June 1944; IWMDoD. Field Marshal Viscount Montgomery of Alamein mss. BLM 183/2. Memorandum. Tour in Africa in November/December 1947 by Field Marshal Viscount Montgomery of Alamein, CIGS, 19 December 1947; TNA WO 216/193. VCIGS to Irwin, 24 July 1946; TNA W0 216/242. PUS to CIGS and Irwin, 27 November 1947.

[160] IWMDoD. Field Marshal Viscount Montgomery of Alamein mss. BLM 183/10. Minutes of the CIGS's meeting with heads of Departments in room 218 on 23 December 1947.

that the War Office would continue to control and administer African, but not Malayan, colonial forces. Each colony would be responsible for paying for those troops it needed to maintain internal security, although if the burden was too great the Colonial Office might provide a subsidy. The British government, through the War Office budget, would pay for any colonial forces needed for imperial defence.[161] The details of just who should pay for what and how much were left to be settled in a series of conferences, but the War Office never got what it wanted, colonial soldiers free of charge.[162]

The second constraint limiting the number of colonial soldiers who could be raised was the shortage of officers to lead them. To the War Office it was axiomatic that African soldiers, and to a lesser extent South East Asians, had to be led by British officers, if for no other reason than that there were too few Africans with a sufficiently high level of education to do the job. (Suitably qualified Gurkha and Malay candidates were allowed to attend Sandhurst and were then commissioned into their own regiments.)[163] Before 1939 generous scales of pay and allowances, and low rates of colonial income tax, had meant that there was no shortage of talented officers ready to fill the comparatively limited number of vacancies in the colonial forces.[164] After 1945 that was no longer the case. In 1952 the GOC West Africa explained that service with colonial troops was unpopular, partly because of the climate, partly because of the lack of family accommodation and partly because the financial incentives that had existed before 1939 were no longer available.[165] Officers married younger than they did before 1939 and were reluctant to subject their families to the discomforts of life in the tropics, especially if when they did so their pay was subject to high rates of British income tax.[166] Furthermore, the demand for British officers to serve in the colonies had increased. Whereas before 1939 the War Office had only to allocate 3 per cent to its officer corps to the colonial forces, by 1955 it needed to find 5 per cent, or 1,700 officers. Because

[161] TNA CAB 130/44/GEN 264/1 meeting. Financing of Colonial Defence. Minutes of a meeting of ministers held at 10 Downing Street, 10 December 1948; TNA T 220/1395. CO Memorandum, Future of the Colonial forces, n.d. but *c.* January 1955.
[162] TNA WO 163/108/ECAC/M(49)1. Minutes of 384 meeting ECAC, 14 January 1949; TNA CAB 131/7/DO(49)44. Alexander, Colonial Forces, 16 May 1949; TNA CAB 131/8/DO(49)17 meeting Cabinet Defence Committee, 1 July 1949; TNA CAB 131/7/DO(49)52. Alexander, Colonial Forces, 19 July 1949; TNA CAB 131/8/DO(49)18 meeting Cabinet Defence Committee, 27 July 1949; TNA CAB 131/9/DO(50)3. Colonial Secretary, Report on African Forces Conference, 1949, 14 January 1950; TNA CAB 131/8/DO(50)2 meeting Cabinet Defence Committee, 23 January 1950; TNA WO 163/113/ECAC/P(50)105. PUS, East African Forces. Nairobi Conference—October, 1950, 6 November 1950; TNA CAB 131/11/DO(51)45. Memorandum by Secretary of State for Colonies, East and Central African Forces, 5 April 1951; TNA CAB 131/10/DO(51)10 meeting Cabinet Defence Committee, 23 April 1951; D. Killingray, 'The idea of a British Imperial Army', *Journal of African History*, vol. 20 (1979), 421–36.
[163] TNA WO 163/104/M(47)37. Minutes of the 327 meeting of the ECAC, 10 October 1947.
[164] D. French, *Military Identities. The Regimental System, the British Army, and the British People c. 1870–2000* (Oxford: Oxford University Press, 2005), 159–60.
[165] TNA WO 216/514. Notes on the CIGS's Conference with Army Commanders 1952, 7 August 1952.
[166] TNA CAB 129/76/CP(55)89. Lord Chancellor, Security in the colonies, 22 July 1955; TNA WO 163/630/ECAC/P(58)58. Adjutant-General, Adviser on the provision of seconded personnel for Commonwealth and Colonial forces, 21 July 1958.

volunteers were in short supply, the shortfall had to be made good by compelling some National Service officers to serve with colonial units.[167]

Shortages of money and of British officers thus limited the size of the colonial forces that the British could raise. Political considerations constrained where those forces could be deployed. This was especially apparent in the case of the Gurkhas. Nepal was landlocked, but under the terms of the November 1947 Tripartite agreement signed with the Indian and Nepalese governments, the Indian government allowed the British to continue using on a temporary basis two existing Gurkha recruiting depots in northern India, and they also gave the British transit rights through India to and from Nepal.[168] But that also meant that the Indian government had a veto over the kinds of operations that the Gurkhas could be employed to conduct. They were willing to see them employed to suppress the Communist insurgency in Malaya, but even before independence Indian politicians had made it plain that they would not welcome them being used to suppress colonial freedom movements elsewhere.[169] By 1953 left-wing political parties in India were pressuring the Indian government to stop the British recruiting Gurkhas, and the British had to enter into tortuous negotiations to ensure they could continue doing so.[170] Furthermore, the British were also aware of Nepal's basic geo-strategic position, sandwiched between two dominant neighbours, India and China, and, as the Ministry of Defence noted in 1958, 'One policy which they share in common is a deep mistrust of "colonialism" or "imperialism". India's foreign policy moreover is based upon neutralism.'[171] In practice, therefore, it was impossible to employ Gurkhas outside the Far East.[172]

Political constraints also limited the utility of other colonial forces. In 1951 Slim did consider sending Royal West African Frontier Forces units to the Far East. But the rapid movement towards independence in West Africa, coupled with the need to maintain a strong internal security force in the region following the Gold Coast riots of 1948, meant that they remained at home.[173] Local security commitments meant that the Malay and Federal Regiments, and the Aden Protectorate Levies and its successor, the Federal Regular Army, never served outside their own country.

[167] TNA WO 163/635/ECAC/G(57)2. Adjutant-General, Report on the financial conditions of service by the sub-committee on terms of service for British personnel serving in Commonwealth, colonial and other national forces, 8 January 1957; TNA WO 163/630/ECAC/M(58)9. Minutes of the 629th meeting of the ECAC, 4 July 1958.
[168] TNA WO 163/60/AC/P(54)9. Note by Secretariat, Recruitment of Gurkhas to the British Army, 9 April 1954.
[169] IWMDoD. Field Marshal Viscount Montgomery of Alamein mss. BLM 181/5. CIGS to Attlee, 24 June 1947.
[170] TNA WO 216/652. VCIGS, Recruitment of Gurkhas to the British army, 1 December 1952; TNA WO 216/652. A. C. B. Symon to Harding, CIGS, 9 December 1952 & Harding to A. C. B. Symon, 11 December 1952; TNA WO 216/652. Lt.-Gen. H. Redman to Maj.-Gen. L. E. C. M. Peronne, 12 January 1953; TNA WO 163/617/ECAC/M(53)9. Minutes of the 536 meeting of the ECAC, 3 May 1953.
[171] TNA DEFE 7/680. Questions raised by the Minister of Defence on army deployment, 15 January 1958.
[172] TNA CAB 131/23/D(60)12 meeting Cabinet Defence Committee, 7 December 1960; TNA CAB 131/25/D(61)4 meeting Cabinet Defence Committee, 17 February 1961.
[173] TNA W0 216/439. CIGS to VCIGS. Notes of talk with Gen. Keightley, 13 October 1951.

Only in East Africa was it possible to deploy colonial units with some degree of freedom outside their own region. Three King's African Rifle battalions served at different times in Malaya, while units of the same regiment recruited from outside Kenya joined the Kenya-raised battalions in fighting the Mau Mau.

In 1957 the Sandys defence reforms threatened to reduce the army's manpower to only 165,000 men, a figure that the Army Council thought was about 15,000 men too few, and which they were in any case not certain they could fill with British recruits. They therefore explored the possibility of raising colonial units for employment outside their country of origin.[174] But the advice of the Colonial Office, the Commonwealth Relations Office and the Foreign Office sank the idea. If Gurkhas were stationed in Kenya and used in the Arabian Peninsula, the Indian and Nepalese governments would complain that they were being used to crush the legitimate aspirations of subject peoples. Furthermore, their presence in Kenya or Aden would be unwelcome to the indigenous populations. The Germans would react badly if they were stationed in BAOR, and India would object because it disliked NATO. The latter consideration also ruled out their being stationed in Britain as part of the army's Strategic Reserve. In general colonial governments would object on political grounds to the use of teeth arm units raised in their territories in other theatres. Arabs generally regard Africans as slaves, and so it was not advisable to station African troops in Arabia, and the Prime Minister of Malaya had asked that no African units be stationed in Malaya.[175] Colonial units were useful but, as the PUS of the War Office had concluded in 1952, 'However useful these local forces were, they could not be compared with British units which could be employed anywhere in the world.'[176]

Although the navy played no part in land-locked theatres such as Kenya, elsewhere it did serve an important function. Insurgents in need of supplies in Malaya and Cyprus, in the 1950s and East Malaysia in the 1960s looked overseas, to China, Greece, and Indonesia, for them. The navy, assisted by RAF maritime reconnaissance aircraft, weakened their insurgencies by preventing, or at least minimizing, the smuggling of weapons and supplies by sea. In the case of East Malaysia they also deterred or intercepted Indonesian raiders.[177] Operation 'Whisky Galore', a combination of maritime reconnaissance aircraft, frigates, minesweepers, and other patrol craft fitted with radar, operated in deeper waters offshore and acted as mother craft for shallow-draught boats and river craft operating inshore, and a coast-watching organization provided by the police,

---

[174] TNA WO 163/634/AC/M(57)20. Minutes of the 183 meeting of the Army Council, 25 July 1957.
[175] TNA WO 163/634/AC/P(57)67. VCIGS, Resources in non-UK manpower, 4 October 1957; TNA WO 163/634/AC/M(57)24. Minutes of the 187 meeting of the Army Council, 24 October 1957; WO 163/634/AC/P(57)79. PUS, Resources in non-UK manpower, 18 November 1957.
[176] TNA WO 163/118/ECAC/M(52)20. Minutes of the 513 meeting of the ECAC, 25 July 1952.
[177] T. Benbow, 'Maritime forces and counter-insurgency', in T. Benbow and R. Thornton (eds), *Dimensions of Counter-insurgency. Applying Experience to Practice* (London: Routledge, 2008), 74–89; C. Tuck, 'The Royal Navy and Confrontation, 1963–66', in G. Kennedy (ed.), *British Naval Strategy East of Suez, 1900–2000* (London: Frank Cass, 2005), 199–220.

civilians, and army units ashore, worked together to prevent the Indonesians infiltrating raiders into Sarawak and Sabah by sea.[178]

CONCLUSION

Those British colonial regimes that were confronted by insurgents were not failed states, but they were often fragile states. The government remained viable, but its capacity to protect and govern the civil population had been significantly degraded, insurgents called into question its legitimacy, and it had lost its monopoly over the legitimate use of violence.[179] They were fragile for several reasons. They were poor. The Colonial civil service was tiny compared to the territory and the number of people that it governed. Colonial police forces were small, and usually badly trained, poorly housed, and inadequately equipped, and their domestic intelligence services were frequently inadequate. In an emergency they could summon military help. But the number of soldiers that could be sent was limited, by the strategic necessity of deploying most of the army in a conventional role in Europe, by shortages of money that made it impossible to tap more than a small proportion of the potential military manpower of the colonies themselves, and by political constraints on deploying that manpower even when it had been raised. The next chapter will examine the aims and strategies of Britain's enemies, how the British (mis)understood those aims and objectives, and the mindsets that conditioned how they responded when their right to govern was openly challenged.

[178] TNA WO 305/2530. Director of Borneo Operations to Brigadier Ibrahim bin Ismail Pis, 20 January 1964.
[179] MOD, *Security and Stabilisation*—Lexicon 9 & 10.

2

Gangsters, Thugs, and Bandits: The Enemies of the Colonial State

In June 1950 the Colonial Secretary, James Griffiths, visited Singapore and Malaya to see the emergency for himself. At the end of his visit he told an audience in Singapore that the war in Malaya was 'clearly part of an attempt to impose a totalitarian Communism on the world. It is not a Nationalist movement at all.'[1] He was not speaking merely for public consumption. This was the private opinion of many ministers and officials. Eight months earlier David Rees-Williams, a junior minister in the Colonial Office, asserted that 'In Colonial territories Communism is more of a menace than is often realised. I am not mixing it up with nationalism.'[2] It was not only in Malaya where British ministers and officials believed they had detected a 'red' menace. In July 1949, the COS of MELF, Maj.-Gen. Harold Pyman, thought that he had found it in Kenya. 'The Kikuyu', he wrote, 'consider themselves the most politically advanced natives in Kenya, and are excellent material for the Communist inspired agitators who are now trying to work up discontent and to promote strikes.' He noted that 'At a meeting on 1 May 1949 at Nairobi, five leading trade unions announced the formation of an "East African Trades Union Congress". One of the principal union leaders is a well-known Communist—Jomo Kenyatta, formerly the secretary of the Kikuyu Central Association.'[3] Cyprus also seemed to be fertile ground for Communist subversion. 'The Cyprus problem', the COS insisted in June 1955, 'has long been over-simplified as one of British resistance to an overwhelming desire for Enosis on the part of the inhabitants of Cyprus. It is not, in general, sufficiently realised that of the two sections of Greek-speaking Cypriots demanding Enosis, the Communist [sic] has the more potential power; that, to that section the exploitation of the Enosis agitation is only a means by which it hopes to achieve the withdrawal of the British forces and the establishment of Communist control over Cyprus, with the strategic implications that this involves; and that, even the grant of an elective constitution might involve a risk of Communist seizure of power.'[4] In Borneo in 1963 both army commanders and the head of the Malaysian Special Branch recognized that

[1] *Manchester Guardian*, 9 June 1950.
[2] TNA CO 537/4401. Mr D. Rees-Williams to Sir T. Lloyd, 10 October 1949.
[3] LHCMA. Gen. Sir H. E. Pyman mss 7/1/298. Diary note, n.d. but *c*. July 1949.
[4] TNA CAB 21/2889/COS(55)153. Enc.: Conclusions of the BDCC (Middle East) on the effect of possible political developments on the security of the British base in Cyprus, n.d. but *c*.27 June 1955.

local insurgents were their immediate problem, 'but ultimately it is Communism from Indonesia and/or China which will pose the greatest threat.'[5]

THE COLD WAR AND THE ROOTS OF INSURGENCY

It is easy to understand why many ministers and officials thought they saw Communist conspiracies whenever a colony burst into unrest. The Gold Coast riots and the opening of the Malayan emergency coincided with the start of the Cold War in Western Europe and the coming to power of Mao Zedong and the Communist party in China. The spread of thermo-nuclear weapons in the mid-1950s seemed to make the threat worse. In October 1955 the COS concluded that, because the Soviet Union knew that the USA had thermo-nuclear weapons and was prepared to use them, they had decided to change their tactics. Overt expansion would give way to more emphasis on subversion and efforts to bring about disintegration of the western powers from within. 'Their aim', warned the COS, 'is world revolution leading to international Communism under Russian leadership. In Asia Communist China has a somewhat similar objective.' Their tactics include spreading dissension between nations, exploiting national and racial movements, and backing them if necessary by the clandestine supply of arms and money.[6]

There were sceptics who did not accept this consensus. Some Colonial Office officials thought that MI5 and the MOD did not really understand what was happening in the colonies, and were apt to mistake every manifestation of local nationalism for Communism.[7] In November 1955, having perused a list of lectures that MI5 training officers proposed to give to colonial police officers, one Colonial Office official asked plaintively if it might be possible to include a single lecture on the threat posed by colonial nationalism which he thought was becoming a growing problem.[8] But, the Colonial Office agreed that even if Communists had not instigated unrest, they would be quick to take advantage of it.[9] Elsewhere a Manichaean view of the struggle between Communism and the western powers was commonplace. Communism was an evil philosophy, according to a manual issued for the guidance of British troops operating in South East Asia in 1962, because if it triumphed 'it means the elimination of free societies everywhere—it spells the end of freedom, it spells the end of a way of life, it spells the end of all the

---

[5] TNA WO 305/2520. HQ British Forces (Borneo). Joint Perintrep no. 10. 11 March 1963; IWMSA. Accession No. 10175. R. J. W. Craig, Transcript, 31.

[6] TNA DEFE 32/4/COS(55)262. Memorandum by the COS, Cold War—countering covert aggression, 12 October 1955.

[7] TNA CO 1035/1. Committee on Security in the Colonies, Briefing paper for Colonial Secretary, n.d. but *c.* 1 May 1956; TNA CO 1035/118. Minutes by J. Barton, 28 May & 16 October 1956.

[8] TNA CO 1035/55. Watson to Hollis, 5 November 1955.

[9] TNA CO 968/244. Minute by J. Barton, 18 February 1953.

powers for goodness in the world—Christianity, Islam, Buddhism, Hinduism, Judaism—it spells the end of our birthright.'[10]

In Malaya, Britain's opponents were Communists and they did try to pursue the kind of Maoist strategy that Thompson outlined in his book. During the Second World War the MCP, which was largely a Chinese-ethnic organization, had taken to the jungle, and spearheaded the resistance to the Japanese occupation. In 1945 it acquiesced in the British re-occupation of Malaya and reverted to its pre-war policy of permeating by covert means the Malayan trades union movement. By 1947 it controlled the great majority of trades unions through its front organizations. But in March 1947 its successes turned to ashes, when the party discovered not only that its secretary general had disappeared, taking with him most of the party's funds, but that he had been a double agent who had worked for the British. The strategy of peaceful penetration was rendered nugatory by this defection, and thereafter the party turned to a new and more militant policy. This development was actually hastened by a government clamp-down on the party and trades unions, and in May and June 1948 local leaders increasingly took matters into their own hands.[11] The resulting strikes and assassinations produced an outcry from the European community that forced the colonial government to act without much planning and declare a state of emergency in mid-June. It was these local developments, not some long concocted plot by the Kremlin, that created the situation that led to the emergency.[12]

Following the declaration of the emergency and a wave of arrests by the security forces, many members of the party still at large, including the new secretary-general, Chin Peng, withdrew into the jungle. There the insurgents' organization evolved into three mutually supporting groups. The MCP was organized on orthodox Communist party lines through a hierarchy of committees. Its armed wing, the MRLA, according to a British intelligence estimate in 1948, numbered between 3,000 and 5,000 armed men. When it first took to the jungle it was organized at least notionally into large units, self-styled 'regiments', but it more usually operated in groups of between 10 and 50. During the Japanese occupation of Malaya about half a million Chinese labourers had become squatters, occupying land they did not own on the fringes of the jungle and where, beyond the control of the government, they eked out a precarious existence growing food and doing labouring jobs. Many other Chinese worked as rubber tappers, and lived in

---

[10] TNA WO 291/2480. Anti-guerrilla operations in South East Asia. Part 1. Tactics. (First edn, April 1962.)

[11] R. Stubbs, *Hearts and Minds in Guerrilla Warfare. The Malayan Emergency 1948–60* (Oxford: Oxford University Press, 1989), 42–59.

[12] A. J. Stockwell, 'A widespread and long-concocted plot to overthrow government in Malaya? The origins of the Malayan emergency', *JICH*, vol. 21, no. 3 (1993–4), 66–88; Stubbs, *Hearts and Minds*, 42–61. For the Kremlin plot thesis, see TNA CAB 21/1681/MAL.C(50)27. Colonial Secretary, Cabinet Malaya Committee: General Background, 14 July 1950; TNA KV 4/408. J. P. Morton, Malayan emergency, n.d. but *c*.1960; L. Efimova, 'Did the Soviet Union instruct Southeast Asian communists to revolt? New Russian evidence on the Calcutta Youth conference of February 1948', *Journal of South East Asian Studies*, vol. 40 (2009), 449–69; P. Deery, 'Malaya, 1948. Britain's Asian Cold War?', *Journal of Cold War Studies*, vol. 9 (2007), 29–54.

plantation labour lines. Mired in poverty, and treated as second-class citizens, they provided an essential reservoir of supporters for the MRLA. The insurgents established their own organization, the Min Yuen (Masses Organization) to tap into this reservoir and to gather the food, money, intelligence, and recruits that the MRLA needed. Sometimes the help was freely given, sometimes it was not. Anyone who refused it was liable to be abducted and assassinated. The party's greatest weakness was and remained that it was an overwhelmingly ethnic Chinese organization with few Malay members.[13]

In December 1949 the party's Central Committee issued 'The supplementary views on the Strategy of the Malayan Revolutionary War', in which it posited a three-stage campaign. In the first phase they would wage widespread guerrilla warfare across Malaya from temporary bases. These operations would not only wear down the security forces, they would also enable the MRLA to seize arms and grow in strength, and allow the Min Yuen to expand. Phase two would be an extension of this process until, in phase three the Min Yuen would gradually assume government powers as it took control of areas abandoned by the security forces. This would permit larger concentrations of Communist forces, and guerrilla warfare would develop gradually into a war of movement. The MRLA would establish permanent bases and the guerrillas would evolve into a regular fighting force.[14]

This was a classic Maoist strategy, and the MCP did seek to establish a Communist regime in Malaya. But elsewhere Rees-Williams and those who thought like him were apt to confuse Communism with nationalism. Direct Communist involvement in most of the other insurgencies that the British confronted was slight. In British Guiana, where the British declared a state of emergency in October 1953, they called the PPP a Communist organization. Some of its leaders were probably fellow-travellers, but its friends, with more justice, thought it was simply a radical nationalist movement giving voice to the frustration and disillusionment resulting from the slow pace of social and economic development under colonial rule. In fact, British Guiana is the odd man out in this study. It was the insurgency that never was. In October 1953 the British government thought that the PPP was but one step away from effecting a Communist take-over of British Guiana, and declared a state of emergency to forestall it.[15] However, a

---

[13] TNA WO 279/241. Director of Operations, Malaya, Conduct of anti-terrorist operations in Malaya (Malaya: Kuala Lumpur, 3rd edn, 1958); TNA CO 537/3692. Commissioner General South East Asia to CO, 26 June 1948; TNA DEFE 11/33. A paper on the dimensions and nature of the security problem confronting the government of the Federation of Malaya, 16 September 1948; T. Harper, *The End of Empire and the Making of Malaya* (Cambridge: Cambridge University Press, 1999), 160–1.

[14] TNA CO 537/5975/JIAC(50)1(Final). Joint Intelligence Advisory Committee, Malaya, The potential of the Malayan Communist Party, 24 October 1950; C. Peng, *My Side of History* (Singapore: Media Masters, 2003), 238.

[15] J. G. Rose, 'British colonial policy and the transfer of power in British Guiana, 1945–1964' (Ph.D. dissertation, University of London, 1992), 129–31; F. Furedi, *Colonial Wars and the Politics of Third World Nationalism* (London: I. B. Tauris, 1998), 43–4, 164–6; TNA CAB 129/63/C(53)261. Memorandum by the Colonial Secretary, British Guiana, 30 September 1953; TNA CAB 195/11/CC54(53). Cabinet meeting, 2 October 1953; TNA CAB 128/26/CC(53)54 meeting.

correspondent of the *Times*, hardly a newspaper likely to favour the Communist cause, reported from the capital, Georgetown, that that the situation was perfectly normal. 'There are no signs of impending crisis such as would justify a revocation of the constitution, nor of any disorder necessitating additional troops.'[16] Nor did the situation on the ground seem to justify such drastic steps. Forbes Burnham, a minister in the PPP government, denied that the party planned a Communist coup, pointing out that coup plotters needed arms and the PPP had none.[17] It was the British, not the PPP who were the insurgents in 1953. The PPP had won power legitimately in a general election in April 1953. It was the first held in British Guiana on the basis of universal suffrage and the PPP gained a clear majority of all votes cast. It therefore had greater claims to political legitimacy than Britain's own government. In the October 1951 election, thanks to the anomalies of the British first-past-the-post electoral system, Churchill's party had won more seats than their Labour opponents, but on a smaller share of the vote.[18]

Direct Communist involvement in insurgencies was equally limited elsewhere. Formed in 1951, by 1962 the CCO in Sarawak consisted of a cadre of 800 members, who in turn controlled small cells of 'activists', who tried to infiltrate and take control of Chinese schools, trades unions, newspapers, and other organizations. Leading Communists also held senior positions in the ostensibly moderate Sarawak United People's Party (SUPP), which had been formed by a group of English-speaking Chinese with the aim of working towards independence for Sarawak by constitutional means. But the CCO drew its support almost entirely from the ethnic Chinese community, and won little support in the majority Malay community.[19] The other two groups involved in the Borneo insurgency were but little influenced by Communism. They were the nationalist Partai Rakyat Brunei (PRB), established in 1956 by Sheikh A. M. Azahar, and the Indonesian government, led by President Sukarno, although lurking behind the latter was the Indonesian Communist Party. What the three groups had in common was their opposition to British plans to create a Malaysian Federal State out of the existing Federation of Malaya, and the British protectorates of Brunei, Sabah, and Sarawak. They regarded the British plan as a neo-colonial enterprise designed to perpetuate British influence in the region.[20]

Cabinet Conclusions, 2 October 1953; TNA CO 115/215. *The Official Gazette of British Guiana*, 9 October 1953.

[16] *Times*, 7 October 1953.

[17] *Times*, 9 October 1953; TNA WO 336/1. Brigadier A. C. Jackson to WO, November 1953; TNA WO 336/1. HQ Caribbean Area. Windsor Log; TNA CO 1031/780. Sir A. Savage to Colonial Secretary, 14 October 1953.

[18] The PPP won 51% of the valid votes cast in British Guiana in 1953. Rose, 'British Colonial Policy', 165. The Conservatives in 1951 won 48% of the total share of the vote in Great Britain, compared to Labour's total of 48.8%. D. Butler and G. Butler, *British Political Facts 1900–1985* (London: Macmillan, 1988), 26.

[19] TNA CO 1030/1105. Secretariat, Kuching, Paper for the Information of the Malaysia Commission, 12 March 1962.

[20] H. A. Majid, *Rebellion in Brunei. The 1962 Revolt, Imperialism, Confrontation, and Oil* (London: I. B. Tauris, 2007), 23–5; TNA CO 1030/1540. Sir A. Waddell to CO, 3 December 1962; C. Tuck, 'Borneo 1963–66: counter-insurgency operations and war termination', *SW&I*, vol. 15 (2004), 91;

Azahari mounted a failed coup in Brunei on 8 December 1962. He was driven to such extremes because, despite the fact that his party, which had stood on an anti-Federation platform, had swept the board in elections held in August 1962, the Sultan of Brunei had ignored the election results and used his built-in control of the Executive Council to press forward with his pro-federation policy.[21] Indonesia announced the start of the 'Confrontation' on 20 January 1963. But Sukharno did not pursue a Maoist strategy. He was intent on avoiding a conventional war, knowing that the British were bound to win. Instead he chose to place pressure on the British by a combination of diplomacy and low-level military activity. The later involved a mixture of covert military attacks, riots, sabotage, subversion, and economic boycotts. The military confrontation, which began in April 1963, took place along the 970 miles of land frontier that separated Sarawak and Sabah (or Eastern Malaysia, as they became after the creation of the Malaysian Federation in September 1963), and Indonesia. Operations took two forms: an internal threat mounted by the CCO and an external threat posed by cross-border raids carried out by local volunteers from Borneo, trained and often led by Indonesian regular soldiers.[22]

Elsewhere there is even less evidence that the opponents of the colonial state were either Communists or committed to a Maoist strategy. This is a significant point. The 'Malayan model' of counter-insurgency laid great emphasis on the need to defeat the political subversion, not just the guerrillas. But if the British did not understand, or take seriously, the political aims of their opponents, their counter-insurgency strategy was likely to go awry.

In Palestine the election of a Labour government in Britain in 1945 encouraged the Yishuv to believe that a pro-Zionist solution to the Palestine problem was possible. They were, therefore, understandably disappointed when in September 1945 it became clear that the Attlee administration would not lift the limits on Jewish immigration into Palestine that had been in place since 1939 and allow 100,000 Holocaust survivors to enter Palestine without delay.[23] The insurgents' common aim was to create an independent Jewish state in Palestine but they were divided over the lengths to which they were prepared to employ violence against the British administration to secure their goal. The largest group, the Haganah, numbered about 45,000 members in 1945. The armed wing of the officially sanctioned Jewish Agency, most of its members were tied down protecting Jewish settlements. But it also contained an elite mobile force, the Palmach, of about 1,500 men. There were two other small groups. The Irgun Zvai Leumi (IZL) numbered about 1,500 members. They hoped that, by raising the military, economic, and human cost of remaining in occupation of Palestine, they could

J. Subritzky, 'Britain, Konfrontasi, and the end of Empire in South East Asia, 1961–65', *JICH*, vol. 28, (2000), 213–14.

[21] Majid, *Rebellion in Brunei*, 79–86; P. Keatley, 'Fears of Brunei rebels', *Manchester Guardian*, 11 December 1963.

[22] Tuck, 'Borneo', 92.

[23] N. Rose, *'A Senseless, Squalid War': Voices from Palestine 1945–1948* (London: Bodley Head, 2009), 71–4.

demonstrate to the British that, far from being a strategic asset, it was a political liability, and thus persuade them to withdraw. The third group, variously known as the Stern Gang or Lohmei Cheruth Israel (Fighters for the Freedom of Israel or LECHI), numbered only 250–300 people. It fought what it regarded as an anti-imperialist war for the liberation of the Jewish people.[24] In the autumn of 1945 the three groups came together in the United Resistance Movement, and between November 1945 and the end of May 1946 they mounted some 50 major operations. The Haganah attacked the system of immigration control, while the LECHI/ IZL, which had less compunction about inflicting casualties on the security forces, attacked military and police targets.[25] But in July 1946, following an Irgun bomb attack on the British headquarters at the King David Hotel in Jerusalem that left 91 British, Arabs, and Jews dead, this precarious unity collapsed. Henceforth the IZL and LECHI went their own way, and the Haganah focused its attention on organizing the mass immigration of Jewish refugees into Palestine.[26]

In Palestine the British found themselves with the impossible task of balancing the interests of the Jewish and Arab communities. In Cyprus they faced a similar conundrum. Eighty per cent of the island's population were ethnic Greeks and wanted *enosis* (union) with Greece. The remaining 20 per cent were ethnic Turks and vehemently opposed them. There was a strong Communist trades union movement on the island, but by 1950 the politics of left and right had given way to the politics of communalism, and enosis was the only thing that could satisfy the aspirations of the majority of the Greek-Cypriot population.[27] On 10 November 1954 a right-wing, nationalist, and vehemently anti-Communist former Greek army-officer, Colonel George Grivas, landed secretly on the island and began to organize small groups of EOKA insurgents in Nicosia, and some of the larger villages. In January 1955 he met the leader of the Greek-Cypriot community, the Greek-Orthodox Archbishop Makarios, and they agreed that a campaign of violence to publicize the cause of enosis would begin on 25 March, Greek Independence Day, although it was later postponed to 1 April.[28]

Grivas knew that Cyprus was no place to pursue a Maoist strategy. Although parts of it were mountainous and forested, it was too small for such a strategy to succeed. Instead he opted for a strategy similar to that pursued by the Zionist insurgents in Palestine. Realizing that it would not be possible to drive the British from the island by military operations alone, his strategy was directed towards mounting such sustained opposition to the continued presence of the British that they would come to accept that the political cost of their remaining outweighed the

[24] Charters, 'Eyes of the Underground', *INS*, vol. 13 (1998), 163–5; Y. Bauer, 'From Cooperation to Resistance: the Haganha 1938–1946', *Middle Eastern Studies*, vol. 2 (1966), 205–6.

[25] Y. S. Brenner, 'The "Stern Gang" 1940–48', *Middle Eastern Studies*, vol. 2 (1965), 2–30.

[26] Rose, *'A Senseless, Squalid War'*, 113–19.

[27] D. M. Anderson, 'Policing and communal conflict: the Cyprus emergency, 1954–60', in D. M. Anderson and D. Killingray (eds), *Policing and Decolonisation. Politics, Nationalism and the Police, 1917–1965* (Manchester: Manchester University Press, 1992), 187–92.

[28] TNA WO 33/2736. History of EOKA, 1954–1959, 20 April 1960; C. Foley (ed.), *The Memoirs of General Grivas* (London: Longman, 1964), 24–9.

benefits. By provoking the security forces into mounting reprisals, he hoped to discredit the British in the eyes of world opinion at the UN and ensure that the Greek government continued to pressurize the British to withdraw.[29] EOKA pursued a flexible tactical policy to achieve these objectives. They mounted sabotage operations against government and military installations. They organized passive resistance and demonstrations against the government. Many of those taking part in these demonstrations were schoolchildren and students, employed by EOKA in the hope that the security forces would react in a heavy-handed manner against 'innocent' victims and deliver a propaganda victory to the insurgents.[30] They also imposed ruthless discipline on their own members. They were required to swear an oath of absolute obedience and anyone who broke it was marked down for assassination. They gathered intelligence by penetrating the police and administration, and they killed members of the security forces and Cypriot civilians whom they believed were 'traitors' because they were suspected of collaborating with the British or were simply guilty of careless talk.[31] Many of the victims, according to a confidential report produced by the Cyprus Intelligence Committee in January 1957, were innocent.[32] But they did not rob or steal from the civilian population. Funds provided by the Church and sympathizers in the USA meant they could pay for what they needed.[33] EOKA thus pursued a carefully considered strategy, military operations and diplomatic initiatives being carefully phased to assist Makarios in extracting concessions from the British.

With the exception of Aden State, none of Britain's opponents in Arab countries were tainted by Communism. What drove them all, in Egypt, Oman, and Aden, was a sense that the foreign presence in their country was a humiliation that had to be ended. Egyptians of almost every class and occupation regarded the British presence as a national disgrace. Any Egyptian government that appeared to be willing to tolerate it had little chance of remaining in power. A US State Department official who visited Egypt in 1951 found that 'The British are detested. The hatred against them is general and intense. It is shared by everyone in the country.'[34] Detestation turned to outright hostility when, in October 1951, the Egyptian government unilaterally abrogated the 1936 Anglo-Egyptian treaty. Egyptian nationalists were determined to demonstrate to the British that, far from being an asset, the Canal Zone base was a liability. They crippled the work of the base facilities by organizing the withdrawal of local labour, anti-British riots

---

[29] Foley (ed.), *The Memoirs of General Grivas*, 37–8.
[30] Foley (ed.), *The Memoirs of General Grivas*, 28–9, 34–5.
[31] TNA WO 33/2736. History of EOKA, 1954–1959, 20 April 1960; TNA CO 926/670/CIC (56)38. Cyprus Intelligence Committee. Intelligence Review for the second half of December 1956, 7 January 1957; Foley (ed.), *The Memoirs of General Grivas*, 25–6.
[32] TNA CO 926/670/CIC(57)2. Cyprus Intelligence Committee. Intelligence Review for the first half of January 1957, 22 January 1957.
[33] TNA CO 926/937/CIC(57)12. Cyprus Intelligence Committee. EOKA accounts, 8 May 1957; TNA WO 33/2736. History of EOKA, 1954–1959, 20 April 1960.
[34] Quoted in Wm. Roger Louis, *The British Empire in the Middle East 1945–51. Arab Nationalism, the United States, and Post-war Imperialism* (Oxford: Oxford University Press, 1984), 742.

took place in several towns in the Canal Zone, and armed insurgents began to shoot at British troops.

One of the leaders of the Egyptian nationalist movement was Colonel, later President, Gamel Abdul Nasser. After negotiating the British withdrawal from the Canal Zone in 1954, he inflicted a second humiliation on them in 1956 when they tried to return during the Suez crisis, and over the next decade he did his utmost to drive them from South Arabia. The SAF had few active supporters beyond the sheiks and emirs of the protectorates. The tribes of the interior disliked it because it threatened their autonomy. Aden's neighbour, the Imam of Yemen, had long claimed Aden and the protectorates as part of his territory, and periodically encouraged tribes within the protectorates to fight the British. Between 1954 and 1958 the British conducted an undeclared border war with the Yemen which eventually persuaded the Imam to withdraw his active support for dissident tribes-men within the WAP, and the frontier remained quiescent.[35] But after his over-throw in 1962, the same cause was taken up by the Republican government that toppled him, now with the support of Nasser. In June 1963, Sana' Radio an-nounced the establishment of the National Liberation Front. Its aims were to liberate the 'South', that is, the Federation of South Arabia, all of which it claimed belonged rightfully to Yemen; to oppose the Federal government, which it believed was bent on continued collaboration with the British; to bring about the removal of the British base in Aden; and to establish a single state embracing Yemen and the 'South'.[36]

These aims had great appeal to much of the Arab population of Aden colony itself, many of whom were Yemeni immigrants. Encouraged by the spread of pan-Arab nationalism across much of the Middle East in the 1950s, they recognized the Federation for what it was, a way of perpetuating British power and influence under a new guise. But, denied the opportunity by the government of pursuing their goals by constitutional means, the nationalists of the Adeni Trades Union Congress and the People's Socialist Party had no option other than to turn to extra-parliamentary means, and, in the case of some groups, to embrace Marxist-Leninism. By 1962 the British knew that most people in Aden opposed the merger of the colony and the protectorates, but they went ahead none the less.[37] The constitution sought to perpetuate the rule of tribal rulers, but the latter proved themselves singularly unable to reach a workable accommodation with the forces of Arab nationalism in the region.[38]

[35] TNA CAB 195/13/CM17(55). Cabinet Conclusions, 23 June 1955; TNA CAB 131/16/DC (55)4 meeting. Cabinet Defence Committee, 27 June 1955; TNA CAB 131/16/DC(55)18. Memorandum by the COS, Aden Protectorate, 8 July 1955; TNA CAB 131/16/DC(55)5 meeting. Cabinet Defence Committee, 11 July 1955; S. Mawby, 'Britain's Last Imperial Frontier: The Aden Protectorates, 1952–59', *JICH*, vol. 29 (2001), 89, 96.
[36] TNA CAB 191/12. LIC Aden, The National Liberation Front for the Liberation of the Occupied South, or the NLF, 25 January 1965.
[37] TNA CAB 128/36/CC(62)52 meeting. Cabinet Conclusions, 1 August 1962.
[38] TNA CO 1055/195. Trevaskis to Greenwood, 28 October 1964.

The merger passed off peacefully in January 1963, partly because many Adeni's regarded it as a *fait accompli*, and partly because many opposition leaders were in custody. A handful of bomb attacks shortly after the merger did nothing to shake the determination of the British and their Federal allies to close off avenues of peaceful protest.[39] However, repression was unavailing. In November 1963 large-scale strikes crippled the Port of Aden. Ostensibly this was an industrial dispute. But the governor, Sir Kennedy Trevaskis, thought that the strikers, who he believed were controlled by Egypt and the Yemen, were intent on arousing popular emotions against the British base and the Federation. The strikers did receive some outside help, but so obsessed were the British with their external enemies, that they were blind to the fact the strikers also had their own domestic socialist agenda.[40] Trevaskis was on the point of seizing what he thought was a great opportunity, to crush the strike, punish its leaders, and restore British prestige, when it collapsed of its own accord.[41] But less than a week later, on 10 December, he was given a second opportunity, which he did not fumble.

At 0850 hours the governor and several Federal Ministers were at Khormaksar civil airport in Aden waiting to board BAOC Flight BA 237 to London where they were due to take part in discussions about future constitutional developments in the Federation. A grenade was thrown at the party. Trevaskis was lucky. He only sustained a minor wound to his hand. Others standing nearby were not. The Deputy High Commissioner died of his injuries, an Indian woman was killed outright, and 24 civilians, including the Federal Minister of the Interior, were injured.[42] Trevaskis and the Federal ministers saw this as a marvellous opportunity to hit back at their nationalist opponents. They immediately declared a state of emergency, arrested over 140 local nationalist and trades union leaders, despite the fact that there was no real evidence to connect them to the attack, and deported a number of Yemenis living in Aden as a way of putting pressure on the Yemeni government.[43]

The insurgency in Aden was waged in two places. Up country in the Federation, the NLF recruited tribesmen who were then given guerrilla training by Egyptian and Yemeni instructors. The Egyptians wanted these groups to switch operations from one part of the Federation to another, taking advantage of local circumstances, so as to stretch British and Federal Forces. Inside Aden State, the NLF was organized on a cell basis and waged a campaign of urban terrorism, propaganda

---

[39] TNA CO 1055/62. Aden Intelligence Summary No. 1 for the month of January 1963, 31 January 1963; TNA CO 1055/196. Assistant High Commissioner Aden to CO, 1 February 1963.

[40] S. Mawby, 'Orientalism and the failure of British policy in the Middle East: the case of Aden', *History*, vol. 95 (2010), 342–4.

[41] TNA CO 1055/196. Trevaskis to CO, 28 November 1963, and CO to Trevaskis, 29 November 1963.

[42] TNA CO 1055/196. GOC Aden to DMO, 10 December 1963; TNA CO 1055/196. Trevaskis to CO, 10 December 1963.

[43] TNA CO 1055/196. Trevaskis to CO, 10 December 1963;TNA CO 1055/197. Trevaskis to CO, 13 & 19 December 1963.

and industrial action.[44] British security officials in Aden State divided their opponents into two groups: the largest was 'a floating group of amateurs, from 50 to 200 strong, who are apparently engaged in odd-job terrorism for cash and are thought to account for most incidents.' The second, smaller, but more dangerous group were better trained and carried out 'gangland style assassinations of the Arab police and security officers who work with the British.'[45] By 1965 the Egyptians were finding it increasingly difficult to control their protégés of the NLF and so in January 1966 in order to maintain their influence in Aden, they established a rival organization, the Front for the Liberation of South Yemen (FLOSY). It, too, consisted of a combination of fighters trained in Egypt or the Yemen, and 'casuals', who barely understood how to throw the grenades that were their favourite weapon.[46] What drove them to fight the British was, according to one of the more perceptive British security officials, not just sympathy for pan-Arabism, but a fierce determination to see the back of the British. 'The involvement in terrorism of the more sophisticated', he wrote, 'is readily comprehensible. Most of those in this category have strong anti-British and anti-Federal feelings, allied to sympathies for the Socialist Egypt and things Egyptian and an admiration for Nasser as the leader of militant Pan-"Arabism".'[47]

Oman was even less 'infected' by Communism than was Aden. The British presence in Oman was less obtrusive than it was in Aden, and it was the British-supported sultan who was the focus of the insurgency. The Sultanate of Muscat and Oman was situated between South Yemen and the Persian Gulf. It was sparsely populated, its three-quarters of a million inhabitants being divided into about three dozen tribes, many of which were themselves further sub-divided into smaller clans. Its people were poverty stricken, poorly educated, and disease-ridden. The foundation of the modern polity was the Treaty of Sib, signed in 1920 between the Sultan of Muscat and most of the leading Omani tribes of the interior. The Treaty established the sultan's paramountcy and his right to represent the tribes in external affairs. In return the tribes were granted a large measure of autonomy. They had the right to elect their own Imam, and he had the right to appoint his own Wali (Governors). But the boundaries between those areas under the Sultan's direct administration, and therefore the effective limits of British paramountcy, and areas under tribal administration, were not precisely defined.[48]

Just as in Aden, the British in Oman threw their support behind the most backward and conservative members of the local political elite. The sultan, Said bin Taimur, was reputed to be determined 'to preserve his country from the

[44] TNA CAB 191/12. LIC Aden, The National Liberation Front for the Liberation of the Occupied South, or the NLF, 25 January 1965; TNA CO 1035/178. Report of IS interrogation in Aden, 2–30 January, 30 January 1965.
[45] TNA CO 1055/220. H. Smith, 'Arab Terrorists in Aden stepping up attacks', *New York Times*, 8 June 1965.
[46] TNA FO 371/185233. J. V. Prendergast, A note on terrorism in Aden, 6 December 1966.
[47] Ibid.
[48] Smiley, *Arabian Assignment*, 8; TNA DEFE 7/2415. D. T. West to Maj. P. G. Castner, 9 August 1957, and enclosure, The Sultanate of Muscat and Oman.

contamination of modern ideas.'[49] He succeeded until the early 1950s, when the status quo created by the Treaty of Sib broke down. In 1954 the old Imam died. Encouraged and funded by the Saudi Arabian government, who wanted to secure control of oil deposits in the Buraimi oasis, which was partly owned by the Sheik of the Abu Dhabi and partly by the Sultan of Muscat, the new Imam, Ghalib bin Ali, and his energetic and charismatic brother Talib, mounted a rebellion against the Sultan. Said bin Taimur was widely unpopular.[50] Matters came to a head over oil concessions sought by a British oil company. Both the Sultan and the Imam claimed the right to control the concession. In 1956 Talib began to organize Omani exiles living in Saudi Arabia into the Omani Liberation Army. Supported by the Saudis, he demanded independence for the interior of Oman and the withdrawal of all British and Muscat troops from their territory. In 1957 the insurgents returned to Oman and established themselves on the Jebel Akhdar, a limestone plateau which was a huge natural fortress. Measuring 50 miles by 20 miles, its peaks rose to 10,000 feet before descending to a plateau at 6,000 feet where there were villages, cultivated land that could feed the insurgents, as well as caves to shelter them from air attacks. The only approaches to the plateau were up a small number of narrow ravines that were easily defended. By July 1957 the insurgents had occupied Nizwa, a key town in the interior, and ambushed and virtually destroyed the Sultan's army, at which point the Sultan appealed to the British for military assistance.[51]

Communists were also suspected of being responsible, at least to some degree, for unrest in Africa. Reference has already been made to Kenyatta's supposed Communist sympathies.[52] He had studied in the Soviet Union, but the experience had left him disillusioned with Soviet Communism. Dr Hastings Banda, the leader of the Nyasaland African Congress, was also suspected of having Communist sympathies. In December 1958 he attended the All-African People's Conference in Accra, where he was alleged to have held a secret meeting with Russian officials, arousing the fears of the administration in Nyasaland that the Soviets were ready to fish in troubled waters.[53] In reality both men were African nationalists who wanted to see an end of the control of their countries by a small minority of European settlers.

In Kenya some 42,000 European settlers dominated a population of about 5.6 million Africans. By the early 1950s a combination of population increase and land seizures by European settlers had produced a gnawing land hunger amongst the Kikuyu, Embu, and Meru. The best agricultural land in Kenya, the 16,000 square

[49] Smiley, *Arabian Assignment*, 40.
[50] D. F. Eickman, 'From theocracy to monarchy: authority and legitimacy in inner Oman, 1935–57', *International Journal of Middle Eastern Studies*, vol. 17 (1985), 3–24.
[51] TNA DEFE 7/2415. No. 73. Acting Political Resident Muscat to FO, 16 July 1957; J. E. Peterson, *Oman's Insurgencies. The Sultanate's Struggle for Supremacy* (London: Saqi, 2007), 54–84.
[52] Although Erskine explicitly denied that he was a Communist. IWMDoD. Gen. Sir G. W. Erskine mss 75/134/4. 'Notes for British Units coming to Kenya' [n.d. but *c*.1 August 1954].
[53] C. Baker, *State of Emergency: Crisis in Central Africa, Nyasaland, 1959–60* (London: I. B. Tauris, 1997), 8–9.

miles of the White Highlands, supported about two Europeans per square mile. By contrast, the 52,000 square miles of the less productive land in the Native Reserves had to support a population density of between 275 and 300 Kikuyu per square mile.[54] The situation for many of the KEM was worsening because European farmers were trying to dispose of many of those who lived as squatters on the edges of their farms and force them to return to the Native Reserves. But evictions only shifted the land hunger problem from the edge of the areas of European settlement to the Reserves, where there were no jobs or land. Conservative African landowners in the Reserves would not surrender any of their own land to help relieve population pressure, and the colonial administration would not force them to do so, for it could not afford to lose the support of these vital collaborators. Efforts by the government to impose more productive farming methods on the KEM so as to ensure that the land could support more people were not the answer. They were deeply unpopular, not least because in order to implement them chiefs were required to organize forced labour. Those conscripted often revolted, directing their ire against the chiefs, and their protests sometimes became violent. Other landless KEM found their way to Nairobi, where they swelled the growing population of the unemployed, under-employed and the criminal underworld. By the late 1940s much of the city's shanty areas was dominated by Kikuyu gangs, often composed of ex-servicemen, and the KEM had also become involved in militant politics and trades union activities.[55]

By 1950 Kikuyu society had divided into three parts. There was a conservative group of headmen, chiefs, senior churchmen, prominent businessmen, and landowners, whose authority rested on their willingness to collaborate with the colonial state. There was a group of moderate nationalists, of whom Kenyatta was the most prominent. They had formed the Kikuyu Central Association, which the government had promptly banned, and a pan-ethnic organization, the Kenyan African Union. Finally, in the 1930s a group of more militant nationalists had emerged whose views were to shape Mau Mau. They sought to protect the interests of those KEM who were being marginalized. They attacked the conservatives as having betrayed them, and the moderate nationalists because their agenda seemed to overlook their own needs for land and better wages. They drew support from the poor and landless peasants in the Reserves, from the urban unemployed of Nairobi, and from squatters dispossessed from European farms in the White Highlands. They were unpopular not just with Europeans, but also with Kikuyu landowners.[56]

Mau Mau adherents, drawn almost exclusively from the KEM, began administering secret oaths binding their supporters to the cause at some indeterminate

---

[54] TNA WO 291/1670. Operational Research Unit (Far East). Report Number 1/57. A comparison of the emergencies in Malaya and Kenya, 6 June 1957.

[55] D. Anderson, *Histories of the Hanged. Britain's Dirty War in Kenya and the End of Empire* (London: Weidenfeld & Nicolson, 2005), 3–37; D. Branch, *Defeating Mau Mau, Creating Kenya. Counterinsurgency, Civil War, and Decolonization* (Cambridge: Cambridge University Press, 2009), 6–8.

[56] Anderson, *Histories of the Hanged*, 11–13; Branch, *Defeating Mau Mau*, 28–35.

point between late 1948 and early 1950.[57] The oaths obliged people to reject all things European and oppose the government by violence if necessary. Those who took the oaths were promised that they would receive grants of European land when Kenya achieved self-government. Intimidation was applied to anyone who was reluctant to take an oath willingly. In August 1950, when it was apparent that the police could not stop the process of oath taking, the government banned the Mau Mau. But banning had little effect on the movement. By early 1952 Mau Mau adherents were openly attacking European farms and property and Kikuyu who were government supporters.[58] When the police investigated the attacks, they often met a wall of silence. Even chiefs and headmen were becoming intimidated by threats and were unwilling to co-operate with government.[59] But for some months the outgoing governor, Sir Philip Mitchell, and most of the central secretariat in Nairobi, were reluctant to acknowledge that there was a real danger of a breakdown of law and order. To do so would be tantamount to admitting that they had lost control of the situation, and, as late as 9 September 1952, Oliver Lyttelton, the Colonial Secretary, echoing their views, told Churchill that 'I do not take a very alarmist view of the situation in Kenya.'[60]

But their colleagues in the provincial and district administration in Central Province and the Rift Valley had no such scruples. Underpinning their fears of a breakdown of law and order was their deep resentment at the implied claim put forward by Kikuyu politicians that the British administrators had failed in their duty to protect the interests of the tribes they were governing. To add weight to their arguments they enlisted the support of settler politicians, who threatened to take matters into their own hands if the government did not act.[61] There were lurid debates in the Legislative Council in June and July 1952 and alarmist reports in the press.[62] They maintained their pressure for strong action throughout the emergency, so much so that Sir George Erskine, the GOC from 1952 to 1955, referred to them as 'the White Mau Mau'.[63] It was their uncompromising determination to retain their grip on power, coupled with half-submerged fears that, as a tiny minority, they could be swamped by the indigenous population, that help to explain why the emergency in Kenya was fought with more bitterness than any other campaign.

What finally broke the impasse in the administration was the arrival of a new governor, Sir Evelyn Baring. Even before he arrived he had been told by a District Commissioner on leave from Kenya that 'We were on the brink of a Kikuyu rising'.[64]

---

[57] D. A. Percox, *Britain, Kenya and the Cold War. Imperial Defence, Colonial Security and Decolonization* (London: Tauris Academic Studies, 2004), 30–6; Elkins, *Britain's Gulag*, 22–7.

[58] TNA CO 822/501. *Times*, 19 April 1952; Branch, *Defeating Mau Mau*, 21–4.

[59] TNA CO 822/2104. Draft letter from Acting Governor to P. Rogers, 17 August 1952.

[60] TNA PREM 11/472. Lyttelton to Churchill, 9 September 1952.

[61] TNA CO 822/2104. European Elected Members Organization. Notes on discussion at Government House on 8 August 1952.

[62] TNA PREM 11/472. J. Redfern, 'Colony calls for strong man', *Daily Express*, 6 September 1952; PREM 11/472. 'Double danger in Kenya', *Daily Express*, 26 September 1952.

[63] IWMDoD. Field Marshal Lord Carver mss. Box 17 file 1.Erskine to Carver, 18 September 1953.

[64] IWMSA. Accession No. 10224 . Sir A. Swann, Transcript 9.

As soon as he arrived in Nairobi Baring bypassed the secretariat and went on a personal tour through Central Province. This allowed the provincial administrators to make their case to him directly. The assassination of Senior Chief Waruhiu, who was one of the government's most influential supporters, on 7 October 1952, provided the pretext he needed to secure agreement from London for decisive action. Convinced that the KAU was no more than a front organization for the Mau Mau, Baring sought, and received permission, to declare an emergency, and arrest Kenyatta and the leaders of the KAU, whom he believed were the leaders of the Mau Mau. This, he hoped would quieten matters by restoring the confidence of loyalist Kikuyu and Europeans in the government.[65]

In Nyasaland the focus of African resentment was the Central African Federation. Created in 1953 by the Churchill government, the CAF consisted of the European-settler dominated self-governing colony of Southern Rhodesia, and the protectorates of Northern Rhodesia and Nyasaland. The British government hoped that the Federation would shun South African-style apartheid and embody the principle of racial partnership. But many European-settler politicians rejected that principle in favour of creating a European-dominated Federation. Both the Northern Rhodesian and Nyasaland African Congresses wanted to leave the Federation, seeing in it nothing more than a vehicle designed to perpetuate European domination.[66] In July 1958 Dr Hastings Banda, Nyasaland's leading African nationalist politician, returned to Nyasaland after 40 years living abroad, and took over the leadership of the NAC. A conference to review the constitution was due to be held in London in 1960 and African nationalists had good reason to fear that the Federal government, led by Sir Roy Welensky, would press for independence, as a step towards entrenching European power throughout the Federation.[67] Banda's immediate objective, which he tried to achieve in a series of meetings with government officials, was to secure an African majority in the Nyasaland Legislature before the conference met. He would then not only have a powerful voice in its deliberations, but the NAC could also pass resolution in the Legislative Council that would enable Nyasaland to secede from the Federation.[68]

In his public speeches Banda did no more than threaten a campaign of non-violent civil disobedience if the government did not accept his aims.[69] But by

[65] B. J. Berman, 'Bureaucracy and incumbent violence: colonial administration and the origins of the Mau Mau emergency', *British Journal of Political Science*, vol. 6 (1976), 143–75; TNA CAB 129/55/C(52)332. Governor Baring to Colonial Secretary, 10 October 1952; TNA CAB 128/25/CC(52)85. Cabinet Conclusions, 14 October 1952.

[66] TNA CO 1035/119/GEN 520. Draft by Commonwealth Relations Office and Colonial Office, Cabinet Committee on counter-subversion in the colonial territories. The Federation of Rhodesia and Nyasaland, July 1956; R. Hyam, 'The geopolitical origins of the Central African Federation: Britain, Rhodesia and South Africa, 1948–63', *Historical Journal*, vol. 30 (1987), 145–72.

[67] TNA CAB 21/4043. Record of a meeting held at 10 Downing Street, 21 November 1958.

[68] TNA CAB 129/98/C(59)124. Colonial Secretary, Report of the Nyasaland Commission of Inquiry, 17 July 1959; Baker, *State of Emergency*, vii–viii.

[69] TNA CO 1035/143. Extract from weekly review of current intelligence, 24 February 1959; TNA CAB 129/98/C(59)124. Colonial Secretary, Report of the Nyasaland Commission of Inquiry, 17 July 1959.

September 1958 the English-language press and European members of the Legislative Council, reacting against a background of a breakdown of law and order in the Congo and memories of the Mau Mau in Kenya, were pressing the government to take strong measures against the NAC, whom they accused of stirring up mob violence and racial hatred. By mid-February 1959 the Governor, Sir Robert Armitage, was convinced that the police could no longer cope with what he believed was a planned campaign not just of civil disobedience, but of anti-government rioting and mob violence. In fact, in the six months before the declaration of the emergency, only four Africans and not a single European had been killed in riots.[70] The critical piece of evidence that convinced Armitage that the only way to save the situation was to declare a state of emergency was a Special Branch report, based on tendentious and hearsay evidence, that the leaders of the NAC were plotting to assassinate government officials.[71]

Armitage's decision to declare an emergency on 3 March 1959 had the full support of the Colonial Secretary.[72] But 'Operation Sunrise', the arrest of 250 NAC leaders and the arrival of troops and police from Northern and Southern Rhodesia, only served to provoke the very breakdown in public order that Armitage hoped to avoid. When crowds tried to release detained NAC leaders, troops and police sometimes opened fired to prevent them. During one such incident on 3 March at Nkata Bay, a crowd tried to rush a jetty to release detainees who were being transferred by boat. Soldiers opened fire, killing 20 people and wounding another 25.[73] It was a measure of the one-sidedness of the violence meted out during the Nyasaland emergency that not a single member of the security forces was killed.[74]

The reality, therefore, was that apart from Malaya, Communism played a small, and often non-existent, part in inspiring most of the insurgents who fought the British. Radical nationalism was a far more common motivating force. Similarly, and again with the exception of Malaya, Britain's opponents did not pursue a Maoist strategy of trying to create liberated areas within which they could muster their own forces, establish a parallel government, and eventually send forth armies

---

[70] TNA CO 1016/1516. Morgan to Armitage, 11 March 1959.

[71] TNA CO 1035/148. A/Superintendents C. L. Humphreys and R. Mushet to Head of Special Branch, 3 February 1959; TNA CO 1035/143. Special Branch Nyasaland, The Emergency Conference of the Nyasaland African Congress held at Blantyre on 24/25 January 1959, 13 February 1959; TNA CO 1035/148. Statement of A.101, dated 11 February 1959; TNA CO 1035/143; TNA WO 32/18515. Extract from Colonial Intelligence summary No. 10 for September 1958 and No. 11 for October 1958; TNA CO 1015/1515. *Nyasaland Times*, 28, 31 October & 14 November 1958; TNA CO 1015/1515. Armitage to J. Morgan, 19 February 1959; TNA CO 1015/1515. Armitage to Colonial Secretary, 21 February 1959; TNA CO 1015/1515. Colonial Secretary to Armitage, 25 February 1959; TNA CO 1015/1515. Armitage to Perth, 26 February 1959.

[72] TNA WO 32/18515. Extract from Colonial Intelligence summary No. 12 for November 1958; TNA CO 1015/1515. Colonial Secretary to Armitage, 27 February 1959; Baker, *State of Emergency*, 1–41.

[73] TNA CO 1015/1515. Armitage to Secretary of State, 3 & 4 March 1959.

[74] TNA CO 1015/1517. Armitage to Secretary of State, 25 March 1959; TNA CAB 129/98/C(59)124. Secretary of State for the Colonies, Nyasaland Commission of Inquiry, 17 July 1959. Report of the Nyasaland Commission of Inquiry.

to defeat the imperialists in a conventional war. The second point was something that in practice the security forces generally recognized and, with varying degrees of success, they adapted their own tactics accordingly. But the former was something that they took longer to understand. In any case, the ways in which the British conducted their counter-insurgency campaigns was only partly determined by the reality of their enemies' aims. Far more important were two other factors: what the British thought were their enemies' aims, and what strategies they believed would be effective in defeating them.

THE ROOTS OF COERCION

Conscious of the fragility of their state apparatus, handicapped by inadequate means of gathering domestic intelligence, and living in the midst of a 'cold war', colonial governments were all-too-prone to give way to alarmism, and to be influenced by demands from different quarters to take stern action when British authority was challenged. Their common response was to try to nip trouble in the bud by arresting small numbers of 'trouble-makers' who, they believed, were leading the great mass of docile and loyal inhabitants astray. In May 1958, for example, Sir William Luce, the Governor of Aden, when faced by a handful of grenade attacks on British service personnel, reported that 'The public, both Arab and European, are alarmed and look to the Government for firm action and I consider it of greatest importance to try and nip this threat in the bud. I have therefore decided to proclaim a state of emergency throughout the Colony to enable the police to take certain action such as detention of suspects.'[75] The same imperatives drove Luce's successor, Trevaskis, in December 1963. Stung by a suggestion from the Colonial Office that he had over-reacted to an isolated incident, he sternly rebuked them. 'We have gathered here', he wrote on 13 December, 'from Colonial Office telegram to me Personal No. 305 that the view in London was that we were making heavy weather of an isolated incident and that the Federation was acting too drastically. I would, however, assure you that strong action at the outset is the course best calculated to stop the rot and to prevent the public in general and indeed our weaker friends going over to the other side.'[76]

In Kenya, so Lyttelton believed, the smack of firm government would soon intimidate the cowardly Kikuyu. 'The Kikuyu is not a warlike tribe', he insisted in November 1952:

Their history was that they cultivated land near the fringes of the bamboo forests, and, when the warlike Masai appeared, they fled to the forest. They are the most advanced tribe and give the best work, and, since, they have not lived by the spear, they have had to live by their brains. From having their ears to the ground to listen for the approach of the Masai, they have learned to have their ears to the ground to listen for any

[75] TNA CO 1015/2088. Sir W. Luce to CO, 2 May 1958.
[76] TNA CO 1055/197. Trevaskis to CO, 13 December 1963; TNA CO 1055/196. CO to Trevaskis, 10 December 1963.

political tremors and turn them to their advantage. They are sometimes said to be like the Irish in politics, without their humour, and like the Jews in commerce, without Leviticus. They are disliked and despised by nearly all the other tribes, particularly the Luo and the Masai.[77]

Evidence collected by the police seemed to implicate Kenyatta and the KAU in Mau Mau, but the hold of the Mau Mau over the Kikuyu could be broken by banning the KAU, bringing Kenyatta and his colleagues to trial, detaining those who could not be tried for lack of evidence, and placing the school system more securely under government control.[78]

Similarly in Sarawak, the governor, Sir Alexander Waddell, had been waging a propaganda war against the CCO since 1960, but with little success.[79] He therefore eagerly seized the opportunity offered to him by the failed coup in Brunei in December 1962 to act against the CCO. Once again, a colonial government that felt itself embattled responded by trying to nip trouble in the bud by arresting the leaders of its opponents. 'In view of general Communist support of the insurrection and the likelihood of the CCO exploiting the situation, an operation was mounted to arrest the more important and dangerous members of the organisation.' But, as in the case of Malaya and Kenya, operations by the security forces only served to drive their opponents underground. The security forces could uncover no evidence that the CCO had been planning outright violence or guerrilla operations, and their arrest programme only netted 49 of the party's leaders. Another 11 escaped arrest and went into hiding, as did groups of Chinese youths, who fled because they were afraid of being caught in the police round-up. Together they formed the basis for a guerrilla movement that had hitherto been non-existent.[80]

Where they failed to nip trouble in the bud, the colonial authorities pursued strategies based on a paradoxical combination of western liberal thinking and repression. They constructed their counter-insurgency strategies within a political framework founded on the Enlightenment belief that governments derived their legitimacy from a contract struck between individuals and the state. The former surrendered some of their autonomy, and the latter offered them certain benefits, the most important of which was physical security and prosperity. Government and insurgents were struggling for legitimacy, and the side that could offer the greater degree of protection and prosperity would win. But such a framework had one major shortcoming. It could not explain why some people rejected as illegitimate governments which, in the eyes of colonial power, were working hard to provide

[77] TNA CAB 129/57/C(52)407. Colonial Secretary, Kenya, 14 November 1952.
[78] Ibid.
[79] TNA CO 1030/1105. Sir A. Waddell, Extract from Sarawak Despatch no. 313, 20 May 1960; TNA CO 1030/1105. Sessional Paper No. 3 of 1960. Sarawak Council Negri, Subversion in Sarawak. Presented by Command of HE The Governor, 22 July 1960; TNA CO 1030/1104. Sir A. N. A. Waddell to W. I. J. Wallace, 24 June 1961; TNA CO 1030/1105. Extract from Sarawak Monthly Intelligence Report for September 1962.
[80] TNA CO 1030/1105. Extract from Sarawak Monthly Intelligence Report for December 1962.

good governance, prosperity, and security.[81] It could not accommodate those groups who placed their ethnic and religious identities above what the British regarded as the tenets of good governance.

Far from accepting their enemies had genuine grievances and that their readiness to resort to violence was an expression of them, the British explained this otherwise inexplicable phenomenon by marginalizing and criminalizing their opponents. They were 'thugs', 'bandits', 'gangsters', or 'terrorists'. Shortly after the destruction of the King David Hotel, the High Commissioner in Palestine, Sir Andrew Cunningham, denounced the leaders of the Jewish Agency as being guilty of 'criminal folly', for they had 'fostered political gangsterism in this manner.'[82] At the end of the first year of the Malayan Emergency, Sir Neil Ritchie, the C-in-C FARELF, wrote of his opponents that 'They are terrorists and thugs, and showed no more courage than any others of that ilk.'[83] 'Bandit' was an appellation applied to insurgents in both Malaya in the early 1950s and in Borneo in the mid-1960s.[84] In the Canal Zone the British damned their enemies as 'terrorists', 'thugs', and 'pseudo-patriots'.[85] Governor Savage of British Guiana dismissed supporters of the PPP as 'thugs'.[86] In Kenya the Mau Mau were 'criminals', 'gangsters' or 'the straight thug element'.[87] Less than a week after the first EOKA bomb attacks on government installations, the Colonial Secretary, Alan Lennox-Boyd, described them as 'criminals' who were responsible for 'wicked and malicious activities'.[88] Maj.-Gen. Kenneth Darling, the Director of Operations in Cyprus, thought that 'A high proportion of militant EOKA is little better than a rabble which has been taught some unpleasant tricks.'[89] By 1962 active insurgents in South East Asia were described in one army doctrinal publication as 'misfits maladjusted to normal society, the selfish, the too ambitious, and the discontented or the ill advised minorities.'[90]

The use of such language by senior officials and in official publications was neither accidental nor meaningless. Terms such as 'bandit', 'gangster', 'terrorist', and 'thug' accorded with the government's propaganda objectives. In 1948,

---

[81] M. Fitzsimmons, 'Hard Hearts and Open Minds? Governance, Identity and the Intellectual Foundations of Counterinsurgency Strategy', *JSS*, vol. 31 (2008), 341–3, 351–2.

[82] TNA CO 537/2287. Cunningham to Colonial Secretary, 29 July 1946.

[83] TNA WO 106/5884. Gen. Sir Neil Ritchie, Report on operations in Malaya, June 1948 to July 1949, 6 September 1949.

[84] IWMDoD. Maj.-Gen. Lewis Owain Pugh 67/67/1–5(1). Brig. Pugh, Operational Standing Orders. 26 Gurkha Infantry Brigade. 1 June 1950; TNA WO 305/2525. HQ British Forces Borneo. Joint Intsum no. 4, 10 August 1963.

[85] TNA WO 236/11. Erskine to all formations Canal Zone, 14 November 1951; TNA WO 236/25. BGS, BTE to all formations under command, 17 November 1951.

[86] TNA CO 1031/780. Savage to Secretary of State Colonies, 15 October 1953.

[87] TNA WO 32/14635. HQ East Africa Command to WO, 21 January 1953; TNA WO 276/449. Appreciation by the Commander-in-Chief of the operational situation in Kenya in June 1955, 11 June 1955; IWMSA. Accession No. 10224 . Sir A. Swann, Transcript, 15.

[88] *Hansard* HC Deb. 6 April 1955 vol. 539, col. 100.

[89] TNA CO 926/1077. Report on the Cyprus Emergency, 31 July 1959. Enc. Directive no. 5 of the Director of Operations, n.d.

[90] TNA WO 291/2481. Anti-guerrilla operations in South East Asia. Part 2. Tactics. (First edn, May 1962.)

anxious to refute suggestions that events in Malaya were a genuinely popular movement, Colonial Office officials insisted that 'On no account should the term "insurgent", which might suggest a genuine popular uprising, be used.' 'Bandit' and 'terrorist' were to be preferred because they denied the insurgents the status of being a genuinely popular movement and reduced them to the level of common criminals.[91] In mid-1952 the authorities in Malaya replaced the term 'bandit' as the official designation of their opponents with 'Communist Terrorist' (or CT for short). Again, they did so for specifically propagandistic reasons. They wanted to teach audiences outside Malaya, especially in the USA, where there were criticisms that the British were not pulling their weight in the struggle against world Communism, that the British were indeed doing their utmost, and that Malaya was part of the frontline in the West's struggle to prevent the spread of Communism in South East Asia.[92]

The language that senior officials used to describe their opponents was in turn underpinned by one of the fundamental assumptions that sustained the whole British colonial enterprise. It was an empire sustained by an ethos of paternalism.[93] The peoples of the empire were socially, economically, and politically backward. It was the mission of the 'White Man' to steer them towards a higher level of civilization. 'What was important to us', Sir Richard Catling, who held senior police posts in Palestine, Malaya, and Kenya remembered, 'was that we had absolute faith that what we were doing was the right thing to do. We may have given the impression of superiority and we did see ourselves as superior to the local citizens, I suppose, but I don't think it was an offensive attitude, more paternal than anything else.'[94] Whether colonial subjects would have agreed with him that such attitudes were not offensive is questionable. 'The African', British soldiers serving in Kenya were warned, 'is simple, not very intelligent, but very willing if treated in the right way. Do not regard him as a slave or as an equal. You will find that most Africans have an innate respect for the White Man.'[95] In June 1938 the then Colonial Secretary, Malcolm Macdonald, had told a summer school of British colonial administrators at Oxford that the purpose of the British empire in Africa was 'the ultimate establishment of various colonial communities as self-supporting and self-reliant members of a great commonwealth of free peoples and nations.'[96] By 1957 this had become one of the army's official missions as defined in its most up-to-date counter-insurgency manual, *Keeping the Peace*.[97]

---

[91] S. L. Carruthers, *Winning Hearts and Minds. British Governments, the Media and Colonial Counter-Insurgency 1944–1960* (Leicester: Leicester University Press, 1995), 77–8.

[92] Carruthers, *Winning Hearts and Minds*, 84–5; P. Deery, 'The terminology of Terrorism: Malaya, 1948–52', *Journal of South East Asian Studies*, vol. 34 (2003), 231–47.

[93] IWMSA. Accession No. 4716. N. Harvey, Transcript, 5.

[94] IWMSA. Accession No. 10392. Sir R. Catling, Transcript, 26.

[95] TNA WO 276/454. *A Handbook of Anti-Mau Mau Operations* (Kenya: East Africa Command, n.d. but c. 1954).

[96] J. Flint, 'Planned decolonisation and its failure in British Africa', *African Affairs*, vol. 82 (1983), 389–411.

[97] TNA WO 296/23. General Staff, *Keeping the Peace (Duties in Support of the Civil Power)* (London: War Office, 1957).

From this mission there sprang the conviction that anyone who opposed the British was blocking the path to a higher form of civilization, and they were probably motivated by criminal intent. In British Guiana the ministers of the PPP were damned because they 'showed no concern for the true welfare of the colony and threatened its progress as an orderly state. It had seriously endangered the economic life of the country and had set it on the road to collapse.'[98] The propensity of the Mau Mau to bind their members by oaths persuaded the colonial authorities that it was rooted in superstition, witchcraft and a backward mentality that rejected modernity. A parliamentary delegation that visited Kenya in January 1954 concluded that 'Mau Mau intentionally and deliberately seeks to lead the Africans of Kenya back to the bush and savagery, not forward into progress.'[99] Templer's directive in Malaya told him that

> Communist terrorism is retarding the political advancement and economic develop-
> ment of the country and the welfare of its peoples. Your primary task in Malaya must,
> therefore, be the restoration of law and order, so that this barrier to progress may be
> removed. Without victory and the state of law and order which it alone can bring, there
> can be no freedom from fear, which is the first human liberty.[100]

The consequences of this mindset were far-reaching. It meant that when Mena-chim Begin, the leader of the Irgun, insisted that he was fighting 'for the dignity of man, against oppression and subjugation',[101] or when George Grivas railed against the way the British treated Greek-Cypriot claims for enosis with 'patronising indifference or outright rejection', and 'denied even the hope of freedom to my fellow countrymen in Cyprus',[102] or when Chin Peng wrote that he and his supporters 'were truly convinced of the morality of our position. There was no question in our minds about the injustices of the colonial system', the British thought their claims were literally incredible.[103] They preferred to believe that the great mass of people in their colonies were content and that trouble-makers were a small and unrepresentative minority. In Malaya, support for Communism was thought to be confined to a minority within the Chinese population. The Malays wanted nothing to do with it and most Chinese wanted to sit on the fence until they saw who was winning.[104] In Egypt, Erskine, who served as GOC BTE from 1949 to 1952, believed that the anti-British agitation in the Canal Zone was organized by an unrepresentative minority of 'students [who] are a mere handful but they have been nourished on extreme Nationalistic lines and regard themselves

---

[98] TNA CO 859/772. [Cmd 8980]. *British Guiana. Suspension of the Constitution*, 20 October 1953.
[99] TNA CAB 21/2906. [Cmd. 9081] *Report to the Secretary of State for the Colonies by the Parliamentary Delegation to Kenya in January 1954*, February 1954.
[100] TNA CAB 21/2884. Directive to Gen. Sir Gerald Templer, High Commissioner in and for the Federation of Malaya, by the Secretary of State for the Colonies, 8 February 1952.
[101] M. Begin, *The Revolt* (London: W. H. Allen, rev. edn, 1979; first published 1952), 60.
[102] Foley (ed.), *The Memoirs of General Grivas*, 1, 12.
[103] Peng, *My Side of History*, 279.
[104] TNA DEFE 11/33. A paper on the dimensions and nature of the security problem confronting the government of the Federation of Malaya, 16 September 1948.

as leaders of an Egypt which had been held down by the British.'[105] After visiting Cyprus in November 1958 the CIGS, Sir Francis Festing, was similarly dismissive of the Greek-Cypriot community. 'The Greek Cypriots in my view lacks the moral and physical stamina indefinitely to conduct a successful resistance movement'.[106] In Nyasaland the Devlin Commission that investigated the background and conduct of the emergency discovered that 'Every member of the Government believes that at bottom in Nyasaland there is government by consent and would not be happy if he thought otherwise; his view is based on the assumption that, apart from a small minority of self-seeking troublemakers, the African wants what is best for him and that the Government knows what that is.'[107] In Sarawak the administration believed the CCO had its roots in the Chinese community 'but it is far from representing them as a whole. The Chinese have contributed inestimably to the development of Sarawak in the past and are making good progress in integrating themselves into the community as a whole. If unchecked the clandestine movement will destroy this peaceful progression.'[108]

From this there sprang a second belief that coloured British understanding of the problems they faced, their reluctance to accept that some of their colonial subjects had their own political agendas, and entertained a genuine desire for independence. In 1952 the author of the Colonial Office's survey of Communism in Africa insisted that, with the possible exception of the Gold Coast and Nigeria, 'in most of the African Continent the idea of a nation is as yet almost unknown'.[109] Instead they saw their colonial subjects as an inert and amorphous mass, waiting to be controlled by either the insurgents or the administration.[110] Communism in Malaya, according to Templer, was not an indigenous development, 'It is the result of a direct infection of Communist virus into a small section of the Chinese community, through the agency of the Communist Party of CHINA.'[111] In the Canal Zone the army's Field Security sections estimated that, although there were large numbers of thieves bent on making life difficult for the British by stealing goods from their depots, there were only between 20 and 30 active insurgents who had taken up arms against them, and that much of the rest of the population only supported them because they had been terrorized.[112] The leaders of the Mau Mau were condemned for having 'incited the people to indignation and revolt over a bogus issue (they asserted, quite falsely, that land had been stolen from the

---

[105] TNA WO 236/14. Erskine, Review of present situation January 1952.

[106] TNA CO 926/1004. Report by CIGS on visit to Cyprus, 23 November 1958 to 27 November 1958, dated 28 November 1958.

[107] TNA CAB 129/98/C(59)124. Secretary of State for the Colonies, Nyasaland Commission of Inquiry, 17 July 1959. Report of the Nyasaland Commission of Inquiry.

[108] TNA CO 1030/1105. Sessional Paper No. 3 of 1960. Sarawak Council Negri, Subversion in Sarawak. Presented by Command of HE The Governor, 22 July 1960.

[109] TNA CO 968/244. Survey of Communism for 1952—Colonial Empire, n.d. but *c*.18 February 1953.

[110] IWMSA. Accession No. 10175. R. J. W. Craig, Transcript, 3–4; IWMSA. Accession No. 10243. A. H. P. Humphrey, reel 1.

[111] NAM 7410-29-2. Sir Gerald Templer mss. Text of speech on situation in Malaya, n.d. but *c*.1953–54.

[112] IWMSA. Accession No. 17650. Sgt R. Knutsen, reel 4.

Kikuyu), skilfully interweaving the movement with elements of the Spiritualist cult that appealed strongly to the African natives.'[113] Harding believed that EOKA garnered much of its support because of its success in intimidating the Greek Cypriot population.[114] In Aden, a British staff officer believed, 'the majority, who were carefully orchestrated by, I can only use the word terrorist, although I don't think that was a popular word at the time, would wish to see us go and would have said so.'[115]

There was an element of truth in their assertion that the insurgents terrorized people to gain their support. In Malaya, the Canal Zone, Kenya, Cyprus, and Aden, although not in British Guiana or Palestine, they did use some degree of terror to silence opponents within their own communities. But to insist, as so many British observers did, that fear was the only reason why people supported the aims of the insurgents, was a self-serving delusion. It took no account, for example, of the fact that in a plebiscite held in January 1950, four years before the start of violence on the island, 96.5 per cent of the Greek-Cypriot population voted for enosis.[116] In other cases it is probably reasonable to assume that while some people supported the aims of the insurgents, even if they did not approve of their methods, or were personally reluctant to take up arms alongside them, some opposed both the aims and methods of the insurgents, and many wished to remain neutral, at least until they could see who was winning.

In principle the colonial authorities' willingness to distinguish between a guilty minority and an innocent majority terrorized into supporting them should have produced counter-insurgency strategies that tried to divide the minority of active insurgents from the inert mass of the population by courting rather than coercing them.[117] It should, therefore, have been a recipe for a strategy of focusing upon the hearts and minds of the people. By the 1960s this was indeed explicitly part of the army's written doctrine. In 1962, 28th Commonwealth Brigade, which was stationed in Malaya and had the task of coming to the aid of any friendly government in the region beset by an insurgency, was told that

> We cannot win counter-insurgency operations without helping to eliminate the poverty, disease, illiteracy and social inequality that breeds unrest. Military action alone will be unsuccessful. It must be co-ordinated at the national level with programmes of social reform and economic development aimed at satisfying the national aspirations of the people. Experience has clearly shown that guerrilla warfare cannot be won unless the people of the country are won over and desirous of victory by our forces.[118]

[113] S. Hosmer and S. O. Crane (eds), *Counterinsurgency: A Symposium, April 16–20, 1962* (Santa Monica, CA: Rand Corporation, 1963/2006), 125.
[114] IWMSA. Accession No. 8736. Field Marshal Lord Harding, Transcript, 352–3.
[115] IWMSA. Accession No. 11092. D. J. Wood, reel 3.
[116] R. Holland, *Britain and the Revolt in Cyprus 1954–59* (Oxford: Oxford University Press, 1998), 18–19.
[117] R. Schultz, 'Force and military strategy: deterrence logic and the cost-benefit model of counterinsurgency warfare', *The Western Political Quarterly*, vol. 32 (1979), 444.
[118] TNA WO 291/2481. Anti-guerrilla operations in South East Asia. Part 2. Tactics. (First edn, May 1962.)

But there was a large gap between the recognition of the need to win the hearts and minds of the innocent majority and what colonial governments and their security forces actually did. The cornerstones of most British counter-insurgency campaigns were coercion and counter-terror, not kindness and economic development. Such policies had a long and not always unsuccessful history. In 1906, summarizing the lessons of nineteenth-century colonial wars, culminating in the Anglo-Boer War of 1899–1902, Sir Charles Callwell wrote that once an insurgency had begun, and the enemy could not be defeated in a conventional battle, 'It is then that the regular troops are forced to resort to cattle lifting and village burning and that the war assumes an aspect which may shock the humanitarian. . . . If the enemy cannot be touched in his patriotism or his honour, he can be touched through his pocket.'[119] Soldiers might find this distasteful, but they accepted that it might be the necessary. 'I dislike it intensely', admitted Sir Andrew Skeen, reflecting in 1932 on his own experiences on the North West Frontier of India, 'but after the enemy's will to stand and take punishment is broken, there is no other way to make him watch his step in the future, or if there is we have not found it out in the past eighty years.'[120] Nor did they discover anything better in Palestine during the Arab Revolt between 1936 and 1939.[121]

A commitment to waging counter-insurgency operations by employing coercion and intimidation continued to be a mainstay of British practice after 1945. Policy-makers remained convinced of its efficacy. They assumed that their subject populations were rational beings who would calculate that any benefits they might gain in the future by supporting the insurgents would be outweighed by the immediate costs of doing so. That the innocent were bound to suffer alongside the guilty was inevitable, acceptable and could be beneficial. In 1946 the General Staff recognized that in Palestine 'It is inevitable that in the course of such action certain law abiding Jewish citizens may be molested, but it may serve to bring home to them the fact that terrorism does not pay and that the community itself should give practical effect to their denunciation of terrorism.'[122] Such beliefs were underpinned by orientalist assumptions about the mind-sets of whole communities. In February 1949, Gurney wrote to the Colonial Secretary

---

[119] Col. C. E. Callwell, *Small Wars. Their Principles and Practice* (London: General Staff, War Office, 1906, reprinted 1914), 40.

[120] Gen. Sir A. Skeen, *Lessons in Imperial Rule. Instructions for British Infantrymen on the Indian Frontier* (London: Frontline Books, 2008), 125. This was first published in 1932 under the title *Passing It On: Short Talks on Tribal Fighting on the North West Frontier of India* (Aldershot: Gale & Polden, 1932).

[121] M. Hughes, 'The banality of brutality: British armed forces and the repression of the Arab revolt in Palestine, 1936–39', *EHR*, vol. 124 (2009), 313–54; M. Hughes, 'The practice and theory of British counterinsurgency: the histories of the atrocities at the Palestinian villages of al-Basa and Halhul, 1938–39', *SW&I*, vol. 20 (2009), 528–50. I am most grateful to Dr Hughes for sharing his insights and conclusions with me. See also J. Norris, 'Repression and rebellion: Britain's response to the Arab revolt in Palestine of 1936–39,' *JICH*, vol. 36 (2008), 25–45.

[122] TNA WO 32/10260. Army Council Secretariat. Brief for Secretary of State, Palestine. Use of armed forces, 31 December 1946.

A report from Sitiawan illustrates the way in which the Chinese mind works. 'A person arrested by the government gets adequate food and is not beaten up, but if one offends the bandits and is arrested, starvation, assault and probably death may result, for which reason it is better to offend the government than the bandits'. This puts in a nutshell the problem of how to convince somebody who thinks like this without descending to Japanese methods. On the other hand, in dealing with Oriental terrorism armed with modern weapons our traditional British methods will always be too little and too late.[123]

In 1950 Griffiths believed that 'The dominant motive among the Chinese population, particularly the unprotected "squatters" in the rural areas, is fear. The terrorist threat is certainly nearer and greater in some places than that of the Government and the Chinese mentality naturally tends to ensure more heavily against the Communists than ourselves. It is also true that the Asiatic mind understands force.'[124] Surrounded by a potentially hostile African population, the handful of European settlers in Kenya had habitually relied on violence to maintain their hegemony.[125] The Emergency only further encouraged them to do so. During a debate in the Legislative Council in November 1952, one European Member, Colonel E. S. Grogan, 'said he could not understand "all this frightful complexity" of legislation to deal with the trouble, and he was sure the African could not. The Kikuyu were regarded as the most cowardly tribe in Africa, he said, and he advocated charging "about a hundred of these rascals" with treason and hanging twenty-five per cent of them in front of the remainder who should then be sent back to the tribal Reserves to tell the rest.'[126] The GOC East Africa, Lt.-Gen. Sir Alexander Cameron, shared his belief in the efficacy of exemplary violence, lamenting that the Mau Mau had not reacted more violently. 'This passive attitude of the Kikuyu is probably, from our point of view, the worst line that they could have taken', for 'If they had assembled in force and being disorderly in only one place we could have hit them and it is probable that the effect would have spread all over the reserve and brought them to order. As it is we have not yet had an opportunity to use the Government's strength and to demonstrate that the Government is much more to be feared than the Mau Mau.'[127]

In 1955, with the emergency dragging on, a staff officer in Nairobi recommended further increasing the pressure on the Kikuyu. 'Our actions against Passive elements have been based, so far', he wrote

> on the physical control of the population. These actions must be intensified. In addition, disciplinary control must be introduced whereby the population will be forced to withdraw its support from Mau Mau, because of the risk of extreme

[123] TNA CO 537/4750. Gurney to Creech Jones, 14 February 1949.
[124] TNA CAB 21/1681/MAL.C(50)25. Colonial Secretary, Cabinet Malaya Committee: Various matters discussed with the authorities in Malaya, 14 July 1950.
[125] M. J. Wiener, *An Empire on Trial. Race, Murder, and Justice under British Rule, 1870–1935* (Cambridge: Cambridge University Press, 2009), 193–221; J. Mcculloch, 'Empire and Violence, 1900–1939', in P. Levine (ed.), *Gender and Empire* (Oxford: Oxford University Press, 2004), 226–7.
[126] *Manchester Guardian*, 27 November 1952.
[127] TNA WO 216/811. C-in-C MELF to VCIGS, 5 November 1952.

punishment. What is required is harsher treatment on a more selective basis. Whereas earlier in the Emergency this was wholly impracticable, due to lack of information, the latter is now sufficient for us to identify Passive organisations and their more important members.[128]

Officials in Palestine, Kenya, and Malaya were not unique in believing that coercion would work.[129] In Cyprus, Governor Harding believed that 'Apart from their intrinsic justification, one of the results of the various measures such as collective fines, curfews and other restrictions that have recently been increased is the restoration of respect for authority.'[130] His Director of Operations, Brigadier George Barker, agreed. Collective punishments might be 'contrary to the principles held by civilised countries of individual responsibility and the rule of law, [and] are regarded as illiberal by the free world', but they did 'bring home to the ordinary people the hard fact that the results of terrorism include hardship to themselves and so create conditions predisposing people in favour of a political settlement.'[131]

Some members of the security forces on the ground agreed that coercion worked. The commanding officer of 8/Parachute Regiment remembered that

No matter what the politicians say, every soldier who served in Palestine during the recent trouble knows, unfortunately by bitter experience, that when the security forces have to deal with a thoroughly non-cooperative, unscrupulous, dishonest and utterly immoral civil population such as the Jewish Community in Palestine, who systematically and continually hide and refuse to give up for justice the perpetrators of murderous outrages, reprisals are the only effective weapon to employ, saving time, money and unnecessary bloodshed.[132]

Reprisals that involved killing of innocent civilians was repugnant and out of the question, but destroying their property was not, and his men destroyed houses or orange groves from which they had been attacked in the belief that this would be enough to encourage the civilian population to turn against the 'thugs'.[133] A British missionary in Kenya taxed a policeman that 'the people were becoming almost more frightened of the police than they were of Mau Mau.' The answer he received was '"Good, that is what we want; when they are more afraid of us we shall get the information we want." . . . "We must combat force with force and the strongest force will win the day."'[134] Similarly, a journalist in Cyprus was told by British

[128] TNA WO 276/430. Lt.-Col. H. A. Hope, GSO1 (Operations) to COS GHQ East Africa, 12 February 1955.
[129] For Aden, see Mawby, 'Orientalism and British policy', 344–8.
[130] TNA CAB 21/288. Harding, The future of Cyprus, 4 April 1956.
[131] TNA CO 968/690. Brigadier G. Baker, A review of the Cyprus Emergency April 1955–March 1958.
[132] LHCMA Stockwell mss 6/26/13. Lt.-Col. J. M. H. Hackett to Stockwell, Lessons learned in Palestine, 17 November 1948.
[133] Ibid.
[134] TNA CO 822/471. Canon T. F. C. Bewes, African Secretary, Church Missionary Society, to Baring, 28 January 1953.

soldiers that 'We won't get anywhere with these until they fear us more than they fear EOKA.'[135]

These attitudes point towards a second reason why the British persisted in employing coercion. Senior officers and their political masters were persuaded that if they did not do so, discipline amongst members of the security forces might crumble and they would take matters into their own hands. A company commander with 2/Lincolnshire Regiment remembered the sense of frustration felt by his men, many of whom had just emerged from fighting a conventional war against the Germans, when they discovered in Palestine that they could not shoot their enemy on sight.[136] The GOC, Sir Evelyn Barker, insisted that in such a situation official reprisals were necessary because of 'the need to maintain morale of the troops.'[137] A. V. Alexander, the Minister of Defence, agreed, telling the Cabinet that 'he thought that all necessary discretion should be given to the Army to prevent and punish terrorism. He reminded the Committee of the cruelty and indignities to which members of the Armed Forces were being subjected. These must be having a most serious effect on our prestige in the Middle East and, if we did nothing, might well lead to a situation in which members of the Armed Forces would take things into their own hands.'[138] John Lawson, the Secretary of State for War, put it more briefly. 'If B[ritish]. troops begin to retaliate, you'll get a Black & Tan situation.'[139] Even the Lord Chancellor, Lord Jowitt, accepted that permitting the security forces to mount cordon and search operations was 'Necessary if troops are not to take the law into own hands.'[140] Similar concerns informed operations in the Canal Zone, where the BDCC(Middle East) noted that,

> Continued experience confirms beyond any doubt that the appropriate response to Egyptian generated incidents is firm and instant action. It is largely because GOC BTE has pursued this policy that the situation has not deteriorated further than it has, and that the morale of the troops is high despite the heavy and exacting demands of internal security duties which have already continued for several months passed and which at present showed no signs of easing.[141]

A British civil servant working in the Canal Zone agreed. His morale was certainly improved by the anti-terrorist measures he witnessed. 'It is quite heartening to see local buses stopped and the passengers searched by the Army as we come along the road to and from the office (about 12 miles each way)', he wrote in October 1951.[142]

[135] M. Faber, 'Cyprus forces are foiled by silence', *Observer*, 15 April 1956.
[136] IWMSA. Accession No. 10109. Col. J. B. Buckmaster, reel 1.
[137] TNA PREM 8/864. Telegram no. 1961: Cunningham to Colonial Secretary, 23 November 1946.
[138] TNA CAB 131/5/DO(47)1 meeting. Cabinet Defence Committee, 1 January 1947.
[139] TNA CAB 195/4. Cabinet Secretary's notebook. CM 60(46), 20 June 1946.
[140] TNA CAB 195/5/CM6(47). Cabinet meeting, 15 January 1947.
[141] TNA FO 371/1102852/JE11914/132/COS(53)379. Report by the BDCC, Review of the present situation in the Canal Zone of Egypt, 6 August 1953.
[142] TNA AIR 2/11415. L. D. Millo to C. J. Pridmore, 18 October 1951.

However, not every soldier and junior officer shared his sentiments. Senior officers and administrators had created an atmosphere in which coercion seemed to be both necessary and acceptable. But it was up to their subordinates in the security forces to carry them out. Many soldiers and policemen knew little about the politics of the situation in which they found themselves, and their superiors did not go out of their way to enlighten them.[143] 'Weren't told a blind thing about the local situation', remembered John Rymer-Jones, who was posted to Kenya in 1953.[144] Such briefing as they were given was on the need to avoid heat exhaustion, excessive drinking, and venereal disease, rather than the local political situation.[145]

Soldiers and policemen on the ground were thus left to a considerable extent to make up their own minds, and they did not reach a single agreed conclusion. Asked about the behaviour of men in his unit towards the people of Malaya, a trooper in the King's Dragoon Guards believed that 'I think it would be true to say that there was a certain feeling that they were let's say "wogs" and a bit inferior natives, but I think that was only true of a minority. As soon as troops had had some experience in the country they did see them as people just like themselves and their own families.'[146] In Palestine a minority of soldiers and policemen were inclined to dislike Jews even before they arrived, and they soon had their prejudices confirmed when the insurgents attacked them. But an equally significant minority were pro-Jewish, admiring their industry and ingenuity, and sympathizing with their plight.[147] Some soldiers took the deaths of their comrades at the hands of insurgents stoically. 'What could your reaction be?' asked Alec Beechey. 'You just had to put up with it.'[148] It was quite possible for the same man to feel sorry for the Jewish refugees he was preventing from landing in Palestine, and to regard members of the Stern gang as 'really nasty people'.[149] A Field Security sergeant in the Canal Zone decided that, although some Egyptians were 'a pretty bad lot', on the whole 'I quite liked them, actually', and felt sorry for them because they lived in such poverty.[150]

Many ordinary soldiers and policemen in Malaya had no particular feelings of hatred towards their enemies even after they had seen the ways in which they terrorized the civilian population. They regarded their time there as a job of work

[143] IWMSA. Accession No. 31504. K. Thorley, reel 3; IWMSA. Accession No. 9821. J. D. Mercer, reel 1; J. Chynoweth, *Hunting Terrorists in the Jungle. The Experiences of a National Service Subaltern in Malaya in the 1950s* (Stroud, Glouc.: Tempus, 2005), 13; TNA WO 261/640. 1. British Infantry Division. Officers' study days, Palestine, 15–17 September 1946. Maj.-Gen. W. P. Oliver, Some problems of the Middle East Command.
[144] IWMSA. Accession No. 13087. J. A. Rymer-Jones, reel 2.
[145] IWMSA. Accession No. 20320. Gen. Sir D. Thorne, reel 4.
[146] IWMSA. Accession No. 10107. N. J. D. Baptiste reel 1.
[147] D. Cesarani, 'The British security forces and the Jews in Palestine, 1945–48', in Claus-Christian W. Szejnmann (ed.), *Rethinking History, Dictatorship and War* (London: Continuum, 2009), 191–210; IWMSA. Accession No. 12208. J. A. S. Adolph, reel 2; IWMSA. Accession No. 10300. J. Sankey, reel 1; IWMSA. Accession No. 12367. J. J. West, reel 1.
[148] I am grateful to Mr Beechey's daughter, Mrs Helen Matthews, for passing on to me a record of her father's recollections.
[149] IWMSA. Accession No. 18047/4. Brigadier W. C. Deller, reel 1.
[150] IWMSA. Accession No. 17650. Sgt. R. Knutsen, reel 3.

that they had been told to do by their government.[151] Michael Gilbert, who served
with 1/Suffolk Regiment in Malaya in 1950–1, thought that the insurgents 'were
my enemy, and it was my job to do something about it if the situation came my
way. But I had no particular feeling as such of hatred, or anything like that. I did
not like what they were doing to my colleagues. They were killing them, of
course.... But that, I'm afraid is war. You know, I think you can get too
emotionally involved in things. You have got to see it for what it is. If they got a
chance to kill you they would. If you got a chance to kill them that was your job.'[152]
A company commander in the same battalion echoed the idea that they had a job of
work to do. After a successful patrol 'It was not the killing that pleased them. That
was merely an unpleasant part of their job. It was the success which had at last
attended so much grinding toil and wasted effort.'[153] A Gurkha officer thought that
his men respected the toughness of their opponents in the jungle but were
contemptuous of the ways in which they terrorized civilians.[154] A British policeman
who spent a year in Cyprus respected EOKA for the fact that they were fighting for
a cause they believed in, even if he did not approve of the methods they were using.
He felt sorry for an insurgent who was ambushed and killed by the army after he
threw bombs at the security forces three nights running from the same place.[155]
The men of the Royal Norfolk Regiment referred to Grivas as 'uncle George. Not
some fearsome enemy but someone who was almost looked upon with a certain
amount of respect and one day we would catch him, so to speak.'[156] Such men
applied the kinds of coercive measures that will be examined in Chapter 4
reluctantly, but apply them they did. Obedience to orders had been ingrained
into them during their basic training and, as one soldier admitted, 'the rules is the
rules. That was what was laid down', while another explained that 'you were just
the little soldier carrying out the command, you know'.[157]

However, there were other junior soldiers and policemen, the men who actually
fought the insurgents, who shared the more robust attitudes of some of their
seniors. An officer who served with the Parachute Regiment in Palestine dismissed
the Stern gang as 'a lot of straight murderers'.[158] Another officer who served with
the KAR in Kenya never accepted that the Mau Mau were nationalist freedom
fighters. They had to be defeated because they were 'a perverted organization of the
Kikuyu for the Kikuyu and to hell with it'.[159] In Malaya an officer thought that his

[151] C. Siver, 'The other forgotten war: understanding atrocities during the Malayan Emergency'
(Prepared for delivery at the 2009 Annual Meeting of the American Political Science Association,
September 3–6, 2009), 40–1; IWMSA. Accession No. 12367. J. J. West, reel 4; IWMSA. Accession
No. 14053. D. E. Henderson, reel 2; IWMSA. Accession No. 10232. L. O. Crosland, reel 2.
[152] IWMSA. Accession No. 18208. M. Gilbert, reel 2.
[153] A. Campbell, *Jungle Green* (London: Allen & Unwin, 1953), 108.
[154] IWMSA. Accession No. 10727. Col. A. S. Harvey, reel 4.
[155] IWMSA. Accession No. 9821. J. D. Mercer, reel 2.
[156] IWMSA. Accession No. 20320. Gen. Sir D. C. Thorne, reel 4.
[157] IWMSA. Accession No. 10043. D. Kelly, reel 2; IWMSA. Accession No. 17833. R. N. Kemp,
reel 3; D. French, *Military Identities. The Regimental System, the British Army, and the British People c.
1870–2000* (Oxford: Oxford University Press, 2005), 61–2.
[158] IWMSA. Accession No. 16395. Lt.-Gen. Sir N. Crookenden, reel 1.
[159] IWMSA. Accession No. 10091. A. L. Liddle, reel 4.

men believed that 'A dead one [i.e. insurgent] was a good one and when one was killed they were usually brought in on the back of a 3-tonner or something and dumped in front of the mess steps and the guys would shake their hand and have their picture taken before they were taken off to the police station. There was considerable hatred, probably stemming, you know, from the fact that on the first patrol one or two of your colleagues, or compatriots, or chums, had been shot dead. It predisposes you not to like the people, of course. Overall we were extremely keen to get at them.'[160] A British officer serving with a police jungle company in Malay came to share the hatred of his men for the insurgents once he 'heard first-hand accounts of the police stations being burned down with women and children trapped inside; of convoys attacked on lonely jungle roads and the wounded thrown into blazing vehicles.'[161]

Some National Servicemen resented being forced into uniform and sent to a far-away place and took out their resentment on the locals.[162] A private in the King's Own Yorkshire Light Infantry thought that he and his comrades respected the insurgents as a skilful and cunning opponent. 'But you know, you never gave a toss for him. If you could have got hold of him, you would have shown him how much you loved him like.'[163] In retrospect an officer who served with the Parachute Regiment in Cyprus in 1956 acknowledged the courage of EOKA insurgents, but 'At the time we had no regard for the EOKA terrorist. He was a terrorist. I mean women had been murdered. People had been shot in the back of the head in the cinema, and so on. They were carrying out acts of terrorism and were loathed by us all.'[164] To a sergeant serving with a Field Security section they were 'thugs' and 'gangsters'.[165]

Soldiers and policemen in the frontline who thought like that—and not all of them did—developed their own language to describe their opponents. In Palestine they were 'Yids'.[166] Egyptians were 'wogs', 'gypos', and 'a-rabs'.[167] In Malaya an insurgent might be a 'murderer', a 'thug', a 'sadist', or a 'chink' who 'were all two-faced beggars, sitting on the fence, waiting to see who was going to get the upper hand'.[168] In Cyprus the insurgents were 'gollies', and operations were 'golly bashing'.[169] In Aden they were 'gollies', 'blackies', 'third-rate, flyblown chaps', and 'smelly, dirty people'.[170] The use of such language was significant. By

[160] IWMSA. Accession No. 17571. N. Dobson, reel 3.

[161] R. Follows, *The Jungle Beat. Fighting Terrorists in Malaya* (Bridnorth, Shrops.: Travellers Eye Ltd, 1999), 62–3.

[162] IWMSA. Accession No. 10043. D. Kelly, reel 2.

[163] IWMSA. Accession No. 20260. E. W. Slade, reel 2.

[164] IWMSA. Accession No. 11147. Col. P. Field, reel 1.

[165] IWMDoD. 86/85/1. Maj. C. R. Butt, 'Cyprus Drafts (I)', 86.

[166] Maj.-Gen Dare Wilson, *Tempting the Fates. A Memoir of Service in the Second World War, Palestine, Korea, Kenya and Aden* (Barnsley: Pen & Sword, 2006), 141.

[167] A. L. Macfie, 'My orientalism', *Journal of Postcolonial Writing*, vol. 45 (2009), 88.

[168] Campbell, *Jungle Green*, 33, 46; R. Miers, *Shoot to Kill* (London: Faber & Faber, 1959), 57.

[169] A. Walker, 'The intelligent way'. Downloaded 20 April 2009 at www.britains-smallwars.com/cyprus/Davidcarter/Walker/intelcorps.html.

[170] B. Roy, *Empire Warriors. Aden: Mad Mitch and his Tribal Law*, BBC, 2004.

denigrating their opponents, it legitimized the coercive measures that the security forces were ordered to mete out to them.

But in Kenya the security forces did not merely denigrate their opponents by labelling them as 'bastard golliwogs', and describing patrols that killed Mau Mau as 'dropping micks'.[171] In Kenya they used zoomorphic language that damned their opponents as atavistic savages and animals. The Mau Mau were not just 'micks', but, dressed in skins, 'their existence had become completely animal-like', and 'They looked in fact almost like animals, they really did, when they'd been in the bush for a long time. And of course they smelt.'[172] These attitudes were the product of two factors. The settler regime in Kenya was, even before the emergency, probably the most openly racist regime in the British empire. One British junior officer who served in Kenya thought that most settlers treated Africans as on a par with animals, 'with no respect at all'.[173] Secondly, many Mau Mau victims were hacked to death by pangas, a sharp cutting tool resembling a machete that left their victims with gaping and bloody wounds. A British officer serving with the KAR thought that the sight of Mau Mau victims appalled his askaris.[174] African policemen who saw the bodies of the victims of the Lari massacre in March 1953 were physically sick and said 'These people are animals. If I see one now I shall shoot with the greatest eagerness and killness [*sic*] and no hanging back.' They kept saying, 'Si bin adamu', 'They're not men, they're not human.'[175] That was an important distinction. Labelling their enemies as wild animals, rather than merely 'wogs' or 'gollies', helps to explain why it was possible for the security forces to employ a far higher degree of coercion in Kenya than elsewhere.

CONCLUSION

The British fought their counter-insurgency campaigns against a background of the Cold War. It is therefore easy to understand why so many British officials thought they saw Communist conspiracies behind almost every manifestation of colonial unrest. But it was only in Malaya that the British confronted an insurgency inspired by a Communist programme and insurgents who were intent on pursuing a Maoist strategy. Elsewhere their opponents pursue a variety of mostly radical nationalist programmes and none of them sought to implement them by following the precepts of Mau Tse-tung. This is a significant point because the 'Malayan-model' of counter-insurgency laid great emphasis on the need to defeat the political subversion, not just the guerrillas. But if the British did not understand, or take seriously, the political aims of their opponents, their counter-insurgency strategy was likely to be

---

[171] P. Hewitt, *Kenya Cowboy. A Police Officer's Account of the Mau Mau Emergency* (London: Avon Books, 1999), 33.
[172] Faulkner, *A Two-Year Wonder*, 170; IWMSA. Accession No. 10224. Sir A. Swann, Transcript, 37.
[173] Private information.
[174] IWMSA. Accession No. 10091. A. L. K. Liddle, reel 4.
[175] IWMSA. Accession No. 10224. Sir A. Swann, Transcript, 29.

misconceived. Furthermore, the methods the British employed to conduct their counter-insurgency campaigns were not just determined by their enemies' aims. Of equal, or even greater importance in determining how they reacted were what the British believed were their enemies' aims, and what strategies they thought would work. Convinced of the moral righteousness of their own imperial mission, and equally convinced that anyone who opposed then was criminally inclined, they found it difficult to accept that their opponents had a legitimate political programme of their own. But their acceptance that the great mass of the colonial peoples were content with their rule and did not accept the political programmes of the minority of active insurgents did not lead, as logically it might have done, to counter-insurgency strategies in which coercion was only employed against the 'guilty'. Experience had taught them that coercion and counter-terror worked and, as the following chapters will demonstrate, they remained cornerstones of most British counter-insurgency campaigns in the post-war era.

3

The Legal Context and Counter-insurgency by Committee

The British did conduct their counter-insurgency operations according to the rule of law. However, the implication is questionable that by doing so they acted in ways that were likely to enhance the legitimacy of the colonial state in the eyes of its subjects. The British did not shun the application of martial law because of some high-minded preference for preserving legal norms. They did so partly for practical reasons, but mainly because they had found a better strategy. The 1939 Emergency Powers Order-in-Council, and local legislation based upon it, allowed them to maintain the outward appearance of legality and simultaneously employ as much or as little coercion and violence as they chose. The real significance of their refusal to apply martial law lay elsewhere. Without martial law the civil power was not subordinated to the military. They therefore had to find other ways to co-ordinate the operations of the administration, the police and the army. In Malaya they created a system that brought together in a pyramid of committees representatives of each of those three branches of government. It seemed to work, but circumstances in Malaya were especially propitious, and elsewhere it was applied inconsistently or not at all.

MARTIAL LAW

In 1934 soldiers who might be summoned to conduct counter-insurgency operations were told that they were likely to do so under legal authority provided by a declaration of martial law, which

> is in reality not 'law' at all in the accepted sense of the term. It denotes the suspension of ordinary law and its suppression by military rule during the war or rebellion, and amounts merely to the exercise of the will of the military commander upon whom has fallen the task of ensuring the safety of the State and the restoration of law and order. It may apply to all persons within the area controlled by the military commander, whether they be civil officials, ordinary citizens, soldiers, rebels or enemies.[1]

---

[1] TNA WO 279/796. War Office, *Notes on Imperial Policing 1934* (London: War Office, 1934), 29.

However, Britain's post-war counter-insurgencies were not conducted under martial law regimes. Thompson has implied that the British avoided declaring martial law as a matter of high principle, but their reasoning was more complex. It was based upon a combination of political and practical calculations. The European community in Malaya clamoured for it in the early days of the emergency, but Gurney refused to listen to them.[2] Reflecting in May 1949 on his experiences in Palestine and Malaya, he explained that the political issues were that 'the withdrawal of the civil power and the substitution of military control represent the first victory for the terrorists.' It was essential to retain as much as possible of the outward appearance of normality. 'Unfriendly propagandists paint the picture of political failure and of resort to force and repression.'[3] By the middle of the twentieth century martial law was, therefore, politically obsolete.

But there were two other considerations at work. Senior soldiers were far from unanimous in wanting it. They remembered the fates of Governor Eyre in 1865 and Brigadier-General Dyer in 1919, men whose careers had been wrecked when they were held to account for having inflicted what was held to be excessive violence on the colonized at a time when martial law had been declared.[4] They realized that, after the event, their men could be held accountable in a court of law for any illegalities they had committed during a period of martial law if the government of the day did not see fit to pass an act of indemnity.[5] Thus when in December 1951 Churchill, contemplating the complex legal situation facing the British garrison in the Canal Zone, told the Cabinet that they should 'Pig it: take a chance: don't be too scrupulous about the law,' he provoked an immediate reaction from the CIGS. Sir William Slim was not prepared to see the GOC, Sir George Erskine, thrown to the wolves at some future date. '[I] Don't want Erskine used' he retorted.[6]

The practicalities of administering martial law were also daunting. In Palestine in March 1947, following a spate of successful insurgent attacks, the administration imposed statutory martial law on Tel Aviv and part of Jerusalem. The civil government remained in existence but the army suspend all public services, closed all post and telegraph offices and telephone exchanges, withdrew all customs, port and railway facilities, and stopped the movement of all people and goods with the exception of foodstuffs.[7] The economic life of the area came to a standstill, and search operations led to the arrest of several dozen suspects. But the experiment lasted for only two weeks. Insurgent attacks continued elsewhere and the Yishuv were not, as the administration had hoped, intimidated into co-operating with the security forces. Furthermore, the government itself suffered because no revenues

---

[2] IWMSA. Accession No. 10243. A. H. P. Humphrey, reel 3.

[3] TNA CO 537/5068. Gurney to Colonial Secretary, 30 May 1949.

[4] D. G. Boyce, 'From Assaye to Assaye: reflections on British government, force and moral authority in India', *Journal of Military History*, vol. 63 (1999), 643–8; B. A. Knox, 'The British Government and the Governor Eyre Controversy, 1865–1875', *Historical Journal*, vol. 19 (1976), 877–900.

[5] WO 279/796. *War Office, Notes on Imperial Policing 1934* (London: War Office, 30 January 1934), 35.

[6] TNA CAB 195/10/CC15(51). Cabinet meeting, 7 December 1951.

[7] TNA CAB 129/18/CP(47)107. COS, Palestine, Imposition of Martial Law, 26 March 1947.

could be collected. The operation also tied down an enormous number of troops, a whole division in the case of Tel Aviv, at a time when the British army was being rapidly run down.[8] Similarly, the manpower demands of imposing martial law on the Canal Zone in 1951 were discovered to be so immense—they would have required the government, which had only a precarious majority in the House of Commons, to take the politically unpopular decision to mobilize part of the Territorial Army—that the idea was quietly dropped.[9]

EMERGENCY POWERS

But the most significant reason why the British did not resort to martial law was that they had discovered a more attractive way of giving the security forces nearly all of its advantages with few of its disadvantages. The jurist A. V. Dicey may have been right to insist that British domestic law did not recognize the continental concept of a 'state of siege', but British colonial law did.[10] In October 1896 an Order-in-Council was promulgated conferring on the governors of several fortress colonies such as Gibraltar, Malta, Hong Kong, and Ceylon the power to issue a proclamation giving them control of all property and persons in the colony, and making the latter liable to trial by a court martial.[11] In 1916 the geographic scope of the Order was extended to other colonies and protectorates and in 1928 the legislation was consolidated and it remained on the statute book until 1939.[12] In March 1939 it was replaced by the Emergency Powers (Colonial Defence) Order-in-Council, 1939, which itself was based upon a modified version of the Palestine (Defence) Order-in-Council that had been promulgated in 1937.[13]

The March 1939 Order-in-Council, and its subsequent amendments, became the legal basis of the emergencies in Kenya, Cyprus, and Nyasaland. Elsewhere, local legislation held sway. In Palestine it was a revised version of the Palestine (Defence) Order-in-Council, 1937.[14] In Malaya, the incoming military administration that took control of the country after the Japanese surrender in 1945 governed under an Essential Regulations Proclamation. In July 1948, a few weeks after the declaration of a state of emergency, it was replaced by a Federal

---

[8] TNA CAB 21/1686. Sir A. Cunningham to CO, 4 August 1947; TNA WO 216/221. C-in-C Middle East to VCIGS, 3 August 1947; TNA WO 32/15037. Appreciation by GOC Palestine on 5th August 1947.

[9] TNA CAB 128/23/CC(51)1. Cabinet Conclusions, 30 October 1951; TNA WO 163/364/ COS(51)681. Note by the War Office for the COS committee, The implications of establishing military government in the Suez Canal Zone, 12 November 1951; TNA WO 216/800. VCIGS to Robertson, 1 December 1951; TNA CAB 129/48/C(51)40. Eden, Egypt, 6 December 1951

[10] A. V. Dicey, *Introduction to the Study of the Law of the Constitution* (London: Macmillan, 1914), 283.

[11] TNA CO 323/1594/3. Order-in-Council, 21 October 1896.

[12] TNA CO 323/1594/3. The British Protectorates (Defence) Order-in-Council, 1916; TNA CO 323/1594/3. The Defence (Certain British possessions) Order-in-Council, 1928.

[13] TNA CO 323/1594/3. W. L. Dale to Sir G. Bushe, 13 January 1938.

[14] Downloaded 25 September 2008 at: http://avalon.law.yale.edu/20th_century/angcov.asp; Townshend, 'The defence of Palestine', 927.

Emergency Regulations Ordinance.[15] In British Guiana the governor acted under the British Guiana Act, 1928, and section 94 of the British Guiana (Constitution) Order-in-Council, 1953.[16] In North Borneo the governor took emergency powers under the Preservation of Public Security Ordinance, 1962.[17] But all these ordinances had one thing in common. They gave the governor the arbitrary power to make such regulations as he thought 'necessary or expedient for securing the public safety, the defence of the territory, the maintenance of public order and the suppression of mutiny, rebellion and riot, and for maintaining supplies and services essential to the life of the community.' He could 'provide for amending the law, for suspending the operation of any law and for applying any law with or without modification'. The only thing that a governor (other than in Palestine where it was permitted) specifically could not do was to establish military courts to try offenders.[18]

The way in which the 1939 Order was drafted and enacted demonstrated the underlying unease with which politicians and civil servants regarded such measures. They might be necessary, but they ran contrary to their deepest constitutional instincts. The Order began life as part of a wider exercise designed to prepare an Emergency Powers Bill to give governments in the UK and its colonies the arbitrary powers they might need when faced by a major international war. But so drastic were these powers that in 1938 Neville Chamberlain, the Prime Minister, baulked at introducing them to Parliament in peacetime for fear that they would be thrown out.[19] Instead he decided that the Bill should be introduced when war was imminent and when the need for such powers was unmistakable. But what might happen if war came suddenly, perhaps when Parliament was not sitting? The solution was to by-pass Parliament, for the executive to act without Parliamentary assent, and to use the Royal Prerogative to enact an Order-in-Council.[20] Originally the Order was not intended to be used in the case of a local emergency, but the Colonial Office quickly saw that it could be. As the Colonial Secretary explained in July 1938, it could confer 'upon Governors wide powers to make regulations for securing public safety and public order, whether in war or in purely

[15] TNA CO 717/167/5. ? to Sir M. Logan, 16 November 1948.
[16] TNA DEFE 11/94. Colonial Secretary to Savage, 24 & 26 September 1953; TNA CO 115/215. *The Official Gazette of British Guiana*, 10 October 1953: The British Guiana (Emergency) Order in Council, 1953.
[17] TNA CO 936/854. Colony of North Borneo. Preservation of Public Security Ordinance, 1962, 11 May 1962.
[18] TNA CO 822/729. Emergency Powers (Colonial Defence) Order-in-Council, 9 March 1939; TNA CO 1031/122. Sir A. Savage to Sir T. Lloyd, 17 September 1953; A. W. B. Simpson, 'Round up the usual suspects: the legacy of British colonialism and the European convention on human rights', *Loyola Law Review*, vol. 41 (1995–96), 652–78.
[19] TNA PREM 1/331/CID Paper 1411B. War Emergency Legislation, 18 March 1938; TNA PREM 1/313. Minutes of 315 meeting of the CID, 25 March 1938; N. Stammers, *Civil Liberties in Britain During the Second World War* (London: Croom Helm, 1983), 7–10.
[20] TNA CO 323/1594/3/ODC No 1559. J. A. Calder Colonies, etc. War Emergency Legislation, 4 July 1938; TNA CO 323/1594/3. Extract from the minutes of the 328 meeting of the CID, 30 June 1938.

local emergencies.'[21] However, that was something the Colonial Office was careful to hide from Parliament. When he sent the final draft to the Privy Council for formal approval, Sir John Shuckburgh, a senior Colonial Office official, reminded the Lord President of the Council that it must 'be kept a secret until such time as an emergency may arise in which it would be necessary for it to be proclaimed by the Governor of a Dependency to which it applies. It is a Prerogative Order, publication of which is not necessary.'[22]

The use of Emergency Powers continued to cause governments embarrassment after 1945. The very fact that a state of emergency had been proclaimed and emergency powers introduced was tantamount to a public declaration that normal government had broken down. In 1950 the Colonial Secretary, Arthur Creech Jones, therefore recommended that colonies should place on their statute books permanent laws giving the government a full battery of legal powers just short of those a governor could exercise under a state of emergency.[23] This package was intended to give a colonial government the legal powers to forestall subversion before it could develop into a full-blown insurgency. But even the architect of the plan was unhappy with this threat to traditional political liberties in the name of security. In a deeply confused admission, Creech Jones explained that 'I do not suggest that powers of this kind should be taken merely because there is a possibility that the need for them may arise. On the contrary, I must emphasise the necessity of adhering, as far as possible, until the stage is reached at which an emergency has to be declared, to the normal principles of English law by which the rights and liberties of the individuals are maintained. Any derogation from these rights and liberties is quite properly the occasion of criticism in Parliament and in the press, and it must be borne in mind that measures such as those outlined below should not be introduced unless the case is sufficiently strong to justify overriding the objections of principle.'[24] How governors were expected to secure the powers to forestall the need to declare an emergency, and square it with his injunction that they adhere to 'the normal principles of English law by which the rights and liberties of the individual are maintained' was left unexplained.

Outside the confines of the empire, the legal basis of British operations was less clear. The Anglo-Egyptian treaty of 1936 conferred on British military personnel in the Canal Zone immunity from civil or criminal prosecutions in the Egyptian courts for any actions they committed while on duty. British military camps were inviolate, and the British were given unrestricted rights of access and communications throughout the Canal Zone. Following Egypt's unilateral abrogation of the treaty in October 1951 the British based their actions on the legal argument that the treaty gave the Egyptians no right of unilateral abrogation, and so the privileges

[21] TNA CO 323/1594/3. Colonial Secretary to Governor, Northern Rhodesia, 16 July 1938.
[22] TNA CO 323/1659/10. Sir J. Shuckburgh to Lord President of the Council, 15 February 1939; TNA CO 323/1659/10. Colonial Secretary to Governors of Colonies, 20 March 1939.
[23] TNA CAB 134/535/ODC(50)14. A. Creech Jones, Powers for Dealing with Subversive Activities, 18 February 1950.
[24] Ibid.

the treaty had granted the British remained valid.[25] This, Erskine reasoned, meant that 'if the Egyptian authorities failed to maintain law and order in the part of Egypt in which we were, we had an inherent right to take such action as was necessary to protect and maintain our forces there.'[26] The legal context of operations in Oman were even more obscure. The sultan enjoyed full domestic autonomy and the British seem to have assumed that his word was the law. In November 1950 the states comprising the Council of Europe, signed their own Convention for the Protection of Human Rights and Fundamental Freedoms. But the signatories, including Britain, were not obliged to extend the Convention to their overseas possessions, and in 1953 Oman was one of the colonies and protectorates that they excluded from its provisions.[27]

The Emergency Powers Orders-in-Council and related local legislation gave rise to elaborate sets of emergency regulations. By the early 1950s, colonial governments were consciously looking back to the experience of Palestine and Malaya and using their regulations as a model for their own. Broadly speaking they fell into two categories. Control regulations gave the security forces the legal powers to employ exemplary force to intimidate the civilian population with the power of the state, to disrupt the insurgents' organization, and arrest suspected insurgents. They allowed the security forces to limit the freedom of movement of people and goods, to impose curfews, to introduce compulsory identity cards, to restrict the possession of foodstuffs and other articles of possible use to insurgents, to inaugurate various forms of censorship of the media and means of communication, and to ban suspect organizations. Policemen and soldiers could search premises and arrest suspects without a warrant. They could also mount cordon and search operations, and impose a variety of collective punishments. Counter-terrorist regulations went much further in the ways they allowed the security forces to employ coercion. They gave them the legal authority to take offensive measures against suspected insurgents. The administration could detain suspects without trial and, in cases where the latter were not citizens of the colony, deport them. In Malaya, Kenya, and Borneo they gave the government the power to enforce wholesale population resettlements, and in those colonies, Cyprus, and Nyasaland they could create free-fire zones where the security forces could engage suspected insurgents with lethal force.[28] Finally, the regulations were part of the legacy that the British bequeathed

[25] TNA CAB 129/48/C(51)40. Eden, Egypt, 6 December 1951; TNA WO 106/5993. Diary of events. Civil affairs—Legal branch, Appendix A: Summary on the legal position of the British Army in the Canal Zone. The establishment of military government, n.d.
[26] TNA WO 163/364/CGSZ/M(51)3. Ad hoc committee on military government in the Canal Zone, 28 November 1951; TNA WO 106/5993. Lt.-Col. A. H. Campbell to Brigadier Hinde, 8 January 1952.
[27] Convention for the Protection of Human Rights and Fundamental Freedoms as amended by Protocol No. 11. Rome, 4.XI.1950. Article 63. Accessed 4 November 2007 at www.conventions.coe.int/Treaty/en/Treaties/Html/005.htm; K. Vask, 'The European Convention of Human Rights beyond the Frontiers of Europe', *The International and Comparative Law Quarterly*, vol. 12, no. 4 (October, 1963), 1210.
[28] Copies of the detailed regulations can be found at: (Palestine) Defence (Emergency) Regulations. The Palestine Gazette, No. 1442. Published by the British Government, Palestine (September 27, 1945), Regulations 12–65. Downloaded on 16 September 2008 at: www.geocities.com/savepalestinenow/

to some post-colonial governments.[29] After independence in August 1957, the government of the Federation of Malay, for example, incorporated almost all of the emergency regulations into its own statute book, and granted the Commonwealth forces that remained stationed in the Federation the same legal powers and immunities they had enjoyed before independence.[30]

Emergency Regulations not only criminalized behaviour that would not otherwise have been illegal. They also allowed the authorities to inflict a range of punishments on wrong-doers far in excess of those they would have faced in more normal times. These ranged from fines and periods of imprisonment for minor offences, up to the death penalty for offences involving committing or threatening violence, or associating with those committing or planning to commit violence. In Malaya, less than a month after the declaration of the emergency, the High Commissioner withdrew the discretion of courts to impose prison sentences on those found guilty of firearms offences and imposed a mandatory death penalty.[31] In June 1950, as part of the government's campaign to deny food and supplies to the insurgents, the death penalty was extended to apply to anyone found guilty of extorting food or money on behalf of the insurgents. Shortly afterwards the onus of proof was thrown onto suspects to demonstrate their innocence.[32] Superficially, punishments in Kenya appeared to be more lenient.[33] However, the definition of an insurgent in Kenya was set extremely widely. It included anyone

---

emergencyregs/emergencyregs.htm and TNA CO 717/471/13. Supplement No 2. Palestine Gazette Extraordinary No. 1470 of 28 January 1946. Defence (Emergency) Regulations; (Malaya) TNA CO 717/161/1. The Essential Regulations Proclamation, 18 June 1948; TNA CO 717/167/3. Federation of Malaya. Regulations made under the Emergency Regulations Ordinance, 1948 together with the Essential (Special Constabulary) Regulations 1948, incorporating all amendments up to 22 March 1949 (Kuala Lumpur: Government Press, 1949); TNA CO 717/167/3. Federation of Malaya. Emergency (Amendment no. 13) Regulations, 1949, 24 May 1949. (Kenya) TNA CO 822/729. Emergency Regulations made under the Emergency Powers Order-in-Council, 1939 (Nairobi: Government Printer, 1953). (British Guiana) TNA CO 115/215. The Official Gazette of British Guiana, 10 October 1953. (Cyprus) TNA CO 926/396. A Law to make provision for the Detention of Persons in certain circumstances. No. 26 of 1955, 15 July 1955; TNA CO 926/561. Emergency Powers (Public Safety and Order) Regulations, 1955, 24 November 1955. (Nyasaland) TNA CO 1015/658. Footman to Gorrell-Barnes, 25 September 1953 and enc.; TNA CO 1015/1516. Emergency Powers Order-in-Council, 1939 and 1956. Emergency Regulations 1959; (North Borneo) TNA CO 936/854. Second Supplement to the Government Gazette, 8 December 1962; (Aden) TNA CO 1055/207. The Constitution of the Federation of South Arabia. Public Emergency Decree, 1963, 10 December 1963; (Aden) TNA CO 1055/207: Public Emergency Amendment Decree, 1965, 16 February 1965.

[29] Simpson, 'Round up the usual suspects', 632–3.
[30] Laws of Malaysia. Act 296. Public Order (Preservation) Act 1958; [Cmnd] 264. *Arrangements for the Employment of Overseas Commonwealth Forces in Emergency Operations in the Federation of Malaya after Independence*, September 1957; Laws of Malaysia. Act 82. Internal Security Act 1960; TNA DO 35/9937. Group Captain A. J. Trumble to Air Ministry, 23 July 1959; TNA DO 35/9937. H. Ellsley to D. R. E. Hopkins, 19 November 1959; TNA DO 35/9935. Ministry of External Affairs, Federation of Malaya to Sir G. Tory, 16 November 1959; TNA DO 35/9935. Extract of a letter from G. E. Crombie to G. W. St Chadwick, 14 January 1960.
[31] TNA CO 717/161/1. High Commissioner Malaya to Colonial Secretary, 2 July 1948.
[32] TNA CAB 21/1681/MAL.C(50)23. Federation Plan for the elimination of the Communist Organization and armed forces in Malaya, 24 May 1950; *Times*, 13 July 1950.
[33] TNA CO 822/729. Emergency Regulations made under the Emergency Powers Order-in-Council, 1939. Regulation 33.

who used, or carried firearms, ammunition or explosives, or acted in a manner prejudicial to public safety, or incited others to do so. All such people were liable to the death penalty, as was anyone guilty of conspiring with them, or impeding the operations of the security forces.[34] Furthermore, the list of offensive weapons, possession of which also carried the death penalty, was extended to include not only firearms and explosives, but also spears, swords, and normal agricultural implements such as pangas and axes. The burden of proof was also reversed, and it was for the accused to demonstrate that they had not acted unlawfully.[35]

Governance through emergency regulations amounted to a wholesale repudiation of many of the human rights enshrined in the UN 1948 Universal Declaration of Human Rights. It was, as a group of Colonial Office officials agreed in October 1948, tantamount to 'police state controls'.[36] They were admitting in private what Lord Devlin, investigating the Nyasaland emergency, was to assert in public, to the utmost embarrassment of the Macmillan government, in 1959. Once a proclamation enforcing the 1939 Order-in-Council had been issued, a colonial government could set aside existing laws and exercise almost unlimited powers. As Gurney admitted, in Palestine emergency regulations were continually being added to, 'so that at the end it might almost have been said that the whole book of Regulations could have been expressed in a single provision empowering the High Commissioner to take any action he wished.'[37]

The British had always used the law as a way of maintaining their hegemony in the colonies, and the Emergency Regulations regimes were just more instances of them doing so.[38] The colonized might sometimes have been able to turn British notions that all were equal before the law against the colonizers. But one of the main purposes of the Emergency Regulations was to deprive them of opportunities to do that. Some of the officials who formulated and wielded these powers had no doubt that they exposed a gaping hole in British rhetoric between their commitment to the rule of law and the reality that the empire was ultimately sustained by force. Trafford Smith, an Assistant Secretary at the Colonial Office with responsibility for Palestine, minuted in real anguish about the detention of Zionist insurgents in Eritrea that

> The plain truth to which we so firmly shut our eyes is that in this emergency Regulation Detention business we are taking a leaf out of the Nazi book, following the familiar error that the end justifies the means (especially when the means serve current expediency). We are out to suppress terrorism, and because we can find no better means we order measures which are intrinsically wrong, and which, since their

---

[34] TNA CO 822/729. Emergency Regulations made under the Emergency Powers Order-in-Council, 1939. Regulations 3, 8; TNA CO 822/728 Baring to Colonial Secretary, 1 May 1953.

[35] TNA CO 822/729. Emergency Regulations made under the Emergency Powers Order-in-Council, 1939. Regulation 3(A)1, 4.

[36] TNA CO 111/736/4. Note of a meeting held on security matters in British Guiana in Mr Seel's room, Church House, on 28 October 1948.

[37] TNA CO 537/5068. Gurney to Colonial Secretary, 30 May 1949.

[38] B. Ibhawoh, 'Stronger than the maxim gun. Law, human rights and British colonial hegemony in Nigeria', *Africa*, vol. 72 (2002), 55–81.

consequence is evidence to the whole world, let us in for a lot of justifiable and unanswerable criticism.[39]

They also understood that the purpose of enacting Emergency Regulations was neither to hasten the liquidation of the British Empire nor sustain the rights of the indigenous peoples. As one Colonial Office official admitted in 1956, 'These sweeping powers were designed and have when necessary been used to preserve the ultimate authority of the metropolitan power and of the Governor as its representative.'[40] But if it was legal, was what they were doing also legitimate? Again, the officials charged with implementing the regulations had their private doubts. In Malaya, 'the Police and Army are breaking the law every day', Gurney admitted in January 1949. 'A spate of Emergency Regulations to provide legal cover could if necessary be issued, but to give the sanctity of all to pieces of paper signed by the High Commissioner only and not subject to ratification by any legislature must lead, if taken too far, to justified criticism and misconceptions derogatory of the law itself.'[41]

In the short term the expression of these qualms was confined to a small group of senior officials and ministers. Their misgivings did not prevent them from enacting and administering the wide range of coercive measures defined by the emergency regulations. But they did establish limits beyond which they did not go. They ensured that, although they may have taken 'a leaf out of the Nazi book', they did not follow Nazi policies chapter and verse and practice genocide in their colonies. They also ensured that when, from the mid-1950s, as Chapter 8 will show, emergency regulations came under increasing attack at the UN, their confidence in the morality of Britain's imperial mission was increasingly undermined.

MINIMUM NECESSARY FORCE

The claim that British security forces eschewed employing excessive violence because their actions were constrained by the common law principle that they were only allowed to employ the 'minimum necessary force' cannot be accepted at its face value, for there was no consensus about what that principle meant. 'The British Army', Lord Harding believed, 'has had widespread experience of these problems, and I think there is what is called the doctrine or the philosophy of minimum force. And that is applicable to situations of these types. Sometimes it's interpreted by critics and journalists in the wrong way, in my opinion. But who is to decide what is minimum force.'[42]

If that decision was left to the military authorities, the limit might be fixed very high, for minimum necessary force was not the army's default setting. By 1945 soldiers had learnt that massive firepower won battles. Confronted by insurgencies

---

[39] TNA CO 537/1825. Minute by Trafford Smith, 10 December 1946.
[40] TNA CO 1037/19 J. S. Bennett (CO official) to C. G. Eastwood, 21 December 1956.
[41] TNA CO 537/4753/BDCC(Far East). 16 meeting, 28 January 1949.
[42] IWMSA. Accession No. 8736. Field Marshal Lord Harding, Transcript, 406.

in Athens in December 1944, and in Surabaya in the Netherlands East Indies in November 1945, they had no compunction about employing artillery, air power, and naval gunfire with little real discrimination between civilians and armed insurgents.[43] An after-action report on operations in Athens told troops that 'In such fighting, our own t[roo]ps must be prepared at all times for such abuses, and must NOT be squeamish about killing anyone carrying a weapon—civilian, woman or child. All occupants of a house from which fire has been coming must be arrested or killed.'[44] As one infantryman who fought in Athens remembered, 'We tried to avoid civilian casualties but people don't pay a lot of attention to that. I've got to be truthful! I mean you wouldn't deliberately shoot at civilians, but if there's any doubt in your mind and you might be wrong, then it's better to be safe than sorry—you'd let fly!'[45] Such attitudes were endorsed at the highest level. In February 1945, Sir Robert Scobie, the British commander in Greece, issued a training circular suggesting that when the army encountered guerrilla opponents indistinguishable from the civilian population, the latter should be warned that anyone captured under arms and not wearing a clear distinguishing mark would be treated as a war criminal and executed.[46]

Senior soldiers wanted to continue some of these practices. In August 1945 the Commander-in-Chief's committee in the Middle East asked the Cabinet whether, 'in view of the greater precision of modern weapons', they might be allowed to employ aerial bombs, naval gunfire, mortars and artillery to quell serious disturbances, although they did promise not to do so in politically sensitive places such as Jerusalem, Bethlehem, and Nazareth.[47] A horrified Cabinet refused.[48] The message got through to troops on the ground, but they did not always like it.[49] Following the deaths of a dozen soldiers in a single incident in the Crater district of Aden in June 1967, troops in Aden were reported to be angry that they were not permitted by their rules of engagement to fire anything heavier than a general purpose machine gun.[50] Refraining from employing the heaviest available weapons had to be imposed on the army by their political masters.

---

[43] TNA WO 204/1909. Operations in Greece, 15 October 1944 to 7 January 1945. 23 Armoured Brigade. On the fighting in Indonesia see: R. McMillan, *The British occupation of Indonesia 1945–1946* (London: Routledge, 2005); TNA CAB 69/7/DO(45)42. Note by the Secretary, Situation in Java, 1 December 1945, and enc. report by Lt.-Col. G. S. Nangle.

[44] TNA WO 204/1909. Lessons from fighting in Greece', n.d. but *c*.15 January 1945.

[45] P. Hart, *The Heat of Battle: 16th Battalion Durham Light Infantry 1943–45. The Italian Campaign* (London: Leo Cooper, 1999), 202.

[46] TNA WO 204/1909. Training Instruction no. 11. Operations in a built-up area against a partisan rising, 20 February 1945.

[47] TNA CAB 69/7/DO(45)40. Note by the Secretary, Use of appropriate weapons in the Middle East, 30 November 1945.

[48] TNA CAB 69/7/DO(45)17 meeting. Cabinet Defence Committee, 12 December 1945.

[49] IWMSA. Accession No. 10109. Col. J. B. Buckmaster, reel 1.

[50] TNA DEFE 24/1896. Anon., 'One shell allowed and that's dud', *Daily Express*, 24 June 1967; DEFE 24/1896. C. Munnion, 'Frustration rises on Aden Army Curbs', *Sunday Telegraph*, 25 June 1967; DEFE 24/1896. S. Harper, '"Soft-pedal" angers our Aden troops', *Sunday Express*, 25 June 1967.

Matters were further complicated because the concept of minimum necessary force, as explained in successive editions of *King's* and *Queens Regulations*, the *MML*, and the army's doctrinal manuals, was so ill-defined that it could not constitute an effective guide for the action of security forces on the ground.[51] The soldier or policeman on the spot was to be left to assess the situation for himself and do what he thought necessary. He had to hope that someone above him, probably far removed from the action, and at some later date, did not find his actions (or inactions) wanting, and hold him accountable. A company commander who served in Palestine concluded that putting the onus in this way on the soldier was no more than 'a most convenient umbrella for the politician and for the civil power, leaving the military holding the baby. If anything went wrong the military could be held to blame, for using either too much or too little force, or for not taking action or, alternatively, using no force when it should have done so.'[52]

The legal niceties in the manuals had to be translated into simple, easily understood, rules of engagement. That was easier said than done. This was graphically illustrated by a brigade commander in a covering note he issued with his rules of engagement in Kenya. The army, he explained was not at war in Kenya, but was carrying out duties in aid of the civil power. 'The principle of the "minimum force necessary" must apply in all circumstances and each of the cases described below. This principle is not really restrictive in fact the minimum force necessary might be the maximum force a soldier or party of soldiers could muster.'[53] Politicians' pronouncements were no clearer. Soldiers in Cyprus were issued with a red card laying down the circumstances in which they could and could not open fire.[54] But commenting on those circumstances in the Commons in 1958, the Secretary of State for War, Christopher Soames, managed to say in the same breath that, 'It is known by every soldier in Cyprus that, whatever action he is called upon to take, he has to do it with the minimum of force', and that, 'We must never forget that the role of the security forces is to conquer terrorism, and there will be many incidents when the minimum force necessary will be quite a lot of force.'[55] Anyone

[51] The analysis in this paragraph is based upon War Office, *Manual of Military Law, 1951–59. Part (II). 1951. Section V. Employment of Troops in Aid of the Civil Power* (London: War Office, 1955). The law as expounded in this edition of the manual differed only in minor respects from the analysis in the preceding edition of the manual, War Office, *Manual of Military Law, 1929* (London: HMSO, 1929), 246–69; War Office, *King's Regulations for the Army and the Royal Army Reserve 1940* (London: HMSO, 1940), 450; War Office, *Queen's Regulations for the Army 1955* (London: HMSO, 1955). The manuals contained summaries of the relevant sections of the *MML*. See, TNA WO 279/796. War Office, *Notes on Imperial Policing 1934* (London: War Office, 30 January 1934); TNA WO 279/470. War Office, *Duties in Aid of the Civil Power, 1937. Reprint incorporating amendments (No. 1) 1945* (London: War Office, 1945); TNA WO 279/391. War Office, *Imperial Policing and Duties in aid of the civil power, 1949* (London: War Office, 1949), and TNA WO 296/23. War Office, *Keeping the Peace (Duties in Support of the Civil Power) (1957)* (London: War Office, 1957)

[52] Maj. V. Dover, *The Silken Canopy* (London: Cassell, 1979), 128.

[53] TNA WO 32/21721. OC, 39 Infantry Brigade to CO's 1/Buffs, 1/Devons, 1/Lancashire Fusiliers, 20 April 1953.

[54] IWMDoD. Misc 93. Item 1391. 'Instructions to individuals for opening fire in Cyprus. Issued by Chief of Staff to H.E. the Governor', December1955.

[55] *Times*, 7 July 1958.

reading the Brigadier's orders or listening to Soames might think that the troops were operating in Wonderland under the command of the Mad Hatter.

Finally, in a colonial emergency what was legal or illegal behaviour was not determined by the *MML*, but by a battery of emergency regulations. The practical issues concerning when and how much lethal force to use that faced the security forces in Malaya, Kenya, Cyprus, Nyasaland, and Borneo were simplified because the emergency regulations defined when and where they could open fire and gave them wide latitude to do so. The security forces could operate a shoot to kill policy in two kinds of places. These were first defined in Malaya in 1948. In July the government issued an emergency regulation declaring specified locations, such as army camps, police stations, government offices, and prisons, to be 'protected places.' Anyone who entered them without a permit, or who failed to stop after being challenged three times, 'may be arrested by force which force may, if necessary to effect the arrest, extend to the voluntary causing of death.'[56] But by November 1948 the security forces had driven the insurgents out of towns and cities into the jungle fringes, where they were attacking rubber plantations and tin mines, the life-blood of the Malayan economy. Consequently, Gurney told the Colonial Secretary, 'I am making new Emergency Regulations under which a Chief Police Officer may declare an area to be a special area, in which, in effect, any person who when called upon fails to stop and submit to search may be shot.'[57]

Elsewhere the nomenclature differed. Nyasaland followed the Malayan example and created 'Special Areas', although in 1960 the Federal Malayan government changed the nomenclature it used to 'security areas'.[58] In Kenya the forests of the Aberdares mountains and the area around Mount Kenya were labelled 'Prohibited Areas'.[59] Initially the security forces were expected to challenge anyone found there before opening fire, but in February 1953 Baring removed even that safeguard.[60] 'Special Areas' in Kenya, which in practice meant the Native Reserves, differed from 'Prohibited Areas' only in that the legal obligation on the security forces to issue a challenge before opening fire was maintained.[61] In Cyprus in 1956 the mountains and forests of the island became 'Danger areas'.[62] But no matter what

[56] TNA CO 717/167/3. Federation of Malaya. Regulations made under the Emergency Regulations Ordinance, 1948, together with the Essential (Special Constabulary) Regulations 1948, incorporating all amendments up to 22 March 1949 (Kuala Lumpur: Government Press, 1949). Regulations 9.
[57] TNA CO 717/210/4. Gurney to Colonial Secretary, 26 November 1948; TNA CO 717/167/3. Federation of Malaya. Regulations made under the Emergency Regulations Ordinance, 1948 together with the Essential (Special Constabulary) Regulations 1948, incorporating all amendments up to 22 March 1949. (Kuala Lumpur: Government Press, 1949). Regulations 10A(2).
[58] TNA CO 1015/1516. Emergency Powers Order-in-Council, 1939 and 1956. Emergency Regulations, 1959, Regulation 11; Laws of Malaysia. Act 82. Internal Security Act 1960.
[59] TNA CO 822/729. Emergency Regulations made under the Emergency Powers Order-in-Council, 1939. Regulation 22A.
[60] TNA CO 822/442. Telegram, OAG Kenya to Colonial Secretary, 24 February 1953.
[61] TNA CO 822/729. Emergency Regulations made under the Emergency Powers Order-in-Council, 1939. Regulation 22B.
[62] TNA CO 926/561. The Emergency Powers (Public Safety and Order) (Amendment No. 8) Regulations, 22 May 1956. Regulation 38A; TNA CO 926/1083. Sir H. Foot (Governor Cyprus) to

name was attached to them, what they had in common was that they were all remote, allegedly sparsely populated, and anyone found in them who did not halt when challenged could be shot. In each case the administration was supposed to give the inhabitants ample warning of the dangers they faced if they entered one of these areas. But, as one Colonial Office official minuted, 'There is an obvious risk of innocent persons being shot through disregard or lack of knowledge of warnings, but that is a risk that I think must be faced.'[63]

ABSENCE OF CHECKS AND BALANCES

Within each colony there were three legal institutions which might have constrained the exercise of the almost untrammelled powers that emergency regulations granted to the security forces. They were the civil courts, coroners' inquests, and, in those colonies where suspects were subject to detention without trial, the advisory committees established to make recommendations about the continued detention of detainees. While the civil courts did sometimes offer protection against the government's exercise of arbitrary power, the other two institutions were much less effective.

In Palestine and Malaya, emergency regulations permitted a coroner to dispense with an inquest if he believed that a person had been killed in the course of security force operations.[64] In Kenya the security forces were ordered to report the deaths of any Mau Mau suspects they had killed to the nearest magistrate, but 'Provided they report any casualties inflicted on the enemy as soon as they can to the Police, the Police will then inform a magistrate who will accept the report and, unless there are exceptional circumstances, will decree that no inquest is necessary. The case is then legally closed and no subsequent charges can affect the issue.'[65] In Cyprus coroners' courts were suspended, but inquests could still be held in a Special Court in Nicosia.[66] This irritated the security forces, but there is no indication that anyone was held to account for their actions by those courts. In Nyasaland coroners functioned, but appear to have found in favour of the security forces. In June 1959 the coroner for Northern Province enquired into events at Nkata Bay, which saw the largest single loss of life during the emergency, but blandly recorded a verdict of justifiable homicide, concluding that, 'I am satisfied the amount of lethal force used

Colonial Secretary, 17 October 1958; TNA CO 926/1083. Emergency Regulation (Public Safety and Order) Amendment No. 5) Regulation, 15 October 1958. Regulation 21.

[63] TNA CO 926/561. W. A. Morris to Sir T. Lloyd, n.d.

[64] Defence (Emergency) Regulations. The Palestine Gazette, No. 1442. Published by the British Government, Palestine (27 September 1945). Reg. 133. Downloaded on 16 September 2008 at: www. geocities.com/savepalestinenow/emergencyregs/emergencyregs.htm; TNA CO 717/167/3. Federation of Malaya. Regulations made under the Emergency Regulations Ordinance, 1948 together with the Essential (Special Constabulary) Regulations 1948, incorporating all amendments up to 22 March 1949 (Kuala Lumpur: Government Press, 1949). Regulation 36.

[65] TNA WO 32/21721. Adjutant, 23/KAR, to all company commanders, 14 May 1953.

[66] TNA CO 926/561. Emergency Powers (Modification of the Coroners Law, 1953) Regulations, 1955, 7 December 1955.

was necessary to disperse the crowd and prevent it from affecting its unlawful purpose.'[67] The same verdict, or a verdict of accidental death, was brought in at 45 of the 47 inquests held on people killed by the security forces in Nyasaland.[68]

In those colonies where detention without trial was introduced, it was accompanied by the establishment of advisory committees who could make recommendations to the Governor about the need or otherwise to detain individuals. They rarely acted as an effective check on the government's arbitrary powers of arrest and detention. In broad terms, they worked in much the same way as similar committees had worked in Britain during the Second World War when they had heard appeals from people detained under Defence Regulation 18B.[69] Their membership was weighted heavily towards the administration and against the detainees. In Cyprus the committee consisted of a retired judge, a retired senior civil servant, and a military lawyer from the Judge Advocate General's Branch. Although they were chaired by judges, the committees were administrative, not judicial, tribunals. They were not bound by the procedures and rules of evidence that applied in courts of law, and their proceedings were not open to the press or public. Detainees were usually only given very general indications of the grounds upon which they had been detained, and they were not permitted to cross-examine witnesses. In Malaya, Kenya, British Guiana, Cyprus, Nyasaland, and Aden, detainees were permitted to consult a lawyer in preparing their cases. But only in Malaya and British Guiana could they be accompanied by a lawyer when they appeared before the committee.[70] In 1953 Governor Baring in Kenya even wanted to deprive detainees of the right of making a personal appearance before the committee, but the Colonial Office insisted that Kenya should follow the Malayan example.[71]

The work of the committees was guided more by political and security goals than by legal or judicial considerations. A Special Branch policeman was often present throughout the hearing, but the detainee was not permitted to hear his evidence, ostensibly because doing so might compromise sensitive intelligence sources.[72] In Aden even the members of the advisory committee complained that they were kept in the dark about some of the evidence collected by the security forces.[73] In Malaya the committees were instructed to give the benefit of any doubt to the government. When some of the committees began to ignore police recommendations in favour

[67] TNA CO 1015/1523. *News Chronicle*, 9 June 1959.
[68] TNA CAB 129/98/C(59)124. Colonial Secretary, Nyasaland Commission of Inquiry, 17 July 1959. Report of the Nyasaland Commission of Inquiry.
[69] Stammers, *Civil Liberties in Britain*, 3–73.
[70] TNA CO 822/451. Colonial Secretary to Baring, 12 March 1953; TNA CO 115/215. *The Official Gazette of British Guiana*, 26 October 1953. Constitution of Advisory Committee established under Regulation 13(2); TNA CO 1015/1517. Armitage to Secretary of State 18 March 1959; TNA CO 1055/207. Aden emergency Regulations 1965, 5 June 1965; TNA CO 1055/209. POMEC Aden to CO, 30 December 1965.
[71] TNA CO 822/451. Baring to Colonial Secretary, 23 February 1953.
[72] TNA CO 822/451. Colonial Secretary to Baring, 12 March 1953; TNA CO 822/451. Crawford to David, 28 August 1953; TNA CO 1031/1425. Procedure to be followed by the Advisory Committee appointed by the Governor under Section 13 of the Emergency Order, 1953, 10 November 1953.
[73] TNA CAB 148/29/OPD(66)128. Bowen to Foreign Secretary, 14 November 1966.

of continued detention, Gurney established a second tier of committees to overrule them.[74] In Cyprus the chairman of the advisory committee concluded in June 1958 that as decisions on whether to release a detainee were taken on political grounds, his committee served no useful purpose. The governor agreed and decided that henceforth he would make the decisions himself, advised by Special Branch.[75] In Kenya, in reaching their recommendations, the advisory committee was told to take into account not only the detailed grounds for detention and any evidence raised at the hearing, but also the detainee's behaviour during detention, and the likely effect of his release on the people of his home district.[76] In general, therefore, the first priority of the committees was not to see that justice was done. It was to maintain public order and there was ample justification for the accusation levelled by the Labour MP and lawyer Dingle Foot that 'the Advisory Committee is in no sense a judicial body and that the procedure by which every detainee asks for it to review his case is mere whitewash.'[77]

The ordinary courts were only marginally more effective in constraining the powers of the executive and bringing its agents to account. As long as the government did not declare martial law, the civil courts remained open, and it was in theory possible for the judges to act as a check on the administration and the security forces. They might demand reasonable proof before punishing an alleged insurgent, and they sometimes did so. In November 1950, Emanuel Shinwell, the Minister of Defence, complained that the civil courts in Malaya were being too lenient. The Director of Operations, Sir Harold Briggs, defended them, insisting that when they had adequate proof of guilt he was satisfied that they were not lenient. 'The difficulty lay in obtaining the proof.'[78] Securing a conviction even of an insurgent caught under arms was far from straightforward. The security forces had to follow proper procedures. As one soldier recounted,

> Capturing guerrillas was not just a simple task of physically apprehending them, with or without a struggle. They always had to be 'processed' so that, legally, the charge of carrying a weapon, which carried the death sentence, could be made to stick in court. If there was no proof of a soldier being detailed personally to carry the guerrilla's weapon, it could be argued in court that that weapon was not the one the guerrilla was alleged to have been carrying, so the charge was unproven.[79]

A further complication arose when the suspect was being interrogated. This was normally done by either Special Branch personnel or army interrogators. But their

---

[74] TNA CO 717/167/4. Chief Secretary to Chairman of each State Advisory Committee, 6 August 1948; TNA CAB 21/1681/MAL.C(50)6 meeting Malaya Committee, 19 June 1950; TNA CAB 21/1681/MAL.C(50)24. Colonial Secretary, Cabinet Malaya Committee: Detention Procedure, 10 July 1950.
[75] TNA CO 926/872. Governor's Advisory Committee on Detainees, 27 June 1958.
[76] TNA CO 822/1234. Deputy Governor to Colonial Secretary, 5 February 1957.
[77] TNA CO 822/1234. Minute by J. F Buist, to Cahill, 7 February 1957.
[78] TNA CAB 130/65/GEN 345/1. Note by the Secretary, Meeting with the Director of Operations, Federation of Malaya, 27 November 1950.
[79] P. Cross, *'A Face Like a Chicken's Backside'. An Unconventional Soldier in South East Asia, 1948–1971* (London: Greenhill Books, 1996), 31; IWMSA. Accession No. 11146. Col. M. Gray, reel 3.

main concern was to secure information about insurgent plans and organizations, not to gather evidence to prosecute individuals. Consequently they did not conduct interrogations under judges' rules and so statements obtained during their interrogations were not admissible as evidence in a court of law.[80]

Whether defendants got a fair hearing depended on whether they had access to a lawyer. Important defendants like Kenyatta could attract distinguished expatriate lawyers. The defendant accused of throwing the grenade that wounded Trevaskis in December 1963 was defended by a British barrister, Christopher French, who ended his career as a High Court judge.[81] But most defendants had to rely on local legal talent. In this respect, Cyprus and Palestine on the one hand, and Nyasaland on the other, were poles apart. In Cyprus most Greek-Cypriot lawyers were sympathetic towards EOKA, and in every capital case except one enough money was collected to make an appeal to the Privy Council.[82] At the other extreme the security forces in Nyasaland quickly took care to place the only trained African barrister in detention.[83]

Complaints by members of the security forces that their actions were unreasonably constrained by the letter of the law, and that they could be unfairly penalized by the courts for doing their duty if they harmed someone, are not new.[84] Soldiers in Palestine, who had recently been using every weapon to hand to fight the Germans, were intensely frustrated that henceforth they could not return fire without a specific order to do so.[85] Twenty years later in Aden, Brigadier C. W. Dunbar, a senior staff officer at MELF, complained that 'As soon as a soldier uses his weapon a mass of false evidence appears and HQ MELF have to plan to avoid an indictment for murder or attempted murder against him.'[86] In fact such prosecutions were comparatively rare because, as Dunbar intimated, the colonial and military authorities went out of their way to provide legal cover for the men on the ground. In normal peacetime circumstances both civil courts and military courts martial could exercise jurisdiction over servicemen. But servicemen committing serious crimes, such as murder, manslaughter, treason, or rape, were nearly always prosecuted before a civil court, whose jurisdiction was paramount.[87] But, in an emergency, this opened the possibility that a soldier who shot a local national might be tried before a jury composed of local nationals who were already biased

[80] TNA WO 32/19064. War Office, *Intelligence in Internal Security Operations* (London: War Office, 28 August 1963).
[81] TNA CO 1055/200. Acting High Commissioner Aden to CO, 29 February 1964.
[82] TNA CO 968/690. Brigadier G. Baker, A Review of the Cyprus Emergency April 1955–March 1958.
[83] TNA CO 1015/2053. Secretary of 'Justice' to Lennox-Boyd, 13 March 1959.
[84] R. Kerr, 'A Force for Good? War, Crime and Legitimacy: The British Army in Iraq', *Defense and Security Analysis*, vol. 24 (2008), 401–19; J. K. Wither, 'Basra's not Belfast: the British Army, "small wars" and Iraq', *SW&I*, vol. 20 (2009), 626; D. Whetham, 'Killing within the rules', *SW&I*, vol. 18 (2007), 721–33.
[85] IWMSA. Accession No. 10109. Col. J. B. Buckmaster, reel 1; IWMSA. Accession No. 11133. Col. H. J. Sweeney, reel 1.
[86] TNA DEFE 11/526. Brigadier N. Gribbon to VCDS, 5 April 1967, quoting a letter from Dunbar.
[87] TNA DEFE 13/468. Colonial Secretary to PM, 24 April 1965.

against him. That this rarely happened was because once an emergency had been declared, the security forces enjoyed a high degree of legal immunity. In Palestine, Malaya, Kenya, and Cyprus the army was declared to be on active service.[88] Soldiers were then immune from prosecution in civil courts for offences committed in the course of their duties, although they might, if their commanders chose, be answerable before a court martial.[89] In Cyprus to avoid any further confusion, the government enacted emergency regulations ensuring that no member of the security forces could be prosecuted for anything he had done in the course of his official duties except with the consent of the Attorney-General.[90] The language of an EOKA propaganda leaflet published in December 1956 may have been intemperate, but it contained more than a grain of truth: 'If you have been unjustly treated or ill-treated, if you are the victim of a theft or of the English justice, you have no right to take the persons responsible to court. The Attorney-General's permission is required beforehand, which, however, is not given. It is an ideal and at the same time sly method of covering their disgraceful acts.'[91]

The security forces sometimes also believed that the wheels of justice in the civil courts ground too slowly. Senior officers warned that this built up a sense of frustration amongst the rank and file, and that unless something was done, they might take matters into their own hands. 'In an Emergency', one Director of Operations in Cyprus wrote, 'it is very important that the wheels of justice should turn as quickly as possible otherwise there is the danger that the Security Forces will lose faith in the judicial system and might attempt to mete out rough justice themselves.'[92] And in Aden the C-in-C Middle East complained that 'If the grenadier, who has been captured at great personal risk rather than gunned down, is allowed to go free we shall run a grave risk of drawing dangerously upon the British soldiers['] reserves of patience and good sense, and the circumstances of this could be more damaging to HMG than any consequences which might arise from justice being meted out to the grenadier.'[93]

In Palestine Cunningham could defuse such criticisms by sending insurgents for trial before military courts. They could impose penalties up to and including death by hanging. There was no appeal from their decision, although their findings had to

[88] TNA WO 106/5884. Gen. Sir N. Ritchie, Report on operations in Malaya, June 1948 to July 1949, 6 June 1949; TNA WO 32/15556. Erskine to CIGS, 9 July 1953.
[89] TNA CO 926/544. Sir R. Armitage to Colonial Secretary, 26 Sept; 1955; TNA CO 926/544. Minute, J. H. Crutchley, 27 September 1955; TNA CO 926/544. Colonial Secretary to Harding, 26 November 1955; *Manchester Guardian*, 29 November 1955.
[90] TNA CO 926/561. The Emergency Powers (Public Officer's Protection) Regulation, 1956, 24 November 1956; TNA CO 926/1086. Sir J. Henry to Sir K. O. Roberts-Wray, 15 April 1957; TNA CO 926/1084 The Emergency Powers (Public Safety and Order) (Consolidation) Regulations, 1958, Regulation 77; TNA CO 926/1084. Foot to Colonial Secretary, 15 July 1958.
[91] TNA CO 926/670/CIC(56)38. Cyprus Intelligence Committee. Intelligence Review for the second half of December 1956, 7 January 1957. Enc. PEKA leaflet, 'The ridiculing of justice', 16 December 1956.
[92] TNA CO 926/1077. Report on the Cyprus Emergency, 31 July 1959.
[93] TNA DEFE 11/524. C-in-C Mideast to CDS, 18 February 1967.

be confirmed by the GOC.[94] In January 1946, these three-man military courts were supplemented by a second tier of military courts presided over by a single officer empowered to try lesser offences and to impose lesser penalties.[95] In 1955 some members of the Cyprus administration, convinced that local judges were being so intimidated that they could no longer deliver impartial justice, wanted to follow this example.[96] But neither the Colonial Secretary nor Harding thought that the moment was opportune to make such a public confession of failure.[97] Instead, they imported a handful of British lawyers as judges and installed them in Special Courts to try offences under the emergency regulations.[98]

Elsewhere criticism that the delivery of justice was too slow was met by a whittling down of judicial safeguards. Even though there was very little actual violence in British Guiana, in April 1954 the Chief Justice thought it necessary to appoint a special magistrate to deal with such cases as they arose.[99] In Malaya and elsewhere, magistrates and district judges confronted by a case that might carry the death penalty were required to dispense with any preliminary inquiries and to transfer it immediately to a higher court.[100] District Courts in Malaya were empowered to hear some cases that would previously have been reserved for the High Court, and could try any offence under the emergency regulations other than those carrying the death penalty.[101] Cases were also tried in camera, allegedly because of the threat that witnesses would otherwise be intimidated.[102] In Kenya special Emergency Assize Courts were established to hear Mau Mau-related offences, and special sittings of the Appeal Court in Nairobi were held to hasten appeals. Aden was the one exception. Despite the unanimous recommendations of the Chief Justice, the Commissioner of Police, and successive High Commissioners that jury trials should be suspended on the grounds that juries were either hopelessly biased or intimidated, ministers and officials in London refused to agree. Abolition would give Britain's foreign critics yet another stick with which to beat

[94] Defence (Emergency) Regulations. The Palestine Gazette, No. 1442. Published by the British Government, Palestine (27 September 1945), Regulations 72–83. Downloaded on 16 September 2008 at: www.geocities.com/savepalestinenow/emergencyregs/emergencyregs.htm.
[95] TNA CO 717/471/13. Supplement No 2. Palestine Gazette Extraordinary No. 1470 of 28 January 1946. Defence (Emergency) Regulations 3–4.
[96] TNA CO 926/542. Acting Governor to Colonial Secretary, 29 September & 1 October 1955.
[97] TNA CO 926/541. Acting Governor to Colonial Secretary, 1 September 1955.
[98] TNA CO 926/542. Colonial Secretary to Acting Governor, 2 October 1955; TNA CO 926/542. Harding to Colonial Secretary, 4 October 1955; TNA CO 926/542. Colonial Secretary to Acting Governor Cyprus, 31 October 1955.
[99] TNA CO 1031/1435. Savage to CO, 6 April 1954.
[100] TNA CO 717/167/1. Emergency (Criminal Trials) Regulation, 1948, 19 July 1948; *Times*, 16 September 1955.
[101] TNA CO 717/167/3. Federation of Malaya. Regulations made under the Emergency Regulations Ordinance, 1948 together with the Essential (Special Constabulary) Regulations 1948, incorporating all amendments up to 22 March 1949 (Kuala Lumpur: Government Press, 1949). Regulation 32.
[102] TNA CO 717/167/1. Emergency Regulations, 1948. Regulations 33(1), 35, 15 July 1948.

them, and in any case suspects could be kept out of circulation until the British left by the simple expedient of detaining them.[103]

The readiness with which the courts and colonial governors, who retained the final right to exercise clemency, inflicted the death penalty varied between colonies. The terms of the Royal Prerogative issued to every governor required him to take account of every private and public circumstance in considering such cases.[104] In Palestine the courts sentenced 28 insurgents to death, although only four were executed.[105] In Cyprus in 1957, Harding reprieved at least seven EOKA members convicted of capital crimes.[106] It is likely that the authorities exercised the prerogative of mercy at least in part because they knew that the course of the emergency was being carefully and critically watched by outside observers. In the case of Palestine this was the USA, in the case of Cyprus the Greeks, and in both cases by the UN.[107] In Palestine military courts 'had instructions from HMG that the death penalty should be avoided if at all possible.'[108] The lengths to which the authorities in Palestine went to avoid international embarrassments was shown in September 1946, when military courts had sentenced 18 members of the Stern Gang to death. The authorities then tried to persuade some of them to plead that they were under-age and so could not be executed. They refused, and eventually the GOC commuted all 18 sentences.[109] However, governors also had to take account of countervailing pressures from within their own security forces. Having exercised his prerogative of mercy in several cases, there is at least a suggestion that Harding confirmed the death sentences on two insurgents in May 1956 because the police and army were becoming impatient with such leniency. 'A reprieve would have seriously affected the morale of the armed forces,' wrote one journalist on the island, 'many of whom consider, rightly or wrongly, that the attitude of the authorities towards the terrorists is already too lenient. Some contend that gunmen caught in action should be shot on the spot as in war instead of being granted the full legal facilities of normal citizens.'[110]

The Mau Mau enjoyed no such outside protectors. Colonial officials, both in Kenya and elsewhere in Africa, had often made use of the death penalty to deter

[103] TNA CO 1055/207. Turnbull to CO, 10 Sept, 22 October & 13 December 1965; TNA CO 1055/207. A. N. Galworthy to Turnbull, 16 November 1965; TNA DEFE 11/524. Turnbull to FO, 15 February 1967; TNA DEFE 11/524. Foreign Secretary to Turnbull, 16 February 1967.
[104] IWMSA. Accession No. 8736. Field Marshal Lord Harding, Transcript, 386.
[105] *Hansard* HL Deb 23 April 1947 vol. 147 cols. 55–6.
[106] TNA CO 926/672/CIC(57)16(Final). Cyprus Intelligence Committee. Intelligence Review for the First Half of May, 1957, 22 May 1957; TNA CO 926/673/CIC(57)26(Final). Cyprus Intelligence Committee. Intelligence Review for the first half of Sept, 1957, 21 October 1957; TNA CO 926/673/CIC(57)28(Final). Cyprus Intelligence Committee. Intelligence Review for the first half of October, 1957, 11 October 1957.
[107] *Hansard* HC Deb 2 July 1947 vol. 439 cc 160–1.
[108] IWMSA. Accession No. 11077. R. A. A. Smith, reel 3.
[109] *Manchester Guardian*, 1 September 1946; H. Rettig, 'Pre-state fighters enjoy rare return to spotlight. Third annual gathering of prisoners of Zion and other activists', *Jerusalem Post*, 22 December 2006.
[110] *Manchester Guardian*, 14 May 1956.

Africans from challenging the colonial order.[111] Kenya had long been a colony in which the judicial system had employed exemplary violence against Africans. As David Anderson has demonstrated, some members of the security forces had little compunction about bending the evidence, and the judicial system willingly co-operated with them to find defendants guilty as charged.[112] The Kenya government was intent on using exemplary executions to overawe the Kikuyu. Ten days after the declaration of the emergency they asked the War Office to lend them a blueprint for a new gallows, explaining that, 'Hitherto all executions have taken place in Nairobi. It is now desired to execute certain murderers in the areas in which the murders occurred.'[113] The readiness of the colonial authorities to take exceptional measures was underlined by the fact that, whereas in normal times about half of all death sentences imposed in Kenya were commuted, during the emergency, 1,068 Mau Mau prisoners were executed out of 1,468 Mau Mau tried and found guilty of capital charges. Mau Mau prisoners convicted of capital crimes were also much more likely than non-Mau Mau prisoners convicted of the same kinds of crimes to be executed.[114]

The same could have happened in Malaya, but it did not. In the course of the emergency 226 people were executed for insurgent offences, of whom 62 died in the first 11 months.[115] In that initial period, the death penalty served a covert political function. The Federal government was under pressure from the British community to use it as a deterrent. One of the unofficial members of the Federal Executive Council called for the introduction of summary trials and contended 'that judicial arrangements should be made whereby, without sacrificing any of the principles of British justice, clear-cut cases of possession of arms and murder should be immediately brought to trial, and if convictions are secured the sentences be immediately carried out.'[116] However, unlike in Kenya, the administration in Malaya was prepared to go only so far in appeasing the British community. Following Gurney's assassination in October 1951, half a dozen members of the Federal Legislative Council insisted that the government had to retaliate by speeding legal processes so that the public could see that punishment would swiftly follow the crime.[117] But Briggs wanted nothing to do with suggestions that he thought were 'largely a result of panic and emotion', and a meeting of senior British officials from each of the Malay states rejected them.[118] 'A "drumhead" trial [and]

---

[111] S. Hynd, 'Killing the condemned: the practise and process of capital punishment in British Africa, 1900–1950s', *Journal of African History*, 49 (2008), 403–18; *idem*, 'Decorum or deterrence? The politics of execution in Malawi, 1915–66', *Cultural and Social History*, vol. 5 (2008), 437–48.

[112] Anderson, *Histories of the Hanged*, passim.

[113] TNA WO 32/20624. GOC East Africa to VAG, WO, 31 October 1952.

[114] TNA CO 822/1256. Governor of Kenya to Colonial Secretary, 17 January 1957; Hynd, 'Killing the condemned', 404–5.

[115] D. Bonner, *Executive Measures, Terrorism and National Security. Have the Rules of the Game Changed?* (London: Ashgate, 2007), 147; *Hansard* HC Deb 18 May 1949, vol. 465 c 20.

[116] TNA CO 537/3692. Minutes of an extraordinary meeting of the Federal Executive Council held at Kuala Lumpur on 26 June 1948.

[117] TNA CO 1022/58. Six members of the Federal Legislative Council resident in Penang to Colonial Secretary, 24 October 1951.

[118] TNA CO 1022/58. Minute, [illegible], 21 November 1951.

execution (which some had in mind) was out of the question.' Not only would such proceedings be of doubtful legality, they would also be counter-productive. Prisoners could provide the security forces with useful intelligence. Corpses could not.[119] It was one of Sir Gerald Templer's most significant contributions to the conduct of the emergency that he was able to stem this 'panic and emotion', with the result that Malaya witnessed far fewer executions than Kenya.

Finally, some explanation is necessary as to why the British persistently referred to their counter-insurgency campaigns as 'Emergencies'. By any commonsensical definition they were wars. The reason they adopted this terminology was mundane, but significant for what it implied about how they believed success could be achieved. During an insurgency there was bound to be considerable damage to the property of British commercial interests. But London insurance brokers were reluctant to offer war-risk insurance. They refused to offer insurance cover in Palestine between 1945 and 1948, and by 1949 were reluctant to continue to offer cover in Malaya. Without insurance the morale of major property owners might collapse and the economy would suffer, thereby handing a major victory to the insurgents. Consequently, Gurney concluded 'it is therefore advisable to avoid the use of terms in official statements which might serve as a handle to the insurance companies. These terms include "enemy", "war", "insurrection", "insurgents", "rebellion".'[120]

COUNTER-INSURGENCY BY COMMITTEE

In 1935 a major riot occurred in the Indian city of Bombalpur. The police could not cope and the army was summoned. But operations were handicapped throughout the crisis by a lack of co-operation between those charged with organizing the response. The District Commissioner was an Indian Muslim, competent but lethargic, struggling with the demands of his own community, and privately resentful of past slights from British officials. The Superintendent of Police was young, British, enthusiastic, and resentful at being under the authority of an Indian whom he thought of as 'an old woman'. He had little understanding of soldiers, and tried to use them as reserve policemen. There was a timorous Hindu City Magistrate, and a biased Muslim Special Magistrate. Communications between the police and the army failed. The soldiers consisted of Indian cavalry and infantry, a single company of British infantry, a section of light tanks, and some local territorials. Looking over the commanding officer's shoulder was Major-General Bullhead-Buttit, who 'has the reputation of being somewhat impatient'.[121]

---

[119] TNA CO 1022/47. Record of conference with the Mentri Besar and Resident Commissioners and British Advisers on the intensification of the Emergency Effort held on 26 October 1951; TNA CO 1022/58. Officer Administering the government of Malaya to Colonial Secretary, 2 November 1951.

[120] TNA CO 537/5068. Gurney to Colonial Secretary, 30 May 1949.

[121] Joint Services Command and Staff College: Staff College, 1935, Senior Division, Volume I, File 18, Items 5a, Appendix B, quoted in S. B. Shoul, 'Soldiers, riots and aid to the civil power, in India, Egypt and Palestine, 1919–1939' (Ph.D. dissertation, London University, 2006), 186.

'Bombalpur' did not in fact exist, and the riot never took place, at least outside the imagination of Lt.-Col. William Slim, then an instructor at the Staff College, and between 1948 and 1952, the CIGS. The events at 'Bombalpur' were part of a role-playing exercise he staged for the benefit of his students to teach them some of the complexities of civil–military relations when soldiers were summoned to give aid to the civil power. What the scenario that Slim chose demonstrated was that there is nothing new about soldiers being required to work with a multitude of civilian agencies, usually with conflicting agendas, when engaged in counter-insurgency operations. Those who took part in Slim's exercise should have found it valuable, for anyone turning to the official manuals in the 1930s would have found scant guidance about how to ensure effective multi-agency co-operation. All that existed were vague recommendations that the commanders of troops called out in aid of the civil power should maintain close contact with the civil authorities and rely on the police for local intelligence. Exactly how this was to be done was left to the man on the spot.[122]

The reason why pre-war manuals were silent on the need to construct adminis-trative machinery to co-ordinate the work of the police, civil administration and army when assisting the civil power, was simple. The authors of those manuals assumed that in a serious crisis the civil power would yield its authority to the military. Martial law would be declared, and the police and civil authorities would come under the army's orders.[123] Counter-insurgency by committee was developed after 1945 because the British did not impose martial law. The civil authorities and police were not subordinated to the army, but some way of harmonizing their activities still had to be found. It is generally supposed that it was not until the Malayan campaign that the British found the answer. Beginning in 1950, they established a pyramidal structure of committees, at Federal, State, and District levels.[124] The chairman of each committee was the leading representative of the civil authorities, put there to ensure that no one was allowed to forget that the purpose of the whole exercise was to establish a favourable political outcome. His colleagues consisted of the local military, police, and special branch commanders, and key personnel drawn from the civil administration. To facilitate regular meet-ings the soldiers were required to establish their headquarters next door to the police and civil administration. This system was supposed to produce a chain of command to ensure that Federation-wide plans were carried out with due regard to local needs, and that the activities of the different arms of government worked in concert.[125] An even greater harmony was secured in Malaya in 1952 when Sir

---

[122] TNA WO 279/796. War Office, *Notes on Imperial Policing 1934* (London: War Office, 1934), 8; TNA WO 279/470. *General Staff, Duties in Aid of the Civil Power, 1937. Reprint Incorporating Amendments (No. 1) 1945* (London: War Office, 24/07/1945), 18–19.
[123] TNA WO 279/796. War Office, *Notes on Imperial Policing 1934* (London: War Office, 1934), 28–41.
[124] T. R. Mockaitis, *British Counterinsurgency, 1919–60* (London: Macmillan, 1990), 117–18.
[125] TNA WO 279/241. Director of Operations, Malaya, *Conduct of Anti-terrorist Operations in Malaya* (Malaya: Kuala Lumpur, 3rd edn, 1958), ch. 3; Sir R. Thompson, *Make for the Hills. Memories of Far Eastern Wars* (London: Leo Cooper, 1989), 92.

Gerald Templer became the political and military supremo, combining in his own person the roles of High Commissioner and Director of Operations.

Attempts to run campaigns through committees had been tried before 1950. The British political and strategic elite had developed a culture of defence by committee at the beginning of the twentieth century.[126] It was applied hesitantly in the first post-war counter-insurgency when, in Palestine in the spring of 1946, Cunningham established a Central Security Committee. It replaced the hitherto ad hoc meetings of the various agencies concerned with internal security. Chaired by the High Commissioner, its weekly meetings were attended by the Chief Secretary (the head of the civil administration), the Inspector-General of Police, the senior military intelligence officer, and the local representative of MI5. The GOC also attended, although he was not formally a member. Similar committees were established at District level, although they were chaired by the local military commander and their effectiveness was problematic. One police officer, the second in command of a police district, even thought that there was less co-operation between the police and the civil administration during the final years of the mandate than in more normal times.[127]

Co-operation between the army and civil authorities in Malaya began badly because the civil authorities had kept the army in the dark about growing security problems until after they had declared an emergency. To try to prevent similar breakdowns of communications in the future, by 1949 a series of local Defence Committees, drawing their membership from the army and civil authorities, had been established to plan operations.[128] But these were ad hoc responses to immediate crises. Failures in Palestine and Malaya persuaded the army that it needed to up-date its doctrine, but its first post-war manual, issued in 1949, was only a little more specific on how to achieve civil–military co-operation than its pre-war predecessors. Commanders were told to hold daily conferences with the police and civil authorities, 'to seek and respect the advice of civil and police authorities. The establishment of mutual confidence between the civil, the police and the military authorities at all levels is of the first importance.'[129] The Colonial Office asked Gurney to fill that gap for them on the basis of his experience in Palestine and Malaya.[130] He recommended a two-tiered administrative structure. At the top Gurney himself held weekly meetings with the GOC, the Commissioner of Police, the Chief Secretary, and the Federal Secretary for Defence. Below this committee, the Federal Secretary for Defence presided over an Internal Security Committee with police, service, and unofficial representatives. This was a channel through

[126] P. Smith (ed.), *Government and the Armed Forces in Britain 1856–1990* (London: Hambledon Press, 1996), *passim*.
[127] D. A. Charters, *The British Army and Jewish Insurgency in Palestine, 1945–47* (London: Macmillan, 1989), 84–5; IWMSA. Accession No. 12208. J. A. S. Adolph, reel 3.
[128] TNA WO 106/5884. Gen. Sir N. Ritchie, Report on operations in Malaya, June 1948 to July 1949, 6 September 1949.
[129] TNA WO 279/391. War Office, *Imperial Policing and Duties in Aid of the Civil Power, 1949* (London: WO, 1949), 4, 11.
[130] TNA CO 537/5068. Sir T. I. K. Lloyd to Gurney, 9 April 1949.

which the views of planters, miners, and others could be made known. Each State and Settlement had similar committees with similar representation, and the Federal Secretary for Chinese Affairs presided over an Emergency Chinese Advisory Committee.[131]

Gurney did not make clear the extent, if any, to which these committees were responsible for planning operations. But he was emphatic that responsibility for executing them must remain with the police. The army disagreed, and after nine months of trying to make the system work, Gurney accepted he was wrong.[132] The committee system was right in principle, but the Commissioner of Police could not simultaneously control the counter-insurgency operations of the security forces and command the police. In February 1950, Gurney therefore asked the Colonial Office to send him an experienced soldier to fill the new civil post of Director of Operations. He was to prepare a plan to eliminate the insurgents, to allocate tasks to the various components of the security forces, and, in consultation with the heads of the police and fighting services, decide priorities between these tasks and establish the timing and sequence of their execution.[133]

Initially the post was filled by a former Indian army officer, Sir Harold Briggs. Briggs made two major contributions to the conduct of the emergency. The first was the Briggs Plan, which will be examined in Chapter 4. The second was to determine that the work of the different parts of the security forces and civil administration should be co-ordinated by a series of committees at Federal, State, and District level.[134] On 16 April 1950 he issued his Directive Number 1, establishing a Federal War Council, and also State and Settlement War Executive Committees. The Federal Council consisted of the Director of Operations, the Chief Secretary, the GOC, the Air-Officer-Commanding, the Commissioner of Police, and the Secretary for Defence. It was serviced by a secretariat in the office of the Director of Operations. The same basic structure was replicated at State or Settlement and District levels. The task of the Federal War Council was to produce policy and to provide the lower level executive committee with the resources they needed. 'It is the responsibility of the State and Settlement Executive Committees', he told them, 'to wage the "war" in their own territories.'[135] In the past co-ordination through committees had been tried before and found wanting. Briggs began to make it work better by insisting that, at all levels, the civil administration, police, and army

---

[131] TNA CO 537/5068. Gurney to Colonial Secretary, 30 May 1949.
[132] TNA CAB 134/534/ODC(49)6 meeting Overseas Defence Committee, 25 August 1949; TNA CO 537/5068. Sir T. Lloyd to Gurney, 17 March 1950; CAB 134/535/ODC(50)14. Note by the Secretary, Guidance to colonial governments on the preservation of internal security, 19 May 1950.
[133] TNA WO 216/333. Gurney to Secretary of State for Colonies, 23 February 1950.
[134] TNA CO 537/5975. Briggs, Outline of future anti-bandit policy in Malaya, n.d. but *c*.1 April 1950.
[135] TNA CAB 21/1681/MAL(50)10. Note by the Joint Secretaries, Malaya Committee, 2 June 1950. Director of Operations, Malaya: Directive No. 1, 16 April 1950.

now had to go a step further and establish joint intelligence and operations rooms where they could plan and work side by side.[136]

The new system was not an immediate success. The 1948 Federation Constitution had created a weak Federal government at the centre and strong state governments at the periphery. The politically dominant Malay community resented pressure from the Federal government to spend money on the mainstay of the Briggs Plan, the resettling of Chinese squatter communities.[137] Briggs could issue orders to the police and army, but although he was expected to maintain close contact with the civil organs of government, Gurney would not allow him to issue orders to them.[138] The result was a log-jam. When Briggs's successor as Director of Operations, Sir Rob Lockhart, arrived in Malaya in November 1951, he reported that 'If Emmett and Heath-Robinson had been asked jointly to devise a comic constitution I don't think they could have thought of one more extraordinary than this one—13 Governments in a country about the size of the N[orth] W[est] F[rontier] P[rovince]! The effect of it is to make actions slow.'[139]

Templer broke the log-jam that Briggs had faced. The new High Commissioner did not have any doctrinaire commitment to command by committee, but he did recognize that given the government's federal structure, it was the only way to ensure proper co-ordination between all sections of the administration and the security forces.[140] He embodied both the civil and military authorities in his own person, he overrode the objections of local politicians and merged the Federal Executive Council and Federal War Council, he brought into it leaders of the Chinese Community, and he established a smaller Director of Operations committee, which met thrice-weekly, to direct military operations.[141] Equally important, he did what Briggs had advocated as early as November 1950, he put the government on a war footing and infused it with his own energy. Templer was a soldier and he therefore knew the value of visiting his subordinates on the ground. His charisma and energy did the rest. A policeman remembered that 'You felt that you were in touch with him, he knew your Christian name, he came on you without warning and you knew that if you had any problem that he would listen to it.'[142] In the opinion of an admittedly biased witness, his aide, Major David Lloyd Owen, 'Life out here is incredibly hectic. H[is]. E[xellency]. works from 8 am to 8 pm every day which I find a bit of a strain. He is quite tireless and it is entirely due to him that there is a complete change of attitude throughout the country. There are a lot of good people among thousands of quite useless ones, but until he arrived there

---

[136] TNA CAB 21/1681/MAL(50)10. Note by the Joint Secretaries, Malaya Committee, 2 June 1950. Director of Operations, Malaya: Directive No. 1, 16 April 1950.
[137] TNA CAB 131/9/DO(50)93. Colonial Secretary, Chinese detainees in Malaya, 15 November 1950.
[138] TNA WO 216/333. Gurney to Sir J. Harding, 13 February 1950; TNA WO 216/333. Gurney to Secretary of State for Colonies, 23 February 1950.
[139] TNA WO 216/806. Lockhart to Slim, 14 January 1952.
[140] LHCMA Liddell Hart mss 1/682. Templer to Liddell Hart, 8 June 1955.
[141] J. A. Nagl, *Learning to Eat Soup with a Knife. Counterinsurgency Lessons from Malaya and Vietnam* (Chicago: University of Chicago Press, 2002/5), 87–90.
[142] IWMSA. Accession No. 10175.R. J. W. Craig, Transcript, 18.

was NO leadership, policy, enthusiasm or desire to do anything other than live their own fat, idle, useless lives. Now people realize they can't do that unless they help themselves—which is, at least, something.'[143] 'Soon after his arrival', according to a senior staff officer, 'he was sweeping through the whole country like the wrath of God.'[144] An instance of how he achieved a real impact was recounted by a district officer in Negri Sembilan. Templer visited him and spent a morning listening to his plans. After lunch Templer told him 'Well, I've thought about your plans and I fully agree with all of them, and if you have any trouble with those buggers up in K[ular] L[umpur] [the Federal capital] he said "Here is my personal telephone number. Just give me a ring and I'll fix them." And of course everybody knew what he was doing and so nobody did give you any trouble.'[145]

By 1957 the 'Malayan model' of pyramidal committees and joint headquarters and operations rooms was firmly embedded in Malay, in the army's written doctrine, and in the syllabus at the Joint Services Staff College.[146] But the full 'Malayan model', in which operations were directed at every level by committees and harmony was ensured at the very top by one man combining both civil and military authority, only operated in Malay, and even then only during Templer's tenure as both High Commissioner and Director of Operations. After he left in 1954 the committees remained, but the roles of High Commissioner and Director of Operations were divided. Sir Donald MacGillivray, Templer's Deputy High Commissioner, became High Commissioner, and the post of Director of Operations was combined with that of GOC Malaya Command, initially held by Lt.-Gen. Sir Geoffrey Bourne and then by Lt.-Gen. Sir Roger Bower. This division of responsibilities was not to Bower's liking. He complained that he had too little say over civil appointments 'and this has undoubtedly sapped much of the impetus from the Emergency, which depends largely on the ability and energy of the Chairmen of State and District War Executive Committees and on their perma-nence of tenure in these appointments. There have recently been frequent postings and replacements, not always by suitable men. This has sometimes been mitigated by good police or army members of the Committees, but they cannot enforce civil measures, nor can they make up for weak or incompetent leadership.'[147] Bower's

---

[143] NAM 8301–6. Sir Gerald Templer mss. Major D. L. Lloyd Owen to Brigadier J. R. C. Hamilton, 19 September 1952.

[144] Maj.- Gen. J. Frost, *Nearly There. The Memoirs of John Frost of Arnhem Bridge* (London: Leo Cooper, 1991), 104.

[145] IWMSA. Accession No. 9141. J. M. Patrick, reel 3.

[146] TNA WO 279/241. Director of Operations, Malaya, *Conduct of Anti-terrorist Operations in Malaya* (Malaya: Kuala Lumpur, 3rd edn, 1958); TNA WO 296/23. General Staff, *Keeping the Peace (Duties in Support of the Civil Power)* (London: War Office, 1957); TNA WO 279/398. War Office, *Keeping the Peace. Part 1. Doctrine* (London: War Office, 7 January 1963); TNA WO 291/1670. Operational Research Unit (Far East). Report Number 1/57. A comparison of the emergencies in Malaya and Kenya, 6 June 1957; IWMDoD. Gen. Sir G. W. Erskine mss 75/134/3. Erskine, Lecture to the Joint Services Staff College. Military Aspects of the Cold War, n.d. but *c*.1956; IWMSA. Accession No. 10175. R. J. W. Craig, Transcript, 13; IWMSA. Accession No. 9141. J. M. Patrick, reels 3–4.

[147] TNA WO 106/5990. Director of Operations Malaya, Review of the Emergency in Malaya from June 1948 to August 1957, September 1957.

strictures point to an important truth. Getting administrative structures right was important. But it was even more important to get the right people to run them.

During the Confrontation, the whole system of committees at federal, state and district level and joint police–army headquarters was imported into Brunei and Borneo where it continued to function, with only minimal changes, even after the establishment of the Federation of Malaysia in September 1963.[148] The contrast with the comparatively effective working of this apparatus, and what happened in the Federation of South Arabia, was instructive, because it highlighted the extent to which the success of the 'Malayan model' depended on the existence of a co-operative and compliant local partner. The British had such a partner in Malaya and Malaysia, but they did not in South Arabia. In the latter responsibility for internal security was dangerously divided between Federal and State authorities and the British High Commissioner in Aden.[149] Emergency policy was determined by a bewildering variety of committees. Initially Trevaskis himself tried to co-ordinate the work of the police, military, and intelligence services, and it was only in May 1964, six months after the start of the emergency, that an officer was appointed to act as his Security Operations Adviser to plan and co-ordinate operations.[150] It was not for another year that a single officer, Major-General John Willoughby, the GOC MELF, was appointed as the Security Commander, with executive command of both the police and army units engaged in internal security operations. But co-ordinated effort under a single commander was never achieved. The High Commissioner retained control of other government departments.[151] Any possibility of running the emergency through the 'Malayan model' of committees was ruled out by 1965 because there were no political officers available on the ground in Aden State. The army had to go to the police for political guidance, hardly a satisfactory solution as police loyalties were deeply divided.[152] D. J. McCarthy, a British diplomat attached to the High Commissioner's staff, wrote in December 1965 that 'The British machine, as distinct from Arabised British, is ramshackle and running down and lacks most elements of normal infrastructure (i.e. career subordinate staff, automatic distributions, coherent command structure, etc.). The successor Arab administrative machine barely exists yet.'[153]

In Kenya and Cyprus the authorities created diluted versions of the 'Malayan model'. But they acted only after much hesitation, and probably because its

[148] TNA WO 305/2519. Director of Operations (Borneo) Instruction no. 1, 29 December 1962. Restoration of civil administration; TNA WO 305/2529. Directive for the Director of the Borneo Operations, 6 December 1963; TNA WO 305/2526. Command Structure Borneo Territories, 12 September 1963; TNA WO 32/19269.C-in-C Far East to CDS, 19 December 1963.
[149] TNA CO 1055/207. Federation of South Arabia (Accession of Aden) Order, 1963, 17 January 1963; TNA CO 1055/198. W. H. Formoy, Responsibility for Internal Security in Aden and the Federation of South Arabia, 8 January 1964; TNA DEFE 13/570. Draft Report on the Ministry and Force HQ Organization of the security forces of the Federation of South Arabia, 17 June 1964.
[150] TNA CO 1035/181. Extract from COS(64)14 meeting, n.d. but *c.*13 February 1964; TNA CO 1035/185. Trevaskis to CO, 7 May 1964.
[151] TNA CO 1035/179. Sir R. Turnbull, to J. Marnham, 25 May 1965.
[152] Ibid.
[153] TNA CO 1035/184/JIC(IAF)(65)3. D. J. McCarthy, Intelligence Organization in Aden, 17 December 1965.

wholesale imposition robbed local politicians and administrators of much of their power, something they naturally resented.[154] It was also a public admission that things were seriously amiss in the colony, something no government wished to have known. In July 1955, Lyttelton was reluctant to appoint a Director of Operations in Cyprus, because 'by placing too heavy an emphasis on the dangers of the internal situation, [it] might do more harm than good.'[155] Harding eventually replicated something like the 'Malayan model' during his governorship, but he was never able to infuse the civil administration with the same energy that Templer injected into Malaya.[156] The opening stages of the Kenya emergency were organized in a somewhat chaotic manner by a series of ad hoc committees of varying membership and competence.[157] When Baring asked for a senior army officer to act as a Director of Operations, the COS initially refused. They were wary of highlighting direct parallels with Malaya, the CIGS insisting that the situation was not sufficiently serious to justify such an appointment.[158] It was not until June 1953, eight months after the start of the emergency and after further experiments, that Erskine was sent to Nairobi, but without the same powers that Templer had enjoyed in Malaya. Although Erskine was charged with the conduct of all military measures to restore law and order in Kenya and could issue orders to the security forces, Baring retained full responsibility for the government and administration of the colony.[159] It was only in 1954 that full control over all emergency measures in Kenya was concentrated in the hands of a small committee at the top of the administration.[160] By June 1955, Erskine's successor, Sir Gerald Lathbury, found that the emergency administrative machinery worked reasonably effectively. But what it was not always able to do was to fetter the habitual latitude, that long pre-dated the emergency, with which Provincial and District Commissioners interpreted orders from Nairobi.[161]

Compliant local partners were also thin on the ground outside the confines of the formal empire. Their solution was to construct ad hoc arrangements to fuse the service and diplomatic chains of command. In the Canal Zone nothing like the 'Malayan model' was adopted for the obvious reason that the civil authorities and

[154] TNA WO 216/879. Erskine to CIGS, 20 December 1954; TNA CO 968/690. Sir H. Foot to Sir J. Martin, 22 April 1959.
[155] TNA CAB 130/109/GEN 497/2. Meeting. Ministerial Committee on Cyprus, 21 July 1955.
[156] IWMSA. Accession No. 8736. Field Marshal Lord Harding, Transcript, 372–3; N. Crawshaw, 'Cyprus and its crisis. II—Barriers to progress', *Manchester Guardian*, 23 January 1956.
[157] TNA WO 276/411. Memorandum on the organisation dealing with the Emergency, 2 January 1953.
[158] TNA WO 216/560. VCIGS to C-in-C MELF and GOC East Africa Command, 28 November 1952; TNA WO 216/560. C-in-C MELF to CIGS, 29 November 1952; TNA WO 216/560/COS (52) 163 meeting, 1 December 1952.
[159] TNA PREM 11/472. Secretary of State War to Minister of Defence, 27 May 1953; TNA CO 822/442. WO to GHQ MELF, 3 June 1953.
[160] TNA WO 291/1670. Operational Research Unit (Far East). Report Number 1/57. A comparison of the emergencies in Malaya and Kenya, 6 June 1957; IWMDoD. Gen. Sir G. W. Erskine mss 75/134/4. Lecture to the Police College. Army Aid to the Civil Power in Colonial and Protected Territories', n.d. but *c*.1956.
[161] TNA CO 822/782. Lt.-Gen. G. W. Lathbury to CIGS, 14 June 1955.

the Egyptian police were themselves the enemy. Command and control of the security forces was exercised through the normal military chain of command in the hands of the GOC BTE, who reported to the War Office through the C-in-C, MELF. But because the Canal Zone was part of a foreign country, army commanders were also expected to determine and co-ordinate their policies with two diplomatic agencies in Cairo, the British embassy and the British Middle East Office. They in turn were responsible to the Foreign Office in London.[162] Similarly in Oman policy was made by senior service officers and diplomats. The Commander British Forces Arabian Peninsula reported through the BDCC (Middle East) to the Ministry of Defence, while Political Residents in Muscat and the Persian Gulf reported to the Foreign Office. These men, together with the single service commanders and the British commander of the sultan's armed forces, but bereft of any Omani representatives, constituted the Military Co-ordinating Committee (Persian Gulf).[163] Sometimes they consulted the sultan, but other times they ignored him.[164]

Committees were needed because soldiers, policemen, and civil administrators did not necessarily agree about how best to conduct an emergency. At the start of an emergency the civil authorities were likely to insist that the army provide large numbers of static guards to protect people and installations. The army objected, convinced that only by taking offensive measures could they defeat the insurgents.[165] The police and the army were also often at loggerheads. 'The most narrow-minded type of soldier', one senior policeman wrote, 'thinks of guerrillas as a purely military force, and measures success in terms of the "bag" recorded in the battalion game book.' But there were faults on his own side. 'His equally narrow-minded police colleague regards the guerrillas as criminals—very dangerous and highly organised criminals, no doubt, but in essence no different from the extortioners, murderers, thieves and cheats who are his traditional foes.'[166]

When the committee system worked, operations were planned and conducted jointly by the police, army, and civil administration. In Malaya this meant that every agency was scrupulous about co-ordinating its plans with every other agency.[167] But this ideal was not always achieved. The creation of administrative structures was an important step on the road to better co-ordination. But personalities matter as much as committees. A District Officer who was the chairman of a DWEC thought that 'There must have been many instances when, the meeting over, the top soldier got straight on the blower to his brigadier and said "I wont stand for this. I wont

[162] M. T. Thornhill, *Road to Suez. The Battle of the Canal Zone* (Stroud, Gloucs: Sutton Publishing, 2006), 44.
[163] TNA DEFE 7/2415. Political Resident Bahrain to FO, 2 March 1958.
[164] TNA DEFE 7/2413.COS(58)227. Directive for Commander British Forces Arabian Peninsula. Responsibilities towards the Sultan of Muscat's armed forces, 3 October 1958.
[165] TNA WO 279/391. War Office, *Imperial Policing and Duties in Aid of the Civil Power, 1949* (London: War Office, 1949), 15.
[166] S. Hutchinson, 'The police role in counter-insurgency operations', *JRUSI*, vol. 114, no. 656 (1969), 58.
[167] S. Hosmer and S. O. Crane (eds), *Counterinsurgency: A Symposium, 16–20 April 1962* (Santa Monica, CA: Rand Corporation, 1963/2006), 96.

have this bloody D[istrict] O[fficer] doing this, or I wont have the policeman doing that."'[168] In Kenya Maj.-Gen. 'Looney' Hinde, who had been sent to the colony in early 1953 as Director of Operations, was widely liked by civilian officials for his lack of pomposity, approachability, and readiness to show that he sided with the settlers. 'Now he was a helluva chap,' felt one Provincial Commissioner. 'And he got on with the police, he got on with the administration, he got on with everybody.'[169] Erskine, who privately despised many settlers, was regarded with much less favour.[170] Reflecting on his own experiences in Malaya and Borneo, Sir Walter Walker, the Director of Operations in Borneo between 1962 and 1965, sadly concluded that 'Some army officers can be far too dictatorial and unbending in their manner. They must overcome this failing and go out of their way to be diplomatic, patient and courteous; and they must have a complete grasp of the functions, capabilities and limitations of the civil police and civil administration.'[171] Walker might have been thinking of a brigade major who, after attending District Committee meetings with his brigadier, concluded that the soldiers had two enemies, the insurgents, and their own 'political masters', by whom he meant the senior civil servants, policemen, and Special Branch officers who also sat on the committee. 'The second problem always seemed to be a greater pain in the buttocks to the "on-the-spot" Commander!'[172]

CONCLUSION

The British did not refrain from conducting counter-insurgency campaigns under martial law as a matter of principle. They did so as a matter of expediency. Emergency powers regulations gave the security forces plenty of latitude but with few of martial law's drawbacks. Thus the security forces operated within a clearly defined legal framework. But a close examination of both the regulations promulgated under the 1939 Emergency Powers Order-in-Council (and related local legislation) and the meaning of the concept of 'minimum necessary force', suggests that these imposed only very loose constraints on the kinds of coercion that could be employed. They did preclude the British from employing genocidal methods against their opponents. But they also permitted them to employ a very high degree of often lethal force.

Where their refusal to impose martial law did have important consequences was in the manner in which counter-insurgency operations were planned and controlled. As the civil administration and police were not subordinated to the army, colonial governments had to develop a form of machinery to enable them to co-ordinate and harmonize the activities of the army, police, and civil administration.

---

[168] IWMSA. Accession No. 9141. J. M. Patrick, reel 4.
[169] IWMSA. Accession No. 10224. Sir A. Swann, Transcript, 38.
[170] IWMSA. Accession No. 11074. R. E. Wainwright, Transcript, 25.
[171] Gen. Sir W. Walker, 'Borneo', *British Army Review*, no. 32 (August. 1969), 14.
[172] Colonel P. Hall, *Jungle Jim* (Privately Published, 1995), 133.

The result was counter-insurgency by committee. This meant that the British never followed the French in Algeria and gave hegemonic power to the army to control operations.[173] However, the ways in which British emergency regulations suspended civil liberties were markedly similar to steps that the French colonial authorities adopted in Algeria in 1955 and 1956.[174] This suggests that, at least in this respect, insistence on British exceptionalism can be overdone. The following chapter examines how the security forces interpreted the orders they received from the committees and what use they made of the emergency regulations.

[173] C. Cradock and M. L. R. Smith, '"No fixed values": A reinterpretation of the influence of the theory of guerre révolutionnaire and the Battle of Algiers, 1956–1957', *Journal of Cold War Studies*, vol. 9 (2007), 68–105.

[174] M. Lazreg, *Torture and the Twilight of Empire from Algiers to Baghdad* (Princeton, NJ: Princeton University Press, 2008), 36–7.

4

Varieties of Coercion: Exemplary Force, Counter-terrorism, and Population Control

In 1956 a senior Colonial Office official explained that, 'Without being hypocritical, I think we can say that there is no doubt at all that when unfortunately we have disturbances in a Colony we seek to maintain humanitarian principles at least to the extent that the circumstances permit.'[1] In writing that he was closing his eyes to the fact that colonial governments were predisposed to employ coercion to combat insurgencies, and they were well provided with legal justifications for doing so. The forms of coercion they employed ranged from the use of exemplary force to intimidate the civil population into withdrawing its co-operation from the insurgents and giving it to the government, to the imposition of a lock-down on whole ethnic groups they had identified as supporting their enemies. The pursuit of humanitarian principles came a long way second.

EXEMPLARY FORCE AND COUNTER-TERRORISM

The first task facing the security forces was to implement anti-terrorist measures to protect key installations and loyalists, and to convince the civilian population that the government could protect them from intimidation by the insurgents.[2] Without such measures civilians would feel defenceless and too frightened to give the security forces information and without information the task of the security forces was 'reduced to conditions akin to searching for a needle in a haystack'.[3] But who was to provide this protection? The army preferred that the weight of anti-terrorist operations should fall onto the shoulders of the police. They necessitated what was in the army's eyes an undesirable degree of dispersal of effort, and they savoured too much of passive defence, which would embolden the insurgents and undermine the soldiers' morale.[4]

The army and most policemen believed that victory required them to take war to the enemy. The second task was, therefore, to harass the insurgents, deter further attacks, 'Disrupt his training, and his organisation into large bodies,' drive them

---

[1] TNA CO 936/391. Minute, E. Burr, 23 May 1956.
[2] TNA CO 537/3692. Commissioner-General South East Asia to CO, 26 June 1948.
[3] TNA WO 106/5884. Gen. Sir N. Ritchie, Report on operations in Malaya, June 1948 to July 1949, 6 September 1949.
[4] Maj.-Gen. Sir C. W. Gwynn, *Imperial Policing* (London: Macmillan, 1934), 19; TNA CAB 131/1/DO(46)33 meeting. Cabinet Defence Committee, 20 November 1946.

from populated areas, and provide the security forces with the intelligence that they habitually lacked at the start of an insurgency.[5] As a policeman in Kenya explained, 'Wily "micks" had to be continually harried, their sources of food denied them, their access to farm labour lines and wheat stores sealed, and their cunningly situated hideouts located and destroyed. They had to be moved on, out of your area, anywhere, it was no good feeling chagrin or defeat if killing figures were low, or even negative. What mattered was that Mau Mau gangs be prevented from becoming too comfortably ensconced.'[6]

But offensive operations had another purpose. Exemplary force was employed to intimidate the civilian population into helping the security forces to suppress the rebellion by making the cost of supporting the insurgents, or even tolerating their presence, too heavy to bear.[7] As Brigadier Baker, the Director of Operations in Cyprus, explained, security forces operations were designed 'To bring home to the ordinary people the hard fact that the results of terrorism include hardship to themselves and so to create conditions predisposing people in favour of a political settlement.'[8] The use of exemplary force to do this was promoted by those at the top. In Palestine Sir Miles Dempsey, the C-in-C MELF, wanted, 'to bring home to the people their responsibility for these murders and outrages'.[9] In Nyasaland, Governor Armitage decided that he wanted not only to arrest NAC leaders and to mount 'Firm but friendly displays of force in quiescent areas', but also to see 'Tough, punitive action in areas where lawlessness and acts of violence are perpetrated or planned.'[10]

What this meant in practice was explained in a pamphlet issued by GHQ Middle East in 1945.

> When the essentials have been organised it will be necessary to take more offensive action to break up hostile bands and capture the leaders. One or more of the following measures may be employed:
> Restrictions on the liberty of the individual by curfews, cordoning an area, etc.
> Searching an area for individuals or arms.
> Offensive military action against armed bands waging guerrilla warfare.[11]

---

[5] TNA CO 537/3692. Commissioner-General South East Asia to CO, 26 June 1948; TNA WO 106/5884. Gen. Sir N. Ritchie, Report on operations in Malaya, June 1948 to July 1949, 6 September 1949; LHCMA Stockwell mss 6/2. Lt.-Gen Sir E. Barker to High Commissioner, Palestine, 3 February 1947; TNA WO 305/2526. Walker, Appreciation of force requirements in Sarawak, Sabah and Brunei up to March 1964, 27 September 1963; IWMSA. Accession No. 10727. Col. A. S. Harvey, reel 3; IWMSA. Accession No. 10300. J. Sankey, reel 3.

[6] P. Hewitt, *Kenya Cowboy. A Police Officer's Account of the Mau Mau Emergency* (London: Avon Books, 1999), 98.

[7] H. Bennett, '"A very salutary effect": the counter-terror strategy in the early Malayan emergency, June 1948 to December 1949', *JSS*, vol. 32 (2009), 415–44.

[8] TNA CO 968/690. Brigadier G. Baker, A Review of the Cyprus Emergency April 1955–March 1958.

[9] TNA WO 216/194. Dempsey to Montgomery, 21 November 1946; LHCMA Stockwell mss 6/2. Lt.- Gen. Sir E. Barker to GOCs 1 & 3 Infantry Divisions, 6 Airborne Division, 9 Infantry Brigade, 23 January 1947.

[10] TNA CO 1015/1494. Nyasaland Operations Committee. Operation instruction No. 2/59, 7 March 1959.

[11] TNA WO 169/19521. *Middle East Training Pamphlet No. 9, Part XIII. Notes for Officers on Internal Security Duties* (May 1945).

The degree of coercion that the security forces employed varied depending on the attitude of the civil population. Road blocks were established not only to intercept insurgent couriers and arms smugglers, but also to place pressure on the inhabitants to co-operate. In the Canal Zone troops were told that 'Lack of civil co-operation will be met by tightening control and search of traffic around area concerned.'[12] Motorists who disobeyed instructions to stop did so at their peril, as the driver of a car on the road from Cairo to Ismalia discovered on the evening of 27 October 1951. When he ignored an order to stop at an army road block, the soldiers manning it opened fire, killing a female passenger and wounding the male driver.[13] Towns and villages were subjected to cordon and search operations. Troops surrounded them to prevent anyone entering or leaving, and groups of policemen and soldiers searched every house and 'screened' the inhabitants. 'Screening' involved placing the men in a wire 'cage', and the women and children in another, and then questioning everyone individually. Hooded informers sometimes accompanied the police to identify suspected insurgents who were then taken away for closer questioning.[14]

Cordon and search operations were themselves a form of collective punishment. The inhabitants of a town or village were subjected to the trauma of being forced to leave their homes, which were then searched from top to bottom by complete strangers. The searches were often accompanied by a good deal of sometimes incidental, and sometimes deliberate, destruction of property. Troops knew that such work entailed turning innocent old people, women, and children from their beds. Some soldiers were uncomfortable with this practice, for 'there was no satisfaction or pride in rooting through a poor family's few precious possessions.'[15] Officers and NCOs were supposed to maintain rigid discipline amongst their men to forestall allegations that they had stolen or wantonly destroyed property. But such allegations were too frequent to have been merely an incidental part of such operations.[16] In Cyprus one officer denied that his men mounted punitive raids on villages looking for EOKA suspects, but thought that when they searched villages

---

[12] TNA WO 236/11. GOC BTE to formations under command, 19 October 1951; TNA WO 106/3107. CIGS Summary No. 13, 6 November 1945; TNA WO 106/3107. CIGS summary No. 35, 5 March 1946.

[13] *Manchester Guardian*, 30 October 1951.

[14] Captain E. G. D. Pound, 'Operations in the Troodos sub-area', *British Army Review*, No 3 (September 1956), 12; Anon., 'Malaya Section', *British Army Journal*, no. 5 (January 1951), 50; TNA WO 169/19521. *Middle East Training Pamphlet No. 9, Part XIII. Notes for Officers on Internal Security Duties* (May 1945); TNA WO 279/391. War Office, *Imperial Policing and Duties in Aid of the Civil Power, 1949* (London: WO, 13 June 1949), 37–40; *Manchester Guardian*, 29 September 1955; TNA CAB 129/98/C(59)124. Colonial Secretary, Nyasaland Commission of Inquiry, 17 July 1959. Report of the Nyasaland Commission of Inquiry; IWMSA. Accession No. 11092. D. J. Wood, reel 2; IWMSA. Accession No. 26853. T. Hewitson, reel 7; IWMSA. Accession No. 20320. Gen. Sir D. Thorne, reel 6; IWMSA. Accession 14750. W. R. Watton, reel 2; IWMSA. Accession No. 18021. F. G. Green, reel 3.

[15] R. Redgrave, *Balkan Blue. Family and Military Memories* (Barnsley: Leo Cooper, 2000), 159; IWMSA. Accession No. 15576. F. C. Hayhurst, reel 3; TNA WO 32/20987. Colonel, GS, MO4 to Head of DS 6, The Bowen report, 21 November 1966.

[16] TNA WO 169/19521. *Middle East Training Pamphlet No. 9, Part XIII. Notes for Officers on Internal Security Duties* (May 1945).

'I'm not sure that everybody was as careful with hindsight as they might have been once they got into the village.'[17] In Nyasaland the Devlin Commission concluded that

> there was a great deal of aggressive and bullying behaviour, frequently accompanied with blows from fists and rifle butts inflicting minor injuries which sometimes necessitated medical treatment. Men were herded into the middle of the village, shouted at, told to stand up, sit down, hold their hands over their heads and so on, and if they were not completely submissive, they were beaten. They were also struck for 'not being cooperative'. Not being cooperative embraced such things as not at once giving information about where people who were wanted by the security forces might be found or giving it in a manner which the questioner found unconvincing. It was not cooperative to protest if other people were being struck.[18]

Collective punishments were not an incidental part of these operations, they were a deliberate and calculated part of the security forces' policy. According to a battalion commander who served in Malay, the degree of pressure to be applied to the civil population was nicely calculated by the District War Committee. 'While every kind of tactical and strategic psychological warfare was being used against the terrorists in the jungle', he explained, 'the very simple carrot-and-stick principle was effective with the civilians. The nature of punishments and rewards had to be worked out with the aforementioned committee, which included the District Officer and the Chief of Police, that is to say, men who were in touch with the people. Punishments often had to be severe, and supervision close.'[19] Harding explained the dynamic even more starkly. In Cyprus he tried to strike 'what I call the balance of fear, fear of punishment by the court, fear of defeat by the security forces, on the one hand, and fear of retribution or punishment by EOKA on the other hand.'[20]

Other forms of collective punishment included curfews, the closing of shops and businesses, and the imposing of collective fines.[21] The latter might be levied in cash or kind. In December 1950, new emergency regulations in Malaya gave magistrates wide-ranging powers. After they had held an enquiry, they could impose collective fines, order shops to be shut, or billet police on the inhabitants of any village. This could be done to any village where they believed people had abetted or consorted with the insurgents, suppressed evidence, failed to give information to the police, or not taken steps to prevent the escape of insurgents. There was no right of appeal against their awards. Anyone who did not pay his share of the fine could have his

[17] IWMSA. Accession No. 11092. D. J. Wood, reel 2.
[18] TNA CAB 129/98/C(59)124. Colonial Secretary, Nyasaland Commission of Inquiry, 17 July 1959. Report of the Nyasaland Commission of Inquiry.
[19] S. Hosmer and S. O. Crane (eds), *Counterinsurgency: A Symposium, 16–20 April 1962* (Santa Monica, CA: Rand Corporation, 1963/2006), 73–4.
[20] IWMSA. Accession No. 8736. Field Marshal Lord Harding, Transcript, 407.
[21] TNA CO 926/543, Reuters telegrams, 16 March & 18 April 1956; *Manchester Guardian*, 17 March 1956.

property seized or be required to give labour in lieu of money.[22] The Malayan, Kenyan, and Cypriot authorities made wide use of such regulations.[23] In Kenya in 1952 the government levied an annual tax of 20 shillings per head on every Kikuyu. Ostensibly this was to help to pay for the cost of emergency measures. In reality, as District Commissioners could exempt those Kikuyu known to be supporting the government, it was a collective fine levied on those members of the tribe who were not actively supporting the government.[24] In Cyprus between December 1955 and June 1956 the administration imposed 17 collective fines, totalling £108,000.[25]

At their most extreme collective punishments took the form of the destruction of buildings or whole villages. The army used 40 lbs of high explosives in August 1947 to demolish a house in the Givat Shaul quarter of Jerusalem in which arms and explosives had been found.[26] In Malaya in 1948 and 1949 the security forces burnt several villages as reprisals and in the hope that they would persuade people to provide them with information.[27] Templer did not immediately stop this practice. He ordered the destruction of the small village of Permatang Tinggi in August 1952 when the inhabitants had refused to supply information about the murder of a government official.[28] In December 1951, troops were ordered to destroy the village of Kafr Abdou in the Canal Zone after some soldiers passing through it had been killed by gunmen.[29] The operation was condoned at the highest level. The VCIGS writing that it was entirely justified and that Erskine had 'acted with admirable restraint considering the treacherous attacks and brutal murder which took place in that area.'[30] Aircraft dropped leaflets in Nyasaland warning people that 'All of you in the areas where buildings, [and] houses have been burned will be fined. Fines will be levied on all people in the areas where roads are blocked. All of you who are in the areas where looting have taken place will be fined.'[31] On 9 March 1959, on the instructions of the District Commissioner, the security forces burnt 38 houses in the Mlanje district of Nyasaland because their inhabitants were suspected of being NAC supporters.[32]

---

[22] TNA CO 537/6007. Collective Punishment. Notes of a meeting held in the Attorney-General's Chamber on 10 November 1950; TNA CO 537/6007. Emergency Regulation Ordinance, 1948. Emergency Regulation (Amendment no. 18) Regulations, 1950, 20 December 1950.

[23] *Manchester Guardian*, 21 January 1951; TNA CO 537/7280. Collective Punishments, n.d.

[24] *Times*, 23 December 1952.

[25] TNA CO 926/543. Appendix A to COS/1229, May 1956; TNA CO 926/543. Deputy Governor to Colonial Secretary, 21 & 22 June 1956.

[26] *Palestine Post*, 5 August 1947.

[27] *Manchester Guardian*, 7, 11 & 13 August 1948; TNA CO 537/4750. High Commissioner, Federation of Malaya to Colonial Secretary, 3 January 1949.

[28] TNA CO 926/561. Cahill to Neale, 21 November 1955; TNA CO 537/7280. Gurney to Colonial Secretary, 25 February 1951.

[29] TNA WO 236/15. Lecture, Erskine, Narrative of events in the Canal Zone, October 1951–April 1952, 21 November 1952.

[30] IWMDoD. Gen. Sir G. W. Erskine mss 75/134/3. VCIGS to Erskine, 14 December 1951.

[31] TNA CO 1016/1516. Colonial Secretary to Armitage, 12 March 1959.

[32] TNA CAB 129/98/C(59)124. Colonial Secretary, Nyasaland Commission of Inquiry, 17 July 1959. Report of the Nyasaland Commission of Inquiry; Colin Legum, 'Security forces "clean up" two provinces', *Manchester Guardian*, 15 March 1959.

Where exemplary force did not seem to work, the government opted for other means, including mass arrests, wholesale detention without trial, deportations, forcible population resettlement, and at their most extreme, the creation of free fire zones.

By April 1953 the security forces in Kenya had already arrested nearly 83,000 people.[33] In Brunei, in the first three weeks of the emergency, they had arrested more than 2,200.[34] If, as was the case with most of those arrested, there was insufficient evidence to place them before a court, they could either be detained without trial or, if they were not citizens of the colony, be deported. The largest use of deportation was made in Malaya, where, by 1955, 31,245 had been deported, the vast majority to China.[35] The scale of deportations was reduced following the victory of the Communists in the Chinese civil war, but, by dint of bribing Chinese Communist officials, some deportations continued even after 1949. 'It cost as much to send a Chinese deck passenger back to China as it cost to send a European passenger first class to Colombo', remembered one British official who organized the voyages. 'But it did not matter. It was worth it. When you are in a fight of that sort. It was a war. You don't let relatively small financial considerations stand in your way.'[36] In Aden, immediately after the grenade attack on Trevaskis, the Federal government deported nearly 300 Yemenis. Their link with the attack was unproven, but the government acted 'with the object of embarrassing the Yemeni Government and demonstrating that Yemenis here are likely to suffer as a result of further outrages'.[37] In the Canal Zone and Kenya the security forces pursued a policy of internal displacement. In Egypt they dumped suspects on the frontier between the Zone and Egypt proper, while in Kenya large numbers of Kikuyu living on the edge of European farms in the settled areas were deliberately driven from their homes and back to the Reserves by police and army operations in the early months of the emergency.[38]

Table 4.1 illustrates the extent to which colonial authorities made use of detention without trial to intimidate the civil population. Column 1 shows the highest number of detainees held at any one time during nine of the emergencies examined in this book. Column 2 shows the size of the 'target' population from amongst whom the detainees were arrested, and column 3 shows the maximum number of detainees as a proportion of the 'target' population.

The figures in column 1 underestimate the real burden of detention without trial on the target populations. Reliable statistics for the *total* number of people who

[33] *Times*, 30 April 1953.

[34] TNA WO 305/2519. Perintrep. n.d. but *c*.6 January 1963; TNA CO 1030/1540. Sir A. Waddell to CO, 14 December 1962.

[35] TNA WO 291/1670. Operational Research Unit (Far East). Report Number 1/57. A comparison of the emergencies in Malaya and Kenya, 6 June 1957.

[36] IWMSA. Accession No. 10243. A. H. P. Humphrey, reel 2.

[37] TNA CO 1055/197. Trevaskis to CO, 13 December 1963; TNA CO 1055/199. Trevaskis to CO, 3 February 1964.

[38] TNA CO 717/210/4. N. D. Watson to F. Mayell, 17 January 1949; TNA WO 236/11. HQ BTE to formations under command, 30 October 1951; TNA CO 822/445. Notes of a meeting held in the Secretary of State's Room, 15 December 1952.

Table 4.1. Detentions without trial

Country	1. Maximum number of detainees	2. Size of 'target' population	3. Maximum number of detainees per 100,000 of 'target' population
Palestine	1,924[a]	544,000 Yishuv[b]	354
Malaya	9,782[c]	2,413,325 Chinese[d]	405
Canal Zone	1,303 [e]	c. 300,000[f]	434
Kenya[g]	70,922	1,550,000 KEM	4,575
British Guiana	5[h]	425,000[i]	1.2
Cyprus	2,109[j]	369,854 Greek-Cypriots[k]	570
Nyasaland	1,029[l]	2,049,459[m]	50
Brunei	3,453[n]	220,000[o]	1,570
Aden	158[p]	220,000[q]	72

[a] TNA CO 537/2287. Cunningham to Colonial Secretary, 29 July & 29 Sept. 1946.

[b] TNA CAB 129/9/CP(46)175. Report of the Anglo-American Committee of Inquiry, 26 April 1946. Figure for 1944.

[c] TNA WO 291/1670. Operational Research Unit (Far East). Report Number 1/57. A comparison of the emergencies in Malaya and Kenya, 06/06/1957. Figure for Jan. 1951.

[d] TNA WO 279/241. Director of Operations, Malaya, *Conduct of anti-terrorist operations in Malaya* (Malaya: Kuala Lumpur. 3rd edn, 1958). figure for 1956.

[e] TNA WO 106/5993. Diary of events. Civil affairs—Legal branch, nd but *c*.21 Mar. 1952. Figure for Jan. 1952.

[f] TNA WO 163/364/COS(51)681. Note by the WO for the COS committee, The implications of establishing military government in the Suez Canal Zone, 12 Nov. 1951.

[g] *Sources*: TNA WO 236/17. Secretary, War Council, to members of War Council, 7 Dec. 1954; TNA WO 276/92. W. F. B. Pollock-Morris to Undersecretary of State for the Colonies, C-in-C East Africa, Attorney-General, Commissioner of Police, et al, 25 June 1955.

[h] TNA CO 1031/1202. Savage to Colonial Secretary, 12 July 1954. Figure for 26 Oct. 1953.

[i] WO 336/1. Landing and support of troops in British Guiana. Appendix C. British Guiana—Intelligence Brief, 6 Oct. 1953.

[j] TNA CO 926/872. Sir H. Foot to CO, 20 Sept.1958. On 20 Sept. 1958 a total of 2163 persons were in detention, of whom 54 were Turks. They have been deducted from the total in column 1.(TNA CO 926/872. Sir H. Foot to CO, 16 Aug. 1958).

[k] *Whittakers' Almanac*, 1951.

[l] TNA CO 1015/1518. Armitage to Secretary of State, 30 April 1959. Figure for 30 April 1959.

[m] 1945 Census.

[n] TNA WO 305/2519. HQ British Forces Borneo, Joint Perintrep No. 4, 26 Jan. 1963. Covered week ending 26 Jan. 1963. Figure for week ending 26 Jan. 1963.

[o] N. van der Bijl, *Confrontation. The War with Indonesia 1962–1966* (Barnsley: Pen & Sword, 2007), 2.

[p] TNA CO 1055/260. Acting HC to CO, 4 Jan. 1965.

[q] T. R. Mockaitis, *British counter-insurgency in the post-imperial era* (Manchester: Manchester University Press, 1995), 56.

passed thorough the detention systems during each emergency are unobtainable. One estimate for Kenya suggests that as many as 150,000 KEM were detained at one time or another, and another for Brunei puts the figure there at anything between 2,000 and 6,000.[39] The figures also take no account of how long detainees

[39] D. Anderson, *Histories of the Hanged. Britain's Dirty War in Kenya and the End of Empire* (London: Weidenfeld & Nicolson, 2005), 5; H. A. Majid, *Rebellion in Brunei. The 1962 Revolt, Imperialism, Confrontation, and Oil* (London: I. B. Tauris, 2007), 98.

spent in detention before they were released. Some detainees were released quite quickly. Five leaders of the PPP who were arrested in British Guiana on 26 October 1953 had all been released by 12 January 1954. The majority of detainees held in Palestine spent only a few months behind wire in the summer of 1946 before being released, although about 250 who had been arrested in 1944–5 and were then deported to Eritrea and Kenya were imprisoned until the end of the British mandate.[40]

Comparisons with Britain during the Second World War and Algeria during the Algerian War of Independence (1954–62) are also instructive. When British ministers were taxed with their willingness to ignore the normal workings of the law and to detain people without trial, they responded by insisting that what they were doing in the colonies was only what their predecessors had done in Britain during the Second World War. In an emergency the state claimed it had the right to take extraordinary measures to protect the public. During the Second World War the British government had applied this principle to the inhabitants of the British Isles, and suspected Nazi and Fascist sympathizers had been detained under Defence Regulation 18B of the Defence of the Realm Act.[41] But in Britain the maximum number of detainees held at any one time under Regulation 18B was 1,450, or 2.9 per 100,000 of the population. Thus, with the exception of British Guiana, ministers who claimed that they were only doing unto others as the British had done unto themselves during the Second World War were being disingenuous. The scale on which detention without trial was practised in the colonies far exceeded what was done in Britain between 1939 and 1945. However, with the exception of Kenya and Brunei, the British made less use of this form of coercion than did the French. In Algeria, for example, one estimate suggests that approximately 100,000 Algerian Muslims were in detention at any one time, giving a ratio of approximately 1,190 per 100,000 detained.[42]

The administration used detention orders because they believed that the insurgents had been so successful in intimidating juries that they would refuse to convict, or because evidence against the accused could not be disclosed in open court without endangering the lives of informers and witnesses.[43] This meant that many people were detained on the basis of flimsy evidence or mere suspicion. In Malaya, according to one journalist, 'A denunciation, former membership of a Communist organization (in the days when the Communists were still esteemed for their "heroic record" against the Japanese), a former connection with

---

[40] TNA CO 537/2287. Cunningham to Colonial Secretary, 29 July 1946; TNA CO 537/3866. Cunningham to Colonial Secretary, 2 April 1948.

[41] TNA CAB 21/1681/MAL.C(50)21. Secretary of State for War, Malaya Committee, The military situation in Malaya, 17 June 1950; TNA CAB 128/17/CM(50)37. Cabinet Conclusions, 19 June 1950.

[42] There were approximately 8.4 million Algerian Muslims in Algeria. See I. F. W. Beckett, *Modern Insurgencies and Counter-Insurgencies. Guerrillas and Their Opponents since 1750* (London: Routledge, 2001), 160. The figure of 100,000 detainees is derived from L. Lazreg, *Torture and the Twilight of Empire from Algiers to Baghdad* (Princeton, New Jersey: Princeton University Press, 2008), 49.

[43] IWMSA. Accession No. 4716, N. Harvey, Transcript, 12; IWMSA. Accession No. 8736. Field Marshal Lord Harding, Transcript, 399.

a Communist-dominated trade union—any of these things can bring a man into a detention camp.'[44] J. P. Morton, the Director of Intelligence in Malaya between 1952 and 1954, privately admitted that information about suspects, particularly in the early stages of the emergency, had been so imprecise 'that many of the prisoners were innocent', but, incarcerated behind barbed wire for an indeterminate period, they 'were now being converted into thoroughly embittered Communists'.[45] In Kenya in January 1954, Erskine urged the detention of 'Any Kikuyu against whom there was the slightest suspicion.'[46] The outcome, according to Richard Catling, who later became Commissioner of Police in Kenya, was that 'The cases against these people were paper thin in hundreds, thousands of cases. They wouldn't have stood up anywhere under examination by people who knew what a sound case is for putting somebody away in detention without trial on those grounds.'[47] In Cyprus Harding ordered the detention of AKEL's leaders, 'irrespective of evidence of active participation'.[48]

Exemplary force met with mixed results. In British Guiana and Nyasaland it could be claimed that it was a total success, but as neither the PPP nor the NAC had made plans or preparations for an insurgency, such claims are fatuous. In Palestine large-scale cordon and search operations, such as AGATHA in June 1946, SHARK in July and August 1946, ELEPHANT and HIPPOPOTAMUS in March 1947, and TIGER in July 1947, did uncover some arms caches and some active insurgents.[49] But they did not succeed in crushing the insurgency. On the contrary, the number of security incidents, which had totalled 78 between October 1945 and July 1946, rose to 286 over the next year.[50] By February 1947 the British were reduced to evacuating all non-essential personnel and concentrating those remaining into a handful of heavily guarded camps. Similarly, in Cyprus cordon and search operations and sweeps yielded some prisoners, weapons, and intelligence, but not enough to destroy EOKA.[51] Collective punishments also failed to

---

[44] *Manchester Guardian*, 5 July 1950.

[45] TNA KV 4/408. J. P. Morton, Malayan emergency, n.d. but *c*.1960.

[46] TNA WO 216/863. Erskine to CIGS, 27 January 1954. Enc. Appreciation on future military policy in Kenya.

[47] IWMSA. Accession No. 10392. Sir R. Catling, Transcript, 42.

[48] IWMDoD. Field Marshal Lord Harding mss AFH 10. Harding to Colonial Secretary, 3 December 1955.

[49] TNA WO 275/120. GHQ MELF Weekly Int. Reviews (Palestine Extracts). No. 67. Issued 5 July 1946; TNA WO 275/114. 6 Airborne Division, Operation Agatha, 29/06/1946, 1 July 1946, Report of OC, 1st Para Brigade; TNA WO 275/120. GHQ MELF Weekly Int Reviews (Palestine Extracts). No. 68. Issued 12 July 1946; TNA CO 537/1719. High Commissioner Palestine to Colonial Secretary, 1 July 1946; TNA WO 275/120. GHQ MELF Weekly Int. Reviews (Palestine Extracts). No. 70, 26 July 1946; TNA PREM 8/864. High Commissioner to Colonial Secretary, 2 March 1947; TNA WO 32/15037. Maj.-Gen. R. N. Gale, GOC 1 Infantry Division. Operation Elephant, General report, n.d. TNA WO 32/15037. Maj.-Gen. R. N. Gale, GOC 1 Infantry Division. Operation Tiger, 2 August 1947.

[50] D. A. Charters, *The British Army and Jewish Insurgency in Palestine, 1945–47* (London: Macmillan, 1989), 60.

[51] TNA CO 926/521. Sinclair to Colonial Secretary, 17 June 1956; TNA CO 926/521. Chief of Staff to Governor, 12 June 1956; TNA CO 926/521. Harding to Colonial Secretary, 10 October 1956; P. Dimitrakis, 'British Intelligence and the Cyprus Insurgency, 1955–1959', *International Journal of Intelligence and Counter Intelligence*, vol. 21 (2008), 381–2.

intimidate the population into co-operating with the security forces. Events at the village of Frenaros near Famagusta, were typical. Following the assassination of two soldiers outside the village on 27 March 1956, troops searched the village, detained 16 people, and found six shotguns, two home-made bombs, and three grenades in a nearby field. The village was put under curfew, and each villager was given a blank sheet of paper and an envelop and told to provide information about the ambush that had killed the soldiers. No information was forthcoming. The authorities could respond only by imposing a collective fine of £1,500.[52] There are two possible explanations for the refusal of the villagers to yield to pressure. They are not necessarily mutually exclusive. One was fear of retaliation by EOKA. The other was that, although they may have felt unease at the violent methods the insurgents employed, they, like the Yishuv in Palestine, shared the insurgents' goals and were not willing to betray them.

There were similar failures in the Canal Zone. The destruction of Kafr Abdou further soured Anglo-Egyptian relations at governmental level, and was followed by an increase in the number of attacks on British personnel.[53] By January 1952, cordon and search operations were developing into small-scale battles.[54] The largest of these, Operation 'Eagle', an attempt by the army to disarm the Egyptian police in Ismalia (whom Erskine suspected were insurgents in disguise), was a disaster. The British employed not just infantry but also armoured cars and tanks in an effort to intimidate the police into surrendering.[55] They refused to be overawed, the British opened fire, and the Egyptians shot back. The police suffered 40 killed and 65 wounded.[56] In Cairo and Alexandria enraged Egyptians attacked British businesses and symbols of British power such as Shepherd's Hotel. The British press thought the army had used too much force and even some senior officers in the Canal Zone thought that '[I] feel sure the aim could have been achieved by the exercise of greater finesse; as it is we have made these miserable people martyrs and no doubt have inflamed world opinion against us.'[57] The clumsy use of force was not going to solve the problem, and henceforth the British had only one option: 'sitting it out', maintaining the garrison and conducting a low-intensity counter-insurgency campaign, while trying to negotiate a settlement about the future of the base with the Egyptians.[58]

---

[52] *Manchester Guardian*, 29 March 1956; TNA CO 926/543. Reuters telegram, 29 March 1956.
[53] TNA WO 236/15. Lecture, Erskine, Narrative of events in the Canal Zone, October 1951–April 1952, 21 November 1952.
[54] *Manchester Guardian*, 5, 14, 15 January 1952; TNA WO 236/12. Erskine to British ambassador, Cairo, 12 January 1952.
[55] TNA WO 236/12. Erskine to British Ambassador Cairo, 19 January 1952; TNA WO 236/13. Brigadier R. K. Exham, Report on Operation Eagle—25 January 1952. The disarming of the civil police in Ismalia, n.d.
[56] TNA WO 236/13. Brigadier R. K. Exham, Report on Operation Eagle—25 January 1952. The disarming of the civil police in Ismalia, n.d.; TNA WO 216/801. Robertson to CIGS, 29 January 1952.
[57] TNA WO 216/802. CIGS to Robertson, 28 January 1952; IWMDoD. Gen. Sir K. Darling mss IX. Darling to parents, Darling to parents, 29 January 1952.
[58] TNA WO 216/554. Robertson, Implications of 'Sitting it out', 19 September 1952.

In Malaya sweeps and cordon and search operations had, by mid-1949, driven the insurgents out of the towns and into the jungle, ending their efforts to create a liberated area in North Pahang.[59] But despite the fact that well-to-do Chinese had formed the Malay Chinese Association and called on their compatriots to support the government, most of the Chinese community remained sitting on the fence.[60] Meanwhile the MRLA regrouped and in October 1949 re-emerged from its jungle bases to renew its offensive.[61] Civilian casualties mounted and public morale fell, as did the amount of information they were prepared to give to the security forces.[62]

In Kenya the emergency began in October 1952 with Operation JOCK SCOTT. It involved the arrest of KAU leaders and security force sweeps. Coupled with the propensity of panic-stricken European farmers to drive Kikuyu labourers from their homes in the settled areas, it encouraged many young Kikuyu to flee to the forests, where they coalesced into Mau Mau gangs. 'In the course of operations of this nature', Governor Baring admitted, 'numbers of Africans were manhandled and the sympathies of the loyal Kikuyu alienated.'[63] Erskine's arrival did not initially mark a fundamental change in the strategy of the security forces, for he continued to maintain constant pressure on the gangs.[64] He re-organized the security forces so that a series of mobile columns could operate across designated areas. The army tried to drive out and destroy the armed gangs by applying what he called 'special treatment'. But that was only half the job. 'As I give special treatment to an area I expect to leave it with Home Guard and Police firmly established and military support remote or at least more concentrated.' Their task was to conduct pacification operations. 'There may', he warned, 'be a tendency to cry "Don't be too beastly to the Mau Mau" which we must resist. The loyal Kikuyu must be given opportunity in every area, to tidy up their own affairs—they will do this much better than the Government, and my operations are designed to give them the opportunity.'[65]

This worked to the extent that by early 1954 intelligence reports suggested that Mau Mau gangs were smaller and more dispersed than in the past.[66] However, operations in the reserves and on the fringes of the forests had contained the insurgents, they had not defeated them.[67] To achieve that Erskine had to attack their main source of supplies, money, and recruits, the African population of

---

[59] TNA WO 106/5884. Gen. Sir N. Ritchie, Report on operations in Malaya, June 1948 to July 1949, 6 September 1949.

[60] TNA DEFE 11/33/COS(49)180. Memorandum by the Colonial Office on the security situation in the Federation of Malaya, April 1949, 17 May 1949.

[61] TNA CO 537/5974. Commissioner of Police to GOC Malaya, 16 February 1950; TNA CO 717/119/4. Gurney to CO, 7 January, 18 & 27 March 1950.

[62] TNA CO 537/5975/JIAC(50)1(Final). Joint Intelligence Advisory Committee, Malaya, The potential of the Malayan Communist Party, 24 October 1950; TNA CO 537/5974. Commissioner of Police, The Armed Communist situation in Malaya, 14 February 1950.

[63] TNA CO 822/445. Notes of a meeting held in the Secretary of State's Room, 15 December 1952.

[64] TNA WO 216/860. Erskine to CIGS, 9 November 1953.

[65] TNA WO 216/853. Erskine to CIGS, 14 June 1953.

[66] TNA CO 822/782. Erskine to CIGS, 4 January 1954.

[67] TNA WO 216/860. Erskine to CIGS, 9 November 1953.

Nairobi. Operation ANVIL was designed not only to destroy the Mau Mau's infrastructure in the city, but also to deal a fatal psychological blow to them. Nairobi was the centre of government, and to live and work in the city symbolized progress to the Kikuyu.[68] No one could accuse Erskine of thinking in terms of half measures. He implemented what was probably the largest cordon and search and mass detention operation in the history of the British Empire. ANVIL began on 24 April 1954. Hooded informers were used to identify Mau Mau suspects, and by 25 May more than 50,000 Kikuyu been screened, of whom 24,100, representing about half the Kikuyu population in Nairobi, were then detained without trial.[69]

POPULATION CONTROL, FORCED RESETTLEMENT, AND FOOD DENIAL

Coercion through exemplary force was everywhere the mainstay of British counter-insurgency policy. It was habitually targeted at individuals or, in the case of collective punishments, at communities, suspected of supporting the insurgency. But in Malaya, Kenya, Oman, and the Radfan, its scope was deliberately widened so that it was directed against entire ethnic groups: Chinese squatters, KEM, and members of Arab tribes who refused to submit to government authority. It was done because, although the use of exemplary force enabled the security forces to contain the insurgents, it did not destroy their capacity to regenerate. To prevent this from happening security force commanders recognized that they had to destroy the link between the insurgents and their support infrastructure. In Kenya Operation ANVIL had begun this process by destroying the Mau Mau logistical base in Nairobi, but the remaining active Mau Mau insurgents could still look to KEM farmers in the Reserves for support. Similarly, in Malaya, MRLA units may have been driven from the towns into the jungle, but they could still draw recruits, supplies and intelligence from the hundreds of thousands of Chinese squatters, miners and rubber tapers living on the fringes of the jungle. In Oman and the Radfan, insurgent tribesmen could draw support and sustenance from the tribes amongst whom they lived.

To break that link in Kenya and Malaya cordon and search operations and disruptive patrolling gave way to 'clear and hold' operations during which the security forces established a permanent framework of troops and police in designated areas. The civil population was then moved into locations variously described as 'resettlement areas' or 'new villages', euphemisms for the fact that hundreds of thousands of civilians were corralled, often against their will, into settlements behind barbed-wire fences and watch towers. The settlements protected government supporters from insurgent intimidation, and prevented the latter from gaining physical access to supplies, intelligence, and recruits. Once the framework had

---

[68] TNA WO 216/863. Erskine to CIGS, 27 January 1954. Enc. Appreciation on future military policy in Kenya.
[69] Anderson, *Histories of the Hanged*, 205.

been established, and resettlement had taken place, the security forces could move to the next phase of their work: a series of surge operations during which they flooded areas in turn with extra troops and police to attack the active insurgents at their most vulnerable point, by denying them ready access to food.

In Malaya this policy will forever be associated with the name of Sir Harold Briggs, a former Indian Army officer called out of retirement to become Director of Operations. Briggs was not the first official to recognize that controlling the Chinese squatter and rubber tappers living on the fringes of the jungle was the key to success.[70] Resettlement had been tried on a small scale before his arrival, but failed for two reasons. It required large numbers of police, soldiers, and administrators, all of whom were then in short supply, and success ultimately depended on the ability of the security forces to protect the settlements from attack.[71] The main elements of what needed to be done had, therefore, been identified before Briggs was appointed and there was, in fact, little that was entirely novel in the plan that he and his small staff formulated in April 1950, shortly after his arrival in Malaya.[72] The Briggs Plan did not mark a fundamental shift in the doctrine underpinning British counter-insurgency doctrine. There was no move from coercion to conciliation. Briggs merely went about coercing the Chinese squatter population in bigger and more effective ways. The crux of his plan was to combine the operations of the police, army, and civil administration in such a way that the government could dominate the rural Chinese population.

The inspiration for the plan came from Burma. Between 1930 and 1932 the British had suppressed a major rebellion when the security forces had created a framework of permanent posts in the disaffected areas, and combined these with a series of sweeps, cordon and search operations, and measures to prevent food and other supplies from reaching the insurgents.[73] The lesson that Briggs drew from this was that

> it was proved in Burma, that if these areas are dominated to such an extent that food, money, information and propaganda were denied the enemy, or even diminished, the task of security troops would be easier and the more loyal elements among the Chinese feel more secure, inducing them to provide us with information and a means of putting out our own propaganda. Furthermore, the Security Forces might get a better and easier chance of engaging the bandit who is forced to fight for his food or else move elsewhere to get it. The initiative then becomes ours.[74]

---

[70] TNA DEFE 11/33. A paper on the dimensions and nature of the security problem confronting the government of the Federation of Malaya, 16 September 1948.

[71] TNA WO 106/5884. Gen. Sir N. Ritchie, Report on operations in Malaya, June 1948 to July 1949, 6 September 1949; TNA WO 216/333. Gurney to Harding, 13 February 1950; TNA CO 537/5974. Gurney to the Chairman, BDCC (Far East), 15 February 1950.

[72] IWMSA. Accession No. 10192. Sir R. Thompson, reel 2.

[73] Gwynn, *Imperial Policing*, 299–330; 'Revolt spreading in Burma. New emergency Powers', *Observer*, 2 August 1931; Anon., 'Burma Ordinance Obligations of civilians,' *Times*, 3 August 1931.

[74] TNA CO 537/5975. Briggs, Outline of future anti-bandit policy in Malaya, n.d. but *c*.1 April 1950.

Coercion would be the key to the successful concentration and control of the rural Chinese. He ordered State and District War committees to make full use of the powers given them by the emergency regulations to compel people to co-operate. Where necessary they were to impose curfews on settlements, close roads at night, erect fences around villages and labour lines, control the movement of foodstuffs, restrict the movement or places of residence of suspects, and if necessary detain them without trial.[75] Lest anyone should doubt the Federal government's ruthlessness, on 1 June they introduced a mandatory death penalty for anyone found guilty of demanding, collecting or receiving supplies destined for the insurgents.

The army had two roles. It was to conduct 'distributed operations', maintaining a permanent framework of troops, deployed in close conjunction with the police, to cover those populated areas which the police could not control.[76] Superimposed on this framework, the army would provide striking forces whose task was to dominate the jungle near potential insurgent supply areas. Battalions were told to establish their headquarters in populated areas, to increase the sense of security nearby, but they were to deploy their companies in bases on the fringes of the jungle up to a distance of about three hours march from roads and main jungle paths. By a combination of patrols and ambushes, companies would dominate the tracks the insurgents used to make contact with the Min Yeun who supplied them. The insurgents would thereby be drawn into a series of killing grounds where soldiers could kill or capture them.[77]

In Kenya there was also a gradual acceptance that only a virtually complete lockdown of a whole ethnic group, the KEM, would undermine its support for the insurgency. In March 1953 security force commanders finally realized that the regular police had to establish a permanent presence in the Reserves, but there was as yet little appreciation of the vital part that denying food supplies to the insurgents might play in defeating them.[78] At the same time as Erskine told the government that the destruction of the Mau Mau infrastructure in Nairobi was essential, he also told them that he wanted to impose an almost complete lockdown on the Kikuyu living in the Reserves. As in Malaya, coercion was the key principle underpinning the Erskine Plan. All those suspected of supporting the Mau Mau were to be detained. The Kikuyu, who lived in small, scattered settlements, were to be forced to live in one of two kinds of protected villages. One sort was erected to protect loyalists, home guards and their dependants. The second were punitive encampments designed to house Mau Mau sympathizers and their families.[79] In the latter the government would make full use of collective

[75] TNA CAB 21/1681/MAL(50)10. Director of Operations, Malaya: Directive No. 2, 12 May 1950.

[76] D. Ucko, 'Countering Insurgents through Distributed Operations: Insights from Malaya 1948–1960', *JSS*, vol. 30 (2007), 48–72.

[77] TNA CAB 21/1681/MAL(50)10. Note by the Joint Secretaries, Malaya Committee, 2 June 1950. Director of Operations, Malaya: Directive No. 1, 16 April 1950.

[78] TNA WO 276/411. Appreciation of the situation by Maj.-Gen. W. R. Hinde, 5 March 1953.

[79] D. Branch, *Defeating Mau Mau, Creating Kenya. Counterinsurgency, Civil War, and Decolonization* (Cambridge: Cambridge University Press. 2009), 107–18.

punishments, including the destruction of all food except the minimum necessary for local consumption, and all movement outside villages and trade between villages would be prohibited.[80]

Two days before ANVIL began the War Council ordered the creation of the kind of permanent security framework that had already been erected in Malaya. With Nairobi under government control, power would be projected outwards from the capital, creating a strong administration and police organization and home guard network. The police were to take over security duties from the army as rapidly as possible so as to free up the latter for surge operations. 'The Role of the Civil Administration will be to bring maximum pressure to bear on the terrorists by the establishment of yet closer and firmer Administration, and to plan the future form of Administration having regard to the social, economic and political aspects.' The army was to support the police and administration by attacking insurgents wherever they found them, 'and generally providing military cover for the establishment of a firm long-term civil administration. In the main the Army and RAF will be responsible for dealing with the more inaccessible places though they will always be prepared to redeploy rapidly to help the civil power.'[81]

Resettlement was done at gunpoint, and not just to prevent the insurgents from interfering. In Malaya, so the Federal government claimed, squatters about to be moved were given several days' notice so they could get their affairs in order. Care was to be taken to explain to them why they were to be moved, where they were going, and that the government would provide them with land and the materials to build new homes. More usually, however, no such warning was given in case the insurgents tried to interfere. Even the official Federal government report admitted coyly that 'Where there was a failure to prepare the people, there was some degree of passive resistance.'[82] Resistance was no more than passive because the authorities mustered an overwhelming force of troops and police and carried out each move as a military operation.[83] Troops surrounded the squatter area at night and policemen went from door to door, telling people to gather their movable belongings and then loading them onto army lorries for the journey.[84] A British official who organized resettlement near Ipoh remembered that 'We had to use a good deal of forceful persuasion to get some of them to move. . . . If you would not dismantle your own house and bring it along and rebuild it in the new village we will just pull it down, and we did.'[85] A Chinese home guard member who helped resettle one village remembered that 'The whole place is surrounded by police and the military to prevent any of the villagers from running away, either due to fear, or due to duress from the Communists. There'd be a lot of crying, you know. Or some of them were

[80] TNA WO 216/863. Erskine to CIGS, 27 January 1954. Enc. Appreciation on future military policy in Kenya.
[81] TNA WO 276/90. War Council directive no. 1. Emergency Policy, 23 April 1954.
[82] TNA CO 1022/29. Resettlement in Malaya, n.d. but c.April 1952.
[83] IWMSA. Accession No. 10175. R. J. W. Craig, Transcript, 10–11; IWMSA. Accession No. 10232. L. O. Crosland, reel 1.
[84] Z. Koya, 'Villagers' sacrifice to beat Reds', *New Straits Times (Malaysia)*, 31 August 1998.
[85] IWMSA. Accession No. 9141. James Marshall Patrick, reel 1.

cursing me. They say, "You're a Running dog."[86] Resettlement in Kenya was similarly coercive. It began in June 1954 when the War Council agreed to enforce resettlement across the whole of Kikuyuland. The Kikuyu normally lived in scattered family settlements and did not welcome being herded together behind barbed wire.[87] In August the government introduced a new Emergency Regulation giving the security forces powers to destroy both the livestock and the property of anyone who refused to move when ordered to do so.[88] The roofs were usually ripped off the huts of those who were reluctant to move.[89]

The attitude of people subjected to this treatment was summed up by a British officer in Kenya: 'Well, you could not expect them to be overjoyed. Their nice homes, which had probably been their homes for some considerable time, in their own chosen parts of their own native country were denied to them other than to work in during the day and they were pretty peeved. . . . Our impression is that they were pretty irritated.'[90] In Malaya, a soldier who assisted in moving squatters into resettlement areas had no doubt that the process involved real hardship. 'I'm certain that it did. Nobody, not even the poorest squatter, likes to be uprooted from the place he may have lived in for years and put in a camp with pretty basic living conditions surrounded by barbed wire.'[91] Just how basic those conditions were was described by Moo Kiaw, who with her family was moved to a new village near Kuala Lumpur where

> all that they saw was a piece of cleared rubber estate land with lots drawn out. 'The tree stumps were still there and the British soldiers pointed to the lots and said Pick your lots and build your houses,' she recalled. Those who could afford it engaged builders but those who could not built their own houses using planks and zinc from their old dwellings.[92]

Forced resettlement represented a massive demographic dislocation. In Malaya about 423,000 Chinese squatters were moved into 410 new villages, and about 650,000 Chinese mine and estate workers were subject to 'regrouping' in wired-in villages. As the total Chinese population in Malay amounted to 2,153,000 according to the 1953 census, the 1,073,000 people forcibly relocated represented almost exactly half of the Chinese population of the country. The proportion of the target population moved in Kenya was even larger. Between June 1954 and October 1955, from a total target population of 1,555,000 (Kikuyu, Meru, and Embu) as measured by the 1948 census, about 1,077,500 people, or 69 per cent, were forcibly moved to one of 854 new villages.[93] This contrasts unfavourably with

[86] K. L. Chye, *Empire Warriors. Malaya 1948: The Intelligence War*, BBC, 2004.
[87] Hosmer and Crane (eds), *Counterinsurgency*, 130.
[88] *Manchester Guardian*, 3 August 1954.
[89] P. Monkhouse, 'Kenya after the Mau Mau. I. The village policy', *Manchester Guardian*, 31 August 1955; TNA WO 291/1670. Operational Research Unit (Far East). Report Number 1/57. A comparison of the emergencies in Malaya and Kenya, 6 June 1957.
[90] IWMSA. Accession No. 10091. A. L. K. Liddle, reel 2.
[91] IWMSA. Accession No. 10107. N. J. D. Baptiste, reel 1.
[92] Z. Koya, 'Life behind a barbed-wire fence', *New Straits Times (Malaysia)*, 31 August 1998.
[93] These statistics are derived from P. Monkhouse, 'Kenya after the Mau Mau. I. The village policy', *Manchester Guardian*, 31 August 1955; TNA WO 291/1670. Operational Research Unit (Far

the application of similar policies by the French and Portuguese colonial authorities. Estimates suggest that by 1961 between a third and a half of the Algerian population had been forcibly resettled by the French authorities. That was about the same proportion of the Chinese population who were resettled in Malaya, but considerably less than the proportion of the KEM who were moved in Kenya.[94] The scale of resettlement in Kenya and Malay also far exceeded Portuguese efforts in Angola and Mozambique, where 20.7 per cent and 14.7 per cent of the population respectively were resettled by the authorities.[95] The argument for British exceptionalism does not apply in the case of their readiness to use forcible resettlement as a counter-insurgency tool.

Once the target population had been resettled, the security forces could mount the next stage of their strategy, denying the insurgents the resources they needed to live and operate. In Malaya the first Federal food denial operation began in June 1951. Typically, such operations fell into three phases. In the initial phase, which might last for two or three months, the Special Branch built up its knowledge of the area and penetrated the Min Yeun. In the second phase, lasting for six months or more, the authorities introduced strict controls over all supplies of food and other essential supplies. Houses were searched and every ounce of surplus food was confiscated. Rice rations were either issued uncooked or families were required to collect a ration of cooked rice that had been prepared in a central village kitchen. Cooked rice could not be passed to insurgents outside the village because it was liable to go bad quickly. Food denial forced the insurgents to rely for food on a limited number of supporters in the villages. As a result of this, and of information obtained from agents and from the public, the security forces were able to mount ambushes, track parties through the jungle and locate and attack insurgent camps.[96] It was a measure of the success of these policies that by December 1955 about 2.5 million people were living in 'white' areas where all emergency restrictions had been lifted.

In Kenya sporadic food control measures had been implemented as early as January and February 1953.[97] They became far more effective once the population had been resettled. For the government, the new villages offered a way of providing security for loyalists and of breaking the link between the passive wing of Mau Mau and the gangs. This was done by a judicious combination of incentives and rewards. As the District Commissioner in Embu explained in orders he issued in May 1955,

---

East); Report Number 1/57. A comparison of the emergencies in Malaya and Kenya, 6 June 1957; R. Sutherland, *Resettlement and Food Control in Malaya* (Santa Monica, CA: Rand Corporation, 1964), 43–52; J. Blacker, 'The demography of Mau Mau: fertility and mortality in Kenya in the 1950s: a demographer's viewpoint', *African Affairs*, vol. 106 (2007), 205–27.

[94] K. Sutton, 'Population resettlement—traumatic upheavals and the Algerian experience', *Journal of Modern African Studies*, vol. 15, no. 2 (June, 1977), 286.

[95] These figures are derived from J. P. Cann, III, 'Portuguese counterinsurgency campaigning in Africa, 1961–1974: A military analysis' (Ph.D. dissertation, University of London, 1996), 5, 11, 296–8.

[96] TNA CO 1022/29. Resettlement in Malaya, n.d. but *c*.April 1952; IWMSA. Accession No. 10175. R. J. W. Craig, Transcript, 12, 21–3; IWMSA. Accession No. 9141. J. M. Patrick, reel 4.

[97] TNA WO 32/14635. HQ East Africa Command to WO, 4 February 1953.

'We must use the successful tactics of relaxing on restrictions wherever the moment is opportune and of increasing the pressure wherever Mau Mau is still being supported.' He had already mobilized local labour to dig a ditch to create a physical barrier between the Reserve and the forest. His aim now was to eliminate the remaining Mau Mau in his district. Food control measures would be intensified. The movement of all foodstuffs except within the confines of towns and villages was prohibited, the sale of foodstuffs was restricted to a three-hour period each afternoon, and only Africans in possession of passes to reside in a particular town or village would be allowed buy food there. He planned to construct food stores, and to fence and to guard fields, so that gangs could not steal food or cattle at night. The movement of people from one district to another would be forbidden without a government pass, and no African, except on government business, would be allowed to travel by bicycle or motor transport without the written permission of a District Officer. This would require money and labour, but resettlement would ensure that it was the KEM who would pay, both in taxes and in forced communal labour.[98]

In Malaya and Kenya, forced population resettlement played a key role in tipping the balance of advantage towards the government. Resettlement meant that in location after location the security forces could establish themselves as the dominant force. The insurgents were denied physical access to supplies of food, money, recruits, and intelligence. The civil population, living behind barbed-wire fences and next to police posts, were no longer subject to intimidation by the insurgents. Loyalists felt safe to show support for the government, those who had tried to be neutral found it might pay them to throw in their lot with the government, however reluctantly, and insurgent sympathizers found it wise to remain passive. People were not free from fear and intimidation. But the sources of that fear and intimidation had switched, from the insurgents to the security forces.

This did not happen overnight. The Briggs Plan did not produce immediate success. The evidence could be read in two ways. The MRLA was not prepared to surrender in the face of the Briggs Plan without a fierce struggle.[99] Pessimists could point to the fact that the number of insurgent-inspired incidents, having fallen in 1949, rose in 1950 and rose even more in 1951. Security forces casualties followed a similar pattern. These trends seemed alarming. But they could also be read as evidence of the success of the plan, for it was achieving what Briggs hoped it would achieve. It was drawing the insurgents onto ground of the security forces' choosing where they could kill or capture them. The average number of insurgents killed, captured, or surrendered fell in both 1949 and 1950, but then rose sharply in 1951.[100] By June 1951 Gurney and Briggs believed that the turning point had been reached. A quarter of a million squatters had already been moved. Since

[98] TNA WO 276/457. District Commissioner's Office, Embu, Intensification of effort against Mau Mau, 27 May 1955.

[99] TNA CO 537/5975/JIAC(50)1(Final). Joint Intelligence Advisory Committee, Malaya, The potential of the Malayan Communist Party, 24 October 1950; TNA WO 216/379. Lt.-Gen. Sir C. Keightley to Lt.-Gen. Sir N. Brownjohn, 26 May 1951.

[100] TNA WO 208/5356. Director of Operations, Review of Emergency Situation at the end of 1956, January 1957: Emergency Statistics.

January 1951 the MRLA had mounted a major offensive to try to disrupt the programme, but that had the effect of bringing them into the security forces' killing fields. The number of contacts between the insurgents and security forces had risen, as had the number of insurgent casualties. The number of civilian casualties was also high, but in the second quarter of the year it had begun to fall, suggesting that the security forces were getting better at protecting the civilian population.[101] By August 1951 the MRLA's leadership had realized that they could not defeat the Briggs Plan, and that, on the contrary, it had defeated them. In October they issued a new directive, signalling a major change of strategy.[102] Such was the shortage of food, and so dangerous had the jungle fringes become, that they decided to withdraw into the deep jungle to grow their own food.[103] By January 1952, civilian confidence in the ability of the security forces to protect them from insurgent intimidation was increasing, shown by the fact that 'in some areas there have been encouraging signs of more information from the civilians'.[104] Thus even before Templer arrived in February 1952 the MRLA had accepted that it could not destroy the resettlement policy.[105]

Resettlement and food denial meant that it was no longer possible for large bands to find sustenance. Compelled to split into smaller groups, the insurgents lost much of their offensive power. By mid-1952 the security forces had discovered that 85 per cent of the insurgent parties they contacted consisted of five or fewer members.[106] The interrogation in the autumn of 1953 of a large number of surrendered insurgents highlighted that shortages of food and manpower were the two most important reasons for the marked drop in insurgent activities. Finding food consumed so much of their time and energy that the jungle fighters had no time to plan and carry out other operations. Without enough food to last them for a period of between 10 and 20 days the insurgents thought they dare not carry out an attack. Their rations would be exhausted before they had evaded the pursuing security forces.[107] They also complained of a lack of intelligence about security forces activities, another sign that forced resettlement had broken the link between the jungle fighters and the Min Yeun.[108] In the jungle the insurgents were left

---

[101] TNA CAB 21/2884/MAL/C(51)1. Combined appreciation of the emergency situation by the High Commissioner and the Director of Operations, 4 June 1951.

[102] C. Peng, *My Side of History* (Singapore: Media Masters, 2003), 279–80.

[103] TNA WO 106/5990. Director of Operations Malaya, Review of the Emergency in Malaya from June 1948 to August 1957, September 1957; TNA CO 1022/210. Pan Malayan review of Political and Security Intelligence. No. 11, 26 November 1952.

[104] TNA WO 216/806. Keightley to Slim, 20 January 1952.

[105] Hack, 'British intelligence and counter-insurgency', 124–55; *idem*, 'Corpses, prisoners of war and captured documents', 211–41.

[106] TNA WO 291/1725. Lt.-Col. C. R. Nicholls, OC Operational Research Section Malaya. Memorandum Number 5/52. Patrolling in the Malayan Emergency, 1 December 1952.

[107] TNA WO 291/1770. ORS(PW) Memorandum 8/53. P.R. Humphrey (officer in command of Interrogation Centre), Some items of psychological warfare intelligence as obtained from surrendered Communist Terrorists in Malaya, 5 October 1953.

[108] TNA WO 291/1770. ORS(PW) Memorandum 8/53. P. R. Humphrey, Some items of psychological warfare intelligence as obtained from surrendered Communist Terrorists in Malaya, 5 October 1953.

isolated, hungry, and dispirited. 'Everything was fine when we lived near to the people', one MCP courier remembered. 'But if the enemy attacked us, we'd be forced to flee to isolated areas deep in the jungle. And then we'd be in trouble. We would survive by eating wild vegetables and animals—everything from rats to elephants.'[109]

Similarly in Kenya, whereas before ANVIL and forced villagization the forest gangs had found that 'life was good, because people had clothing and food and all the supplies they wanted with them', from 1955 onwards, life became very hard.[110] 'I can't begin to explain all the suffering we went through', one gang member remembered. 'By this time, food had become so scarce and we were forced to eat bark from trees. We'd chew it until it became finer than flour. We'd chew any bones we could find, whether they were animal or human ones. When our food supply finally dried up, we'd cut a piece of the skin from our clothes, roast it and eat it.'[111] By August 1955, Baring could write to Lennox-Boyd about the 'sharp improvement in [the] position during last three months'.[112] The most significant feature was the increasing readiness of the KEM living in the Reserves and Settled Areas to co-operate with the security forces. 'There are several explanations', Baring explained, 'but most important is success in most areas of control of movement arrangements. These involve the provision of tribal police of Kikuyu guard escorts for villagers working in fields, herding cattle, and the children going to school. This has cut off physical contact with gangs and to my mind here lies the explanation of remarkable change.' A growing number of senior insurgents were surrendering, the rate of insurgent attacks other than those designed to secure food, 'has become almost negligible and loyalist casualties are very low'.[113] By Christmas 1955, Lathbury agreed that, 'Close administration has broken the back of the Passive Wing and little active help is now given to the terrorists.'[114]

Elsewhere resettlement was either employed on a much smaller scale, or it was not employed at all. Framework operations were used in Sabah and Sarawak, where the army established 27 company-sized fortified posts along the frontier. From them the garrisons dispatched patrols to bolster the confidence of the population and mount ambushes to catch parties of infiltrators as they made their way to and from Kalimantan.[115] The Federal government also prepared an ambitious resettlement programme to move 627,500 people, or about half the population of Sabah

---

[109] Lao Jiang, *Empire Warriors. Malaya 1948: The Intelligence War*, BBC, 2004.
[110] Karari Njama, *Empire Warriors. Kenya: The Hunt for Kimanthi*, BBC, 2004.
[111] Field Marshal Muthoni, *Empire Warriors. Kenya: The Hunt for Kimanthi*, BBC, 2004.
[112] TNA PREM 11/1424. Baring to Colonial Secretary, 25 August 1955.
[113] Ibid.
[114] TNA WO 216/892. Lathbury to CIGS, 5 December 1955.
[115] TNA WO 305/2526. Walker, Appreciation of force requirements in Sarawak, Sabah and Brunei up to 3 March 1964, 27 September 1963; TNA WO 305/2528. Brigadier J. B. A. Glennie, Central Brigade Operations Instruction No. 1, 6 November 1963; TNA WO 291/2407. FARELF. G (Operational Requirements and Analysis) Branch. Report No. 1/69. Lessons learned from Borneo Operations, 17 March 1969; TNA WO 291/2524. FARELF. G (Operational Requirements and Analysis) Branch. Memorandum No. 1/68. Company bases in the Borneo Campaign, 1962–66, 9 February 1968.

and Sarawak. It was not remotely practical for the government had neither the administrators nor the money to carry it out. In May 1964, when they presented a bill for $416 million to the British, an official in the High Commission in Kuala Lumpur rejected the proposal with the comment that it was 'consummate nonsense'.[116] Consequently, by mid-1965 only about 1,100 families had been resettled.[117] In July, a further 1,277 families, or about 7,600 people, were forcibly resettled. This followed an attack by IBT insurgents, assisted by local CCO members, on a police station on the Kuching–Serian road of Sarawak. The Chinese community had given the security forces no assistance and resettlement was intended not only to forestall further attacks, but also to punish them.[118] But anything on a larger scale would have given Sukharno a major propaganda victory, for the target population in Sarawak was not, as in Malaya in the 1950s, illegal squatters, but people who had a legal title to their land.[119]

Forcible resettlement was briefly considered in Aden and quickly rejected. Not only would the cost be prohibitive, but the timing was wrong. Counter-insurgency through population control took several years to work. In Aden the British knew that they did not have that long.[120] Referring to Sheikh Othman, one of the most notorious suburbs of Aden city, the High Commissioner admitted in October 1965 that, 'We might be able to turn it into a model village by close control and lavish expenditure of money and effort but the project would take three years. Alternatively, by massive and indiscriminate deportations, we could make it fairly secure within three months. But second method would not do us much good in long-term.'[121]

Resettlement never seems even to have been considered in Cyprus. Not only would it have been prohibitively expensive, but Cyprus, like Palestine but unlike Malaya or Kenya, was under the constant scrutiny of critical foreign journalists. The level of coercion necessary to implement resettlement would have evoked a greater number of critical stories than the British government could stomach. Resettled communities also had to be protected. In Kenya and Malaya this was done by locally recruited home guards, but in Cyprus the propensity of EOKA to assassinate anyone suspected of helping the security forces meant that the Greek

[116] TNA DO 187/40. Abdul Razak to Lord Head, 22 May 1964; TNA DO 187/40. J. R. A. Bottomley to M. McMullen, 29 May 1964; TNA DO 187/40. M. McMullen to J. R. A. Bottomley, 2 June 1964.
[117] TNA DO 169/435. Note by CRO. Working party on aid for Malaysian Defence Expansion. Resettlement in Borneo, n.d. but *c*.10 May 1965.
[118] TNA WO 305/2547. Director of Borneo Operations weekly assessment of the threat to East Malaysia and Brunei, 26 June 1965 to 3 July 1965; TNA DO 169/435. Punitive regrouping—Kuching/Serian road area. Proposals by operations sub-committee Sarawak SSEC, 3 July 1965; TNA WO 305/2547. Director of Borneo Operations, Quarterly Operation Report, 1 April 1965 to 30 June 1965, 31 July 1965.
[119] TNA WO 305/2530. Minutes of the 15 meeting of Borneo Territories Security Executive Committee (Operations Sub-committee), 19 February 1964; TNA DO 187/68. G. A. T. Shaw to H. P. Hall, 14 July 1964; TNA DO 169/435. J. R. A. Bottomley to A. A. Golds, 21 August 1964.
[120] TNA CAB 148/23/OPD(65)143. A. R. Rushford and A. P. Cumming-Bruce, Report of Security Measures in Aden, 7 October 1965.
[121] TNA CO 1055/208. Turnbull to CO, 23 October 1965.

population was 'utterly intimidated'.[122] Any hope that the security forces could rely on the Turkish-Cypriot community to act as home guards was dashed in January 1958 when Turkish Cypriots, demonstrating in favour of partitioning the island, clashed with the security forces, and Governor Foot began to fear for the loyalty of the Turkish members of the police.[123] Resettlement also required a large number of loyal civil servants and administrators, which Cyprus also lacked. By early 1958, EOKA was mounting a campaign of civil disobedience and civil servants and civic leaders were resigning and were replaced by pro-EOKA men. Greek Cypriots were boycotting government services and substituting their own village committees for government authorities. Foot foresaw the possibility that the government's authority might simply ebb away.[124]

POPULATION CONTROL AND AERIAL PROSCRIPTION

In Malay and Kenya, the British were able to apply population control through forced resettlement because the target population was geographically accessible, because, albeit with some difficulty, they could find the necessary resources, and because the people they were corralling could not readily fight back. The same was also true, to a lesser extent, in Borneo. In Cyprus they could not follow the same policy because although the target population was accessible, the breakdown of relations between the Turkish community and the British in early 1958, and the crumbling of the administration due to EOKA intimidation meant that the government could not command the necessary resources. In addition the kind of measures that would have been required would have brought down upon their heads a torrent of international criticism.

In Oman between 1957 and 1959 and the Radfan in 1964, population control as practised in Kenya and Malay was impossible for different reasons. Both regions were geographically inaccessible, making operations by ground forces difficult. Money and administrators were in short supply. But more important than any of these constraints was the fact that the target populations were armed. Unlike Chinese squatters or KEM peasants, they were unlikely to allow themselves meekly to be put onto army lorries and taken away to begin a new life under government control. On the contrary, the appearance of government forces was likely to spark intense armed resistance. In October 1958 a War Office manual asserted that

> The inhabitants of tribal country are usually Moslem by religion. They are a poor, but hardy, race, brought up in an atmosphere of blood hereditary feuds. They are experts in the art of self-preservation and learn to handle a rifle at an early age. They have many good qualities, among which manliness, hospitality, a sturdy spirit of independence

---

[122] TNA DEFE 11/264. Acting Governor Cyprus to Colonial Secretary, 9 November 1957.
[123] TNA DEFE 11/264. Sir H. Foot to Colonial Secretary, 21 & 28 January 1958.
[124] TNA CO 926/1071. Sir H. Foot to Colonial Secretary, 12 March 1958.

and a good sense of humour predominate, but on the other hand they are often fanatical, cruel and treacherous, *and should always be treated with suspicion.*[125]

The official interpretation of the Jebel Akhdar campaign was that success owed almost everything to the skill, courage, and daring of two squadrons of the SAS who stormed the Jebel in February 1959. 'As for the enemy, they were conquered by surprise, not slaughter: a brilliant example of economy in the use of force.'[126] In a similar vein a senior British commander who led some of the ground forces in the Radfan in 1964 wrote after the operation that the concept that had underpinned it was that his troops had to seize the commanding heights in the region. Once they had done so not only would the insurgents' prestige and morale crumble, but they would fight to reoccupy them, in which case the British could employ their superior firepower to destroy them.[127] Both campaigns were thus portrayed as a fair fight between two groups of armed men. In reality they were nothing of the sort. The British had discovered a way to impose population control measures on geographically inaccessible armed people. If they could not operate easily on the ground, they could do so in the air. This was not new. In the inter-war period the British had shown little hesitation in employing 'air-policing' to impose their will on dissident indigenous groups, especially in the Middle East. Aerial sorties could wreak the same degree of physical damage far more rapidly and at a fraction of the cost of ground-based punitive expeditions.[128] After 1945 the military continued to believe that such operations had an important role. 'Air action', the authors of *Imperial Policing and Duties in Aid of the Civil Power, 1949* asserted,

particularly in undeveloped countries, can be the quickest, cheapest, and most convenient and humane means of imposing a sanction effectively. The severity of air action can be widely varied to suit the circumstances. A show of force alone may prove effective, but if force has to be used the required degree of accuracy and destruction may be achieved by choosing the appropriate weapon. But the difficulty of distinguishing between insurgents and innocent people in built-up areas may make use of offensive air action in urban situations undesirable.

In IS operations air power can have great moral effect on dissidents, particularly in case of native populations to whom it may be an unknown factor.[129]

In July 1957, after rebels had inflicted a major defeat on his forces, the Sultan of Oman asked the British for help. The Commander, British Forces Arabian Peninsula, Air Vice-Marshal M. L. Heath, suggested applying military pressure on the

---

[125] WO 279/742. General Staff, *Local Operations in Mountainous Country, 1958* (London: WO, October 1958). The italics were in the original.
[126] From our Military Correspondent, 'Insurgents surprised. Brilliant but little known British desert action', *Times*, 9 April 1959.
[127] Gen. Sir C. Blacker, *Monkey Business. The Memoirs of General Sir Cecil Blacker* (London: Quiller Press, 1993), 142–58.
[128] D. Omissi, *Air Power and Colonial Control. The Royal Air Force, 1919–1939* (Manchester: Manchester University Press, 1990); J. S. Corum, 'Air control. Reassessing the history', *Royal Air Force Air Power Review*, vol. 4 (2001), 15–36.
[129] TNA WO 279/391. WO, *Imperial Policing and Duties in Aid of the Civil Power, 1949* (London: War Office, 13 June 1949), 35.

insurgents through a calculated plan of escalating air operations. An alternative operation would have involved deploying a whole brigade, but so soon after Suez 'politically they [the British government] could not possibly allow a highly public thing like a brigade to become involved in a little colonial war.'[130] Instead, after locally raised troops had sealed off the dissident areas, aircraft would make demonstration flights and drop warning leaflets to intimidate them. Phase two would consist of more warning leaflets intended to give the dissidents a chance to get clear of the target area, followed by attacks on three forts, which were obvious military objectives. If that failed to induce them to surrender, air power would be used to impose a form of population control over the insurgents and their supporters. Aircraft would destroy civil society on the Jebel Akhdar by targeting the water supply of selected villages and by making it impossible for farmers to gather their harvest. The final phase would be implemented only if earlier operations did not bring the insurgents to heel. It would consist of what Heath euphemistically called the 'denial of selected villages by ultimatum under threat of air attack'.[131] What he meant was that, after yet another round of warning leaflets, the RAF would bomb the villages.[132]

The British pursued a similar policy in the Radfan in 1964. The Radfan was a mountainous region of the FSA, about 60 miles north of Aden. The main tribe in the area, the Quteibi, made their living from subsistence farming and levying protection money from travellers. But in 1962 a Federal customs union was introduced, which threatened their second source of revenue. Resenting any outside interference in their affairs, the Quteibi were happy to take arms from the Yemenis and Egyptians, and to attack symbols of the Federation, in particular forts manned by the Federal Regular Army.[133] The British were not prepared to see their authority flouted, fearing that if they did not act decisively in the Radfan, subversion would spread to other parts of the Federation.[134] Between January and August 1964 they mounted two expeditions. In January Operation NUTCRACK-ER was conducted by Federal forces with limited British ground and air support.[135] It was intended to arrest insurgent leaders, establish a firm base in the region, and compel the tribesmen to make a formal submission to the government. But the Federal forces proved too weak to hold the limited territorial gains they made. Thus, at the end of April a second, larger expedition, with more British ground and

[130] IWMSA. Accession No. 20888. Maj.-Gen. A. J. Deane-Drummond, reel 3.
[131] TNA DEFE 7/2415. Commander British Forces Arabian Peninsula to BDCC (Middle East) to COS, 21 July 1957.
[132] TNA DEFE 7/2415. Commander British Forces Arabian Peninsula to BDCC (Middle East), 24 July 1957.
[133] J. Walker, *Aden Insurgency. The Savage War in South Arabia, 1962–67* (Staplehurst, Kent: Spellmount, 2005), 74; TNA WO 386/22. Intelligence, n.d. but *c*.1 August 1964; TNA CO 1055/197. Trevaskis to CO, 22 & 26 December 1963; TNA CO 1055/200. Radfan Revolt, n.d. but *c*.17 April 1964.
[134] TNA CO 1055/197. Trevaskis to CO, 26 December 1963; TNA CO 1055/197. C-in-C Mideast to CDS, 28 December 1963.
[135] TNA CO 1055/198. Trevaskis to CO, 5 January 1964; TNA CO 1055/62. Trevaskis to Colonial Secretary, 12 February 1964. LIC Aden Int. Sum. for January 1964.

air support, was mounted.[136] The concept that underpinned the second operation was the same as that which had underpinned operations in Oman. As Trevaskis explained in a letter to Sir Charles Harington, the C-in-C MELF,

> Since we ourselves can seldom get to grips with the rebels, our only effective means of damaging them is through those on whose support they rely for food, lodging, information and all the miscellaneous services necessary for the conduct of their guerrilla warfare. In practical terms this means holding the tribal group in whose territory they are based responsible and bringing pressure on them to remove the rebels; making it clear, however, that similar measures will be brought to bear on any other tribal group which may subsequently receive them.[137]

If the British could not break the link between the insurgents and their supporters by placing the latter in wired-in villages, they could achieve the same objective by creating a famine, by attacking the villages that supported the insurgents and by destroying their food supplies. If the insurgents fought back and exposed themselves to the superior firepower of the British and their Federal allies, so much the better. During the first operation warning pamphlets had been dropped telling the inhabitants they had a day to move out of the area as air strikes with machine guns 'will be used to prevent any movement in the area'.[138] International criticism of a subsequent air attack on a Yemen military installation at Fort Harib meant that ministers were reluctant to allow commanders the same freedom of action in April.[139] However, the rules of engagement they agreed permitted air strikes and artillery fire against 'true military targets' or to ensure the safety of friendly ground forces, which gave commanders ample latitude to call down fire from the air. In May, after ground forces had encountered stiffer than expected resistance, ministers agreed to relax their prohibition on air strikes against civilian targets in the hope of bringing the operation to a rapid end.[140]

This policy was endorsed at the highest level of government. The Colonial Secretary, Duncan Sandys, went to Aden himself and agreed that before the second offensive began Radfani soldiers of the Federal army should be sent to the villages to warn people that they might be bombed. 'With some careful official briefing, these messengers could be relied upon to put the fear of death into the villages they visited. The message would quickly spread from village to village and would no

---

[136] CO 1055/199. Trevaskis to CO, 27 January 1964; TNA CO 1055/199. Trevaskis to CO, 30 January 1964; TNA CO 1055/200. HC Aden to CO, 21 March 1964.
[137] TNA CO 1055/1964. Trevaskis to Sir C. Harington, 5 April 1964.
[138] TNA CO 1055/199. Trevaskis to CO, 30 January 1964.
[139] TNA DEFE 13/569. Trevaskis to Colonial Secretary, 5 April 1964; TNA WO 386/22. Appendix 1. Political Directive, 29 April 1964; TNA CO 1055/194. CDS to C-in-C Mideast, 8 April 1964; TNA CO 1055/194/COS(64)29 meeting, 14 April 1964.
[140] TNA CO 1055/194. Acting CDS to Harington, 23 April 1964; TNA WO 386/22. Appendix 1. Political Directive, 29 April 1964; TNA CO 1055/194. C-in-C Mideast to Acting CDS, 1 May 1964; TNA CO 1055/194. Trevaskis to Colonial Secretary, 2 May 1964; TNA CO 1055/194/COS (64)33 meeting, 4 May 1964; TNA CO 1055/194. Trevaskis to Colonial Secretary, 7 May 1964; TNA CO 1055/194. Colonial Secretary to Trevaskis, 8 May 1964; TNA CAB 128/38/CM(64)27 meeting. Cabinet Conclusions, 12 May 1964; TNA CO 1055/194. Colonial Secretary to PM, 13 May 1964; TNA CAB 128/38/CM(64)28 meeting. Cabinet Conclusions, 14 May 1964.

doubt improve with the telling.'[141] Once this had been done and warning leaflets dropped, the proscribed area was subject to 'military control' measures. The political directive issued on the eve of the operation decreed that anything moving on the ground in a proscribed area, be it livestock or human, was fair game. In abandoned villages troops were to 'confiscate property, burn fodder, destroy grain, grain stores and livestock.' Standing crops were also to be destroyed.[142] According to the army's after-action report, 'Grain stores wherever found were burnt, and so were the thorn fences behind which livestock were kept. Livestock were either slaughtered humanely and eaten, or driven away to areas in which there was food and water. The inhabitants were firmly excluded from the controlled areas.' It can have been scant comfort to the tribesmen that 'No permanent damage of any kind was done to buildings, wells or agriculture, unless troops had been fired on from the area in question in which case installations there were of course subject to the risks of battle.'[143] Anyone trying to return to his home or fields was liable to be attacked by ground forces or air strikes.[144] British journalists summed up the policy as 'British try to starve out tribesmen' and '"Hunger War" on Radfan tribes'.[145]

Careful news management meant that there were no such press reports about the campaign in Oman. But intelligence reports indicated that, as well as destroying wells and water courses and killing goats and donkeys, mainstays of local agriculture, the bombing also killed people. How many of these casualties were armed insurgents, and how many were unarmed villagers is unknown.[146] What is clear is that the RAF wrecked the economic infrastructure on the Jebel Akhdar. By September 1958 intelligence estimates calculated that in four insurgent villages between a quarter and a third of their cultivated fields had been destroyed by air attacks, together with many water tanks and irrigation channels.[147] When the SAS arrived at the top of the Jebel in February 1959 they discovered that most of the villages had been destroyed, that cultivation had all but ceased, and that the villagers were facing imminent famine.[148]

The scale and intensity of air attacks suggests that while the force the British employed may have been 'necessary' it can scarcely be described as 'minimum'. In the Radfan the RAF flew 600 air sorties, fired 2,500 rockets and 200,000 cannon shells, and the Royal Artillery fired 20,000 rounds of artillery ammunition.[149] In Oman, employing a mixture of Shackleton maritime reconnaissance aircraft

---

[141] TNA CO 1055/194. Colonial Secretary to PM and Secretary of State for Defence to Harington, 11 May 1964.

[142] TNA WO 386/22. Appendix 1. Political Directive, 29 April 1964.

[143] TNA WO 386/22. Operations in Radfan, 14 April 1964 to 30 June 1964, 1 August 1964.

[144] CO 1055/195. Higham to Huijsman, 27 August 1964.

[145] IWMDoD. 92/15/1. Brig. D. F. A. T. Baines, 'Gunners in South Arabia'; C. Hollingworth, 'British try to starve out tribesmen', *Guardian*, 16 May 1964; TNA CO 1055/201. R. Beeston, '"Hunger War" on Radfan tribes', *Sunday Telegraph*, 1 June 1964.

[146] DEFE 7/2416. British Resident Bahrain to GHQ MELF, 15 & 22 August 1958.

[147] TNA DEFE 7/2413. Political Resident Bahrain, to MOD, 26 September 1958.

[148] LHCMA Maj.-Gen. A. J. Deane-Drummond mss. Deane-Drummond to Hamilton, 12 February 1959; *idem*, Report on reconnaissance operation on the Jebel Akhdar (13–24 February 59).

[149] Walker, *Aden Insurgency*, 110.

carrying 500 lb bombs, and Vampire jets equipped with 60 lb rockets and cannons, the RAF flew 1,635 sorties between July and December 1958 and dropped 1,094 tons of bombs and fired 900 rockets. That was more than twice the weight of bombs that the Luftwaffe dropped on Coventry in November 1940.[150] But, by disclosing the presence of the SAS after the operation was over, the Ministry of Defence could conceal that fact from the wider world, while the SAS was able to use its apparent success to justify its continued existence just as the Malayan campaign was winding down and its future was threatened by the Sandys reforms of the structure of the army.[151]

In the Radfan, just as in Malaya, Kenya, and parts of Sarawak, the British had conducted counter-insurgency by targeting a whole ethnic group and transforming them into refugees, a word that actually began to appear in operational situation reports in May 1964.[152] A senior British official estimated that by April 1964 half of the 20,000 people living in the Radfan had become refugees, and that by August 'There is probably some malnutrition since area is poor, but no signs of actual starvation.'[153] The one difference was that, whereas in Malaya, Kenya and Sarawak the colonial authorities resettled the refugees, in Oman and the Radfan they did not. British officials in Aden knew this, and tried to hide it from the outside world. In early May 1964, Major-General J. H. Cubbon, the GOC Land Forces Aden, had told a press conference that 'all our operations up to now are governed by an embargo on any form of attack on a village', a statement that was hardly consistent with the spirit of the political directive under which the ground forces were operating.[154] The acting High Commissioner was, therefore, most anxious to do all he could to block a proposed inspection of the Radfan by representatives of the ICRC, pointing out to the Colonial Office that

the operations in Radfan, by their very nature, have involved the entire population. Refugees from Radfan had been absorbed into neighbouring, mostly unadministered, tribal areas. When refugees have entered administered areas the Federal Government have allowed them to follow their own choice, i.e. to make their own arrangements in tribal areas. After an initial abortive effort to set up refugee centres, the Federal Government avoided getting involved in creating formal refugee camps and all the miseries they entail, but the refugees have been able to enjoy health and other services not available to them in Radfan. In the context of Arabian tribal life this absorption does not present the same degree of difficulty or hardship that it would in more sophisticated urban societies. Nevertheless, to anyone not versed in the grinding poverty of Radfan in times of peace, the apparent side-effects of out military operations might well seem distressing.[155]

[150] TNA DEFE 7/2314. Background notes for the Minister's information only, n.d. but *c*.12 & 20 January 1959.
[151] IWMSA. Accession No. 20888. Maj.-Gen. A. J. Deane-Drummond, reel 3.
[152] TNA DEFE 11/498. Harington to CDS, 25 May & 1 June 1964.
[153] TNA CO 1055/201. Acting British Agent, WAP, to Foreign Office, 10 November 1964.
[154] TNA DEFE 13/569. Scott Reid to Brigadier Hobbs, 3 May 1964.
[155] TNA CO 1055/260. Acting High Commissioner to Monson, 29 August 1964.

Without the establishment of a permanent security framework allied to the close administration of the population, aerial proscription might damage the insurgents, but it could not stop them regenerating themselves. In Oman the insurgent leaders evaded their SAS pursuers and escaped to Saudi Arabia. By December 1959 they were once again able to mount bomb attacks, one of which went off under the bed of the Omani Minister of the Interior.[156] The insurgents in the Radfan also survived to continue fighting. Lack of troops meant that it was impossible for the security forces to maintain a permanent framework in the Radfan.[157] By March 1965 bands of insurgents between 50 and 60 strong were moving about at night, kidnapping Federal government officials, and attacking government posts and mining roads.[158]

CASUALTIES

Table 4.2 gives some indication of the degree of force that the security forces employed in 11 operations discussed in this book.

Security force casualties included members of the army, the police and, where applicable, the home guard. Insurgent casualties included those people who were killed or wounded and classified by the security forces as taking part in armed attacks on the security forces. Civilians included members of the public killed or wounded by either the insurgents or the security forces.

These statistics must be treated with a good deal of caution. This is especially so in the case of insurgent casualties. The statistics were collected by the security forces, and in the heat of battle it was far from easy for even regular armies and police forces, with all their accompanying bureaucracy, to maintain accurate counts. Furthermore, as will be shown in the next chapter, there is reason to believe that not every corpse that the security forces reported as an insurgent was in fact so. The most that can be claimed for these figures is that they give a rough and ready approximation of the order of magnitude of the loses sustained by each party in active operations. Except in the case of Kenya, we have no statistics for those civilians and insurgents who died from disease or malnutrition caused by security forces operations.[159]

But even in the light of these caveats, the table sheds some light on how the security forces interpreted the principle of 'minimum necessary force'. In the Canal Zone and, to a lesser extent, Aden, there was a close approximation between security forces and insurgent casualties. In Palestine and Cyprus, security forces losses outnumbered those of the insurgents by a considerable margin, although some of the civilian casualties listed in both of these campaigns, as well as in Aden, probably ought to be included in the column of insurgent casualties, as they

---

[156] *Times*, 14 December 1959.
[157] TNA DEFE 11/500. Acting High Commissioner to CO, 9 September 1964.
[158] TNA CO 1055/202. Sir R. Turnbull to CO, 11 March 1965.
[159] J. Blacker, 'The demography of Mau Mau', 205–27.

Table 4.2: Casualties[a]

Campaign	Security force casualties	Insurgent casualties	Civilian casualties
Palestine[b]	1,016	63	493
Malaya[c]	4,341	9,158	4,651
Canal Zone[d]	90	102	–
Kenya[e]	1,166	10,502–20,000	25,000[f]
British Guiana	0	0	0
Cyprus[g]	944	90	823
Oman[h]	133	233	–
Nyasaland[i]	6	130	19[j]
Aden[k]	1,112	1,348[l]	1,059
Brunei[m]	35	50–60	–
Indonesian Confrontation[n]	251	643	42

[a] Casualties are defined as persons killed, wounded, and missing as a result of active military operations. They do not include members of insurgent forces who were captured by the security forces, or, except in the case of Kenya, people who died from disease or malnutrition as a result of forced population resettlement. A dash means that no evidence has come to light.

[b] Charters, *The British Army*, 205. Figures for security forces casualties are combined for army and police and are for the period 31 Oct. 1945 to 31 July 1947 and for 1 Jan. to 7 June 1948. See WO 162/300. Adjutant-General, Statistics, Casualties in Palestine, 15 June 1948.

[c] TNA WO 106/5990. Director of Operations Malaya, Review of the Emergency in Malaya from June 1948 to Aug. 1957, Sept. 1957.

[d] TNA WO 236/8. Problems in the Canal Zone after the abrogation of the 1936 treaty, n.d. but c.1952.

[e] TNA WO 291/1670. Operational Research Unit (Far East). Report Number 1/57. A comparison of the emergencies in Malaya and Kenya, 6 June 1957. These figures are for the period from 20 Oct. 1952 to 12 May 1956. Anderson gives figures of at least 12,000 and perhaps more than 20,000 for Mau Mau Casualties. Anderson, *Histories of the Hanged*, 4.

[f] J. Blacker, 'The demography of Mau Mau: fertility and mortality in Kenya in the 1950s: a demographer's viewpoint', *African Affairs*, vol. 106 (2007), 205–27.

[g] TNA CO 926/1077. Report on the Cyprus Emergency, 1959.

[h] J. E. Petersen, *Oman's Insurgencies. The Sultanate's Struggle for Supremacy* (London: Saqi, 2007), 136–7. Figures are for the period Jan. 1958 to Jan. 1959.

[i] TNA CAB 129/98/C(59)124. Secretary of State for the Colonies, Nyasaland Commission of Inquiry, 17 July 1959. Report of the Nyasaland Commission of Inquiry. Figures for 20 Feb. to 19 Mar. 1959.

[j] TNA CO 1015/1517. Armitage to Secretary of State, 25 Mar. 1959.

[k] TNA CAB 148/31/OPD(67)19. South Arabia. Problems of preparing for independence, 8 Mar. 1967. Annex D. Comparative Table of casualties. Figures for the period Jan. 1964 to 21 Feb. 1967.

[l] Combined figure for killed and wounded in Aden State and the remainder of the Federation.

[m] *Manchester Guardian*, 21 Dec. 1962. Figures for the period 8–20 Dec. 1962

[n] TNA WO 305/3327. Director of Borneo Operations to Commander-in-Chief FE, 11 Sept. 1966. Figures for the period from 11 April 1963 to 31 Aug. 1966.

included insurgent sympathizers injured in the course of anti-government riots and demonstrations. But in Malaya, Kenya, Nyasaland, and the Brunei/Indonesian Confrontation, the reverse was the case. The security forces inflicted far more casualties on the insurgents than they suffered themselves. This suggests that there were two kinds of counter-insurgency campaigns. There were those, such as Palestine, the Canal Zone, Cyprus, and British Guiana, where the security forces operated under constraints, legal and otherwise, that limited the amount of lethal force they could employ, and there were those, such as Malaya, Kenya, Oman, Nyasaland, and Eastern Malaysia, where those constraints were in practice much weaker. Aden seems to fall awkwardly between these two categories. Restraints appear to have operated during most operations in Aden State, but were less in evidence in up-country operations such as the Radfan campaign. But, in general the table supports the argument developed in Chapter 3 that the principle of 'minimum necessary force' was elastic, both in law and in its interpretation. In several instances the practical emphasis seems to have been placed on what the security forces considered to be 'necessary', rather than on what they thought was an acceptable 'minimum'. However, even with that qualification in mind, none of the raw casualty figures for any British counter-insurgency come close to matching what happened in Algeria. Between 1954 and 1962 between 143,000 and 153,000 insurgent died, and the Algerian Muslim population as a whole suffered about 300,000 casualties, both conservative estimates.[160]

The degree of force the security forces employed depended to a large extent on what their opponents did. In general, when confronted by a riot, the initial recourse was to employ exemplary or non-lethal force. This included the use of tear gas, or 'tear smoke' as the COS, sensitive to the political implications of using any kind of gas, insisted it should be called.[161] In June 1948, following the Gold Coast riots, Creech Jones reminded every colony and protectorate that, 'it is a general principle that the police and (if they are called upon) the military, should employ only the minimum degree of force necessary to restore order or protect life and property in the event of riots, and that recourse should be had in the use of firearms only as a last resort', adding that 'One of the most effective and humane weapons available against rioting crowds is tear smoke.'[162] Most colonies held stocks of tear gas, and trained their police in its use and Ministers remained convinced for the next twenty years that it was the preferable method of crowd dispersal.[163]

For a long time the army remained wedded to its doctrine that if the police could not contain a situation and summoned their help, soldiers should be armed with their normal weapons, in which case 'When employed upon Internal Security duties if the Army uses its weapons it must shoot to kill.'[164] One reason that

---

[160] M. Thomas, 'Algeria's violent struggle for independence', in M. Thomas, B. Moore, and L. J. Butler, *Crises of Empire. Decolonization and Europe's Imperial States, 1918–1975* (London: Hodder Education, 2008), 229–30.

[161] TNA WO 106/5176. COS to ALFSEA, 9 November 1945; TNA CO 537/1719. High Commissioner Palestine to Colonial Secretary, 3 July 1946; TNA WO 261/640. 1 Infantry Division. Report on operation Hermon, 17–18 August 1946; TNA CO 537/2712. Creech Jones to all Colonies and Protectorates, 24 June 1948; TNA CO 537/2712. Governor Nyasaland to Colonial Secretary, 3 August 1948; TNA CO 537/2712. Commissioner of Police, Northern Rhodesia to CO, 16 June 1948.

[162] TNA CO 537/2712. Creech Jones to all Colonies and Protectorates, 24 June 1948.

[163] TNA WO 106/5176. COS to ALFSEA, 9 November 1945; TNA CO 537/1719. High Commissioner Palestine to Colonial Secretary, 3 July 1946; TNA WO 261/640. 1 Infantry Division. Report on operation Hermon, 17–18 August 1946; TNA CO 537/2712. Creech Jones to all Colonies and Protectorates, 24 June 1948; TNA CO 537/2712. Governor Nyasaland to Colonial Secretary, 3 August 1948; TNA CO 537/2712. Commissioner of Police, Northern Rhodesia to CO, 16 June 1948; TNA CO 537/2712. Governor Cyprus to Creech Jones, 16 August 1948; TNA CO 537/2712. Governor Aden to Creech Jones, 27 August 1948; TNA CO 537/4401. Memorandum, 20 May 1949; TNA CO 537/6964. Secretariat, Grenada to H. Beckett, 11 December 1951; TNA CO 1055/221. A. Greenwood to P. Stein, 10 November 1965.

[164] TNA WO 216/811. DMO to VCIGS, ? November 1952.

they adhered to this doctrine was their fear that colonial governments would be even less ready than they already were to spend their own money on an adequate police force if they knew that troops could easily be substituted for policemen.[165] But the collapse of the Cyprus police in 1955 meant that Harding had no option but to call on the army to take their place, and the army had no option other than to co-operate, even forming combined police–army riot squads armed with a mixture of rifles, batons, and tear gas.[166]

But just because they were armed with lethal weapons did not mean that soldiers in a riot automatically used them with intent to kill. In the Canal Zone the army had neither batons nor tear gas, but they adopted their own practices in an attempt to minimize casualties. When rioters attacked the houses of British service families in Ismailia on 16 October 1951, 1/Lancashire Fusiliers restored order by trying to intimidate the rioters. They advanced steadily towards them with fixed bayonets and fired bursts from their sten guns into the ground at what they hoped was a safe distance from the crowd. It worked. The noise of the gunfire frightened the crowd into dispersing and there were few casualties.[167] Some units devised novel ways of dispersing rioting crowds. When 1/Parachute Regiment carried out riot duties in Nicosia in late 1955–6 they called at the local Coca-Cola factory and picked up a couple of gross of Coca-Cola bottles. The bottles were made from thick green glass and

> If we expected to get involved in a riot of hostile Greek Cypriots, we left the Coke bottles in the backs of trucks to 'cook' in the hot sun. When a riot got under way, we grabbed a few of these bottles, gave the Coke a good shake and then threw them in the air so that they dropped just in front of the demonstrators. The bottles exploded like hand grenades and laid a carpet of thick glass across the street.[168]

But if they were shot at, the security forces shot back. In October 1955 a crowd in the Cypriot town of Morphou marched on the police station. Shots were fired at the building, and someone in the crowd threw a bomb which wounded three soldiers of 1/Gordon Highlanders. The Gordons then displayed a banner bearing the words 'Disperse or we fire'. When the crowd ignored this, the soldiers fired warning shots over their heads, but the stone throwing only intensified, and they then fired into the crowd, wounding three youths.[169]

In those emergencies, such as Malaya and Kenya, where free fire zones had been established, the security forces had little compunction about employing the full range of their weapons. Most insurgent casualties were probably caused by small arms fire, but commanders were not always chary about using heavier weapons.

---

[165] TNA WO 296/23. E. M. Bastyn to DMO, 8 March 1956.
[166] TNA WO 296/23. Enc. 'Report on the employment of troops in the police role', n.d. but *c*.March 1956.
[167] Anon., 'The Lancs & the tanks go into action'. Accessed 28 April 2002 at http://www.britains-smallwars.com/Canal/ISMAILIA-RIOTS.htm; TNA WO 236/8. Problems in the Canal Zone after the abrogation of the 1936 treaty, n.d. but *c*.1952.
[168] B.Hunter, 'EOKA meets the Parachute Regiment', Downloaded 20 April 2009 at http://www.britains-smallwars.com/cyprus/Davidcarter/hunter/arealisticapproach.html.
[169] *Manchester Guardian*, 29 October 1955.

Erskine's readiness to use the main armament of Centurion tanks at Ismalia in January 1952, and the use of RAF bombers in Oman and the Radfan have already been noted. In Borneo each company base situated along the frontier with Kalimantan had either one or two howitzers to provide close support. They were kept well employed. In one three-month period the guns attached to a single brigade fired nearly 10,000 rounds.[170] Confronted by opponents hiding in dense jungle, it was never likely that artillery or aircraft in Malaya or Kenya would be able to destroy pinpoint targets.[171] But the British did employ aircraft to harass insurgent forces and deny them opportunities to rest.[172] Offensive air strikes achieved little. In Malaya, intelligence reports indicated that aerial attacks accounted for only about 10 per cent of insurgent casualties.[173] In Kenya, when he was pressed to justify using Lincoln heavy bombers, Erskine admitted that the thick tree cover meant that it was not easy to provide tangible proof of the results of bombing. But captured insurgents said that the air strikes had caused heavy losses, the threat of air attacks had forced gangs to split up into small groups and had lowered their morale.[174] That may have been true but the very presence of spotter aircraft also warned Mau Mau gangs of the presence of troops and gave them the opportunity to hide.[175] Most aircraft sorties did not involve the delivery of lethal munitions. Aircraft were used to transport troops, evacuate casualties, perform reconnaissance missions, drop supplies, and assist in psychological warfare operations by relaying messages to insurgents via loud speakers.[176]

[170] TNA WO 305/2541. Director of Borneo Operations, Quarterly Operation Report, 1 October 1964 to 31 December 1964, 27 January 1965; TNA WO 305/3326. Director of Borneo Operations, Quarterly Operation Report, 1 January 1966 to 31 March 1966, 16 April 1966; TNA WO 291/2407. FARELF. G (Operational Requirements and Analysis) Branch, Report No. 1/69. Lessons learned from Borneo Operations, 17 March 1969.

[171] TNA CAB 21/1681/MAL.C(50)21. Secretary of State for War, Malaya Committee, The military situation in Malaya, 17 June 1950.

[172] TNA WO 291/1670. Operational Research Unit (Far East). Report Number 1/57. A comparison of the emergencies in Malaya and Kenya, 6 June 1957; TNA CAB 21/1682/MAL.C (50)31. Note by the Secretary of State for War to the Malaya Committee, Report on the visit of the Australian Military Mission to Malaya: July to August, 1950, 12 October 1950; TNA WO 216/874. Lt.-Gen. Sir G. Bourne, Director of Operations, Directive, February 1955, 14 February 1955.

[173] J. Gordon Simpson, 'Not by bombs alone', *Joint Forces Quarterly* (1999), 95. See also K. Perkins, *A Fortunate Soldier* (London: Brassey's, 1988), 50–2; P. Cross, *'A Face Like a Chicken's Backside'. An Unconventional Soldier in South East Asia, 1948–1971* (London: Greenhill Books, 1996), 39–42; Wing-Commander B. J. Hunt, 'Air Power and Psychological Warfare Operations Malaya 1948–1960', *Air Power Review*, vol. 11 (2008), 15–16.

[174] TNA CO 822/475. Erskine to MOD, 29 December 1953; TNA WO 236/18. Erskine to Governor Kenya and other Kenya government officials, CIGS and Military Members Army Council, Colonial Secretary, etc., 25 April 1955.

[175] TNA WO 276/518. Some points of operational value from the interrogation of 'Brigadier' Thurura, n.d. but *c*.26 April 1956.

[176] A. Mumford, 'Unnecessary or unsung? The utilisation of airpower in Britain's colonial counterinsurgencies', *SW&I*, vol. 20 (2009), 636–55; D. Jordan, 'Counter-insurgency from the air: the postwar lessons', in T. Benbow and R. Thornton (eds), *Dimensions of Counter-insurgency. Applying Experience to Practice* (London: Routledge, 2008), 90–105.

CONCLUSION

The British conducted their counter-insurgency campaigns within the law. But it was a law that they largely created themselves, and it was one that left them with wide latitude to act coercively yet legally. It was not until the second half of the 1950s, as Chapter 8 will show, that international law really began to constrain what they could do. In the meantime coercion was the mainstay of British counter-insurgency practice. The manner and degree to which it was employed varied from place to place. Measured by the number of people detained or insurgents who became casualties, the British behaved at their most benign in British Guiana, and at their most vicious in Kenya. The concept of 'minimum necessary force' was ill-defined both in theory and in practice. In Kenya and Malaya, Oman and the Radfan it did not prevent the security forces from employing a great deal of force. Other campaigns fell between these two extremes. But what the raw and imperfect statistics in Tables 4.1 and 4.2 cannot demonstrate is the degree of psychological insecurity that security force operations inflicted on the civil population. Apparently arbitrary stop and search operations, unpredictable curfews, the daily fear of arrest and interrogation, not to mention the occasional destruction of property, combined, as they were intended to do, to intimidate people. Forced resettlement and food denial operations in Malaya and Kenya not only denied food to the insurgents, they also made it very clear to the civil population that the government now had the whip hand over them.

The claim that the British conducted counter-insurgency campaigns in ways that were somehow more gentle than other colonial powers need to be treated with some caution. The British forcibly resettled a higher proportion of their 'target' populations than did the French or Portuguese, although they killed fewer people than the French. In Algeria the French state employed several of the same methods that the British employed, including the use of various types of exemplary force, the creation of free fire zones, and the forcible resettlement of large numbers of people. The military conduct of campaigns in Oman and the Radfan bore some striking similarities to the French use of razzia in Algeria, 'an attack with overwhelming force against unprepared herdsmen or settlements'.[177] It has also been argued that the commitment of the French colonial state to its own 'Guerre révolutionnaire' theory led inevitably to a parallel commitment to the systematic use of torture.[178] The next chapter will determine whether the British followed them and went beyond state-sanctioned coercion to mount 'dirty wars'.

---

[177] T. Rid, 'Razzia: a turning point in modern strategy', *Terrorism and Political Violence*, vol. 21 (2009), 618.
[178] Lazreg, *Torture and the Twilight of Empire*, 15–33.

5

Britain's 'Dirty Wars'?

At dawn on 8 February 1954 soldiers of 1/Royal Northumberland Fusiliers entered a village near Nairobi, paraded the inhabitants, and asked them to reveal in confidential questionnaires what they knew about the Mau Mau. The regimental band brought a holiday atmosphere to the proceedings and when the forms had been completed the troops gave the villagers tea and buns. One villager told a journalist afterwards 'The gentle treatment, kindness and courtesy of the soldiers and police to-day made a profound impression on all of us. I am sure many of us were able to give valuable information to the authorities under this system of secrecy. In the past we have all been afraid of Mau Mau reprisals if we talked.'[1] Thirteen years later the same unit was serving in Aden, where another journalist saw another side of British counter-insurgency operations. After a grenade had exploded and wounded two members of a patrol

> Across the road Corporal Harry Oliver holds a bloody knee with his left hand as he shouts 'Halt', first in English, then in Arabic, to a man running along a culvert. The man stops at the Arabic command and raises his hands. More Arabs are rounded up. The tough young men of Tyneside are in [an] ugly mood on this second day of the terrorist offensive. To understand just how they feel you need to be in Crater with them, not on the back benches of Parliament in Westminster. There's a lot of boot, gun butt and fist thumping. It isn't a display of brutality—it's a show of righteous human anger.[2]

These were the two faces of counter-insurgency at street level. A free concert and tea and buns looked like 'hearts and minds' in action. Lashing out with gun butts, fists, and boots looked like coercion in its most naked form. The same dichotomy is reflected in the literature, with some writers insisting that behaviour like that just recounted in Aden was the exception, with others claiming that the British sometimes descended to the level of fighting a 'dirty war'.[3]

---

[1] *Manchester Guardian*, 9 February 1954.
[2] S. Harper, *Last Sunset. What Happened in Aden* (London: Collins, 1978), 85.
[3] For contrasting views see Lt.-Col. M. Dewar, *Brush Fire Wars. Minor Campaigns of the British Army since 1945* (London: Robert Hale, 1984), 26; and D. Anderson, *Histories of the Hanged. Britain's Dirty War in Kenya and the End of Empire* (London: Weidenfeld & Nicolson, 2005), the subtitle of which is apposite.

DEFINITIONS AND ALLEGATIONS

Any examination of these issues raises problems of how to define a 'dirty war'. At its most basic level, it implies that members of the security forces operated outside the confines of the law. This is a useful starting point, but only if it is remembered that the law, as it operated during colonial emergencies, had been deliberately manufactured by the colonial state in ways that allowed the security forces latitude to violate many widely accepted human rights. But at least the legal regimes created by regulations issued under the 1939 Order-in-Council and related local legislation did establish minimum standards of conduct to which the security forces were expected to adhere. Nor did soldiers escape from the constraints of the civil law when they donned a uniform. They could be found guilty of offences such as murder, assault, and theft in the same way as any civilian.[4] Furthermore, Article 3 of the 'Geneva Convention relative to the Protection of Civilian Persons in Time of War', laid down that prisoners and detainees should in no circumstances be subjected to

(a) Violence to life and person, in particular murder of all kinds, mutilation, cruel treatment and torture;

(b) Taking of hostages;

(c) Outrages upon personal dignity, in particular humiliating and degrading treatment;

(d) The passing of sentences and the carrying out of executions without previous judgement pronounced by a regularly constituted court, affording all the judicial guarantees which are recognized as indispensable by civilized peoples.[5]

The British did not accede to the Convention and were not bound by its obligations until September 1957. But they were a party to the UN's Universal Declaration of Human Rights, promulgated in 1948, and the European Convention on Human Rights of 1950, which imposed similar obligations.[6] Together the emergency regulations, the Declaration and the ECHR placed certain kinds of behaviour beyond the pale. The extent to which colonial and military authorities knew of instances when members of the security forces had broken these rules, and either condoned or encouraged them to do so, was a measure of their readiness to go beyond waging counter-insurgency by state coercion, and to wage a 'dirty war'.[7]

---

[4] War Office, *MML. Part 1. 1956* (London: HMSO, 1956), 129–96.

[5] War Office, *The Law of War on Land being Part II of the Manual of Military Law* (London: HMSO, 1958), Appendix XIV: 'Geneva Convention relative to the Protection of Civilian Persons in Time of War', Article 3.

[6] Article 3, The European Convention on Human Rights, downloaded 7 February 2010 at www. hri.org/docs/ECHR50.html; 'Universal Declaration of Human Rights', www.un.org/en/documents/ udhr/, downloaded 7 February 2010.

[7] For a helpful discussion of the concept of 'dirty war' see M. L. R. Smith and S. Roberts, 'War in the gray: exploring the concept of dirty war', *Studies in Conflict & Terrorism*, vol. 31 (2008), 377–98.

In public the authorities always insisted that the security forces must maintain strict discipline, whatever provocation they faced.[8] They repeatedly warned the security forces that they must operate within the law, and threatened to hold to account any who did not do so.[9] Army officers under training were told of the importance of maintaining strict discipline and ensuring that the conduct of their men was beyond reproach.[10] Commanders in the field issued similar injunctions.[11] In February and April 1953 the Kenyan government issued an order 'to make it clear, to the public generally, as has already been explained to all ranks of the Security Forces, that it utterly condemns and will not tolerate acts of indiscipline involving the unlawful causing of death or injury, the rough handling of members of the public, suspects, or prisoners, or the misappropriation of or damage to their property.'[12] In Cyprus Harding ensured that 'Instructions have been issued that damage to property is, so far as possible, to be avoided,' and policemen were attached to units to investigate allegations that soldiers had misbehaved during cordon and search operations.[13]

There were instances when members of the security forces were held legally accountable for their actions. In March 1948 an NCO and four soldiers of the Highland Light Infantry were court martialled on a charge of having killed four Haganah men, a deed they were accused of doing in retaliation for the death of several of their comrades.[14] A policeman serving in South Perak found guilty by a court of torturing a suspect was sentenced to a long term of imprisonment.[15] A Malayan policeman was arrested after it was discovered that he had planted evidence on a Chinese peasant involved with him in a love triangle.[16] In Kenya by February 1954 there had been 130 prosecutions brought against the

---

[8] Maj. R. D. Wilson, *Cordon and Search. With 6th Airborne Division in Palestine* (Aldershot: Gale & Polden, 1949), vii. Foreword by Maj.-Gen. H. C. Stockwell; TNA CO 1015/1495. Draft of a letter to be signed by Secretary of State for Commonwealth Relations to Sir Roy Welensky and Sir Edgar Whitehead, n.d. but *c*.27 April 1959; TNA WO 32/20987. Colonel, GS, MO4 to Head of DS 6, The Bowen report, 21 November 1966.

[9] WO, *MML 1951–59. Part II. 1951. Section V. Employment of Troops in Aid of the Civil Power* (London: HMSO, 1955); TNA WO 279/470. General Staff, *Duties in Aid of the Civil Power, 1937. Reprint incorporating amendments (No. 1) 1945* (London: War Office, 1945), chapter 1;TNA WO 279/391. WO, *Imperial Policing and Duties in Aid of the Civil Power, 1949* (London: War Office, 13 June 1949), chapter 1; TNA WO 296/23. General Staff, *Keeping the Peace. (Duties in Support of the Civil Power)* (London: War Office, 1957), ch. 2; TNA WO 279/241. Director of Operations, Malaya, *Conduct of Anti-terrorist Operations in Malaya* (Kuala Lumpur: 3rd edn, 1958), chapter 4.

[10] LHCMA Sir Hugh Stockwell Mss 6/26/9. Lecture, Paragraph headings, n.d. but *c*.1949; IWMDoD. Gen. Sir G. W. Erskine mss 75/134/3. Erskine, Lecture to the Joint Services Staff College. Military Aspects of the Cold War, n.d.

[11] TNA WO 169/19566. Brigadier RAC to CGS, MELF, Notes on IS Duties with armoured units, 6 November 1945; TNA CO 1015/1523. Nyasaland Government, *Instructions to Civil Officers, Military Officers, and Police Officers on the use of Armed Force in Case of Civil Disturbances, 1958* (Government Printer, Zombe, 1958).

[12] TNA WO 32/21721. Press Office Handout no. 68, 17 April 1953; TNA CO 822/474. Kikuyu disorder. Directive by the Governor, 11 February 1953.

[13] TNA CO 926/396. Harding to Colonial Secretary, 20 January 1956; IWMSA. Accession No. 16064. J. Taylor, reels 2, 5.

[14] *Palestine Post*, 17 March & 3 October 1948.

[15] T. Hatton, *Tock Tock Birds* (Lewis, Sussex: Book Guild, 2004), 126.

[16] IWMSA. Accession No. 31504. K. Thorley, reel 3.

police for brutality, 40 cases were pending, and 73 convictions had been secured.[17] In February 1956, after he had shot a youth, a corporal in Cyprus was tried before a civilian court on a charge of murder, although he was subsequently found to have acted in self-defence and was acquitted.[18] Two months later two army officers were less fortunate. They were found guilty by a court martial of assaulting two prisoners and were dismissed from the army.[19] In Nyasaland an inquest found a private of the KAR guilty of manslaughter in March 1959. He had shot an African riding on a bicycle who had refused to halt when he ordered him to do so.[20] In Aden a soldier who had killed an Adeni by hitting him over the head with an iron bar after hearing that some friends had been victims of an insurgent attack, was found guilty of culpable homicide and sentenced to 10 years' imprisonment.[21]

These cases suggest that the authorities did try to ensure that the security forces operated within the law and punished those who broke the rules. But there were a plethora of complaints that they did not do so. They fell into two categories. Soldiers and policemen were accused of employing unnecessary violence, of theft, and of wantonly destroying private property. In December 1946 a Palestine newspaper reported an attack on the village of Masmiya in Gaza district by 'A group of English-speaking soldiers' who, it alleged, opened fire for no good reason.[22] In January 1959 troops searching the village of Argos in Cyprus were accused of injuring 30 people and that 'the extent of the ill-treatment, hardships, humiliation, and suffering to human life cannot be described'.[23] In July 1967, 700 leading citizens in Aden signed a petition citing numerous instances when peaceful citizens 'were "beat up, shot, robbed, harassed, abused, insulted and degraded" by security forces in the name of carrying out their responsibilities'.[24] The security forces were also accused of deliberately ill-treating prisoners. In July 1946 a member of the executive of the Jewish Agency in London described what he called 'mediaeval torture' being practiced by the police at Athlit detention camp in Palestine.[25] Reports smuggled out of prison by Irgun detainees in 1947 claimed that they had been systematically beaten by soldiers and policemen and denied medical treatment.[26] In late October 1955 Athens Radio broadcast a letter said to have been written by an EOKA detainee in which he accused the Superintendent of

---

[17] TNA CAB 21/2906. [Cmd. 9081] *Report to the Colonial Secretary by the Parliamentary Delegation to Kenya in January 1954*, February 1954.

[18] IWMDoD. 86/85/1. Maj. C. R. Butt, 'Cyprus Drafts (I)', 40.

[19] *Times*, 4, 6, 7, & 9 April 1956; C. Foley and W. I. Scobie, *The Struggle for Cyprus* (Stanford, CA: Hoover Institution Press, 1975), 73–4; N. Crawshaw, *The Cyprus Revolt* (London: Allen & Unwin, 1978), 179.

[20] TNA CAB 129/98/C(59)124. Colonial Secretary, Nyasaland Commission of Inquiry, 17 July 1959.

[21] TNA CO 1055/280. High Commissioner Aden to CO, 2 December 1964; TNA CO 1055/280. Reuters telegram, 23–25 February 1965; TNA CO 1055/280. Turnbull to CO, 19 March 1965.

[22] TNA WO 275/72. BGI to 6 Airborne Division. Palestine Press, 26 November 1946.

[23] *Times*, 27 January 1959.

[24] *Times*, 24 July 1967; *Manchester Guardian*, 17 July 1967.

[25] TNA CO 537/1719. Colonial Secretary to High Commissioner, 3 July 1946; *Times*, 3 July 1946.

[26] M. Begin, *The Revolt* (London: W. H. Allen, rev. edn, 1979; first published 1952), 269–72.

Prisons and the Turkish warders of engaging in 'cannibalistic actions' against prisoners.[27] Interrogators were alleged to have beaten prisoners, extracted their teeth without an anaesthetic, made them stand on ice during interrogations, flogged and burnt them, and injected them with truth serum.[28] Detainees in Nyasaland complained they had been handcuffed in pairs, made to sit on the floor for eight hours with their hands on their head, and beaten by prison officers.[29] In Aden 35 detainees held at the Fort Morbut interrogation centre in December 1965 gave evidence to a Special Branch investigation alleging they had been tortured.[30]

The colonial authorities responded in several different ways to such charges. Some allegations made against members of the security forces were so vague that it was impossible to prove whether they were true or propaganda fabrications.[31] Sometimes sufficient details were available, and the authorities could demonstrate that the accusations were untrue. Complaints by Zionist detainees held in a detention camp in Eritrea about being poorly housed and inadequately fed were dismissed by a delegate from the ICRC who visited the camp in June 1946.[32] In 1957 a prisoner in Cyprus alleged that an interrogator had knocked out all of her front teeth. But a doctor who examined her reported that she had all but one of her own teeth, and her own dental records showed that she had lost the missing tooth 11 months before she was arrested.[33] Sometimes the authorities accepted that wrongdoing had occurred, but argued that the ends justified the means. The official diarist of 1/Royal Northumberland Fusiliers admitted that in at least two instances men in the battalion had shot innocent bystanders in the Crater district of Aden in 1966, but justified their actions because the battalion gained a reputation for being willing to use its weapons, and the number of insurgent incidents, at least temporarily, dropped.[34]

[27] TNA CO 926/396. BBC Monitoring Service, Caversham Park, UK: Athens Broadcasts for Cyprus, 25 October 1955.
[28] TNA CO 926/671/CIC(57)9 (Final). PEKA leaflet: 'The methods of the incendiary marshal', 3 March 1957; CO 926/671/CIC(57)10 (Final). PEKA leaflet, 'The Torturers in the Medieval Prisons of Famagusta', 28 March 1957; TNA CO 926/880. Harding to Colonial Secretary, 9 June 1957.
[29] TNA CO 1015/2097. 'Dissent', 4 June 1959.
[30] TNA CAB 148/29/OPD(66)128. Bowen to Foreign Secretary, 14 November 1966. This was one of a series of such allegations. TNA CO 1055/266. Central Office of Information: Cairo's Voice of the Arabs alleged that British authorities were torturing detainees in Aden, 20 December 1964; TNA DEFE 24/252. H. G. Franck, Chairman, Swedish Section Amnesty International, to H. Wilson, 16 December 1966; TNA DEFE 24/252. Foreign Office to High Commissioner Aden, 18 January 1967.
[31] See, for example: TNA CO 926/671/CIC(57)11 (Final). PEKA leaflet, '25th of March', 25 March 1957; TNA CO 926/671/CIC(57)Thirteen (Final). PEKA leaflet 'We report on British justice in Cyprus to the British people and the civilized world', 17 April 1957; TNA CO 926/672/CIC(57)17 (Final). PEKA leaflet, 'British terrorism', 16 May 1957.
[32] TNA FO 371/61872. R. Gallopin, Director Delegate, ICRC, Geneva, to Colonial Secretary, 27 September 1946; TNA FO 371/61872. M. Munier, Jewish political internees detained in Eritrea. Special Camp number 119, n.d. but c.September 1946.
[33] TNA CO 926/881. Harding to Colonial Secretary, 27 June 1957.
[34] TNA WO 305/4301. Historical Record (1 April 1966 to 1 April 1967) 1st Battalion Royal Northumberland Fusiliers.

It was also sometimes claimed that men under pressure were bound sometimes to break the rules. In 1953 and 1954 two separate courts martial in the Canal Zone found soldiers guilty of murdering Egyptians and imposed death sentences. But both courts recommended mercy on the grounds that men serving in the Canal Zone were under exceptional strain, an argument that was accepted by the Solicitor General.[35] In both instances the accused were reprieved, imprisoned and then released before they had served their full term.[36] In neither case did the military authorities cover-up wrongdoing. But there was more than a suggestion that the punishments were symbolic. Members of the Kenya Police excused activities such as exhibiting the head of a dead Mau Mau on a pole outside a police post, or delivering electric shocks to the testicles of suspects, by insisting that these were exceptions, that Africans had different standards of behaviour compared to Europeans, and that those police who did behave brutally were amongst

Those of the security forces who [had] witnessed the horrors perpetrated by Mau Mau and who were aware of the oaths which some had taken, can perhaps have been expected to have been less than gentle when dealing with the terrorists, suspected or otherwise, and of course there was callousness and brutality.[37]

A willingness sometimes to condone breaking the rules went right to the top of government. In a debate in the Commons in June 1956, John Hare, the Minister of State at the Colonial Office, rebutted accusations that the rule of law had broken down in Kenya, by noting that 'Large armed gangs, often 100 strong, roamed the countryside murdering and pillaging and the extent of the terror was only now being fully revealed as the bodies of the victims were discovered. Some things undoubtedly occurred in the heat of the battle and under the strain and influence of the brutalizing conditions which were terrible and inescapable.' But, he maintained, the 'few isolated cases of brutalities and atrocities on the part of Government forces', had been dealt with.[38] Two years later the Prime Minister, Harold Macmillan, made much the same defence of the army in Cyprus following unofficial reprisals by troops in the wake of the assassination of a soldier's wife in Famagusta.[39]

Hare was at least prepared to concede that sometimes members of the security forces had stepped out of line. In other instances the authorities issued an outright denial of the truth of the allegation. Cunningham flatly denied allegations that prisoners were tortured at Athlit and was confident enough to allow journalists to

[35] TNA WO 32/21676. DPS, WO, to Undersecretary of State Air Ministry, 13 December 1954.
[36] TNA WO 71/1212. Lt.-Gen. Sir F. Festing to C-in-C MELF, 4 March 1953; *Times*, 22 February 1953; TNA WO 32/21676. DPS, WO, to Undersecretary of State Air Ministry, 13 December 1954; TNA WO 71/1223. Deputy JAG, MELF, to C-in-C MELF, 12 May 1954; TNA WO 32/21676. Press cutting, 30 July 1959.
[37] C. Faulkner, *A Two-Year Wonder. The Kenya Police 1953–1955* (Livingston: Librario, 2004), 152–3; I. V. B. Peter Mills, *The Dawn Stand-to* (Devon: Edward Gaskill, 2000), 273.
[38] *Times*, 7 June 1956.
[39] *Hansard*, HC Deb 10 December 1958 vol. 597 cols 343–5.

visit the camp to see for themselves.[40] The judge hearing the case of Mau Mau defendants alleged to have murdered a settler family, the Rucks, in January 1953 confessed himself 'heartily sick of repeated allegations of wicked behaviour by persons in authority which cannot stand the test of ventilation in a court of law for a moment.'[41] A willingness to turn a blind eye to misdemeanours sometimes went right to the top of the government. In the Commons in July 1953, Lyttelton brushed aside accusations that the security forces in Kenya were shooting people indiscriminately.[42] The Cyprus government issued a press statement flatly contradicting allegations about the inhuman treatment of detainees.[43]

Finally, officials sometimes insisted that allegations were untrue, or at the very least grossly exaggerated, because they were part of deliberate propaganda campaigns designed to discredit the security forces in the eyes of the world's press.[44] By mid-1956, soldiers in Cyprus were 'conscious that whenever we picked up people they would then try to either damage themselves or pretend that you had damaged them', and as a result tried to prepare careful reports on everything that had happened from the moment an arrest was made in order to refute untrue allegations.[45] Their suspicions were justified. EOKA had developed an organization specifically tasked with spreading propaganda to discredit the security forces.[46] At least one detainee in Aden admitted that he had made false allegations against his interrogators because it 'was "good propaganda for the cause".'[47]

Some prisoners may have fabricated such stories for another reason. Detainees could find themselves in an awkward position. If they did not co-operate with the security forces they might face the death penalty. But if they co-operated, they might face assassination by their former friends.[48] People who had given information to the security forces might try to justify their betrayal by claiming that it had been beaten out of them.[49] It was this that may have been behind a case in Aden in 1966. There a detainee who had supplied his interrogators with much valuable

---

[40] TNA CO 537/1719. High Commissioner Palestine to Colonial Secretary, 3 July 1946; *Manchester Guardian*, 4 July 1946.

[41] *Times*, 25 April 1953.

[42] *Times*, 16 & 19 July 1953.

[43] TNA CO 926/396. Cyprus government communiqué no. 6. The facts about Kyrenia Castle, 24 October 1955; TNA CO 926/396. Lennox-Boyd to Noel-Baker, 26 October 1955; TNA CO 926/396. 'From our special correspondent, "Conditions in Kyrenia Castle. Where troops envy the detainees"', *Manchester Guardian*, 5 November 1955; TNA CO 926/398. *Manchester Guardian*, 8 December 1955.

[44] TNA WO 275/72. Commanding Officer, 3/Para to HQ, 3 Para Brigade, 1 January 1947; TNA WO 275/72. Brigade Commander, 3 Para Brigade to 'G', 6 Airborne Division, 1 January 1947; TNA CO 822/474. [Kenya] Press Office Handout no. 68, 17 April 1953; TNA FCO 8/153. Turnbull, Comments on the sections of the Bowen Report entitled 'Allegations of cruelty and torture', 25 January 1967; TNA DEFE 11/505. Turnbull to Foreign Office, 25 September 1966.

[45] IWMSA. Accession No. 11146. Col. M. Gray, reel 3.

[46] TNA CO 926/675. Weston to Reddaway, 31 May 1958.

[47] TNA DEFE 24/252. Turnbull to Foreign Office, 1 February 1967.

[48] TNA CO 926/670/CIC(57)5. Cyprus Intelligence Committee. Intelligence review for the first half of February 1957, 21 February 1957.

[49] N. Crawshaw, 'Justice in Cyprus. I—an inquiry needed', *Manchester Guardian*, 1 July 1957; TNA CO 926/881. A. S. Aldridge to Canon H. M. Waddans, 4 October 1957.

information subsequently complained to a visiting member of the ICRC that he had been subjected to electric-shock treatment. The detainee and the ICRC delegate were then taken to a hospital where 'Medical evidence (scars at back of neck) do not support allegations. M. Rochat [the ICRC representative] satisfied that allegations not substantiated, and agreed no further investigation necessary.'[50]

INTERPRETING THE EVIDENCE

The historian is thus left walking through a hall of mirrors. Nothing was what it seemed. Protagonists on both sides were intent on distorting the evidence for their own advantage. But the situation is not, in fact, quite so bleak. There were some witnesses who did not have quite such sharp axes to grind, and at least some degree of reliance can be placed on some of the evidence produced by the protagonists themselves.

'Neutral organizations' such as the ILO, the ICRC, and some Christian Churches provided testimony about the behaviour of the security forces in several campaigns. It was not always critical. An ILO representative who investigated allegations made by prisoners detained in the Canal Zone in 1951–2 that they had been subjected to forced labour, dismissed their claims. The most that they had been forced to do was to clean their own cells.[51] But international inspectors did not always report so favourably. An ICRC delegation who visited detention camps in Kenya in June and July 1959 were critical of the use of physical punishments, referring explicitly to 'The abuses committed in applying corporal punishment and subjecting certain detained persons to brutal treatment during questioning;' and noting 'unmistakable traces of brutal treatment'.[52]

Church missionaries in both Kenya and Nyasaland were disturbed by the behaviour of police and soldiers. In February 1953 a British missionary in Kenya received 'a constant stream of reports of brutalities by police, military and home guards'.[53] A Church of Scotland missionary working in Nyasaland in March 1959 reported unprovoked attacks by volunteer policemen on a group of schoolboys, an assault on an elderly African janitor, and a threat made by a European special constable to 'Get the hell out of here or I'll stick a bullet in your guts.'[54]

Some allegations stood up to forensic examination in a court of law. Because of the widespread intimidation of witnesses, prosecutors appearing before courts in

[50] TNA DEFE 24/252. Oates to Brenchley, 17 January 1967.
[51] TNA WO 279/241. Director of Operations, Malaya, *Conduct of anti-terrorist operations in Malaya* (Kuala Lumpur: 3rd edn, 1958).
[52] TNA CO 822/1258. Leopold Boissier, President of ICRC, to Lennox-Boyd, 12 October 1959.
[53] TNA CO 822/471. Extract of a letter from Reverend Neville Langford-Smith to Canon T. F. C. Bewes, 9 February 1953.
[54] TNA CO 1015/1517. By our own reporter, 'Alleged brutality by Nyasaland Police. Mission teacher on "threats, beating, shooting"', *Manchester Guardian*, 6 March 1959; TNA CO 1015/1516. A. C. McAdam, Church of Scotland mission, Blantyre, to editor *Manchester Guardian*, 4 March 1959.

Cyprus had to rely heavily on confessions allegedly made by the accused.[55] In early 1957 there was a spate of cases in which the courts either rejected prosecution cases or allowed appeals against the sentences of lower courts on the grounds that confessions made by the accused had been extracted under duress. In one case the judge rejected a claim by the accused that he had been tied to a bed and beaten by police but accepted that he was taken to Kyrenia Castle with a sack over his head and made to run by being hit with the butt of a gun. Another prisoner, who was arrested in possession of a sten gun and accused of assassinating a policeman, was found not guilty. The judge rejected his complaint that he was tortured, but accepted that the arresting officers, in their desire to ensure he did not escape, made him travel face down in an open truck, without shoes or socks and in the pouring rain, and had refused him a change of clothes or medical treatment for the injuries received when he was arrested.[56] In December 1958 a coroner concluded that during mass arrests following the assassination of a British soldier's wife in Famagusta in October, it was apparent that 'a degree of force that would appear to be entirely unjustified was used by security forces'.[57]

But the most telling testimony was provided by members of the security forces or their superiors, who admitted that they had themselves perpetrated wrongdoings or conceded that they had happened. They had no obvious reason to lie, and indeed, may have had good reason to conceal the evidence. In August 1946, in the aftermath of a large cordon and search operation, the police received complaints of theft from the occupiers of premises that had been searched. The police asserted that they had been committed by civilians during breaks in the curfew, an accusation which provoked indignant denials from the municipal authorities.[58] Senior army officers insisted that such allegations were part of a Zionist campaign to discredit their men.[59] The new commanding officer of 1/Parachute Regiment knew otherwise. He discovered that a group of off-duty soldiers had begun 'to organise their own cordon and search operation, taking a block of flats in Tel Aviv as a target. Unfortunately they did not search for weapons but for money; they were not after terrorists but loot.'[60] Officers and senior NCOs had turned a blind eye to their activities.[61] In 1950 James Griffiths, the Colonial Secretary, admitted that in Malaya 'the police are decidedly corrupt, and if you give them sweeping powers of arrest on suspicion for the period of the emergency, many innocent people will be held.'[62] Erskine knew that soldiers in the Canal Zone had been looting in 1951–2, which was why he

[55] Crawshaw, *The Cyprus Revolt*, 246.
[56] TNA CO 926/881. Memo. Mediterranean Department, CO, Background report on recent cases involving allegations of ill-treatment by Cyprus police, 28 May 1957.
[57] *Manchester Guardian*, 4 December 1958.
[58] *Palestine Post*, 6 August 1946.
[59] TNA WO 275/72. CO, 3/Para to HQ, 3 Para Brigade, 1 January 1947; TNA WO 275/72. Brigade Commander, 3 Para Brigade to 'G', 6 Airborne Division, 1 January 1947.
[60] Maj.-Gen. Sir J. Nelson, *Always a Grenadier* (Privately published, n.d.), 60.
[61] LHCMA Stockwell 6/26/3. Maj. P. M. A. Taylor to Captain P. Cavendish, 6 August 1948.
[62] TNA CAB 21/1681/MAL.C(50)21. Secretary of State for War, Malaya Committee, The military situation in Malaya, 17 June 1950; TNA CAB 128/17/CM(50)37. Cabinet Conclusions, 19 June 1950.

issued orders forbidding it.[63] When he wrote in December 1953 that in the first eight months of the emergency in Kenya he believed that a considerable number of people had been shot indiscriminately by the army and police, and that many detainees had been beaten to extract information, it is reasonable to conclude that he was reporting what had indeed happened.[64] In Aden in 1967 the Chief Justice privately conceded that 'whereas most British Units in Aden have reacted with the utmost restraint in the face of extreme provocation from terrorist organisations, this has not, unfortunately, been the case with every Unit. There are instances, which you will know about, of damage to property, and the rough handling of law-abiding citizens.'[65]

Testimony from those in the frontline made similar points. In Cyprus a soldier who served with the Intelligence Corps in 1958, remembered that

> There is no doubt that torture of suspects was endemic. A certain amount of casual brutality against the 'enemy' by soldiers is inescapable, but some units, as a matter of routine, placed metal buckets on the heads of their prisoners and banged them with rifle barrels until he or she confessed. The Turkish Special Branch, with whom my unit worked, was something else. Its officers were filled with a profound hatred of anything Greek and quite ready to frame suspects.[66]

The last point was confirmed by an RAMC doctor called to examine two Greek-Cypriot detainees arrested by Turkish policemen in 1958. He found both men bruised, one suffering from a broken rib and another with a shoulder injury.[67] But the blame for such misbehaviour could not always be offloaded onto the shoulders of the Turkish-Cypriot police. British soldiers and policemen were usually present when a suspect was interrogated.[68] A British officer who stood by when a Turkish policeman beat a Greek informer with the butt of his rifle to make him reveal the location of an arms dump did not like what he saw, 'but as the munitions were unearthed I reluctantly conceded that the tough line was acceptable'.[69] In Aden in October 1965, the Director of Health Services and the High Commission's Legal Adviser visited the security forces' detention centre at Al Mansoura. There they were told by an army medical officer 'there was some evidence of physical ill-treatment of detainees who had returned from Fort Morbut after interrogation'. From that they concluded that there was sufficient prima facie evidence to justify the opening of a judicial inquiry.[70]

---

[63] TNA WO 236/14. Erskine to all formations under command in Canal Zone and all Lt-Col. commanders, 30 January 1952.

[64] TNA WO 236/18. Erskine to Governor Kenya and other Kenya government officials, CIGS and Military Members Army Council, Colonial Secretary, etc, 25 April 1955; TNA WO 32/15834. Erskine to Secretary of State for War, 10 December 1953.

[65] TNA DEFE 24/1873. Proceedings of an inquiry as requested by the High Commissioner in letter to the Chief Justice, 21 July 1967.

[66] A. Walker, 'The Intelligent Way'. Downloaded 20 April 2009 at www.britains-smallwars.com/cyprus/Davidcarter/Walker/intelcorps.html.

[67] J. Dewhurst, 'Complicity', *British Medical Journal*, 22 January 2005.

[68] Walker, 'The Intelligent Way'.

[69] R. Redgrave, *Balkan Blue. Family and Military Memories* (Barnsley: Leo Cooper, 2000), 159–60.

[70] TNA CO 1055/209. Turnbull to CO, 19 December 1965; TNA FCO 8/153. Turnbull to J. E. Marham, 30 January 1967.

There is thus enough evidence to conclude that although the authorities officially frowned upon members of the security forces who broke the law, there were instances when they did so, and, although some were punished, others were not.

UNOFFICIAL REPRISALS

In October 1946, after several of his men had been killed by an insurgent bomb, the CO of 1/Argyll and Sutherland Highlanders told a journalist that, 'When a thing like this happens our chaps get mad. I have told them not to be biased, but we have got to hit back. When we hit back they keep quiet for 4 or 5 days.'[71] Such a mindset sometimes led members of the security forces to mount their own unofficial and illegal reprisals. Following an attack by the Stern Gang on 6 Airborne Division's car park in Tel Aviv on 25 April 1946, which left seven British soldiers dead, 'feeling has not unnaturally run high amongst our own troops, and there were two small cases of attempted retaliation, one on a Jewish settlement at Beer Tuvyn.' The second was reported to have taken place at Nathanya.[72] In November 1946 members of the Palestine Police Mobile Force left nine people in hospital when they smashed Jewish cafes and a dairy in reprisal for the deaths of three of their comrades.[73] By early 1947 parts of the army and police were locked into a cycle of reprisals and unofficial counter-reprisals.[74] In February 1947, following the sentence of death passed on one of their members, Dov Gruner, the Irgun attacked the HQ of 1/Parachute Regiment and in a separate operation blew up two jeeps. 'The Airborne reaction to this followed five days later, when some 65 men from Tel Aviv were taken to Sarona camp and made to run the gauntlet while being beaten with sticks.'[75] In April two British policemen were shot in Jerusalem. The same night two Jewish youths claimed they had been arrested and beaten by plain-clothes policemen.[76] The hanging of two British sergeants by the Irgun on 31 July 1947 sparked more reprisals. In Tel Aviv on the night of 31 July parties of soldiers, some in civilian clothes, armed with sub-machine guns and batons, assaulted people, smashed shop windows, and stole valuables. In a separate incident three armoured cars appeared and fired in all directions, and in another incident five soldiers in the Hartikva quarter of Tel Aviv fired guns and threw a bomb into a cinema. Meanwhile, in Haifa, troops conducted a cordon and search operation 'during which time they [the inhabitants] were insulted, assaulted and threatened.'[77]

---

[71] TNA CO 537/1719. Eric Grey, 'Lieutenant Colonel Webb calls in the reporters', *Daily Express*, 26 October 1946.
[72] TNA WO 106/3107. CIGS summary No. 43, 30 April 1946; WO 275/120. GHQ MELF Weekly Int. Reviews (Palestine Extracts) No. 58. Issued 3 May 1946.
[73] *Palestine Post*, 19 November 1946.
[74] *Palestine Post*, 3, 5, & 7 January 1947.
[75] Bruton, *A Captain's Mandate*, 79–80.
[76] *Palestine Post*, 9 April 1947.
[77] TNA WO 275/72. Palestine Press, 1 August 1947; *Manchester Guardian*, 1 & 2 August 1947.

There were occasions when the security forces in Malaya were restrained from taking unofficial reprisals only by their officers. In June 1953 a patrol of 6/Malay Regiment discovered a track leading right up to the fence of a new village, and learnt that a group of insurgents had been given food there on the previous evening. The platoon commander found that 'All my men were livid and begged me to open up with our three Bren guns on the village as a salutary lesson. I lost several stone in restraining them—I had visions of a court-martial.'[78] In Kenya some Kikuyu loyalists used their membership of the Home Guard to settle old scores over land disputes or property, or to take vengeance if a friend or family member had been killed by Mau Mau. In October 1956 men of 1/Highland Light Infantry were accused of assaulting large numbers of Greek Cypriots in the village of Lefkoniko following a bomb explosion at the village fountain that had killed one soldier and wounded five others.[79] An officer on the island remembered that, after the explosion, 'The regiment, which was not always noted for its observance of the Queensbury [*sic*] Rules, returned to the village that night and literally took it to pieces with their bare hands. There was never any "trouble" again from the villagers and, although the "Authorities" huffed and puffed, they probably privately thought that retribution had been swift and fair.'[80]

Better known were the events following the re-occupation of the Crater district of Aden by 1/Argyll and Sutherland Highlanders in 1967. After the killing of several of their comrades, together with members of 1/Royal Northumberland Fusiliers in June, the army had temporarily evacuated Crater. But under their charismatic commanding officer, Lieutenant-Colonel Colin Mitchell, the Argylls re-occupied the district, and then imposed what the media dubbed 'Argyll's Law'. Even journalists sympathetic to Mitchell described the operations of his battalion as 'rough justice'. Hints that they were intent on killing a dozen alleged insurgents in revenge for the soldiers that they had lost were later confirmed by soldiers who had served with the battalion.[81] Another added that there were other motives, 'with bodies being stripped of money belts and valuables. Others, he said, were for the initiation of young soldiers on their first active service.'[82] A junior officer from another regiment who complained about their behaviour 'was told to mind my own business'.[83]

---

[78] J. Chynoweth, *Hunting Terrorists in the Jungle. The Experiences of a National Service Subaltern in Malaya in the 1950s* (Stroud, Glouc.: Tempus, 2005), 56.

[79] TNA CO 926/880. Harding to Colonial Secretary, 9 June 1957.

[80] Redgrave, *Balkan Blue*,154.

[81] J. Lynn, *Empire Warriors. Aden: Mad Mitch and his Tribal Law*, BBC, 2004.

[82] G. Goodwin and G. Burke, 'I accuse the Argylls', *Sunday Mail*, 26 April 1981 (I am grateful to Dr Matthew Hughes for providing me with this reference); S. Harper, *Last Sunset. What Happened in Aden* (London: Collins, 1978), 114. Allegations were also made shortly after the battalion had left Aden that soldiers had stolen property from Arab houses, but these were never proven. TNA DEFE 24/1854. Record of conversation between Miss E. Evans and F. P. Baker, 29 August 1967; TNA DEFE 24/1854. Allegation that the large remittance by senior NCOs of 1/A&SH may have been the proceeds of theft during searches of Arabs and Arab property in Aden, 4 September 1967; TNA DEFE 24/1854. D. M. Evans (AUS(GS)) to PS/US of S (Army), 18 October 1968.

[83] 2/Lt N. Stephens, *Empire Warriors. Aden: Mad Mitch and his Tribal Law*, BBC, 2004.

If the security forces were not operating in free fire zones or prohibited areas the most common abuses took place during cordon and search operations. They involved damage to property, and allegations of verbal, physical, and sexual assaults.[84] Insurgents used great ingenuity to conceal their weapons caches and so searchers had to go about their task with great thoroughness.[85] But one side's thoroughness was another side's wanton destruction, and sometimes damage was unnecessary and possibly malicious.[86] During a curfew on the village of Ikos in Cyprus in November 1956 soldiers broke into cupboards, tore clothing, broke pots full of oil, and destroyed the roofs of houses.[87] Using excessive force against civilians was also common. Police in Nyasaland were taught to disable rioters by using their batons to strike them on their collar bones, arms, and legs, not on their heads. But, as the Devlin Report dryly remarked, 'You may be surprised at the number of occasions on which a blow said to be so aimed did in fact strike the head.'[88] The same report also noted nine instances during Operation SUN-RISE, the wave of arrests that accompanied the declaration of the state of emergency, when police and soldiers used batons and rifle butts on individuals who were not resisting arrest.[89]

In prohibited areas the security forces were supposed to challenge a suspect before opening fire.[90] Some patrols did so, except when they were faced 'with an armed person, in which case you just do not take a chance.'[91] But tired soldiers and policemen, frustrated after months of fruitless jungle patrolling, were sometimes apt to shoot first and ask questions later. As one policeman remembered, 'After months of patrolling and ambushing in foul weather against a foe as wily as Mau Mau terrorists, it was inevitable that there were operational encounters where, despite some doubt as to an individual's identity, he was deemed to be Mau Mau and, "bang-bang", eliminated.'[92] Another policeman in Kenya remembered that 'No Mau Mau would ever wait to be challenged, and it was a standing joke that "Simama" (Halt!) meant "goodbye!"'[93] A senior policeman in Malaya told one of his jungle squad commanders that 'All I have ever asked for are dead terrorists and live policemen out of any job.' He hardly needed to say this as his subordinate had

[84] *Manchester Guardian*, 22 December 1947, 27 November 1952, 25 September 1958; *Times*, 17 January 1953; IWMSA. Accession No. 16395. Lt.-Gen. Sir N. Crookenden, reel 1.
[85] TNA WO 33/2736. History of EOKA, 1954–1959, 20 April 1960; Maj. E. A. Cooper-Key, 'Some reflections on Cyprus', *British Army Review*, no. 5 (September 1957), 40–1.
[86] TNA CO 926/396. Harding to Colonial Secretary, 20 January 1956; *Manchester Guardian*, 24 December 1955.
[87] TNA CO 926/670/CIC(57)3. Cyprus Intelligence Committee. Intelligence Review for the second half of January 1957: Enc: EOKA leaflet: 'Some more acts of vandalism', 7 February 1957.
[88] TNA CAB 129/98/C(59)124. Colonial Secretary, Nyasaland Commission of Inquiry, 17 July 1959.
[89] Ibid.
[90] TNA WO 279/241. Director of Operations, Malaya, *Conduct of Anti-terrorist Operations in Malaya* (Malaya: Kuala Lumpur, 3rd edn, 1958); *Times*, 16 July 1953.
[91] IWMSA. Accession No. 10232. L. O. Crosland, reel 2.
[92] Hewitt, *Kenya Cowboy*, 204.
[93] Faulkner, *A Two-Year Wonder*, 55.

already told him that in mounting an ambush 'I shall exercise correct tactics. Shoot first and ask questions afterwards.'[94]

There is evidence that some units, anxious to inflate their 'scores', shot people indiscriminately. An experienced British officer in the Malay police, posted to South Kedah in November 1950, 'was told that the jungle squads lacked discipline and, on examining the operation room records, I discovered that, although they had notched up a remarkable number of terrorist kills, very few arms had been recovered; whereas it had been my previous experience in Selangor that dead terrorists were almost always armed. I found this extremely worrying.'[95] A soldier who served with 1/Argyll and Sutherland Highlanders in Crater in 1967 'spoke of the inter-platoon rivalry which existed for Robertson Jam Golliwog stickers, awarded by an officer to any Argyll who notched up the killing of an Arab.'[96] Nervous soldiers could make mistakes which were subsequently covered up. A subaltern serving with 6/Malay Regiment wrote to his parents in 1953 that 'No Chinese rubber tapper is safe when we search an estate, my men are trigger-happy with Chinese, and several platoon commanders have had to plant grenades on tappers and call them bandits when their men have made "a small error in judgment."'[97]

Exactly how many of the people that the security forces shot were insurgents is open to debate. Someone who was killed in possession of a firearm was probably an insurgent. Someone who was killed without a firearm might possibly have been an innocent bystander. A large discrepancy between the number of people killed by the security forces, and the number of weapons recovered, raises the suspicion that the security forces were killing innocent bystanders. The evidence from Malaya is incomplete, because no detailed records were kept of arms recovered between 1948 and 1953. But from that point until August 1957, the security forces recovered 7,297 small arms. Between June 1948 and August 1957, they inflicted 9,581 casualties on the insurgents. Taking into account an unknown number of weapons recovered between 1948 and 1953, there was a rough correspondence between insurgent casualties and weapons recovered.[98] The same was true for the Confrontation.[99] However, in Kenya between October 1952 and April 1955, the security forces reported that they had killed 8,400 Mau Mau. But they recovered only 1,193 firearms.[100] Erskine suspected that at least one battalion of the KAR had deliberately inflated its successes in the opening months of the emergency by killing innocent people.[101] But that did not stop him from explaining away the discrepancy by insisting that 'We do not report capture of Native weapons such as Pangas,

[94] J. W. G. Moran, *Spearhead in Malaya* (London: Peter Davis, 1959), 125.
[95] Hatton, *Tock Tock Birds*, 157.
[96] Anon., 'They killed for more golliwog badges', *Sunday Mail*, 17 May 1981.
[97] Chynoweth, *Hunting Terrorists in the Jungle*, 57.
[98] TNA WO 106/5990. Director of Operations Malaya, Review of the Emergency in Malaya from June 1948 to August 1957 September 1957.
[99] TNA WO 305/3327. Director of Borneo Operations to Commander-in-Chief Far East, 11 September 1966.
[100] TNA WO 276/457. Casualties to Terrorists, security forces and loyal civilians, n.d.
[101] TNA WO 32/15556. Erskine to CIGS, 9 July 1953.

Simis and spears. These are lethal weapons in the kind of war fought at close quarters. Many of these are captured and handed over to the Home Guard or used ourselves for forest clearance.'[102] What he did not mention was that pangas and simis were common farm implements, and a Kikuyu farm labourer might carry them just as an English labourer might once have carried a scythe or a sickle, or that the Kikuyu usually carried spears for self-protection when travelling thorough the bush.[103]

The number of fatal insurgent casualties may also have been inflated by the fate meted out to some wounded prisoners. Some were fortunate and were carried out of the jungle by their captors who realized that a wounded man who had been well treated might be willing to provide information.[104] But in Malaya and Kenya others were executed on the spot.[105] The dead were also made to serve the purposes of counter-terror. In Malay and Kenya when the security forces had managed to recover the bodies of dead insurgents, they might be exhibited outside a police station, or be tied to the top of a land-rover and taken from village to village. This was done not only to enable the police to discover the identity of the people they had shot. It also reassured government supporters that at least one of their enemies could no longer threaten them, and showed insurgent supporters what might happen to them if they did not change sides.[106]

In Malaya and Kenya the security forces were accused of deliberately mutilating the corpses of dead insurgents. Patrols were ordered to bring back intelligence identifying any insurgents they killed, but in the opening stages of both emergencies they were rarely equipped with either cameras or finger-print equipment. The latter was, in any case, difficult to use in damp jungle conditions. An alternative was to tie the corpse to a pole and carry it out, a nauseating experience for those involved.[107] Consequently, decapitating a dead body, or removing its hands for later finger-print identification, was the preferred method. Some British soldiers found the practice deeply distasteful. In Malaya the British had recruited Iban trackers from Borneo to assist their patrols to find insurgents in the jungle. They had far fewer qualms and indeed hoped that they might be permitted to keep insurgent heads as trophies. An NCO serving with 42 Commando in Malaya remembered that after a successful ambush that left two insurgents dead 'none of our guys were rushing forward to do it and the Iban was asked to cut the head off. Now he was overjoyed because he thought he was being given the head, and they

[102] TNA WO 216/855. Erskine to CIGS, 18 July 1953.

[103] TNA CO 822/474. Minute by Barton, 16 February 1953.

[104] P. Cross, 'A Face Like a Chicken's Backside'. An Unconventional Soldier in South East Asia, 1948–1971 (London: Greenhill Books, 1996), 38–9.

[105] Follows, *The Jungle Beat*, 27; TNA WO 32/21720. Proceedings of the McLean Court of Inquiry. Major D. N. Court, OC 'A' company, 1/Buffs, Lt.-Col. J. F. Connolly, CO 1/Buffs, Major S. J. Squire, OC 'C' Company, 1/Buffs, 29 December 1953; Hewitt, *Kenya Cowboy*, 257.

[106] Yap Yok Foo, 'Bearded terror of Kajang', *New Straits Times (Malaysia)*, 4 January 2004; 'Corpses exposed in public. Malayan terrorists', *Manchester Guardian*, 20 August 1952; G. Greene to editor of the *Times*, 4 December 1953; Nigel Hunt to editor, *Times*, 31 December 1953; Hewitt, *Kenya Cowboy*, 188; *Who Do You Think You Are? Series 7. No. 9, Alan Cumming*, BBC, broadcast 13 September 2010.

[107] Chynoweth, *Hunting Terrorists in the Jungle*, 120.

are native head-hunters. Having cut the head off when the boss wanted the head back to put in this bag and there was quite a little tussle. No, he wanted, the Iban wanted the head. However, the head went in the bag and it was taken back for identification.'[108]

However, in 1952 the *Daily Worker* caused a scandal when it published a photograph of a Royal Marine holding a head, apparently as a trophy.[109] This led to a division in official opinion. Templer wanted permission to continue the practice of decapitation if there was no other way of bringing back an identity, but the Cabinet refused, not because they found the practice morally distasteful, but because it was politically counter-productive. As Churchill told his colleagues, 'Odium is out of all prop[ortio]n to advantage gained. I'm against it. Plays into hands of Communist agitation.'[110] In Kenya in the opening months of the Emergency it was common practice for patrols to cut off the hands of dead insurgents for identification purposes. This continued regularly until the summer of 1953. Security forces units were then issued with equipment so they could finger-print corpses. In August Erskine ordered that where possible the bodies of dead insurgents should be handed to the police, or if that were impossible they should be buried after their finger-prints had been taken.[111] The Mau Mau, if they had time, preferred to bury their own dead, although they too might remove their heads and hands so as to prevent the security forces from identifying the corpse and perhaps directing their attentions to the dead man's family.[112]

The possibility that considerable numbers of innocent people may have been killed by the security forces points to a related question, whether the British authorities deliberately employed death squads, or at least tolerated the operations of out-of-control elements of the security forces.[113] Troops who were fired upon by insurgents had every right to fire back in self-defence. But the only instance when the authorities themselves deliberately established a group of counter-insurgents and gave them permission to use insurgent methods against their enemies took place in Palestine in 1947. Major Roy Farran, a former officer in the SAS, was the commander of one of two special squads established by Bernard Fergusson, a former Chindit commander then serving as the Assistant Inspector-General of

---

[108] IWMSA. Accession No. 18021. F. G. Green, reel 2.
[109] TNA CAB 129/51/C(52). First Lord of Admiralty, *Daily Worker* photographs of a Royal Marine holding the severed head of a bandit, 2 May 1952.
[110] TNA CAB 195/10/CC49(52). Cabinet meeting, 6 May 1952.
[111] TNA WO 32/21720. Proceedings of the McLean Court of Inquiry, Captain J. W. Turnbull, 28 December 1953; TNA WO 32/21722. Extract from GHQ East Africa training Instruction Number 7, 1 August 1953.
[112] TNA WO 276/512. Interrogation of Waruhiu s/o Itote (Alias) 'General China', 26 January 1954.
[113] T. D. Mason and D. A. Krane, 'The political economy of death squads: toward a theory of the impact of state-sanctioned terror', *International Studies Quarterly*, vol. 33, no. 2 (June, 1989), 178; G. Hughes and C. Tripodi, 'Anatomy of a surrogate: historical precedents and implications for contemporary counter-insurgency and counter-terrorism', *SW&I*, vol. 20 (March 2009), 1–35; L. E. Cline, *Pseudo Operations and Counterinsurgency: Lessons from Other Countries* (Carlisle, Penn.: Strategic Studies Institute, 2005), v, 15.

the Palestine Police. Farran was court-martialled in October 1947 for the murder in May 1947 of an alleged member of the Stern Gang, 16-year-old Alexander Rubowitz.[114] Although the Palestine government asserted that Farran had not been authorized to use anything other than ordinary police methods, in February 1947 Fergusson had justified establishing the squads by arguing that the best way to defeat terrorists was by using counter-insurgents who had themselves worked as terrorists.[115]

It may have been that the adverse publicity that attended the Farran case persuaded later governments that resort to such expedients simply did not pay, for there is little evidence that they repeated the experiment. Indeed, elsewhere they went out of their way to try to prevent private vigilantes meting out their own version of 'justice', although not always with complete success. Alarm for their own safety was already growing amongst the settler community in Kenya even before the Rucks were killed. One settler remembered that the murders 'caused a lot of worrying and fury amongst the whites in Nairobi. And they went completely bonkers. They were rushing around in a sort of crazy state . . . handing out petitions that everybody's got to be murdered who had anything to do with this and they were talking much the same sort of way as the blacks were then.'[116] A group of settlers formed the United Kenya Protection Association and established a 70-strong 'Commando'.[117] Concerned that this might be a step towards the settlers forming their own vigilante groups, the government sought to control them by expanding the Kenya Police Reserve and the Kenya Regiment, thus giving settlers the opportunity to fight against the Mau Mau, but within the confines of a disciplined force.[118] However, this was not entirely successful. Erskine believed that in 1953, in at least one area near Nairobi, the local authorities were conniving in the activities of 'a definite gang of settlers operating as a private army in KPR uniform, mostly by night and killing suspected Mau Mau. I was told they openly boasted that they could not wait for the normal legal process.'[119]

There also remains the suspicion that the authorities turned a blind eye to the existence of death squads amongst the police. Another senior policeman reminisced that 'The question as to the existence of "murder squads" has often arisen and I do not know the answer, but I do know that occasionally, a prominent member of the Mau Mau passive wing would disappear to be found later, the victim of a hit and run vehicle or turn up with a knife through his ribs after which, Special Branch Officers would look very pleased.'[120]

[114] TNA CO 537/2302. Cunningham to Colonial Secretary, 13 June 1947. There is an excellent account of the Farran case in D. Cesarani, *Major Farran's Hat* (London: William Heineman, 2009).
[115] TNA CO 537/2270. Memorandum by Fergusson, Secondment of army officers to Palestine Police, n.d. but c.12 February 1947; TNA CO 537/2302. Cunningham to Colonial Secretary, 25 June 1947.
[116] S. Carswell, *Empire Warriors. Kenya: The Hunt for Kimanthi*, BBC, 2004.
[117] *Times*, 26 January 1953.
[118] TNA WO 32/14635. HQ East Africa Command to WO, 28 January & 4 February 1953.
[119] TNA WO 32/15834. Erskine to Secretary of State for War, 10 December 1953.
[120] Mills, *The Dawn Stand-to*, 272.

In Cyprus in September 1958 some members of the security forces tried to form their own private counter-terrorist organization. Leaflets in English signed 'Cromwell' were circulated in Nicosia 'threatening reprisals on prominent Greek-Cypriots in the event of any expatriates being murdered.'[121] In October a group called 'ICO', allegedly 'a British organization whose aim is to deal with the terrorists', also threatened violent reprisals against the Greek community. The fact that the leaflets were in English and printed on Stationery Office paper suggested they had been prepared and distributed by members of the security forces.[122] The military authorities responded by sentencing a corporal to nine months detention for distributing the leaflets.[123] Nor were they willing to tolerate the behaviour of four soldiers of 1/Argyll and Sutherland Highlanders who tried to murder a village headman in Sarawak in 1965 because they suspected him of aiding the Indonesians in killing one of their comrades. They were found guilty by a court martial and sentenced to terms of imprisonment.[124]

EXTRA-JUDICIAL EXECUTIONS

During their campaign in Algeria the French routinely employed torture as a normal means of interrogating prisoners and it was common for prisoners, once they had undergone interrogation to 'disappear', becoming the victims of extra-judicial executions.[125] The evidence that the British did the same is less apparent. Some prisoners were subjected to brutal interrogation methods, although the extent to which these were the norm is unclear. There is also evidence of some extra-judicial executions, but the circumstances in which they took place were not necessarily linked with interrogation procedures. Some seem to have been the result of members of the security forces seeking private revenge. In December 1946, after insurgents had flogged three British soldiers of 2 Parachute Brigade, troops arrested five suspects and an officer serving with the division remembered that 'One died and the others took a long time to recover before their trial.'[126]

One case in which a prisoner was killed after interrogation concerned a Greek-Cypriot detainee who had been in police custody in 1957 for 11 days. Under interrogation he revealed the location of an EOKA arms cache. The police took him to the spot and found a pistol hidden in a wall. As they examined it, the prisoner was alleged to have tried to run away. The British police officer in charge of the party ordered one of his subordinates to open fire, who killed the man at 10 yards'

[121] TNA CO 926/676. Special Branch half-monthly report for the first half of September 1958, 20 September 1958; *Manchester Guardian*, 10 September 1958.

[122] *Manchester Guardian*, 6 October 1958.

[123] *Times*, 6 November 1958.

[124] *Times*, 7, 8, & 9 September and 12 October 1965.

[125] C. Cradock and M. L. R. Smith, 'No fixed values'. A reinterpretation of the influence of the theory of *guerre révolutionnaire* and the Battle of Algiers, 1956–1957', *Journal of Cold War Studies*, vol. 9 (2007), 92–6.

[126] P. Bruton, *A Captain's Mandate. Palestine 1946 to 1948* (London: Leo Cooper, 1996), 75.

range, without, as he admitted to the inquest, attempting to chase him or to fire any warning shots. Lennox-Boyd was understandably sceptical of the official account and asked the Cyprus government to comment on the episode, remarking that 'The phrase "shot when trying to escape" has long had an ugly connotation; in this case, there seems to have been barely even the pretence that it was true.'[127]

Elsewhere the precise circumstances in which victims were killed remains unclear, clouded in official language. Reports from Kenya were peppered with such phrases as: 'In scattered incidents various suspected persons refused to stop when ordered to do so and were shot';[128] or 'a patrol of Lancashire Fusiliers operating north of Kinangop arrested Kikuyu on curfew charge. He attempted to snatch sten gun from one of the patrol. He escaped into the forest, failed to halt when called upon, and was shot dead';[129] 'a prisoner wanted on a murder charge was being conveyed to Nyeri. When the car in which he was travelling slowed down he jumped out. The prisoner failed to halt and was shot dead.'[130] Such incidents were not peculiar to Cyprus or Kenya. In Malaya in 1949 police arrested a suspected insurgent outside a cinema in Pahang when 'he made a break for liberty and was shot dead by a European police sergeant'.[131] During the Radfan operation in 1964 for the army captured 40 tribesmen, but only one was identified as a definite rebel and 'he was killed whilst attempting to escape'.[132] Between September 1966 and July 1967 the security forces admitted either killing or wounding seven Adenis who were alleged to have been trying to escape arrest.[133]

It is impossible to give an overall measure of the scale of such incidents, although in Kenya Baring reported in April 1953 that in the preceding six months 430 suspects had been shot while attempting to escape or resisting arrest.[134] Colonial Office officials were incredulous, one of them minuting that 'I find it increasingly difficult to believe that in the present circumstances all the prisoners concerned would invariably be shot dead and none of them just wounded.'[135] His incredulity was shared by an American journalist who visited Kenya in March 1953 and who pinpointed the implausibility of the security forces' explanations of why so many prisoners were shot. 'The number of Kikuyu "shot trying to escape" has risen,' he wrote,

[127] TNA CO 926/881. Colonial Secretary to OAG Cyprus, 26 July 1957.
[128] TNA CO 822/474. Baring to Colonial Office, 9 February 1953.
[129] TNA CO 822/474. Baring to Colonial Office, 12 February 1953.
[130] TNA CO 822/474. Baring to Colonial Office, 23 February 1953.
[131] *Times*, 25 April 1949.
[132] TNA WO 386/22. Intelligence, n.d. but *c.*1 August 1964.
[133] TNA DEFE 11/505. Commander-in-Chief Mideast to CDS, 20 September 1966; TNA DEFE 11/504. C-in-C Mideast to CDS, 11 October 1966; TNA DEFE 11/506. C-in-C Mideast to CDS, 3 January 1967; TNA DEFE 11/525. C-in-C Mideast to CDS, 2 March 1967; DEFE 11/525. C-in-C Mideast to CDS, 3 March 1967; TNA DEFE 11/526. C-in-C Mideast to CDS, 28 March 1967; *Times*, 17 July 1967.
[134] TNA CO 822/474. Baring to Colonial Office, 20 April 1953.
[135] TNA CO 822/489. Minute by E. B. David, 18 November 1953; TNA CO 822/474. Roger to Potter, 12 February 1953.

in remarkable fashion. One Kenya police reserve unit hauled in four Kikuyu men. The prisoners were taken away in a truck, but when the truck reached its destination, all four Kikuyu were dead. It was said that they had 'tried to escape.' None of the four was armed. Kikuyu (including at least one woman) have also been shot dead 'while trying to wrest a Sten gun from a guard'—although the settlers all swear the Kikuyu are a cowardly, not a desperately suicidal, people.[136]

INTERROGATION AND TORTURE

Interrogation took place in two stages and prisoners were most likely to be ill-treated immediately after their capture. Troops and police who actually captured a suspect usually subjected them to an immediate tactical interrogation to secure information about the location and plans of any nearby insurgents.[137] Not only was time of the essence if they were to make good use of 'hot' contact information, but questioning was usually done by personnel who had no specific training in interrogation techniques. This did not invariably mean that prisoners were ill-treated immediately after they were captured.[138] In 1950 Michael Calvert, the commanding officer of 22 SAS, literally threw a policeman out of his mess when the latter told him that torture was the best way of extracting information from a prisoner.[139] Officers of the Royal Hampshire Regiment 'knew that the information they [i.e. prisoners] had would be far more valuable if given voluntarily than as a result of us doing untrained interrogation, including beating up.'[140] But other units did apply their own crude and violent methods. One NCO in Malaya admitted that he had extracted information from villagers by taking them behind a hut one at a time and firing a shot into the air to intimidate the others into believing they would be executed if they did not talk.[141] During the trial in 1951 of an Australian rubber planter on a charge of consorting with the insurgents, evidence emerged that the Malayan police had resorted to such techniques as 'threats with revolver shots, kickings, punchings, and severe beatings with a rattan cane to the insertion of a needle under the fingernails.'[142]

In Kenya the regular army stood aside and left the process of interrogation to the police, home guard, or the settlers of the Kenya Regiment. This was not because they were more fastidious than their colleagues, but because few British soldiers

---

[136] A. Campbell, 'A Report from Kenya', *Time Magazine*, 30 March 1953. Downloaded 13 March 2009 at www.time.com/time/magazine/article/0,9171,818044-1,00.html
[137] IWMDoD. Maj.-Gen. Lewis Owain Pugh 67/67/1-5(1). Brig. Pugh, Operational Standing Orders. 26 Gurkha Infantry Brigade. 1 June 1950; TNA WO 32/19064. WO, *Intelligence in Internal Security Operations* (London: War Office, 28 August 1963).
[138] IWMSA. Accession No. 11147. Col. P. Field, reel 1.
[139] IWMSA. Accession No. 11127. Col. J. Woodhouse, reel 4.
[140] IWMSA. Accession No. 10106. Col. J. Buckmaster, reel 2.
[141] TNA DEFE 70/101. 'British guilt revealed. Horror in nameless village', *The People*, 1 February 1970.
[142] *Manchester Guardian*, 17 July & 27 August 1951; L. Comber, *Malaya's Secret Police 1945–60. The Role of the Special Branch in the Malayan Emergency* (Victoria, Australia: Monash University Press, 2008), 83–4.

spoke Kikuyu. British soldiers knew that the prisoners they handed over were likely to be ill-treated, but that did not always prevent them from doing so.[143] Some interrogators were not squeamish in the methods they employed.[144] A company commander in the Kenya Regiment denied that he allowed his men to beat suspects, but did admit that they were allowed 'to go as far as giving the man a good fright' to make them talk.[145] An intelligence officer from the same regiment thought that 'a smack over the ear' was quite acceptable.[146] An officer in the Kenya Police Reserve tried to frighten a prisoner into telling him the location of a Mau Mau gang by firing a shot four inches above his head and threatening 'Next one goes through your skull.'[147] Techniques used by the Kenya police included placing an upturned bucket on a prisoner's head and beating it with a metal instrument and forcing a prisoner 'to put his head between his knees, put his arms round the back of his knees and hold his ears, and stay in that position until he gave in.'[148]

In Nyasaland a British army liaison officer reported that troops were continuing to arrest large numbers of people and 'It seems those arrested soon say where others are hiding and Askaris [are] not slow in extracting this information.'[149] While serving in Aden in 1967 1/Parachute Regiment earned the displeasure of the authorities because of 'the vigorous interrogation methods', they employed. To avoid further censure, the battalion adopted a more subtle technique. Prisoners were taken to the local bank, which had a large computer, where they were 'lashed to the main-frame and informed that the radiation from the machine would make him sterile, Arabs being particularly sensitive about their macho image.'[150] A soldier in 1/Argyll and Sutherland Highlanders alleged that the battalion had established its own interrogation centre in a basement and that 'When such suspects were being interrogated, I could hear the stick cracking his skull. The butt of the rifle cracking the chin. You could hear these things. You could hear the questions being asked in Arabic. I didn't know...I couldn't speak Arabic, so I didn't know what they were asking. You could hear the pleading of the Arabs. Another crack on the skull. Another question and an answer.'[151]

Such behaviour happened because at least some senior officers and officials created a permissive atmosphere in which it was acceptable to ill-treat prisoners. Asked about the way prisoners were treated immediately after capture, Harding replied:

---

[143] TNA WO 32/21720. Proceedings of the McLean Court of Inquiry. Reverend F. T. Squire RACD, 29 December 1953.

[144] C. Elkins, *Britain's Gulag. The Brutal End of Empire in Kenya* (London: Jonathan Cape, 2005), 62–90.

[145] TNA. WO 32/21720. Proceedings of the McLean Court of Inquiry, Major N. M. C. Cooper, 21 December 1953.

[146] TNA WO 32/21720. Proceedings of the McLean Court of Inquiry, Captain J. W. Turnbull, 28 December 1953.

[147] T. Symonds, *The Mail on Sunday*, 7 February 2010.

[148] TNA CO 822/471. Canon T. F. C. Bewes to Baring, 28 January 1953.

[149] TNA CO 1015/1494. British Liaison Officer Salisbury to WO, 30 March 1959.

[150] J. Starling, *Soldier On! The Testament of a Tom* (Tunbridge Wells: Spellmount, 1992), 51–2.

[151] J. Lynn, *Empire Warriors. Aden: Mad Mitch and his Tribal Law*, BBC, 2004.

As far as ill-treatment, rough treatment on capture, I think that is something which inevitably does happen. After all if you've got troops or police who are engaged in an anti-terrorist operation and they've seen some of their comrades killed in action, well then they capture some of the enemy responsible, naturally they are liable to be rough handled, and that is a perfectly natural thing to happen, and not something which you can regulate against. I don't think it happened to any serious extent in Cyprus, but certainly there were occasions when a captured EOKA man was pretty roughly handled in the course of his arrest. And that's something which is perfectly natural, and to my mind, acceptable.[152]

But what he believed was not acceptable, and what was specifically forbidden by the official regulations, was the employment of physical duress during the second stage of a prisoner's interrogation.[153] That was intended to produce background information from which the Special Branch could build up a bigger picture of the insurgents' organizations and personalities. It was carried out, once the prisoners had been removed from the frontline, by either Special Branch officers or trained interrogators of the army's Intelligence Corps. How it was done depended not only on the skill and training of the interrogators, but also on the facilities available to them, and whether they merely wanted to secure information from their prisoners, or whether they wished to 'turn' them and employ them as double agents.

During the Second World War MI5 had been highly successful at interrogating and 'turning' captured German agents. In a number of Combined Service Detailed Interrogation Centres, using an excellent records registry, and information provided by signals intercepts, interrogators induced prisoners to talk by simultaneously frightening them and persuading them that, as they already knew a great deal about their activities, it was pointless to remain silent. If that did not work they used other means, including stool pigeons, 'sympathy men', and bugging devices.[154] Similar methods were sometimes used in post-war counter-insurgencies, especially if the interrogators were seeking to build up a sense of trust in the mind of their prisoner which might make them willing to switch sides and work for the Special Branch.[155] Prisoners whom the Special Branch wanted to use as agents were much more likely to be treated in a similar way to those who had surrendered. Both were fed and clothed, and then questioned in a quiet and sympathetic manner. Insurgents who had been indoctrinated into believing that if they were captured they would be tortured, might be 'turned' by kindness when they were well

---

[152] IWMSA. Accession No. 8736. Field Marshal Lord Harding, Transcript, 409.

[153] TNA WO 33/2335. Joint Services Pamphlet, *Interrogation in War*, 1955; TNA WO 208/5572. ? to Inspector of Intelligence, 18 November 1963. IWMSA. Accession No. 10232. L. Crosland, reel. 2.

[154] O. Hoare (ed.), *Camp 020. MI5 and Nazi Spies. The Official History of MI5's Wartime Interrogation Centre* (London: Public Record Office, 2000), 17–21, 105–31; C. Cunningham, 'International interrogation techniques', *JRUSI*, vol. 117 (June 1972), 31–4; K. Fedorowitch, 'Axis prisoners of war as sources for British military intelligence, 1939–42', *INS*, vol. 14 (1999), 156–78; C. Walton, 'Torture and intelligence gathering in Western democracies', downloaded 23 March 2010 at www.historyandpolicy.org/papers/policy-paper-78.html.

[155] IWMSA. Accession No. 10232. L. Crosland, reel 3; IWMSA. Accession No. 10175. R. J. W. Craig, Transcript, 14.

treated.[156] Others agreed to co-operate because of the threat that if they did not they might be tried and executed, or at best interned for a long time, or because they were offered money.[157]

Such methods could yield good results, but they took time and a large investment in resources. They needed skilled interrogators and linguists, ample accommodation, sophisticated listening equipment, and an efficient registry system to provide detailed briefings for interrogators before they questioned prisoners.[158] Facilities based on the CSDIC model were established in Malaya and Aden, but they were rarely available elsewhere, particularly in the early stages of an insurgency, when everything had to be improvised from scratch.[159] The British may have governed the countries in which they fought their counter-insurgency campaigns for many years, but all too often the soldiers and policemen who were rushed into an emergency situation to expand the existing security forces lacked even a rudimentary understanding of the language and culture of the people amongst whom they were operating. In Cyprus the army had so few Greek-speakers that they took National Servicemen with a knowledge of classical Greek learnt at school, gave them a crash course in modern Greek, and sent them to the island as interrogators.[160] In Borneo the handful of trained interrogators available had to work through interpreters, who themselves found it difficult to understand the particular dialect of Malay that their prisoners spoke.[161] The result, according to an MOD psychologist who had been involved in prisoner interrogation, was that interrogation units

> have been expected to operate with minimal resources, poor personnel, often in the most appalling physical condition and usually in great haste. They have been flung prisoners like so many bones to a pack of hungry dogs and ordered to crunch them and make them yield something of substance.[162]

Forbidden to subject prisoners to physical mutilation, interrogators in need of quick results developed a number of other methods of placing pressure on their prisoners which would not leave lasting signs of physical injuries. In 1971 and 1972

[156] *Empire Warriors. Malaya 1948. The Intelligence War*, BBC, 2004; IWMSA. Accession No. 10232. L. Crosland, reel 2.
[157] IWMSA. Accession No. 11162. Anon., reel 1; IWMSA. Accession No. 10175. R. J. W. Craig, Transcript, 14–15.
[158] TNA CAB 163/68/JIC(65)15. Sir B. Burrows, Joint directive on military interrogation in internal security operations overseas, 17 February 1965; TNA CAB 129/161/25/CP(72)25. Cabinet Secretary, The Parker Report, 29 February 1972; B. Stewart, 'The interrogation dilemma', *INS*, vol. 24 (2010), 642. For an example of when 'CSDIC' methods did yield good results see TNA CO 1035/178. Report of IS interrogation in Aden, 2 January 1965 to 30 January 1965 by WO2 Everson, Intelligence Corps.
[159] TNA DEFE 11/33. Sir H. Gurney to Colonial Secretary, 7 July 1949; TNA CO 1035/178. Lt.-Col. R. M. Richards, IS interrogation in Aden, 18 September 1964 to 25 October 1964; Comber, *Malaya's Secret Police*, 85–6.
[160] TNA DEFE 11/181/COS(56)126. Confidential annex, 29 November 1956; LHCMA Ian W. G. Martin mss. I; Martin, 'In the Service of Queen and Country', *Plebs, Journal of the British Library of Social and Political Science*, 1978.
[161] TNA WO 208/5572. Sqr. Leader E. S. Williams to MI7, 16 April 1963.
[162] Cunningham, 'International interrogation techniques', 31.

the Compton and Parker reports on the treatment of detainees in Northern Ireland discovered that, in the course of operations ranging from Palestine to Borneo, the army had applied a number of interrogation techniques including sleep deprivation, a restricted diet of bread and water, being forced to stand for long periods against a wall in a stressful position, hooding prisoners and subjecting them to loud noises for long periods.[163] Their object was to make detainees receptive to interrogation by frightening them, making them realize that they were isolated in a hostile environment, and were at the mercy of their interrogators. As a senior Special Branch officer in Malaya explained 'You would continue to bombard the suspect with questions. You'd keep at him. Tiredness came into it. That was a great weapon. I suppose it could be called cruel. I suppose it was. It has been labelled cruel in Northern Ireland. But you'd keep suspects awake. You'd make sure they suffered from fatigue, and by these means you'd break their resistance down. And in the end, I don't know of one who in the end did not give us some information.'[164]

Whether or not such techniques constituted torture was problematic. Neither the UN Declaration on Human Rights nor the ECHR defined what constituted torture, or inhuman or degrading treatment. This omission was perpetuated in directives issued to interrogators, who were thus given a free hand to employ their own methods.[165] Critics have subsequently termed them as 'torture lite'.[166] A Special Branch officer recalled that at the Holding Centre in Kuala Lumpur, 'I don't think they tortured anybody—not that—but I think they had a masterly control over . . . over their minds. I think, you know, brainwashing, I suppose. They had a very hard time in there. The beds weren't quite straight. They had a room built where the walls weren't even, and the ceiling was on a slope, and the bed was on a slope. They could disorientate people.'[167] A guard at the Aden interrogation centre who saw prisoners before and after they were interrogated thought that afterwards, 'they would look a bit different. Physically they would be . . . they'd been thorough the mill.'[168]

There were no manuals detailing how these techniques should be employed. They were taught at the Intelligence Corps training centre by word of mouth.[169] The centre also taught other techniques which, in view of the physical brutality

[163] These techniques were cited in a petition presented to the Colonial Secretary by detainees held in Aden in November 1964. TNA CO 1055/266. Petition by 27 detainees held at Fort Morbut to 'The Minister for Colonial Affairs', 27 November 1964.

[164] IWMSA. Accession No. 10300. J. Sankey, reel 3.

[165] TNA CAB 163/68/JIC(65)15. Sir B. Burrows, Joint directive on military interrogation in IS operations overseas, 17 February 1965; TNA CAB 163/68. T. Oates, Instructions on Detainees, 30 September 1965.

[166] J. Wolfendale, 'The myth of "torture lite"', *Ethics and International Affairs*, vol. 23 (2009), 47–61.

[167] E. Davies, *Empire Warriors. Malaya 1948: The Intelligence War*, BBC, 2004.

[168] B. Roy, Lt.-Col. C. Mitchell, J. Lynn, *Empire Warriors. Aden: Mad Mitch and his Tribal Law*, BBC, 2004.

[169] TNA CAB 129/161/25/CP(72)25. Cabinet Secretary, The Parker Report, 29 February 1972; TNA CAB 129/159/33/CP(71)133. Home Secretary, Northern Ireland. The Compton Report, 12 November 1971.

they involved, did meet any reasonable definition of torture. In 1960 a National Serviceman who received his Intelligence Corps training in 1949 remembered that

> My platoon was taught, among other things, the way in which to interrogate a prisoner and we were told that, in certain cases, it would probably be necessary for us to use various forms of physical torture. The tortures that were described to us had the advantage of leaving none of the visible traces which might be noticed by members of the International Red Cross and included beating the prisoner after his body had been wrapped in a wet blanket, filling his body with water and holding him against a hot stove. Our instructor, a Regular sergeant in the Intelligence Corps, told us that he had seen these tortures used against Japanese prisoners in Burma. I have since been told by other National Servicemen that the same methods were being recommended as recently as three years ago and there is, of course, every reason to believe that they are still being taught today.[170]

The majority report of the Parker inquiry downplayed the possibility that the techniques the inquiry had discovered might cause physical or mental damage. Compton made a semantic distinction, accepting that they constituted physical ill-treatment, but not 'physical brutality'.[171] Their use was banned by British forces in 1972, although they appear to have been employed in Iraq in 2003.[172] But whatever the semantics of the procedures, the army's own psychiatrists recognized that exposure to the techniques described by Compton and Parker could cause psychotic illness, with episodes of terror, depression, and delusion, and at least one psychologist concluded that they might 'produce a long-lasting post-traumatic neurosis'.[173]

DETENTION

The ordeal endured by prisoners did not end with their interrogation. After being interrogated most prisoners were transferred to detention camps. The conditions under which they were held varied. At one extreme Archbishop Makarios and three associates were arrested and deported from Cyprus to the Seychelles in March 1956. The Colonial Office, determined to ensure that they could not make any propaganda out of their treatment, maintained them in luxury. Housed in the governor's summer house, they were allowed to move about the island, purchase food and other goods from local shops, and were given generous living expenses

---

[170] TNA WO 32/17501. A. Hetherington to Secretary of State War, 3 December 1958.; TNA WO 32/17501. G. Strickland to P. Emery MP, 18 March 1960.
[171] I. Brownlie, 'Interrogation in depth: The Compton and Parker Reports,' *The Modern Law Review*, Vol. 35 (1972), 501–7.
[172] R. Kerr, 'A force for good? War, crime and legitimacy: the British Army in Iraq', *Defense and Security Analysis*, vol. 24 (2008), 412.
[173] TNA DEFE 70/211. Brigadier J. F. D. Murphy (Professor of Army Psychiatry) to Lt.-Col. T. B. Stephens, Notes for Medical Officers on interrogation phase of exercise, 24 February 1969; T. Shallice, 'The Ulster depth interrogation techniques and their relation to sensory deprivation research', *Cognition*, vol. 1 (1973), 385.

sufficient not only to cover food, but also 'wine, tobacco, clothing, books and a taxi fares for sightseeing from advances from account.'[174] At the other extreme were the often appalling conditions and treatment meted out to detainees in Kenya. Even in pre-emergency times African prisoners in Kenya were routinely subjected to unhealthy living conditions, inadequate food, and corporal punishment.[175] Conditions in most emergency detention and rehabilitation camps were even worse, although some administrators persisted in believing that all was for the best. 'I think that three quarters of the Kikuyu that you put into detention were thankful to be there,' recalled one Provincial Commissioner. 'They were no longer intimidated, they were no longer being forced to take these ghastly oaths.'[176] In reality detainees were obliged to do hard manual labour, and to live in overcrowded huts with inadequate food, bedding, latrines, and washing facilities.[177] One camp, built to house 6,000 detainees, actually held 16,000, resulting in a major outbreak of typhoid in 1954 that claimed 115 lives. During the emergency detainees were put through a 'pipeline', a series of camps with regimes of varying severity that were intended to 'rehabilitate' them so that they might eventually be released.[178] Kenyan government pronouncements painted a picture of rehabilitation as a benign process of training and Christian teaching.[179] But it was common for corporal punishment, euphemistically referred to as 'shock treatment', to be used to induce detainees to renounce their allegiance to Mau Mau.[180] In March 1959, in the most scandalous case, 11 detainees were beaten to death by their guards at Hola camp when they refused to work. But even that did not prevent the Nyasaland government from thinking that they had something to learn from their northern neighbour. In April 1959 Nyasaland imported a senior District Commissioner from Kenya with experience of the 'pipeline' system to advise them on how to deal with their detainees, and he recommended establishing the same system wholesale in Nyasaland.[181]

Conditions for detainees in Malaya, Cyprus, Palestine, and Borneo fell between these two extremes. Six detention camps had been opened in Malaya by June 1949. In their public pronouncements, the Federal Government presented a positive and humane picture of conditions in the camps. Detainees could not be compelled to do any work except that necessary to keep their rooms clean. But many undertook voluntary work, for which they received payment. They were also given a plot of

[174] TNA CO 926/532. Colonial Secretary to Harding, 16 March 1956; TNA CO 926/533. Secretary to the Governor of the Seychelles to P. S. Joannides, 14 March 1956; TNA CO 926/533. Governor of the Seychelles to Colonial Secretary, 2 May 1956.
[175] D. Branch, 'Imprisonment and Colonialism in Kenya, *c*.1930–1952: Escaping the Carceral Archipelago', *The International Journal of African Historical Studies*, vol. 38, no. 2 (2005), 239–65.
[176] IWMSA. Accession No. 11074. R. E. Wainwright, Transcript, 34–5.
[177] TNA CO 822/1258. L. Boissier, President of ICRC to Lennox-Boyd, 16 May 1957.
[178] TNA WO 276/92. W. F. B. Pollock-Morris to Under Secretary CO, C-in-C East Africa, Attorney-General, Commissioner of Police, et al, 25 June 1955; TNA CO 822/1273. Report of the Committee on Emergency Detention Camps, 7 July 1959; Elkins, *Britain's Gulag*, 91–191.
[179] *Times*, 1 September 1953.
[180] TNA CO 822/1273. F. D. Webber to Baring, 17 July 1959; TNA CO 822/1258. L. Boissier, President of ICRC to Lennox-Boyd, 12 October 1959.
[181] TNA CO 1015/1839. Armitage to J. C. Morgan, 18 April 1959; TNA CO 1015/1905. J. Pinney, System for the holding, rehabilitation and release of detainees', n.d. but *c*.28 May 1959.

land to cultivate and received the same diet as civilian prisoners in gaol.[182] Detainees who were not identified as hard-core members of the MCP were sent to a rehabilitation camp, where they were exposed to anti-Communist propaganda 'so they would be good lads when they went back. Spread the gospel of the glory of British rule and so on,' and underwent a course of vocational training so that eventually they could be released.[183] The importance of treating detainees in a reasonably humane manner was underlined when a group of insurgents who had voluntarily surrendered were interrogated in the second half of 1954. A quarter of them claimed that they had finally been persuaded to surrender by stories of the good treatment meted out by the government to comrades who had already surrendered.[184] But there was also a 'special camp', the Majeedi detention camp, which was used to discipline those detainees who were not willing to obey the rules of the ordinary camps. At Majeedi discipline was stricter and detainees were required to work (for which they were paid) but had fewer privileges in terms of visits and prison luxuries. Detainees at Majeedi were put through a three-stage process of rehabilitation, with increasing privileges as their behaviour improved.[185] That camp regimes were not always as benign as the government suggested was indicated by events at Ipoh detention camp in June 1955, when detainees rioted and took two warders hostage. In their efforts to restore order, warders, according to the local coroner, over-reacted, killed three detainees and wounded others. The attitude of the detainees the next day was described as being a mixture of truculence and sullen resentment.[186]

Truculence and sullen resentment was also an apt summary of the attitude of detainees in Cyprus. In September 1955 the first group of detainees, held in the Central Prison in Nicosia, complained that they were housed in over-crowded cells with inadequate sanitation and were beaten by their guards. They were then moved to the more forbidding surroundings of Kyrenia Castle.[187] There they created even more trouble for their jailers when 16 of them escaped 'by means of a rope made of blankets'.[188] Those remaining were moved a second time, to specially constructed

---

[182] TNA CO 1022/132. Extract from proceedings of the Malayan Legislative Council, 19 March 1952.

[183] IWMSA. Accession No. 9141. J. M. Patrick, reel 1; TNA CO 1022/132. No. 24 of 1953. Federation of Malaya. Detention and deportation during the Emergency in the Federation of Malaya. Paper to be laid before the Federal Legislative Council by Command of His Excellency the High Commissioner, 9 March 1953; TNA CO 1031/1425. Jerrom to Vernon, 14 January 1954; TNA CO 926/394. Colonial Secretary to Harding, 7 January 1956.

[184] TNA WO 291/1786. ORS(PW), Memorandum 15/54. A study of surrenders amongst Communist Terrorists in Malaya, June to November 1954, 18 November 1954.

[185] TNA CO 1022/132. No. 24 of 1953. Federation of Malaya. Detention and deportation during the emergency in the Federation of Malaya. Paper to be laid before the Federal Legislative Council by Command of His Excellency the High Commissioner, 9 March 1953.

[186] TNA CO 1030/145. High Commissioner Malaya to Colonial Secretary, 5, 6, 7, 9, June & 16 July 1955.

[187] TNA CO 926/396. Acting Governor Cyprus to Colonial Secretary, 3 September 1955; TNA CO 926/396. Governor of Cyprus to Colonial Secretary, 17 October 1955; TNA CO 926/396. Colonial Secretary to Acting Governor, 30 September 1955; TNA CO 926/396. BBC Monitoring Service, Caversham Park: Athens Broadcasts for Cyprus, 1 October 1955.

[188] TNA CO 926/396. Sir R. Armitage to Colonial Secretary, 24 September 1955.

detention camps where they lived in over crowded huts in enclosures ringed by barbed-wire fences overlooked by guard towers equipped with searchlights and automatic weapons.[189] Facilities were basic, and when Sir Lionel Fox, the Chairman of the UK's Prison Commission, visited the camps in March 1956, he recommended a range of essential improvements.[190] The physical conditions of detainees may subsequently have improved, but that did not prevent them from causing serious disturbances on at least two occasions.[191]

By early January 1963 over 2,200 people were in detention in Brunei in often appalling physical conditions.[192] One camp consisted of an open-air tennis court which flooded when it rained.[193] A British staff officer admitted that 'the state of the prisoners in the Detention Camps is pitiful, and many of them will be permanently embittered.'[194] By the end of January, efforts to improve accommodation were underway, two detention camps had been opened, detainees were being screened and classified according to their degree of involvement in the revolt, and plans were being prepared to start a rehabilitation centre, although it was not finally opened until the end of March.[195] Detainees graded as 'white' were released immediately, those classified as varying shades of 'grey' were put through a rehabilitation programme, and some were kept back for police investigations with a view to prosecution.[196] As in Malaya, the authorities tried to present a positive picture of the rehabilitation regime, but again as in Malaya, detainees did not take kindly to their forced incarceration. In July some of them staged a 48-hour hunger strike, protesting at the fact of their detention and alleged ill-treatment by their guards.[197]

But whatever material conditions they enjoyed, all detainees were kept behind barbed wire against their will. Some of them suffered great physical hardships, but all of them suffered the same psychological hardships. Their indeterminate legal status meant that, unlike criminal prisoners who had been tried and sentenced to a term of imprisonment, they had no idea how long they would remain incarcerated. 'They consider themselves', reported an ICRC delegate who visited a camp in Eriterea in June 1946 which held Zionist detainees deported from Palestine, 'as

[189] TNA CO 936/397. Minute, K. J. Neale, 28 September 1956 on Harding to Colonial Secretary, 26 September 1956; TNA CO 926/871. C. Legum, 'Cypriots in Camp K. deny ill-treatment', *Observer*, 3 March 1957.
[190] TNA CO 926/394. Report to the Governor by Sir L. Fox and Mr D. Fairn on the matters referred them concerning the treatment of detainees and the future development of the treatment of offenders, 22 March 1956.
[191] TNA CO 936/397. Harding to CO, 24 October 1956; TNA CO 926/872. Sir H. Foot to CO, 10 April 1958.
[192] TNA WO 305/2519. Perintrep, n.d. but *c.*6 January 1963.
[193] TNA WO 305/2519. HQ British Forces Borneo, Joint Perintrep No. 3, 19 January 1963.
[194] *Manchester Guardian*, 11 December 1962; TNA WO 305/2519. HQ British Forces Borneo, Joint Perintrep No. 2, 12 January 1963.
[195] TNA WO 305/2519. HQ British Forces Borneo, Joint Perintrep No. 4, 26 January 1963.
[196] TNA WO 305/2520. Minutes of a meeting of the Borneo Security Council held at the Office of the High Commissioner for Brunei, 29 March 1963; TNA WO 305/2520. Minutes of a meeting of the Borneo Security Council held at the Office of the High Commissioner for Brunei, 29 March 1963.
[197] TNA CO 1030/1539. Extracts from the Sarawak Monthly Intelligence Report, July 1963, n.d. but *c.*1 August 1963.

outlaws, since they have not been charged and there is no national or international body to which they can appeal. But these people have been cut off from the rest of the world for several years, without any prospect of returning home. This mental condition must be kept in mind.' Several of the detainees were apparently suffering from 'a nervous trouble and hysteria due to prolonged internment (from five to six years) behind barbed wire, and to the uncertainty in which they are regarding the length of their detention.'[198]

COVER-UPS

Coercion in different guises was fundamental to British-conducted counter-insurgency operations. But beyond the officially sanctioned policies of reprisals, collective punishments and population control measures that were designed to intimidate the civil population into withdrawing their support from the insurgents, there were, as this chapter has shown, a range of unofficial acts of brutality committed by members of the security forces. This was nothing new. Similar patterns of behaviour have been documented in South Africa during the Anglo-Boer War of 1899 and 1902, in Ireland between 1919 and 1921, and in Palestine between 1936 and 1939.[199] The attitude of the authorities towards such behaviour was significant. The injunctions in both official manuals and orders issued by commanders in the field that members of the security forces had to maintain proper discipline suggests that they wanted to keep tight control over their subordinates. Their apparent willingness to punish wrongdoers, and, for example, the decision of the Kenya government to expand the KPR, is also evidence that they wanted to prevent the development of vigilante death squads. But there is also evidence that they sometimes went to considerable lengths to cover up wrongdoing, or at least to place limits on what was disclosed. This can be illustrated by looking at five incidents, each of which became a minor *cause célèbre*: the court martial already mentioned of Major Roy Farran in October 1947; the shooting by the army of 24 Chinese rubber tappers, who were allegedly insurgents trying to escape, at the village of Batang Kali in Malaya in December 1948; the shooting in Kenya of two forest workers by Captain G. S. L. Griffiths of 5/KAR in June 1953; the mass assault upon several hundred Greek Cypriots in Famagusta in October 1958 following the assassination of Mrs Cutliffe, the wife of an army sergeant; and the alleged systematic torture of

---

[198] TNA FO 371/61872. M. Munier, Jewish political internees detained in Eritrea. Special Camp number 119, n.d. but *c.*September 1946.

[199] S. M. Miller, 'Duty or crime? Defining acceptable behaviour in the British Army in South Africa, 1899–1902', *Journal of British Studies*, vol. 49 (April 2010), 311–31; P. Hart, *The IRA and its Enemies. Violence and Community in Cork 1916–1923* (Oxford: Oxford University Press, 1998), 95–100; D. Leeson, 'Death in the afternoon: the Croke Park massacre, 21 November 1920', *Canadian Journal of History*, vol. 38 (2003), 43–67; M. F. Seedorf, 'The Lloyd George government and the Strickland report on the burning of Cork, 1920', *Albion*, vol. 4 (1972), 59–66; M. Hughes, 'The banality of brutality: British armed forces and the repression of the Arab revolt in Palestine, 1936–39', *EHR*, vol. 124 (2009), 313–54.

prisoners at Fort Morbut, the security forces' interrogation centre in Aden, in 1965–6.

In Palestine the authorities were less than eager to pursue Farran. They decided that they had to court martial him only after the story broke in the press in Palestine and America.[200] The head of the Palestine Police, Lt.-Col. W. N. Gray, was deliberately slow in pursuing enquiries against Farran, giving priority instead to finding the members of the Stern Gang that Farran had uncovered. Two Palestine policemen had just been assassinated in Jerusalem, and Nicol thought that the arrest of a senior British police officer 'would have had, in my opinion, a disastrous effect on the morale of the Force.'[201] At the trial the prosecution was seriously impeded because Farran's commanding officer, Bernard Fergusson, refused to give evidence on the grounds that he might incriminate himself.[202] Higher up the chain of command the COS of MELF, Major-General Pyman, admitted that he 'was most distressed to hear about Roy Farran, and off the record have been doing all I can to help him.'[203] Farran was found innocent and immediately left the country. The trial was, with some justification, dismissed as a farce by the Yishuv.[204]

In Malaya, shortly after news of what had happened at Batang Kali broke, a British police officer, hearing of what was reported to be a major success by the security forces visited the village where

> I photographed the dead people still piled together on the back of a truck. I was disturbed to see how white were the palms of their hands, and I was surprised to see that they all wore singlets and underpants. I did not wish to determine whether they were men or women. They were not at all like the Gombak Armed Work Force, whose hands were dark and rough. Moreover, no weapons had been found and no one had been wounded. They were all stone dead. I returned to Rawang and discovered that one of my Chinese detectives came from that area and he volunteered to visit his aunt's family. On his return, it was clear to me that these people were not terrorists, but civilian rubber tappers on one of the local absentee landlord Chinese-owned rubber estates.[205]

His misgivings were soon shared by the Malayan press, and the planter who had employed the tappers made a complaint. There were then no fewer than three inquiries: an army court of inquiry, an inquiry by the Attorney-General of Malaya, and a judicial inquiry conducted by a judge from Singapore. The soldiers concerned were exonerated. However, the extent to which the inquiries elicited the truth is open to doubt. The army's own Special Investigation Branch was not asked to examine the evidence, which might suggest that the military authorities were less than enthusiastic about uncovering what had happened.[206] Evidence

[200] Cesarani, *Major Farran's Hat*, 119–22.
[201] TNA CO 537/2302. Nicol to Chief Secretary, Government of Palestine, 24 June 1947.
[202] *Palestine Post*, 9 October 1947.
[203] LHCMA. Gen. Sir H. E. Pyman mss 7/1/9. Pyman to Maj.-Gen J. M. L. Renton, 3 September 1947.
[204] IWMSA. Accession No 29225. E. Yakin, reel 1.
[205] Hatton, *Tock Tock Birds*, 138.
[206] TNA DEFE 70/101. A. C. Burcher to C2(AD), 16 February 1970.

recently uncovered in Malaysia suggests that the Attorney-General was privately convinced that 'there was something to be said for public executions as a legitimate means to demoralise those involved in the insurgency.'[207] There is also one further piece of evidence that points towards a high-level cover-up. On 22 January 1949 the Federal government promulgated a new Emergency Regulation, 27A. Henceforth, after issuing a challenge, soldiers and police were authorized to shoot anyone escaping from their custody. Significantly, this regulation was made retrospective so that, according to Regulation 27A(6), 'Any act or thing done before the coming into force of this Regulation which would have been lawfully done if this Regulation had been in force, shall be deemed to have been lawfully done under this Regulation.'[208] What had been illegal in December 1948, was made legal by the stroke of a pen in January 1949.

In Kenya Griffiths was court-martialled on a murder charge, but was found not guilty on a technicality. Erskine's very real dismay at this, and his insistence that he be retried on a lesser charge, may serve as testimony to his determination to ensure the good behaviour of all members of the security forces. But a different picture emerges if the wider context is explored. In December 1953, because of the public furore created by the news of the Griffiths acquittal, the Cabinet felt compelled to establish an inquiry into the conduct of the army in Kenya.[209] But ministers carefully controlled the composition and remit of the inquiry in order to limit any embarrassing revelations. The Secretary of State for War, Anthony Head, had already made up his mind what he wanted the inquiry to find even before it had been established. 'We sh[oul]d', he told the Cabinet, 'seek to show it [the Griffiths murder] was exceptional,' and not commonplace in Kenya.[210] Despite requests from Labour MPs for a public inquiry, the Cabinet decided that it would take the form of an army court of inquiry presided over by a senior army officer, Sir Kenneth McLean.[211] The army would investigate itself. Furthermore, McLean's terms of reference were deliberately narrowed to exclude all events that had taken place between the start of the emergency and Erskine's arrival in June 1953. This was done at Erskine's insistence. 'There is no doubt', he wrote to Head on 10 December 1953,

> from Oct[ober] 1952 until last June there was a great deal of indiscriminate shooting by Army and Police. I am quite certain prisoners were beaten to extract information. It is a short step from beating to torture and I am now sure, although it has taken me some time to realise it, that torture was a feature of many police posts. I do not believe

[207] R. Verkaik, '60 years on, Malaya "massacre" by British troops to be investigated', *The Independent on Sunday*, 30 April 2009.

[208] TNA CO 717/167/3. Federation of Malaya. Regulations made under the Emergency regulations Ordinance, 1948 together with the Essential (Special Constabulary) Regulations 1948, incorporating all amendments up to 22 March 1949. (Kuala Lumpur: Government Press, 1949.)

[209] TNA CAB 128/26/CC(53)73 meeting. Cabinet Conclusions, 30 November 1953; TNA WO 32/21722. Extract from *Hansard*, Cols. 770–3, 30 November 1953; TNA CAB 128/26/CC(53)77 meeting. Cabinet Conclusions, 8 December 1953.

[210] TNA CAB 195/11/CC73(53). Cabinet meeting, 30 November 1953.

[211] TNA WO 32/15834. Nicholson to Erskine, 9 December 1953.

the regular police were heavily involved although some of them may have been. The real trouble came from the Kenya settler dressed as KPR or in Kenya Reg[imen]t. This example tended to spread and was whipped up by such events as the Lari Massacre and every European murder.[212]

An independent inquiry might insist on investigating everything from the beginning of the Emergency and 'I think the revelations would be shattering.'[213] Erskine got his way. McLean conducted an army inquiry into the army. He confined his investigations to the period after Erskine's arrival and focused on just three issues that had been raised at the Griffith court martial: the offering of monetary rewards to soldiers for Mau Mau kills, the keeping of scoreboards recording kills, and the fostering of a competitive spirit between units to kill Mau Mau.[214] The inquiry lasted 12 days. It interviewed 147 witnesses, from Brigadiers to private soldiers, plus a Roman Catholic bishop. Witnesses gave evidence under oath, but were granted immunity from prosecution. This perhaps explains why instances of casual brutality that they testified to were not followed up by the prosecuting authorities. The inquiry gave the army a relatively clean bill of health. McLean's conclusions served a double purpose. They appeared to vindicate the conduct of the army, but equally important his report served to instruct the troops in appropriate modes of behaviour.[215] The inquiry was not a complete whitewash. But it was certainly not as thorough, penetrating, or revealing as it might have been.

The Cutliffe case demonstrated the limitations of coroners' inquests as a way of getting to the bottom of what happened when discipline amongst the security forces broke down. The wife of a battery commander in which Mrs Cutliffe's husband was serving recorded in her diary that 'All Greek males being rounded up and taken to cages for questioning. Troops not wearing kid gloves and many broken heads.'[216] Shortly after the soldier's rioted, one of them wrote to his father that

I suppose you are heard on the radio about all the trouble we had in Famagusta last Friday. About the two women being shot, one dead and the other very ill. The troops were called out . . . they gave the Greeks a hell of a time. The troops just went mad. There was no order for the first two hours. The officers could not control them. I suppose you heard what the Mayor of Famagusta said, '250 injured,' and I'll bet most of them had their heads split open. The lads all had riot sticks. In the first two hours they hit every Greek male they could lay their hands on.[217]

The inquest heard that two Cypriots had died as a result of injuries they received, injuries that Greek Cypriot witnesses claimed were inflicted by soldiers wielding

[212] TNA WO 32/15834. Erskine to Secretary of State for War, 10 December 1953.
[213] Ibid.
[214] TNA WO 32/21720. Proceedings of the McLean Court of Inquiry, 15 December 1953.
[215] H. Bennett, 'British Army counterinsurgency and the use of force in Kenya, 1952–56' (Ph.D. dissertation, University of Wales, Aberystwyth, 2007), 165–70.
[216] IWMDoD 93/30/1. Mrs J. Sommerville, diary entry, 3 October 1958.
[217] *Manchester Guardian*, 13 October 1958.

wooden sticks, although that was denied by soldiers who gave evidence.[218] Governor Foot subsequently claimed that, although the assassination had angered the troops, 'it did not affect their duties. They carried out their duties with balance and firmness and in a way that was wholly admirable.'[219] An army storeman remembered things differently. He had issued riot batons to anyone in his regiment who wanted one. Later he saw about 350 Greek Cypriots being made to run the gauntlet between a row of 200 soldiers who beat them and later he watched a medical officer tend to the injured. 'On Saturday morning our B[attery] Q[uarter] M[aster] S[ergeant] came into the stores and said he had enjoyed himself. The butt of his Sterling machine gun was bent and covered in bits of skin, hair and blood.'[220] Foot rejected Greek Cypriot demands for a public inquiry into the troops' behaviour, but the government did make ex-gratia payments to the families of the dead men.[221]

So vehement were allegations of torture at Fort Morbut that the Aden government's own Legal Adviser recommended a judicial enquiry. Governor Turnbull, however, rejected that because of the harm it would do to the morale, and hence the effectiveness, of the interrogators.[222] But a complete cover-up was impossible and the Foreign Secretary, George Brown, agreed to an official inquiry. It was marginally more independent than the McLean Inquiry, in that it was conducted by a civilian lawyer and Liberal MP, Roderick Bowen. But he was given what one critic has reasonably described as an 'evasive brief'.[223] Rather than examine specific allegations of torture, he was asked to investigate procedures for dealing with such reports in Aden.[224] He stuck to it and produced a report that exonerated everyone except for a handful of officials, who were accused of sins of omission, and three unnamed interrogators.[225] Under some pressure from the Prime Minister, the MOD then mounted its own, private, inquiry, into allegations that the interrogators had ill-treated detainees, but decided that there was insufficient evidence to try anyone for their actions.[226]

The willingness of the authorities to cover up the fact that sometimes members of the security forces took the law into their own hands points to a systemic problem. Even though emergency regulations gave the security forces considerable latitude, many of them still chafed against what they thought were unreasonable

[218] *Manchester Guardian*, 20 November 1958.

[219] IWMSA. Accession No. 8937. Sir H. Foot, reel 3.

[220] D. Cater, 'After the Cutliffe Murder', downloaded 6 August 2009 at www.britains-smallwars.com/cyprus/Davidcarter/aftercutliffe/aftercutliffe.html.

[221] *Manchester Guardian*, 7 February 1959.

[222] TNA FCO 8/153. Turnbull, Note on the security situation in Aden in December 1965, 25 January 1967.

[223] K. Sellars, 'Human rights and the colonies: deceit, deception and discovery', *The Round Table*, vol. 93 (2004), 717–18.

[224] TNA CAB 148/29/OPD(66)128. Bowen to Foreign Secretary, 14 November 1966.

[225] TNA CAB 148/29/OPD(66)128. Foreign Secretary, South Arabia: Bowen Report on the handling of detainees in Aden, 1 December 1966.

[226] TNA DEFE 13/529. A. M. Palliser to P. D. Nairne, 21 November 1966; TNA DEFE 13/529. G. Reynolds to Healey, 23 November 1966; TNA WO 32/20987. Adjutant-General to Minister (Army), 4 April 1967.

restraints, and were bitter at criticism of their behaviour. After the evacuation of Palestine the official historian of 6 Airborne Division regretted that the army had not been permitted to employ the full range of powers it had nominally been granted under the emergency regulations because of the political repercussions that would have arisen and hinted at the frustration this caused to the troops.[227] The officers and men of 1/Devonshire Regiment were deeply resentful of criticism directed at them by left-wing newspapers in Britain when they learnt that the battalion's commanding officer had offered a reward of £5 to the first patrol to kill a Mau Mau.[228] Similarly, at least one settler cum officer in the Kenya Regiment hankered after what he thought was a golden age of counter-insurgency when the security forces could do as they pleased. 'May I put it this way?' he asked rhetorically.

> When my father came out here years ago we had several small up-risings and regular troops were used to squash those up-risings and they were squashed and it never happened again. Now we have come down to it that this rising has happened and we had to do it legally, follow the band and so on, if you happen to step over a certain mark you spend six months on legal quibbles when you should be doing a job of work, and that is what is getting everybody down.[229]

Similar complaints were voiced by members of the security forces in other campaigns.[230] The authorities therefore had to walk a fine line between maintaining the rule of law as defined by emergency regulations on the one hand, and not undermining the morale of the security forces by punishing those who broke them. It was this concern that led Gurney to admit that he was reluctant to be seen to be criticizing the security forces in Malaya. In January 1949, writing about the 'alleged "bashing" of people picked up during anti-bandit raids', he explained that 'Rightly or wrongly, we feel here that we must be conservative in criticism of the men who are undoubtedly carrying out a most arduous and dangerous job . . .'[231]

The full impact of what might happen to the security apparatus of a colonial state like Kenya if there was a systematic inquiry into the misdeeds of the security forces was exposed in December 1954. Six members of the home guard at Ruthagathi were found guilty of murdering two Kikuyu farmers in their custody, and it became apparent in the course of the trial that this was not an isolated incident.[232] The very fact that even one trial of home guard miscreants had taken place, and that they had been found guilty, led to a serious drop in their morale. On 5 January 1955 a senior chief asked Erskine

---

[227] Wilson, *Cordon and Search*, 17–18.

[228] IWM. Dept of Docs. 90/20/1. J. K. Windeatt mss. Mau Mau rebellion Kenya. 1/Devonshire Regiment Record 1953–55.

[229] TNA WO 32/21720. Proceedings of the McLean Court of Inquiry, Major N. M. C. Cooper, 21 December 1953.

[230] TNA CO 926/1077. Report on the Cyprus Emergency, 31 July 1959.

[231] TNA DEFE 70/101. High Commissioner, Federation of Malaya, to CO, 1 January 1949.

[232] Anderson, *Histories of the Hanged.* 301–5.

How can we finish the Mau Mau terrorism if Home Guards, Chiefs and Headmen are taken to court and accused of beating the Mau Mau supporters and leaders? It has come to my notice that some of the Kangeme loyalists have been accused of the same. I am bitterly pained because the action has been taken in Fort Hall District and it is a pity if such a thing is to be carried out in the District where I am a senior chief. It is quite shameful to the loyalists who have assisted the Government since Emergency was declared and who have suffered mostly on [*sic*] the Mau Mau brutality, to be accused of fighting the lawbreakers. Is it the Mau Mau or the loyalists who will regain peace and order in our country? Surely it will give the terrorists a good chance of getting on with their terrorism activities. And on the other hand it will completely break down the hearts of the loyalists.[233]

By the beginning of 1955 a dozen further such cases were on-going.[234] The government in Nairobi and the administration in the disturbed provinces feared that if they proceeded and the accused were found guilty, large numbers of home guard would refuse to continue to fight and might desert to the Mau Mau.[235] To forestall such a nightmarish possibility, they decided that their only option was to reorganize the home guard so as to tighten its discipline while simultaneously retrospectively condoning its wrongdoings.[236] On 18 January 1955 the government announced a double amnesty in the shape of surrender terms for the Mau Mau and an amnesty for the home guard.[237]

CONCLUSION

Coercion and counter-terror, directed and organized by the state, were the mainstays of British policy. But it was never government policy to allow the security forces to take their own reprisals. However, charges were frequently levelled against soldiers, policemen, and home guards that they went beyond what they were allowed to do by the lax limits fixed by emergency regulations, and meted out their own brands of unofficial and casual brutality on the civilian population. Sometimes such charges were deliberately exaggerated by the insurgents for their own purposes. But there is sufficient independent testimony to suggest that there was a substratum of truth underpinning some of them. Soldiers and policemen might misbehave for a combination of reasons. These ranged from poor training and ignorance of the law, contempt for the indigenous population, fear of an unseen enemy who was killing and maiming their comrades, frustration that

---

[233] TNA WO 216/879. Senior Chief Njiri Karanja to Erskine, 5 January 1955.
[234] TNA WO 216/876. Governor Kenya to Colonial Secretary, 15 February 1955.
[235] TNA WO 216/879. District Commissioner, Fort Hall, to Erskine, n.d.; TNA WO 216/879. Baring to Colonial Secretary, 11 January 1955.
[236] TNA WO 276/90. Governor's Directive No. 4 of 1954, 31 December. 1954; TNA WO 216/879. Erskine to Secretary of State for War, 12 January 1955; TNA WO 236/18. Erskine to Governor Kenya and other Kenya government officials, CIGS and Military Members Army Council, Colonial Secretary, etc, 25 April 1955.
[237] TNA WO 276/430. To all Mau Mau leaders and their followers. New Surrender Terms, 18 January 1955; TNA PREM 11/1424. Acting Governor Kenya to Colonial Secretary, 21 January 1955.

generated a determination to retaliate against anyone they suspected of supporting the enemy, all coupled with senior officers who failed to enforce proper standards of conduct.[238] That they did not perpetrate atrocities on an even larger scale probably owed a good deal to the fact that the intensity of fighting in most campaigns was at a low level and so only rarely generated an uncontrollable sense of outrage amongst the security forces.

The attitude of the authorities towards members of the security forces who were alleged to have committed acts of unofficial brutality was never straightforward. On the one hand they did a good deal to condemn such behaviour, and occasionally they punished wrongdoers. But on the other hand they also sometimes felt obliged to hide evidence of their excesses and to limit punishments for fear that if they went too far they would break the morale of their own forces. If they acted too vigorously against wrongdoers, they might lose the hearts and minds of the security forces. But if they allowed them too much freedom to take unofficial reprisals, they would reduce the chances of winning the hearts and minds of the civil population. The British authorities did not deliberately and systematically direct 'dirty wars'. But, by their readiness to manipulate the law in their colonies and set aside accepted human rights safeguards, they did create an atmosphere within which it was easy for some elements of the security forces to operate in ways contrary to norms laid down in international law, and they did not always do as much as they might have done to forestall or punish such misbehaviour. The next chapter will examine the other side of the coin. Coercion was not the only weapon in the British counter-insurgents' armoury, for they sometimes also tried to 'court' both the insurgents and the civil population.

---

[238] Lt.-Col. R. Rielly, 'The inclination for war crimes', *Military Review* (May–June 2009), 17–23.

6

Winning Hearts and Minds

Within days of his arrival in Malaya, Templer told a group of senior civil servants in Kuala Lumpur that '"I could win this war in three months if I could get two thirds of the people on my side." It is not a military problem, he said. It is a political war. The basic problem is the people. Therefore emphasis must be placed on "political, economic, social and cultural development" of the people.'[1] In January 1953 his Deputy Director of Operations, Sir Rob Lockhart, told another press conference that 'the shooting war in Malaya was only 25 per cent of the struggle against the Communists. Progress had been most pronounced in the other 75 per cent— the struggle for the "hearts and minds of the people." He reviewed progress in health, welfare and educational work, and said the attitude of people resettled in new villages had changed for the better.'[2] The idea quickly spread. In November 1952 the Solicitor General of Kenya told the colony's Legislative Council that he had recently returned from Malaya where the situation had been described as '25 per cent a shooting war and 75 per cent a battle for the hearts and minds of the people. In Kenya he would put these figures at 5 per cent and 95 per cent. The battle for the hearts and minds would be retarded, he added, by injudicious punishment of the innocent.'[3]

The notion that faced by an insurgency governments have to use some force, but that it has to be applied judiciously to avoid alienating the civilian population, has become commonplace. It has been accompanied by the associated notion that governments must also try to raise the living standards and welfare of the population so as to show them that they would enjoy a better future if they threw in their lot with the government.[4] In the post-war era British soldiers were told to make friends with people, and that they had a natural propensity for doing so.[5] They sometimes used unorthodox methods to prove it. In Borneo a journalist noted that 'A large part of the military effort is concerned with "winning the hearts and minds of the people". British troops are good at it. There is now a thick file of stories about

---

[1] M. Davidson, 'Task in Malaya. Basic problem—the people', *Observer*, 10 February 1952.
[2] Anon., 'Winning the shooting war in Malaya', *Observer*, 4 January 1953.
[3] *Manchester Guardian*, 27 November 1952.
[4] T. R. Mockaitis, 'Winning hearts and minds in the "war on terrorism"', *SW&I*, vol. 14 (2003), 21; Gen. Sir Richard Dannatt, 'Setting a date for withdrawal plays into the enemy's hands', *Sunday Telegraph*, 6 December 2009; Professor Donald Wilhelm to the editor, *Evening Standard*, 21 September 2001; Mr Gerry Smallwood to editor, *Financial Times*, 7 October 2009; Damien McElroy, 'Analysis: A long haul, but wooing the Taliban may make it shorter', *Daily Telegraph*, 29 January 2010.
[5] TNA WO 279/121. *The Middle East* (London: War Office, n.d. but *c*.1947).

corporals who have become the unofficial mayors of communities, and of private soldiers acting as midwives and doctors.' Patrols visited villagers and 'A good deal of pleasure usually accompanies the business of obtaining intelligence. The villages will put on a war-dance show. The preserved heads of an earlier phase of Borneo's history are proudly displayed. In return, every member of the patrol is expected to perform a party piece. Experienced patrollers have now perfected various turns guaranteed to make an Iban laugh (this is actually very easy) and less talented newcomers can always just stand on their heads.'[6]

Standing on their heads is an apt metaphor for British efforts to win 'hearts and minds'. Coercion, not conciliation, was the mainstay of British policy. British efforts to deliver on promises of a better life were usually under-funded and under-resourced. Nor did they readily or willingly adopt what Thompson identified as the first principle of successful counter-insurgency operations, the pursuit of 'a clear political aim: to establish and maintain a free, independent and united country which is politically viable and economically stable and viable.'[7] This made it difficult for the British to achieve their real objectives, which were to persuade at least a minority of the civil population to give their active support to the colonial state, to serve in its government machinery and security forces, and to persuade most of the remainder that its claims to govern them were legitimate.[8]

THE CIVIL POPULATION AND COERCION

Being on the receiving end of British counter-insurgency operations was never pleasant. Some measures, like forced resettlement in Malaya and Kenya, were disliked because they imposed real physical hardships on people. In Malaya, the British may have called the settlements 'New Villages', but to their Chinese inhabitants 'they were in actual fact detention camps, with barbed wire and guards at every post. No one was free in a Chinese new village,' remembered one Chinese man whose family were resettled when he was a boy.[9] Another inhabitant remembered that 'Everybody was always under pressure as we were treated like prisoners with all our movements being watched.'[10] Their complaints were echoed by the Kikuyu who were forced to abandon their homes. A British journalist who visited some of the villages in August 1955 found that, 'Most Kikuyu dislike the cramped dwellings, the social and hygienic discipline to which the life compels them, the constant supervision by detachments of the security forces, tribal police, or home

---

[6] Anon., 'Battle for minds in Borneo', *Times*, 14 October 1963.
[7] Sir R. Thompson, *Defeating Communist Insurgency. The Lessons of Malaya and Vietnam* (St Petersburg, FL: Hailer Publishing, 2005; originally published 1966), 51–2.
[8] Major L. V. Packwood, 'Popular support as the objective in counter-insurgency. What are we really after', *Military Review* (May–June 2009), 67–77.
[9] Z. Koya, 'Villagers' sacrifice to beat Reds', *New Straits Times (Malaysia)*, 31 August 1998.
[10] Z. Koya, 'Life behind a barbed-wire fence', *New Straits Times (Malaysia)*, 31 August 1998.

guards.'[11] Conditions were even worse for the families of detainees or suspected Mau Mau supporters, for they were now liable to violent abuse by loyalists and tribal police.[12]

Some communities were at least outwardly phlegmatic. An officer of the Royal Norfolk Regiment found that in the case of Greek Cypriot villagers 'commonsense told them they had to just let it happen, to encourage us to leave as soon as possible, to act on the whole with courtesy. I used to get embarrassed by being offered a little liquor and a cold drink when I left, having been a bloody nuisance to them. I have never forgotten that courtesy. That was the quickest way of getting rid of us.'[13] But other people were openly resentful at what they saw as an affront to their dignity. Living in Jerusalem in December 1945 Arnold Spear experienced what it was like to be on the receiving end of a cordon and search operation. 'The first intimation one has of these things', he wrote,

> are loud bangs with rifle-butts on one's door. When the door happens to be open the guardians of the law just step in without bothering to announce themselves. From then and until your happy return from detention you had best forget that the English language boasts such expressions as 'please', 'thank you', 'sorry', 'if you don't mind'.
>
> The next step is for your visitor to look into each room and then to invite each of his male hosts to 'hurry up' and 'get going'. Where to and why is no concern of yours. In return for such discretion your visitor does not inquire your name, your calling, whether you are ill or healthy, your age or any other particulars which might enable him to form an estimate of you. Accordingly, after being collected in groups—not without encouraging shouts of 'keep together', 'don't fall behind' and the like, apparently acquired on the parade-ground,—you are hustled into trucks which bring you to a military prison somewhere in town.[14]

Once in a detention cage Spear and his companions were kept waiting for five hours without chairs to sit on or food to eat. Those who looked like they were over 40 years old were then sent home without even being asked their names. 'The others are searchingly looked in the eyes by a gentleman in mufti who sends on one side all those who have apparently not reached the age of majority and do not wear a tie— what happens to them is unknown to me.' Of the remainder, some had their identity papers checked, some did not, and all were sent home. 'You of course also wonder why searches had to be carried out behind the back of the owners of the searched premises though the law expressly provides for the opposite, and also at what is told you as regards the manner of the searches. But then why wonder at all, for judging by the display of arms employed it is anyhow a case of do or die.'[15] Sometimes popular reactions were more bitter. Following the destruction of the King David Hotel in July 1946, the army conducted a series of cordon and search

---

[11] P. Monkhouse, 'Kenya after the Mau Mau. I. The village policy', *Manchester Guardian*, 31 August 1955.

[12] C. Elkins, *Britain's Gulag. The Brutal end of Empire in Kenya* (London: Jonathan Cape, 2005), 233–74.

[13] IWMSA. Accession No. 20320. Gen. Sir D.Thorne, reel 5.

[14] *Palestine Post*, 9 January 1946.

[15] Ibid.

operations. At Ruhama Agricultural Settlement a settler remembered that soldiers 'herded all the men together. They shoved us into the pigpen. We shouted at them . . . "Nazi! Nazi!" They replied . . . "Heil Hitler! Heil Hitler!" Of course it made us angry. And both sides were spitting at each other.'[16]

Elsewhere a schoolboy living in Ismalia in 1952 remembered the sense of humiliation felt by many Egyptians at the British military presence. 'City residents could not enter or leave the area without permission from the British army. The British even closed some parts of the city and prohibited Egyptians from going near those areas and from entering social clubs.'[17] In Cyprus a British barrister noticed that the enforcement of petty security regulations was especially galling to Greek Cypriots because the measures were enforced by Turkish Cypriot policemen.[18] An Arab living in Aden remembered that 'these soldiers in the red hat', presumably a reference to the Parachute Regiment, 'They put fear into everyone's hearts.'[19] Arab men felt humiliated that their womenfolk were searched, even though it was done by female police officers.[20]

Successful military operations could persuade people to side with the government. In 1955 a company of 2/6 Gurkha Rifles ambushed and killed two insurgents in the Jelibu district of Negri Sembilan. One of the dead men had lived in a nearby village, which he had terrorized. Hitherto the village had been apathetic towards the British. But on learning of his death 'the whole village came over to the side of the government and it was a great victory, really.'[21] But in other instances coercion bred sullen resentment, and the British privately admitted as much. One senior officer in Malaya believed that '75 per cent of these people are choking with animosity against us, but being Chinese they have got thick enough skins to contain their feeling. Occasionally it bursts out and then a few more young men take to the jungle or even a whole village goes bad.'[22] In 1954 Sir Geoffrey Bourne concluded that the attitude of most Chinese villagers 'towards Government has only changed, however, from non-co-operation and antipathy to one of "reasonably friendly apathy".'[23] On the eve of Malayan independence in 1957, his successor, Sir Roger Bower, was equally candid. While some Chinese villages liked their new homes 'It is undeniable, however, that a large number of these persons feel a nagging resentment of the Government which, as they see it, removed them from their original homes to lie among strangers behind wire. It is among these

[16] E. Knaani, *Empire Warriors. The Jewish War*, BBC, 2004.
[17] Al-Ahram Weekly Online, 24–30 January 2002. Issue No.570. Downloaded on 30 December 2006 at http://weekly.ahram.org.eg/2002/570/sc5.htm.
[18] P. Benenson, 'Stagnation in Cyprus. Seeds of dissension', *Manchester Guardian*, 23 January 1957.
[19] Anonymous Arab witness, *Empire Warriors. Aden—Mad Mitch and his Tribal Law*, BBC, 2004.
[20] TNA CO 1055/220. Hedrick Smith, 'Arab Terrorists in Aden stepping up attacks', *New York Times*, 8 June 1965.
[21] IWMSA. Accession No. 10727 Col. A. S. Harvey, reel 3.
[22] R. Knox, 'Vanishing enemy in Malaya', *Observer*, 4 January 1953.
[23] TNA WO 216/874. Bourne to Harding, 17 July 1954.

people that the CTO finds its greatest support.'[24] A District Officer in Segamat in 1957 thought that the inhabitants of the new villages 'obeyed sullenly the police rules for house and field curfew; resentfully submitted themselves and their houses to spot searches and to a dozen other irksome and humiliating restrictions. The Emergency had blunted their sensibilities; there seemed to them little to choose between bandit and police.'[25]

Officials who oversaw the resettlement of the Kikuyu entertained similar impressions. A policeman thought that, with the barbed-wire fence that surrounded them, and the watch-towers that overlooked them, the resettlement villages resembled prisoner-of-war camps.[26] The author of an official army report admitted that 'the villages were squalid and untidy'.[27] Some villagers became so distraught when the government punished them by seizing their livestock, that they killed the animals themselves with rocks and sticks.[28] In March 1956 the District Commissioners of Paphos and Famagusta reported that the Greek Cypriot reactions to the deportation of Archbishop Makarios were a mixture of sorrow, indignation, and fear.[29] Charles Butt, who served with a Field Security section in Cyprus, recognized that soldiers and civilians were locked into a grim downward spiral of frustration and distrust in which no one's heart was likely to be softened. 'Each villager and townsman', he believed

> lived his life as best he could in the circumstances, farmed his fields, opened his shop, drank in the local coffee house, went to worship and occasionally squeezed into the hot and overcrowded local bus to visit relatives, but always he lived in expectation of impediment from a Government search or curfew or an EOKA inspired strike or raid.[30]

Collective punishments such as fines, the closure of places of entertainment, and the imposition of curfews did little beyond cause growing resentment against the government.[31]

DEVELOPMENT PROJECTS

The British, therefore, had to make great efforts if they wanted to transform sullen resentment into willing co-operation. But they were impeded by two obstacles: a shortage of resources, and their own unwillingness to accept that the insurgents

---

[24] IWMDoD. Lt.-Gen. Sir Roger Bower mss P. 123. Bower to State War Emergency Committees, 17 July 1957. Emergency policy after September 1957.

[25] R. Miers, *Shoot to Kill* (London: Faber & Faber, 1959), 141.

[26] C. Faulkner, *A Two-Year Wonder. The Kenya Police 1953–1955* (Livingston: Librario, 2004), 35.

[27] TNA WO 291/1670. Operational Research Unit (Far East). Report Number 1/57. A comparison of the emergencies in Malaya and Kenya, 6 June 1957.

[28] Faulkner, *A Two-Year Wonder*, 37–8.

[29] TNA CO 926/532. Harding to Colonial Secretary, 20 March 1956.

[30] IWMDoD 86/85/1. Maj. C. R. Butt, 'Cyprus Drafts (I)', 156.

[31] TNA CO 968/690. Brigadier G. Baker, A Review of the Cyprus Emergency April 1955–March 1958. Appendix I: Conclusions regarding the use of collective measures for control of punishment.

were pursuing a legitimate political programme, even if they were doing so by what the British regarded as illegitimate means.

The Colonial Office knew that 'In the long run the best barrier against communist penetration is obviously a spirit of political and industrial contentment amongst Colonial peoples, founded on the knowledge that the development of Colonial resources, with a parallel development of social and welfare services, is proceeding at a satisfactory rate.'[32] But development programmes were expensive, colonial governments rarely had large surplus revenues, and at times of emergency they invariably looked to the British government for money both to fund development projects, and to pay for security forces.[33] In return the Treasury insisted on having detailed oversight of the colony's budget. The latter was 'divided into three parts: ordinary budget, emergency budget, and capital and development budget. All three would be examined in advance here by the Treasury, and would require Treasury approval before being adopted.'[34] Spending under the first two heads had to be met from the colony's ordinary revenues to the maximum extent possible. Only after that source was exhausted would the Treasury provide a grant-in-aid to meet the remaining costs. Colonial governments were expected to fund development projects from normal sources, that is, from money allocated to them through the Colonial Development and Welfare Act, loans they could raise on the London money market, and their own ordinary revenues.[35]

Malaya was fortunate in that the inauguration of the Briggs Plan coincided with the outbreak of the Korean War and a boom in the prices for its tin and rubber exports. That provided the government with some of the funds it needed to pay for the plan, but by 1953, with the price of tin and rubber sinking on world markets, even the Malayan government had to look to the British exchequer for help. By 1960 the British taxpayer had spent £84 million to fund the emergency.[36] Elsewhere, the poverty of most colonies and the Treasury's reluctance to open its purse strings ensured that the rhetoric of killing insurgency through economic development consistently outpaced the reality. Money generated by a colony's own taxes

[32] TNA CO 537/2768. Colonial Secretary, Communist infiltration and the security situation in the colonies, n.d. but *c*.20 July 1948.
[33] TNA CO 1031/1436. Minute by J. A. Armitage-Smith, 11 January 1954; TNA CO 1031/1436. Minute by N. L. Myle, 14 January 1954; TNA CO 1015/2627. Governor Aden to Colonial Secretary, 22 August 1960; TNA CO 968/799. Sir A. Waddell to CO, 15 May 1963; TNA CO 1031/1437. Minute by Mr Melville, 29 January 1954; TNA T 220/573. Minute by Colonel Russell Edmunds on CP(55)82, 19 May 1955; TNA T 220/573. J. G. Thompson to Colonel Russell-Edmunds, 3 November 1955; TNA T 220/573. Minute by A. K. Rawlinson, 9 November 1955; TNA CO 1015/1518. Armitage to Secretary of State, 4 May 1959; TNA CO 968/799. Colonial Office to Governors of Sarawak and North Borneo, 7 August 1963.
[34] TNA T 220/573. A. K. Rawlinson to Sir A. Johnson, 4 November 1955.
[35] TNA CO 1031/1436. Minute by P. Rogers, 17 September 1954; TNA T 220/573. Anon., Cyprus Finance, 12 January 1956.
[36] TNA CAB 131/9/DO(50)94. Colonial Secretary, Political and economic background to the situation in Malaya, 15 November 1950; TNA FO 371/106984/FZ1111/3. Malcolm MacDonald to Lyttelton, 23 July 1953; TNA WO 106/5990. Director of Operations Malaya, Review of the Emergency in Malaya from June 1948 to August 1957, September 1957; R. W. Komer, *The Malayan Emergency in Retrospect: Organization of a Successful Counterinsurgency Effort* (Santa Monica, CA: Rand Corporation, 1972), 23.

that might have been spent on development projects was diverted to security spending. In Palestine, the government's assistant secretary for finance admitted in 1947 that funding emergency-related measures meant that there was little left in the budget for development programmes.[37] When Baring was told by the Colonial Office in December 1952 that his government would have to meet the cost of the troops sent to Kenya, he replied that 'Their resources were limited and the more that was spent on troops the less they would have available for positive development policies.'[38] But he was given no option.[39]

In total, between 1946 and 1957 colonies spent about £1,000 million on projects intended to develop their economies and improve health, education, and housing. But 60 per cent of that money came from their own tax revenues. A further 18.7 per cent took the form of international loans, which represented another burden on each colony's tax revenues, since interest payments on the loans came out of taxes. Despite all the rhetoric of 'hearts and minds', the British taxpayer, through the 1945 Colonial Development and Welfare Act, provided only 13.7 per cent of their development funding.[40] Even when new money was found, priority was usually given to spending on projects directly related to security. In November 1955, Harding announced that the British government would fund a development programme costing £38m in Cyprus, but simultaneously explained that the first charge on the island's revenues under this plan would be the organization of a police force able to maintain public security.[41]

Much has been made of the fact that the Briggs Plan not only physically separated the squatter population from the insurgents, but also raised living standards by providing the inhabitants of the new villages with better health care, education, and social services.[42] Briggs recognized that coercion alone would not win the support of the Chinese community and that the government had to be able to offer them rewards as well as punishments. The Malays had to be persuaded to accept that the Chinese were in Malaya to stay, and that they would keep the land that they occupied. The promise that land would either be retained or taken away, the decision depending on their behaviour, 'would knock the main plank from under the feet of Communist propaganda and deprivation of land might be as effective as the fear of the bandits.'[43] But such was the pressure to break the links quickly between the Chinese rural population and the insurgents in 1950–1, that they were sent to resettlement camps that still lacked basic services.[44] In May 1952

[37] *Times*, 21 May 1947.
[38] TNA CO 822/451. Note of a meeting in Mr Gorrell-Barnes's room on 15 December 1952.
[39] *Manchester Guardian*, 28 March 1953.
[40] [Cmnd 672]. *Colonial Development and Welfare Acts*, February 1959.
[41] *Manchester Guardian*, 17 November 1955.
[42] A. C. Grayling, 'Drying out the insurgency', *New York Times*, 27 March 2006.
[43] TNA CO 537/5975. Briggs, Outline of future anti-bandit policy in Malaya, n.d. but *c.*1 April 1950.
[44] TNA CO 1022/29. Resettlement in Malaya, n.d. but *c.*April 1952; TNA CO 822/481. Notes on planning and housing aspects of resettlement and in the development of 'new villages' in the Federation of Malaya, 1952–53. Prepared by Mr G. A. Atkinson, colonial liaison officer, building research section, and Housing Adviser to the CO, 5 May 1953; T. N. Harper, *The End of Empire and*

the Federal government produced figures that showed that the claim that three-quarters of the government's efforts were being put into providing welfare services or raising living standards to win the 'hearts and minds' of the people were very wide of the mark. By the end of 1951, out of a total resettlement budget of M$41 million, they had spent M$2.38 million on acquiring the land needed build the settlements, M$29.89 million on housing grants, subsistence allowances, transport, preparation of sites, fencing, access and internal roads, and drainage, and M$6.39 million on building police stations. They had allocated only M$1.96 million on schools, M$200,000 on agricultural aid, and M$360,000 on medical and health needs.[45] The Malay Branch of the British Medical Association warned in April 1952 that the lack of medical facilities in the resettlement areas constituted 'a new risk to public health, threatening epidemics which may endanger not only the areas themselves, but also the adjacent populations.'[46] It was voluntary societies, principally the Red Cross and St John Ambulance Brigade, not the government, who filled the gap.[47] Conditions in camps holding resettled Orang Asli (that is, the aboriginal population who inhabited the dense central jungles of Malaya) were particularly poor. They resulted in such alarmingly high mortality rates that the government abandoned efforts to resettle them outside the jungle and instead established military posts in the jungle to prevent the insurgents preying on them for food.[48]

Although by November 1951 all but one Malay state had agreed in principle to give resettled squatters titles to the land they occupied, land tenure remained a problem. Many Malays resented large sums of public money being spent on the Chinese and giving them land titles, refusing to accept that they were in Malaya to stay.[49] As late as 1953, 40 per cent of the settlers still did not have proper land titles.[50] Those that did were usually only given a temporary occupation licence which could be renewed annually, or a leasehold, often for a period that they thought was too short.[51] Many new villages remained economic backwaters for years to come.[52]

---

the Making of Malaya (Cambridge: Cambridge University Press, 1999), 177; R. Stubbs, *Hearts and Minds in Guerrilla Warfare. The Malayan Emergency 1948–60* (Oxford: Oxford University Press, 1989), 159–60, 173–84, 258.

[45] TNA CO 1022/29. Paper to be laid before the Federal Legislative Council by command of his Excellency the High Commissioner. Resettlement and the Development of New Villages in the Federation of Malaya, 1952, 20 May 1952.

[46] TNA CO 1022/31. Extract from *Straits Budget*, 3 April 1952.

[47] TNA CO 1022/31: Memo by the Member for Health, 17 September 1953; K. H. Phau, 'The development of health services in Malaya and Singapore 1867 to 1960' (Ph.D. dissertation, London School of Economics, 1987), 275–81.

[48] Phau, 'The development of health services in Malaya and Singapore', 284–5.

[49] TNA CO 1022/29. Federal Government Press Statement. Titles to land in resettlement areas, 30 November 1951; TNA CO 1022/29. Extract from the Monthly Review of Chinese Affairs for January 1952.

[50] L.H. Wang, 'New Villages Growing Old in Malaysia', *Habitat International*, vol. 12 (1988), 38; TNA CO 1022/29. Penang government press statement, 5 March 1952.

[51] T. N. Harper, *The End of Empire*, 180.

[52] Lim Hin Fui and Fong Tian Yong, *The New Villages in Malaysia—the Journey Ahead* (Kuala Lumpur: Institute of Strategic Analysis and Policy Research, 2005), 27–35; Harper, *The End of Empire*, 179.

None of this prevented the Federal authorities from trying to put the best possible face on their efforts. But the reality was that life in many new villages was grim. According to a British officer who visited a new village near Kluang in Johore in early 1956,

> Living conditions in the villages and estate lines were still very primitive. In some cases long wooden huts were divided into cubicles and shared by several families, one cubicle for a small family, two for a large. Each cubicle was again divided by the tenants into living and sleeping rooms, with a shelf a couple of feet above the floor on which the whole family slept. Except for electric light there was strictly no modern conveniences; water was carried from a tap outside.[53]

Malaya was a relatively wealthy colony. Nyasaland and Aden were not. Efforts to pursue development programmes there barely got off the ground.[54] In the wake of the Radfan campaign Sir Charles Harington, Trevaskis, Lord Mountbatten, the CDS, and the Minister of Defence, Peter Thorneycroft, realized that military victory and the destruction of their food stocks and villages would not win the hearts and minds of the Radfani people. The army and Federal government had to invest in irrigation and agricultural development programmes and improved roads to demonstrate the tangible benefits of being part of the SAF.[55] But it was only after considerable effort that they managed to extract even a fraction of the funding they wanted from the Treasury, and much of that was spent not on irrigation or agriculture, but on bribes to buy the loyalty of tribal leaders.[56] Even the gift of some worn-out trucks was forbidden. As a senior officer in the MOD explained to Harington, 'The great difficulty is of course the usual one, money, and in this connection projects which are essentially matters of development or aid must be funded from the Colonial Office vote and if they are not already covered in estimates require Parliamentary approval. We just cannot spend money from Defence funds on such projects and even in such matters as the gift or loan of part worn military vehicles we cannot naturally depart from this principle.'[57]

When extra development money was made available in the course of an emergency, it was carefully targeted to produce a particular political result. Commenting on plans to increase development spending in Cyprus in 1956, a Treasury official noted that 'The increases, in the main, are based on a political assessment of where development expenditure can do most to influence the political situation.'[58] In British Guiana poor housing on the sugar estates was identified as one of the main reasons why the PPP garnered so much support, so development money was channelled into improving housing.[59] Money spent on agricultural development

---

[53] Miers, *Shoot to Kill*, 35–6.

[54] IWMSA. Accession No. 4716, N. Harvey, Transcript, 30.

[55] TNA DEFE 13/570. Harington to CDS, 11 June 1964; TNA DEFE 13/570. CDS to Secretary of State, 24 June 1964; TNA DEFE 13/570. Thorneycroft to Colonial Secretary, 25 June 1964; TNA DEFE 13/570. Mountbatten to Secretary of State Defence, 30 June 1964.

[56] TNA DEFE 13/570. CO to Acting HC Aden, 24 July 1964.

[57] TNA DEFE 11/500. Sir A. Earle to Harington, 21 August 1964.

[58] TNA T 220/573. Cyprus Finance, 12 January 1956.

[59] *Manchester Guardian*, 18 November 1953; *Times*, 7 December 1953 & 15 March 1954.

in British Guiana, Kenya, and Malaya was spent on schemes to create small family farms, on the assumption that 'a responsible peasant landowning class', would be a politically conservative bulwark against Communism or a resurgence of Mau Mau.[60] In Malaya and Cyprus, the government identified Chinese and Greek-language schools as significant foci of support for the insurgents. Funds were therefore directed towards expanding English or Malay language schools as a way of weaning young people away from supporting them.[61] By 1957 the largest single item in the Cyprus government's development programme was education spending. Templer encouraged the establishment of regional museums in Malaya with a political purpose in view. 'One of the small ways in which I tried to help in the appreciation of the necessity for the gradual formation of a really united Malayan nation', he wrote in 1955, 'was to start regional museums, which I hope in the course of time will be able to illustrate in visual form, the varied part of all the component parts which make up the Malay of today.'[62]

When they were denied the funding needed to support large-scale programmes to raise living standards, the British fell back on cheap, small-scale, civic action programmes run by the military. In Malaya 'efforts were made even in fairly simple ways like a detachment giving a party for the village children which helped bridge the gap between the British and the local people and made the local people realize that the British were not in fact ogres, and that British soldiers were ordinary people like themselves.'[63] In the Radfan, British troops stockpiled supplies of flour, oil, grain, and tea to distribute to the tribes once they had made their peace with the government.[64] A young platoon commander operating in Borneo in 1964 remembered that 'Winning hearts and minds was new then, and we didn't really know what to do. So we decided to provide the villagers with basic needs such as medical care. It worked, and we were treated like their own.'[65]

These operations did sometimes succeed in persuading people that they had more to gain than to lose by siding with the government.[66] But their impact could not always counter-balance wider government failures. In Brunei by March 1963 'maladministration, due to the parsimony and ineptitude of the Government, which was one of the original causes of the revolt, is continuing. This is creating widespread discontent in the country districts, and nullifying to a considerable degree the "Hearts and Minds" campaign conducted by the military.'[67] Other

---

[60] *Manchester Guardian*, 9 February 1954; *Times*, 6 March & 5 July 1954 & 14 January 1957; D. Branch, 'The enemy within: loyalists and the war against Mau Mau in Kenya', *Journal of African History*, vol. 48 (2007), 304–6.

[61] TNA CAB 21/1681/MAL(50)10. Director of Operations, Malaya: Directive No. 2, 12 May 1950; TNA CO 1022/32. Extract from Fed Leg Co Paper 33 of 1952.

[62] TNA CAB 21/2925. Templer to Sir B. Horrocks, 1 April 1955.

[63] IWMSA. Accession No. 10107. N. J. Baptiste, reel 1.

[64] C. Hollingworth, 'British to aid Radfan refugees', *Guardian*, 25 May 1964.

[65] D. Wong, ' "Hearts and minds" way to win battles', *New Straits Times (Malaysia)*, 9 March 2007; TNA WO 291/2407. FARELF. G (Operational Requirements and Analysis) Branch. Report No. 1/69. Lessons learned from Borneo Operations, 17 March 1969.

[66] TNA DEFE 7/2415. Secretary MCC (Persian Gulf) to Secretary BDCC (Middle East), 8 August 1957; TNA WO 305/2519. HQ British Forces Borneo, Joint Perintrep No. 3, 19 January 1963.

[67] TNA WO 305/2520. HQ British Forces (Borneo). Joint Perintrep No. 11, 17 March 1963.

problems emerged elsewhere. In Cyprus in 1955, when a Royal Marine Commando searched the village of Akanthou, their medical officer treated any peasants requiring medical assistance. A British journalist who accompanied the troops wrote that 'the good nature and efficiency shown by the Commandos at Akanthou is expected to characterize all their operations. And this should help to minimize local resentment.'[68] It might have helped to minimize resentment, but at least one officer with the unit was sceptical about its wider impact. He wrote that, 'The problem which still has to be resolved is to win over the civil population to a pro-British attitude. In a small way a start has been made by the unit doctor and his staff, but until the civilian has confidence in the security force and is prepared to deny temporal power to the Church the recruitment and supply of terrorists may well continue.'[69]

The British tried to apply their own notions of good government to wean the civil population away from tolerating or supporting the insurgents. In some instances in Malaya development aid may have contributed to achieving this. Information derived from the interrogation of insurgents who had voluntarily surrendered demonstrated that, over time, welfare improvements in the villages, patchy as they were, had reduced their determination to fight for a change of regime.[70] But elsewhere, ethnic identities and a determination no longer to be ruled by foreigners proved to be more powerful. A microcosmic example of how these two forces could come into conflict was illustrated by a meeting of the District Commissioner of Troodos and the villagers of Kyperounda in January 1959. 'At first the gathering at the coffee shop went as in the pre-Emergency days', he reported.

> We discussed the unemployment with the seasonal closing of the Amiandos mines and the question was raised of asphalting the village square which was in a foul and muddy state. I said I would meet half the cost from the district development fund (£100 out of the £200 which I then thought would be all that will be left after completing the Trimiklini irrigation scheme). At this stage some of the youths started figiting [*sic*] and one of them said they wanted nothing from Government: at this another added that they did not want to see Government propaganda appear in the newspapers that assistance had been given to Kyperounda which was the only purpose of my offer. From then on all toed the party line.[71]

Some people just refused to be bought.[72]

---

[68] *Manchester Guardian*, 29 September 1955.
[69] Capt. E. G. D. Pound, 'Operations in the Troodos sub-area', *British Army Review*, no. 3 (September 1956), 13.
[70] TNA WO 291/1787. ORS (psychological warfare) memorandum No. 16/54. Some statistics relating to Communist terrorist recruitment in Malaya, 21 December 1954.
[71] TNA CO 926/677. District Commissioner Troodos to Reddaway, n.d. but *c*.1 February 1959.
[72] IWMSA. Accession No. 8736. Field Marshal Lord Harding, Transcript, 382–3.

SECURITY SECTOR REFORM

One of the best touchstones of the success of the colonial state in winning the hearts and minds of the civil population was their ability to achieve security sector reform. Not only would locally raised troops, policemen and home guards reduce the need to deploy British soldiers, but they would also associate the civil population with the counter-insurgency effort in ways that really mattered. Such forces could offer people protection from insurgent intimidation, and make siding with the government increasingly attractive.

The record of the colonial authorities in doing this was chequered. In some cases they did not even try. In Palestine, there were no local recruits they could turn to for assistance. As long as they refused to permit large-scale Jewish immigration the Yishuv, much as they might deplore the methods of violence used by the insurgents, were not willing to fight against them.[73] Nor were the British willing to arm large numbers of Arabs, having fought a counter-insurgency campaign against them less than a decade earlier. The same was the case in the Canal Zone, where few Arabs were willing to be seen to be working with the British, either because they were afraid of retaliation, or because like most Egyptians they wanted to see them leave.

In other cases the British tried and failed, or discovered that their success ultimately backfired. In Aden the British had long harboured concerns about the political reliability of locally raised troops and policemen because their sympathies were so obviously with the cause espoused by the insurgents.[74] The FRA also fractured along religious lines between Sunni and Shia. Soldiers and local policemen listened avidly to UAR propaganda broadcast by Radio Sana which told them that the British were fighting for her interests in South Arabia 'to the last Arab', and emphasizing the evil of 'Arab fighting Arab'.[75] There was enough truth in this assertion to make it plausible. In 1964 FRA units did take part in operations in the Radfan and, to the surprise of the British, acquitted themselves well. However, before the operation began, their British officers had taken the precaution of sending all Radfanis in the FRA on paid leave.[76] But between 1965 and 1967 their worst fears came to pass. The FRA and local police were thoroughly penetrated by the insurgents.[77] By the autumn of 1965 FRA units were performing their

---

[73] IWMSA. Accession No. 10392. Sir R. Catling, Transcript, 19–21, 24.

[74] TNA WO 32/18518. GOC MELF to WO, 31 January 1963; TNA WO 32/18518. Captain P. G. Boxhall (Int. Corps, HQ Aden Protectorate Levies) to Col. J. H. S. Bowring (MI11, WO), 29 June 1959; TNA WO 32/18518. MI11 Colonel's tour notes, Notes on the ADL, n.d. but *c.*July 1959; TNA WO 32/18518. Major G. C. Hutson, Half Yearly Report on security of Aden Protectorate Levies, 8 Mar. and 18 October 1960; WO 32/18518. GOC MELF to WO, 31 January 1963.

[75] TNA WO 32/18518. FRA. Quarterly Security Report, 24 April 1964; IWMSA. Accession No. 23811. Maj.-Gen. J. Dye, reel 10.

[76] TNA WO 32/18518. FRA. Quarterly Security Report, 1 September 1963 to 31 December 1963, 22 February 1964; TNA WO 32/18518. FRA. Quarterly Security Report, April–June 1964, 8 August 1964.

[77] TNA CO 1035/183. Extract from JIC(65)40 meeting, 3 September 1965; TNA CO 1035/179. Confidential Annex to COS(65)45 meeting, 9 September 1965; S. Harper, *Last Sunset. What Happened in Aden* (London: Collins, 1978), 88–92.

duties in at best a half-hearted manner, and their officers had organized 'a collective protest about the behaviour of British troops during internal security operations in Aden.'[78] A year later FRA soldiers were throwing grenades at British soldiers.[79] The breakdown in discipline culminated in June 1967 when men of the Armed Police mutinied, ambushed two convoys of British soldiers, and killed more than 20 of them.[80]

In Kenya, where the emergency was in part a civil war fought within Kikuyu society, the British were able to expand locally raised European forces such as the Kenya Regiment and Kenya Police Reserve, and recruit large numbers of Kikuyu home guards. By March 1954 the Home Guard numbered 25,600, and were more numerous than both the forest gangs and the British garrison. Membership of the Home Guard became almost mandatory for Kikuyu, and those who were unwilling to enlist were treated by the police or loyalist chiefs as Mau Mau sympathizers. Once enlisted, they were likely to find themselves being used by their chiefs to inflict abuses on the civilian population, abuses that included extortion, torture, and murder.[81] Similarly in Cyprus the British could recruit large numbers of policemen from the minority Turkish community, but the political cost of doing so was high. The existence of so many Turks in the police served only to widen the already deep rifts between the two communities that bedevilled the island.[82]

It was only in Malaya and Malaysia that security sector reform was an unqualified success. Templer raised the Federation Regiment because 'Until it was started, it was absolutely impossible for any non-Malay-Asian (i.e. Chinese, Indian, Pakistani, etc.) to join the armed forces and do something towards the defence of his country. The Federation Regiment is thrown open to all the various Communities.'[83] But Malay suspicions of their Chinese neighbours remained so deepseated that Templer could not persuade the Malay Sultans to allow him to raise a purely Chinese regiment.[84] The Malayan police force was expanded eightfold between 1948 and 1952, at which time it numbered 75,000 men.[85] But of even greater political significance was the Malay home guard. By 1950 the latter numbered about 100,000. They were ill-trained and poorly equipped, but their

---

[78] TNA CO 1035/183. Review of current intelligence, 28 September 1965.
[79] TNA DEFE 11/504. C-in-C Mideast to CDS, 12 September 1966; TNA DEFE 11/530. CinC Mideast to CDS, Sitrep week ending 15 August 1967.
[80] LHCMA Maj.-Gen. C. W. Dunbar 2/4. 'Staff—in confidence. Some random thoughts about the South Arabian Army and Arab Police Mutiny 20 July 1967'; Walker, *Aden Emergency*, 239–58.
[81] Anderson, *Histories of the Hanged*, 239–43; TNA WO 384/20, Table 13, Strength at home and overseas, 31 December 1953; D. Branch, *Defeating Mau Mau, Creating Kenya. Counterinsurgency, Civil War, and Decolonization* (Cambridge: Cambridge University Press, 2009), 58–76, 108–9.
[82] J. S. Corum, 'Training indigenous forces in counterinsurgency: a tale of two insurgencies'. Downloaded 14 December 2009 at http://www.StrategicStudiesInstitute.army.mil/, 28–30; D. Anderson, 'Policing and communal conflict: the Cyprus emergency, 1954–60', in D. Anderson and D. Killingray (eds), *Policing and Decolonisation. Politics, Nationalism and the Police, 1917–1965* (Manchester: Manchester University Press, 1992), 187–217.
[83] TNA CAB 21/2925. Templer to Sir B. Horrocks, 1 April 1955.
[84] IWMSA. Accession No. 10243. A. H. P. Humphrey, reel 1.
[85] TNA CAB 129/48/C(51)59. Colonial Secretary, 21 December 1951; TNA WO 216/806. Sir R. Lockhart to Slim, 14 January 1952.

mere existence gave the Malay community a badly needed sense of greater security.[86] In June 1950 Briggs decided to raise a similar force in Chinese resettlement areas. Many Chinese were reluctant to join for fear that they would become marked men, so the government made service compulsory. Their reliability varied according to the influence of the insurgents in any particular area, and it was not unknown for them to pass weapons on to them.[87] The nominal strength of the combined Malay and Chinese home guard peaked at about 300,000, although it fell to just over 100,000 by 1957.[88] Only partly trained and equipped with shotguns, their ratio of kills to contacts was the lowest of all elements of the security forces.[89] But that hardly mattered. Their real importance was that they helped sustain the morale of Malaya's population in the face of insurgent intimidation, and forced the Chinese, however reluctantly, to side with the security forces.[90]

The outbreak of the emergency in Brunei and Borneo was quickly followed by equally successful efforts to raise local security forces. In Sarawak nearly 2,000 tribesmen were recruited in December 1962 to assist the security forces in hunting down the remaining insurgents.[91] In 1963 the British began to raise a force of over 1,000 Border Scouts from amongst the inhabitants of the frontier between Borneo and Kalimantan. They had three functions. They provided the security forces with intelligence about the movement of insurgents across the frontier. They engendered confidence in border communities that the government would help them to protect themselves, and thus ensured that the Indonesians and the CCO could not intimidate them. Finally, they shielded the security forces from accusations that repressive and coercive measures such as curfews were imposed on the population by outsiders.[92] They became an essential and successful part of the security forces' operations.

[86] Corum, 'Training indigenous forces in counterinsurgency', 13.

[87] TNA CO 1022/210. Pan Malayan review of Political and Security Intelligence. No. 10, 29 October 1952.

[88] TNA WO 106/5990. Director of Operations Malaya, Review of the Emergency in Malaya from June 1948 to August 1957, September 1957.

[89] TNA WO 208/5356. Lt.-Gen. Sir R. Bower, Review of the Emergency Situation in Malaya at the end of 1956, 12 February 1957.

[90] TNA WO 216/874. Lt.-Gen Sir G. Bourne to Harding, 17 July 1954.

[91] H. A. Majid, *Rebellion in Brunei. The 1962 Revolt, Imperialism, Confrontation, and Oil* (London: I. B. Tauris, 2007), 128; TNA DEFE 6/85/JP.55/63(Final). JPS, Report by the C-in-C Far East on operations in Borneo from December 1962 to February 1963, 5 July 1963.

[92] TNA CO 968/873. Sir W. Goode to Colonial Secretary, 16 February 1963; TNA WO 305/2522. Minutes of a meeting of the Borneo Security Council held at the Office of the High Commissioner for Brunei, 10 May 1963;TNA WO 305/2522. Minutes of a meeting of the Borneo Operations Committee held at HQ COMBRITBOR, 24 May 1963; TNA WO 305/2523. Directive on the employment of the Sarawak Border Scouts in 3 Commando. Brigade Area, 22 June 1963; TNA WO 305/2525. Minutes of a meeting of the Borneo Operations Committee held at HQ COMBRITBOR, 15 August 1963; Cross, P., 'A Face Like a Chicken's Backside'. An Unconventional Soldier in South East Asia, 1948–1971 (London: Greenhill Books, 1996), 139–43, 147, 157.

POLITICAL CONCESSIONS

Shortage of resources was only one reason why any commitment to waging counter-insurgency through a concerted effort to win the 'hearts and minds' of the civil population was more rhetorical than real. Another and perhaps even more important reason was that doing so required the British to make real political concessions to their opponents. But their tendency to regard insurgents as criminal conspirators hardly predisposed them to look for a political solution to their problem. A remark about events in the Canal Zone by Selwyn Lloyd, the Minister of State at the Foreign Office, makes this clear. In replying to a Labour MP who asked him whether he agreed that 'when outrages have a political cause, as is clearly the case in this instance, and as was the case in the past in Ireland and in Israel and on many other occasions, the remedy must be a political question and not merely blind military firmness?' Lloyd, insisted that 'I do not think that all these crimes are political. Very many of them are simply plain thuggery.'[93] The British government did not, at least willingly, negotiate with thugs. It locked them up.

'Blind military firmness' was often the option that British governments preferred. Almost the only occasion when British ministers did consider voluntarily surrendering part of their imperial obligations was in 1946. Driven by economic pressures to save money, and believing that the UN would develop into an effective world security system, Attlee, supported by the Chancellor of the Exchequer, Hugh Dalton, argued that the British should abandon their Middle East commitments.[94] They could not prevail against the combined opposition of Bevin and the Foreign Office, the Colonial Office, and the COS. Not only would such a withdrawal, in their estimation, deliver a fatal blow to British prestige and international standing, but it would also endanger the security of the Middle Eastern oil supplies upon which Britain depended. In addition Britain would forfeit the air bases in the region from which one day it might wish to bomb southern Russia. In January 1947, faced by a threat of resignation by the COS, Attlee abandoned his position of wholesale withdrawal, although he did persuade his colleagues that leaving Palestine was imperative.[95]

But far from reaching this decision as the result of trying to bring an independent Jewish state into existence, the British tacked and tacked again trying to find

[93] *Hansard* HC Deb 17 February 1954, vol. 523, col. 1963.
[94] TNA CAB 131/2/DO(46)27. Attlee, Future of the Italian colonies, 2 March 1946; B. Pimlott (ed.), *The Political Diary of Hugh Dalton, 1918–40, 1945–60* (London: Jonathan Cape, 1986), 368–9. R. Smith and J. Zametica, 'The cold warrior: Clement Attlee reconsidered', *International Affairs*, vol. 61 (1985), 237–52.
[95] TNA CAB 131/2/DO(46)40. Bevin, Memorandum by the Secretary of State for Foreign Affairs, 13 March 1946; TNA CAB 131/2/DO(46)47. Report by the COS, Strategic position of the British Commonwealth, 2 April 1946; TNA CAB 131/2/DO(46)51. Note by the Secretary, Mediterranean Strategy, 10 April 1946; S. Ball, 'Bomber bases and British strategy in the Middle East, 1945–49', *JSS*, vol. 14 (1991), 515–33; H. Rahman, 'British post-Second World War military planning for the Middle East', *JSS*, vol. 5 (1982), 511–30.

a solution that would satisfy the demands of all parties.[96] The Arabs of Palestine and the neighbouring Arab states had made clear their objection to continued Jewish immigration into Palestine in the late 1930s when the former had risen in revolt against the British Mandate administration and the latter had supported them. In 1945 the Yishuv, supported by President Truman, demanded an end to immigration restrictions. The only way in which the British might have been able to defeat the Zionist insurgency was by agreeing to allow large-scale Jewish immigration, for that might have divided the majority of the Yishuv from the minority of active insurgents. But following the destruction of the King David Hotel in July 1946, in which a large number of Arabs were killed, Cunningham insisted that it was imperative to put an end to illegal immigration. The Arabs were, in his opinion, in an ugly mood and might themselves launch an insurrection if the British did not act.[97] However, given their immediate economic difficulties, and the need to seek financial support from the USA, Britain could not afford to alienate the US administration.[98] Despite the COS's insistence that the defence of the Middle East required the British to maintain control over the whole of Palestine, in February 1947 the Cabinet agreed to place the problem before the UN. If that organization could not produce a solution that met British, as well as Arab and Zionist interests, then the mandate should be abandoned.[99] When the UN failed to do that, the British walked away.

That was the first of three withdrawals that the British undertook under pressure from insurgencies in the Middle East over the next decade. The next came in the Canal Zone. The British were intent on staying there. The Egyptians were equally intent on seeing the back of them, and in December 1945 opened negotiations to revise the 1936 treaty.[100] The British did withdraw their troops from Cairo and Alexandria, but wanted a 99-year lease on the Canal Zone.[101] When the Egyptians unilaterally abrogated the treaty in October 1951, the Attlee government was determined to stand fast.[102] By July 1954 their Conservative successors had

[96] D. K. Fieldhouse, *Western Imperialism in the Middle East, 1914–1958* (Oxford: Oxford University Press, 2006), 205–8; R. Ovendale, 'The Palestine policy of the British Labour government, 1945–46', *International Affairs*, vol. 55 (1979), 409–31.
[97] TNA WO 32/10260. Telegram, High Commissioner Palestine to Colonial Secretary, 25 July 1946.
[98] Fieldhouse, *Western Imperialism in the Middle East*, 205–12; Ovendale, 'The Palestine policy of the British Labour government, 1945–46', 409–31; R. Ovendale, 'The Palestine policy of the British Labour government, 1947', *International Affairs*, vol. 56 (1980), 73–93.
[99] TNA CAB 131/4/DO(47)3. Report by the COS, Palestine—strategic requirements, 6 January 1947; TNA CAB 128/9 CM(47)22 meeting, 14 February 1947.
[100] TNA WO 169/22879 War Diary G(Ops)1. GHQ MELF. Minutes of C-in-C 9th Commanders Conference, held at GHQ MELF, 17 April 1946.
[101] TNA CAB 131/1/DO(46)8 meeting. Cabinet Defence Committee, 18 March 1946; TNA CAB 131/3/DO(46)84. Report by COS, Egypt—evacuation plan, 2 July 1946; BLM 211/3 Montgomery, Personal directive to C-in-C Middle East, 26 June 1946.
[102] TNA CAB 131/2/DO(46)56. Report by the COS, Egyptian treaty revision, 15 April 1946; TNA CAB 131/9/DO(50)40. Report by the COS, Co-operation with Egypt, 19 May 1950; TNA CAB 195/8/CM86(50). Cabinet meeting, 14 December 1950; TNA CAB 129/45/CP(51)95. Secretary of State for Foreign Affairs, Egypt: Defence negotiations, 30 January 1951; TNA CAB 129/46/CP(51)214. Foreign Secretary, Egypt: Defence questions and the Sudan, 27 July 1951.

reluctantly recognized that it no longer made sense to do so. Merely defending the base required between 70,000 and 80,000 troops, the equivalent of almost the whole of the army's strategic reserve. Furthermore, such a large, static installation would make a tempting target for a Soviet thermo-nuclear strike. Consequently, the Churchill government, much against the wishes of the Prime Minister himself, opted to negotiate the best settlement they could. The result fell far short of the COS's aims. Not only were all British ground forces withdrawn from the base, but they also had to give up their hope of maintaining air defence facilities. The most that the Egyptians would accept was the presence of British civilian technicians to maintain facilities, that the British would be permitted to reoccupy it in the event of a Soviet attack on Turkey or any Arab state, and that the agreement would run for seven years, rather than the 10 or even 20 years that the British wanted.[103]

In the meantime they opted to build a new base in Cyprus.[104] As in Palestine, the COS insisted that if it were to be viable the British had to retain sovereignty over the whole country, and agreed that Henry Hopkinson, the Minister of State at the Colonial Office, should publicly announce that the British would never accept enosis.[105] In August 1955 Macmillan, then briefly Foreign Secretary, insisted that Britain 'Should be ready to get firm internal control over Island.'[106] But by 1957, now Prime Minister, he was beginning to change his mind. First, he wondered whether the British did need to maintain control over the whole island. Would not possession of just part of it as a military enclave suffice?[107] When Harding and the COS objected, he overrode them.[108] Cyprus was becoming another Canal Zone. Harding estimated that it would need 16,000 soldiers merely to defend it against insurgent attacks. If he was right, that would mean that most of the newer and smaller Strategic Reserve of the post-Sandys all-regular army would be tied down on the island, unavailable for operations elsewhere. Macmillan persuaded his

[103] TNA CAB 128/27/CC(54)43 meeting. Cabinet Conclusions, 22 June 1954; TNA CAB 128/27/CC(54)47 meeting. Cabinet Conclusions, 7 July 1954; J. Kent, 'The Egyptian base and the defence of the Middle East, 1945 to 1954', in R. Holland (ed.), *Emergencies and Disorder in the European Empires after 1945* (London: Cass, 1994), 45–65; P. L. Hahn, 'Containment and Egyptian nationalism: the unsuccessful effort to establish the Middle East Command, 1950–53', *Diplomatic History*, vol. 11 (1987), 23–40; R. Ovendale, 'Egypt and the Suez Base agreement', in J. W. Young (ed.), *The Foreign Policy of Churchill's Peacetime Administration 1951–1955* (Leicester: Leicester University Press, 1988), 135–58.
[104] TNA CAB 128/25/CC(52)91. Cabinet Conclusions, 29 October 1952; TNA CAB 129/56/C (52)382. Alexander, Move of the Middle East Headquarters, 4 November 1952; CAB 128/25/CC(52) 101. Cabinet Conclusions, 3 December 1952.
[105] TNA DEFE 6/14/JP(50)106 (Revised Final). Report by the JPS, Review of Middle East policy and strategy, 1 September 1950; TNA PREM 11/605/CC(54)245. Secretary of State for the Colonies and Minister of State, Cyprus, 21 July 1954; TNA CAB 128/27/CC(54)53 meeting, 26 July 1954.
[106] TNA CAB 195/14/CM28(55). Cabinet meeting, 15 August 1955.
[107] TNA CAB 130/122/Gen 567/1 meeting. External Affairs. Note of meeting held 10 Downing Street, 23 January 1957.
[108] TNA DEFE 11/181/COS(56)426. BDCC (Middle East), Military implications of the partition of Cyprus, 30 November 1956; TNA DEFE 11/181. Secretary, COS to COS, 14 February 1957; TNA PREM 11/1939. Sir N. Brooke to Macmillan, 2 April 1957; TNA DEFE 11/183/COS(57)152. CIGS, Internal Security Problem in Cyprus, 1 July 1957; TNA DEFE 11/183. Harding to Colonial Secretary, 1 July 1957; TNA DEFE 11/183/COS(57)83(Final). Report by JPS, Cyprus—Partition, 3 July 1957; TNA DEFE 11/183/COS(57)53 meeting. Confidential annex, 3 July 1957.

colleagues that Britain could not afford another expensive white elephant, especially one that generated so much political odium.[109] By February 1959 he had negotiated an agreement that temporarily halted the EOKA insurgency, and permitted the British to retain base rights, although at the cost of surrendering sovereignty over the remainder of the island.[110]

Intervention in both British Guiana and Oman saw the British manoeuvre themselves into political culs-de-sac. The Churchill government's coup in British Guiana did not destroy the PPP, which retained its popularity with the electorate.[111] A British constitutional commission made a distinction between the 'communism' of Cheddi Jagan and the moderate 'socialism' of the party's other main leader, Forbes Burnham, a distinction that not accidentally coincided with ethnic divisions in the party between supporters of Indian and African extraction. The result was that in 1955 the PPP split on ethnic lines.[112] But the declaration of an emergency produced only a political stalemate, which meant, to the intense annoyance of Anthony Head, the Secretary of State for War, that the British would continue to have to station British troops in the colony who were badly needed elsewhere.[113] The garrison was reduced to a fraction of its emergency level in 1956, but, as the Colonial Office's Deputy Security and Intelligence adviser reported after visiting the colony in June 1956, 'The "cold war" being waged in British Guiana since 1953 is likely to continue and even intensify.'[114] That he was right became fully apparent in 1957, when Jagan won a general election. The British, nonplussed as to what they might do next, returned to their starting point. In 1960 they restored self-government with a virtual assurance of future independence.[115]

Intervention in Oman produced a similar political stalemate. The sultan wanted nothing less than the complete submission of his enemies. The British insisted that only a negotiated political settlement, coupled with a development programme to raise the abysmally poor standard of living of his people, would bring long-term

[109] TNA DEFE 11/183. Colonial Secretary to Harding, 3 July 1957; TNA DEFE 11/183/CPC (57)25. Sandys, Military Base in Cyprus, 5 July 1957; TNA CAB 129/88/C(57)161. Macmillan, Cyprus, 9 July 1957; TNA CAB 131/18/D(57)3 meeting. Cabinet Defence Committee, 10 July 1957; TNA CAB 128/31/CC51(57) Cabinet meeting, 11 July 1957.
[110] TNA CAB 21/2891. PM, Cyprus, n.d. but *c.*August 1958; TNA CAB 21/2891. Summary of conclusions reached between the PM, Colonial Secretary and Governor of Cyprus, 6 September 1958; TNA CAB 21/2892. Macmillan to Eisenhower, 19 February 1959.
[111] TNA WO 32/161251. Brigadier A. C. F. Jackson, Commander, Caribbean Area, Review of the present political situation in the Caribbean and its effect on the military requirement, 29 December 1953.
[112] J. G. Rose, 'British colonial policy and the transfer of power in British Guiana, 1945–1964' (Ph.D. dissertation, University of London, 1992), 284–5.
[113] TNA CO 968/441. Anthony Head to Lyttelton, 29 January 1954; TNA CO 968/441. Savage to Colonial Secretary, 19 May 1954; TNA CO 1031/1437. Savage to Colonial Secretary, 23 May 1955; TNA CO 1031/1437. Colonial Secretary to Savage, 26 July 1955; TNA CO 1031/1437. Carstairs to Maj.-Gen. N. Poett, 12 October 1955.
[114] TNA CO 1035/102. C. A. Herbert to Governor British Guiana, 23 June 1956.
[115] C. Seecharan, 'Whose Freedom at Midnight? Machinations towards Guyana's Independence, May 1966', *The Round Table*, vol. 97 (October 2008), 719–36; TNA CAB 129/101/C(60)63. Perth, British Guiana, 28 March 1960; TNA CAB 128/34/CC(60) 21 meeting, 29 March 1960.

stability. In 1958 they forced him to accept a subsidy to institute a civil development programme.[116] But his heart was never in it.[117] An uneasy calm was restored,
but, as British officials predicted, the insurgency merely shifted elsewhere, to
Dhofar.[118] The British had to intervene once again. But this time they began
differently. In July 1970 their first step was to depose the sultan and to replace him
with his own son. He had been trained at Sandhurst, where he had learnt that
insurgencies could not be defeated by purely military means, and that he
had to pursue a political settlement acceptable to at least some of the insurgents'
supporters.[119]

Malaya and Kenya are generally regarded as successful counter-insurgency
operations. But in neither case did the British win because they began by laying
down timetables for creating independent states to succeed colonial rule. At the
start of both emergencies the last thing that the British had in mind was to make
political concessions to buy local support. That option was forced upon them only
later, and when other avenues to end the emergencies had been closed off. In
Malaya the British had tried to extend political rights to the Chinese community
before the declaration of the emergency, only to be forced to withdraw in the face of
Malay protests.[120] By 1950, with the emergency under way, political reforms that
would require the Malays to make concessions would be politically dangerous and
'we must not take any risk of alienating the Malays, who were at present very
loyal'.[121] In November 1950 Briggs insisted that the whole focus of the Federal
government had to be on the day-to-day prosecution of the emergency, and plans
for constitutional changes should be shelved until it was over.[122]

The opening stages of the Kenya emergency were characterized by a similar
political stalemate. The British hoped to develop a multiracial state with power
shared between the different ethnic groups, although it would not be distributed
evenly on a recognizably democratic basis with the minority European and Indian
communities retaining a disproportionately large share.[123] But, on the declaration
of the emergency the colonial government proscribed the KAU, and Baring, like
Briggs, decided that there would be no further constitutional changes while the
emergency lasted.[124] Erskine recognized that while the security forces could restore
law and order, peace would not last for long 'unless the people of this Colony have a

---

[116] TNA DEFE 7/2416. Selwyn Lloyd to Sir B. Burrows, 20 August 1958; TNA DEFE 7/2413.
COS(58)227. Directive for Commander British Forces Arabian Peninsula. Responsibilities towards
the Sultan of Muscat's armed forces, 3 October 1958.
[117] TNA DEFE 7/2413. Political Resident, Bahrain, to FO, 20 October 1958.
[118] TNA DEFE 7/2414. Political Resident Bahrain to FO, 3 February 1959.
[119] W. C. Ladwig III, 'Supporting allies in counterinsurgency: Britain and the Dhofar Rebellion',
SW&I, vol. 19 (2008), 62–88; G. Hughes, 'A "Model campaign" reappraised: the counter-insurgency
war in Dhofar, Oman, 1965–1975', *JSS*, vol. 32 (2009), 271–305.
[120] TNA WO 216/806. Lockhart to Slim, 14 January 1952.
[121] TNA CAB 21/1681/MAL.C(50)6 meeting Malaya Committee, 19 June 1950.
[122] TNA CAB 21/1682/COS(50)468. Director of Operations, Malaya, An appreciation of the
military and political situation in Malaya as on 25 October 1950, 16 November 1950.
[123] L. J. Butler, *Britain and Empire. Adjusting to a Post-Imperial World* (London: I. B. Taurus, 2002),
123.
[124] TNA CO 822/442. Baring to Colonial Secretary, 24 February 1953.

long-term policy which is acceptable to the majority'. But by August 1953 he also realized that 'There is no sign of any long term policy emerging at present. In fact the political side of this colony is divided up and down and from right to left in a way which shows no realism and no appreciation of the multi-racial problems in Kenya. A few talk vaguely of partnership in a great East Africa and the rest talk of the ways and means of ensuring European domination. It is most depressing. The colour bar is rigid.'[125]

In both colonies the British tried to break the stalemate by finding and working with collaborators amongst indigenous politicians. In Malaya, not all Chinese were poor squatters. Some lived in towns, and some were prosperous businessmen. In late 1949 Gurney noted that their leaders, the Malayan Chinese Association, 'have come off the fence publicly'. They spoke in public on the side of the government. The Association 'is an indispensable piece of political machinery if we are to ensure that the loyal Chinese leaders rally their people behind them on Federation-wide political issues and if there is to be a popular Chinese anti-Communist platform.'[126] But it was not until the Churchill administration came to power in October 1951 that ministers in London began seriously to try to work with them. Deeply concerned that the emergency was continuing with no end in sight, Lyttelton travelled to Malaya in December 1951. He returned convinced that success would only be achieved if the bulk of the Chinese population began actively to support the government, which they would not do unless the political log-jam was broken. Consequently when Templer was sent to Malaya his directive proclaimed the goal of the creation of a self-governing Malaya within the Commonwealth. To achieve that he must, without sacrificing the interests of Malays, introduce a form of citizenship common to all ethnic groups.[127] With these instructions, and Briggs now departed, Templer could extend Federal citizenship to the Chinese and begin to hold elections, first at municipal, then at state and finally at Federal levels. The elections saw the coming together of the Malay-dominated United Malays National Organization, led by Tunku Abdul Rahman, and the Malayan Chinese Association. They established a formal alliance and in 1953 were joined by Indian National Congress to form the Alliance Party, led by the Tunku. The British were given extra impetus to move down this road by events in Indo-China, where the French position finally collapsed in May 1954. They now knew that, if they did not bolster the constitutional political parties in Malaya, the MCP might be able to look to the Chinese Communists for support.[128]

However, the extent to which the majority of Chinese peasants had been won over remained unclear. In March 1955 Sir Geoffrey Bourne thought that most were

[125] TNA CO 822/442. Erskine to CIGS, 15 August 1953.
[126] TNA CO 537/5974. Gurney to Colonial Secretary, 12 January 1950.
[127] TNA CAB 21/2884. Directive to Gen. Sir Gerald Templer, High Commissioner in and for the Federation of Malaya, by the Colonial Secretary, 8 February 1952.
[128] TNA WO 216/874. Lt.-Gen. Sir G. Bourne to Harding, 17 July 1954; A. J. Stockwell, 'Insurgency and decolonization during the Malayan emergency', *Journal of Commonwealth and Comparative Politics*, vol. 25 (1987), 78.

still sitting on the fence.[129] That was what made the outcome of the first federal election so important. Held in July 1955, it demonstrated that the Alliance, which won 51 out of 52 seats, had seized the political initiative from the MCP. The Alliance's support for self-government undercut much of the MCP's political appeal, and its electoral mandate ensured that the MCP became increasingly a political irrelevance.[130] In December 1955 Tunku Abdul Rahman, now Chief Minister of the Federation, accompanied by the leader of the Malayan Chinese community, and the Chief Minister of Singapore, met the MCP leader, Chin Peng, at the border town of Baling. Increasingly constrained by security forces' successes, Chin Peng sought a way back into political life through negotiating an agreement that would allow the MCP to emerge from the jungle, claiming it was undefeated, and with the right to fight elections. The Alliance government, with a mandate to speak for the whole Malayan people, offered him nothing better than the terms that had been on the table since September 1955. The armed insurgents would have to lay down their arms and face a period of detention while their past behaviour was investigated.[131] The talks collapsed and never resumed. By February 1957, slightly less than half of the population of the Federation were living normal lives in 'white' areas, where all emergency measures had been lifted, and in August the Alliance government led Malaya to independence within the Commonwealth.[132] Ching Peng admitted that with the promise of independence 'the core of our armed struggle had been abruptly extracted'.[133]

In Kenya, Lyttelton hoped to find new African political organizations to replace the KAU, ones which would be 'led by experienced and sober-minded Africans'.[134] Hugh Fraser, his Parliamentary Private Secretary, returned from Nairobi in October 1953 hoping, 'to canalize Kikuyu feeling not into a subservient loyalty to HMG but to create a moderate party who whilst supporting law and order will through constitutional means be able to help plan their future and gain some of their objectives.'[135] In 1954 the British government began to travel a short distance along the road that Fraser had mapped out. Military facts on the ground had changed the political complexion of the colony. Kenya's reliance on British soldiers meant that 'Kenya has placed herself in the hands of HMG in a way which has never happened before,' Erskine concluded. 'If we are providing troops and money to the extent of to-day, I believe we should dictate future policy.'[136] Lyttelton then

[129]   TNA WO 216/874. Lt.-Gen. Sir G. Bourne to Harding, 8 March 1955.
[130]   Stubbs, *Hearts and Minds*, 200–26.
[131]   TNA CAB 131/16/DC(55)30. Memorandum by the Colonial Secretary, Declaration of amnesty in the Federation of Malaya, 24 August 1955; TNA WO 216/875. Lt.-Gen. Sir G. Bourne to Templer, 3 October 1955; TNA CAB 131/16/DC(55)11 meeting. Cabinet Defence Committee, 19 October 1955.
[132]   TNA WO 208/5356. Lt.-Gen. Sir R. Bower, Review of the Emergency Situation in Malaya at the end of 1956, 12 February 1957.
[133]   C. Peng, *My Side of History* (Singapore: Media Masters, 2003), 395.
[134]   TNA CAB 129/57/C(52)407. Colonial Secretary, Kenya, 14 November 1952.
[135]   TNA PREM 11/472. Summary of Report of visit to Kenya by the Hon. H. C. P. J. Fraser, 12 October 1953.
[136]   TNA CO 822/442. Erskine to CIGS, 15 August 1953.

took the colony further down the path of multiracialism, but in ways deliberately benefiting loyalists. Land reforms were introduced with the aim of developing a conservative elite of loyalist landowners, while simultaneously punishing their Mau Mau-supporting neighbours who lost out when existing scattered land holdings were consolidated into larger farms. Poorer loyalists who had no land were rewarded with access to government and other jobs, which were also denied to supporters of the insurgency. The process of 'Africanization' enabled loyalists to colonize the civil service and Provincial Administration.[137] At the centre there was a small increase in African representation, but it was coupled with a promise that there would be no further constitutional changes until 1960.[138]

The settlers thought this was a sell-out to the insurgents. But, as 5.5 million Africans were represented by only one minister and two undersecretaries, whereas 130,000 Asians and Europeans had no fewer than five ministers, it was hardly likely that the former would long be satisfied.[139] Senior security officials agreed. They knew that the army, police, and home guard had done no more than enforce a temporary political standstill. 'Even though the Emergency might be declared officially at an end', Lathbury wrote in December 1955, 'we should have no illusions about the future. Mau Mau has not been killed: it has been suppressed. The thousands who have spent a long time in detention must have been embittered by it. Nationalism is still a very potent force and the African will pursue his aim by other means. Kenya is in for a very tricky political future and it would be dangerous to relax security measures too quickly. They will cost a lot of money for a long time to come.'[140] Lennox-Boyd responded by introducing a qualified form of democracy to Kenya. Different ethnic groups had their own voting rolls and only those Africans who met appropriate property and educational qualifications could vote.

But it proved no more than a temporary expedient. In 1957 a committee of British government officials predicted that Kenya might achieve internal self-government but that 'the devolution of responsibility will largely depend on the growth of inter-racial confidence, which cannot be predicted in terms of time.'[141] But as African representation grew after the 1957 election, so, too, did demands that the majority ethnic group should be given a larger share of representation. Even so, the British government still seemed determined to stay in command. On 22 April 1959 Lennox-Boyd told the Commons that he could not foresee a date when the British government would surrender their ultimate responsibility for Kenya.[142] It took a series of shocks, including the Hola camp atrocities, the fallout from the Nyasaland emergency, and the growing recognition that retaining colonies against the will of the colonized was too politically and financially

[137] Branch, *Defeating Mau Mau*, 120–5, 148–9, 163–74.
[138] *Manchester Guardian*, 11 March 1954.
[139] *Manchester Guardian*, 11 March & 6 October 1954.
[140] TNA WO 216/892. Lathbury to CIGS, 5 December 1955.
[141] TNA CAB 135/1556/CPC(57)30. Future constitutional development in the colonies, 6 September 1957.
[142] F. Heinlein, *British Government Policy and Decolonisation 1945–1963. Scrutinising the Official Mind* (London: Frank Cass, 2002), 190.

196 The British Way in Counter-Insurgency

expensive, to persuade the Macmillan government that they had to sacrifice the European settlers to the demands of African majority rule. This was the only way to secure African goodwill in the rest of the continent. The 'experienced and sober-minded' African they found to lead Kenya to independence in December 1963 was the very man they had locked up in 1952, Jomo Kenyatta.

PSYCHOLOGICAL WARFARE

The tardiness with which the British habitually espoused political remedies to insurgencies was important. It not only contributed to the reluctance of the civil population to provide the security forces with information, but also helped to undermine efforts to use psychological warfare operations to induce armed opponents to surrender.[143] Experience in Malay showed that psychological warfare operations by themselves would rarely suffice to shift the balance of advantage in favour of the security forces, but, if they were coupled with military successes and political initiatives that seemed to offer the insurgents and their supporters a better future, they could do so. Conversely Kenya demonstrated that if the government was slow to offer the insurgents a better political future, the insurgency was likely to drag on.

In Malaya between 1948 and April 1957 the number of insurgent guerrillas at large dropped from about 11,000 to only 2,100. But those who remained were tough and experienced. The Director of Operations had no doubt that the insurgency would not be ended until they had been eliminated. Chasing such a small number of insurgents in the depths of the Malayan jungle was likely to be a thankless task, so the Malayan government opted for an intensified psychological warfare campaign to induce them to surrender. In September 1957 they issued an amnesty for the remaining insurgents and publicised it by air-dropping 34 million leaflets. In the next 15 months the jungle fighters suffered a catastrophic loss of members. By the end of 1958 fewer than 900 remained in the jungle, and they had ceased to function as a guerrilla army. The psychological warfare operation was not solely responsible for the government's success. Independence under the multi-racial Alliance party had robbed the MCP of its ostensible reason for fighting, freeing Malaya from British colonialism.[144] Propaganda operated in conjunction with an effective military strategy that had cut the insurgents off from their main sources of supply and intelligence, driven them into the deep jungle, and left them convinced that they could not win the military struggle. The government

---

[143] S. L. Carruthers, *Winning Hearts and Minds. British Governments, the Media and Colonial Counter-Insurgency 1944–1960* (Leicester: Leicester University Press, 1995), 42, 49–50; K. Utting, 'The strategic information campaign: lessons from the British experience in Palestine 1945–1948', in T. Benbow and R. Thornton (eds), *Dimensions of Counter-insurgency. Applying Experience to Practice* (London: Routledge, 2008), 36–56.

[144] Ramakrishna, 'Anatomy of a collapse', 109–33; K. Ramakrishna, 'Content, credibility and context: propaganda, government surrender policy and the Malayan Communist mass surrender of 1958', *INS*, vol. 19 (1999), 242–66.

also offered amnesty terms that were more attractive than anything hitherto on the table. Surrendered insurgents, no matter what their crimes, would escape prosecution, would be reintegrated into a normal life and reunited with their families.[145]

Psychological warfare operations in Kenya were much less successful, for, although it was plain by 1954 that the security forces were winning the war on the ground, the government did not offer the remaining forest fighters similar inducements to surrender. In August 1953 the government had issued the 'green branch' terms, so called because insurgents were told to carry a green branch to signal their willingness to give themselves up. The terms were hardly attractive. Mau Mau were told that they would not be executed merely for carrying arms, but they might be if found guilty of murder. By February 1954 only 159 insurgents had taken advantage of the offer. About 10,000 remained active.[146] A second set of surrender terms were offered in the spring of 1954, but they were only marginally more attractive. Lyttelton persuaded the Cabinet to agree not to prosecute people who were wanted for murder, but agreed that they would be detained for a long time.[147] A third offer was made in January 1955, as part of the package of measures that also included an amnesty to members of the home guard who had committed crimes.[148] It had more success, not least because it was accompanied by two major security forces operations, HAMMER and FIRST FLUTE, the first large-scale invasion of the insurgents' forest sanctuaries. The result was that whereas between August 1953 and January 1955 only 447 insurgents had surrendered, between January and July 1955 (when the terms were withdrawn) another 979 did so.[149]

Even so, the British were frankly disappointed. Some insurgents were just not convinced that surrender offered them a better option than remaining at large in

---

[145] TNA KV 4/408. H. Carlton Greene, Head, Emergency Information Services, Report on Emergency Information Services, September 1950—September. 1951, 14 September 1951; TNA WO 291/1783. Operational Research Section (Psychological Warfare). P. H. Lakin and G. J. Humphreys, Memorandum number 11/54. A study of surrenders in Malaya during the period January 1949 to June 1954, 14 July 1954; TNA WO 291/1784. Operational Research Section (Psychological Warfare) Memorandum 12/54. An estimate of the effectiveness of Operation Bison as a means of bringing about group surrenders, 18 August 1954.

[146] TNA CO 822/496. DDO to Provincial Commissioners, Emergency Directive No 9. Surrender Policy, 28 July 1953; TNA CO 822/496. Maj.-Gen. W. R. N. Hinde, Emergency Directive no. 10. Directive on the Treatment of Surrendered Terrorists, 28 July 1953; TNA CO 822/496. Secretariat, Nairobi to Provincial Commissioners Central Province and Rift Valley Province, 28 July 1953; CO 822/496. Erskine to CIGS, 20 August 1953.

[147] TNA CO 822/773. Erskine to VCIGS, 13 February 1954; TNA CO 822/773. Erskine to Lt.-Gen. H. Redman, 27 February 1954; TNA CO 822/773. Colonial Secretary to Churchill, 1 March 1954; TNA CAB 195/12/CC13(54). Cabinet meeting, 1 March 1954; TNA CO 822/773. Lyttelton (Kenya) to Churchill, 2 March 1954; P. Catterall (ed.), *The Macmillan Diaries. The Cabinet Years, 1950–1957* (London: Macmillan, 2003), 298.

[148] TNA WO 216/879. Erskine to CIGS, 6 January 1955; TNA WO 216/879. Erskine to CIGS, 9 January 1955; TNA WO 216/879. Baring to Colonial Secretary, 11 January 1955; TNA WO 216/879. Erskine to Secretary of State for War, 12 January 1955; TNA WO 276/430. 'To all Mau Mau leaders and their followers. New Surrender Terms', 18 January 1955; TNA PREM 11/1424. Acting Governor Kenya to Colonial Secretary, 21 January 1955.

[149] Bennett, 'British Army counterinsurgency and the use of force in Kenya', 178–91; TNA WO 276/457. Press Conference (Brief for C.-in-C. on surrenders), n.d. but *c*.20 January 1955; WO 291/1670. Operational Research Unit (Far East). Report Number 1/57. A comparison of the emergencies in Malaya and Kenya, 6 June 1957.

the hope that they would eventually extract political concessions from the government. On one occasion, a security force patrol commander operating in the forest and charged with getting the government's message about surrender terms across to the insurgents, drew

> himself up to his five foot six, reached for his loud hailer, a prized possession that he had been longing to use and putting it to his lips, he shouted in his best Oxford accent that we all hated.
>
> 'Give yourselves up, there's good chaps, you will all be well-treated and be given food and shelter.'
>
> From across the beautiful valley with Mount Kilimanjaro in the background, through another loud hailer, came the casual reply, 'Get stuffed white man.'[150]

CONCLUSION

The mainstay of British counter-insurgency operations was always coercion, and the practical consequences of that—collective punishments, cordon and search operations and perhaps forcible population resettlement—were never welcomed by the people who experienced them. Conciliation, whether it took the form of making carefully calculated political concessions as Thompson advised, or buying support through investment in projects to raise living standards, were practised only on a limited scale. In Palestine the British government refused to allow increased Jewish immigration, the only political concession that might have divided the Yishuv from the Irgun and the Stern Gang. In the Canal Zone, the Attlee and Churchill governments tacked and tacked again in an effort to find a compromise that would satisfy Britain's strategic requirements and Egyptian nationalist aspirations. What they accepted in the 1954 settlement was a virtual surrender to the Egyptians. The pattern of concessions reluctantly conceded was similar elsewhere. Even in Malaya, the British were slow to accept that they had to offer political independence if they wanted to undercut the attractions of the MCP. Almost everywhere attempts to buy support for the colonial regime by promoting investment in economic development foundered on the shortages of money and the reluctance of the Treasury to provide more than the barest minimum of funding. Buying 'hearts and minds' was never a real possibility. The British could not afford the down payments.

Sir Richard Turnbull, who was the Chief Secretary to the government of Kenya between 1955 and 1958, had no doubt that the campaign was won by being nasty, not nice, to the Kikuyu. '. . . we had if I can use a cant phrase to "win the hearts and minds of the people". But how could we as strangers win the hearts and minds of the Kikuyu in opposition to their brothers and cousins who were in the forests? It was a vain hope, all the same in the end we did wear them down and wearing down

---

[150] T. Stack-Hawkley, 'That Time in Kenya?' Downloaded 13 April 2009 at: http://www.nsrafa. org/%5CTimesRemembered.aspx.

is the proper word.'[151] It is a moot point whether, even if they had been able to pour more investment into economic development programmes, it would have made much difference. Visiting Aden in 1964 the journalist Clare Hollingworth listed the grievances of moderate Arab merchants and professional men. She recognized that they did not want to see the back of the British because the British kept them poor, but because they humiliated them. British officials looked down on them as 'natives', when Arabs elsewhere in the Middle East were already their own masters. It was degrading that Aden was the only major city in the Arab world that was not part of an independent state. They were not free to express their own political ideas, for they might be detained without trial if they did so. They were deprived of their political rights by the British, who had rigged the constitution to exclude most people from the franchise. If the British closed the base and left Aden it might indeed harm their prosperity. But, Hollingworth concluded with real insight, 'It is difficult for a Western mind to grasp this fact, and to understand that a Moslem would on the whole prefer to be ruled by co-religionists even if the regime was less beneficial to him personally than a foreign one.'[152] As the next chapter will show, that was not the only thing that the British were slow to grasp and act upon.

---

[151] IWMSA. Accession No. 4742. Sir R. Turnbull, Transcript, 42–3.
[152] C. Hollingworth, 'Aden unrest not only among extremists', *Guardian*, 23 May 1964.

7

Counter-insurgency and the Learning Curve

In 1953 a young National Service subaltern, John Chynoweth, was posted to 6/Malay Regiment. He remembered that

> Our time at Eaton Hall [the training school for National Service officers] had taught us nothing about jungle warfare and nearly all our month at Port Dickson [the Malay Regiment's Depot] had been devoted to acclimatisation rather than training in the jungle. I spent more time on the tennis court and in the sea than I did in the jungle or in the classroom. We were also refused permission to attend a course at the Far East Land Forces School of Jungle Warfare, although National Service subalterns in British regiments were allowed to attend. Instead, we were told to read an Army issue handbook entitled 'The Conduct of Anti-Terrorist Operations in Malaya'. Anyone who has been on active service knows that you cannot learn how to command troops in unfamiliar terrain against an unfamiliar enemy from a handbook—a course on the ground run by experienced campaigners is essential.[1]

Chynoweth might have been surprised to discover that some observers have given the British high marks for their ability to learn from their experiences, and to create and disseminate a successful counter-insurgency doctrine.[2] He might have had more sympathy with the claim that not only were they slow to learn 'lessons' within a theatre, but they were even worse at transmitting them between theatres. These latter failures have been attributed in no small part to a culture within the army that exalted a 'warrior ethos', that made it difficult for soldiers on the ground to deal with the political complexities that confronted them during counter-insurgency operations.[3]

This chapter will examine how the army went about gathering, and analysing, the lessons of its campaigns. It will explore how those lessons were subsequently disseminated to units in the field by looking at what special training they received. But it will also examine another issue that the existing literature has ignored. The army was not the only agency involved in waging these campaigns. The Colonial

---

[1] J. Chynoweth, *Hunting Terrorists in the Jungle. The Experiences of a National Service Subaltern in Malaya in the 1950s* (Stroud, Glouc.: Tempus, 2005), 46–7.

[2] T. R. Mockaitis, *British Counterinsurgency, 1919–60* (London: Macmillan, 1990), 10; D. D. Avant, *Political Institutions and Military Change. Lessons from Peripheral Wars* (Ithaca: Cornell University Press, 1994), 102–29; J. A. Nagl, *Learning to Eat Soup with a Knife. Counterinsurgency Lessons from Malaya and Vietnam* (Chicago: University of Chicago Press, 2002/5), 59–80, 105–7; R. Gregorian, '"Jungle bashing" in Malaya: towards a formal tactical doctrine', *SW & I*, vol. 5 (1994), 338–59.

[3] J. Kiszely, 'Learning about counter-insurgency', *JRUSI*, vol. 151 (2006) 16–21.

Office was also deeply involved, and yet little has been written about how it went about gathering, analysing, and disseminating the lessons of its experiences.

THE ARMY AND GATHERING THE LESSONS OF COUNTER-INSURGENCY

The army was assiduous in garnering the lessons of its operations so that they could be passed on to future generations. This process happened in two stages. Unit and formation commanders were expected to produce reports of their operations while campaigns were still on-going in order that lessons could be put to immediate use.[4] Once a campaign had ended senior commanders and their staffs were required to compile lengthy accounts of their doings and to highlight any lessons that might be of interest to others. There were a number of such reports. The last GOC in Palestine, Sir Gordon Macmillan, produced a lengthy report on the operations preceding the final evacuation.[5] In October 1951 the HQ BTE forwarded to all units a brief report on insurgent tactics as practised by Zionist insurgents in Palestine between 1945 and 1948 in the belief that their opponents in the Canal Zone might behave in similar ways.[6] Erskine wrote two final reports, a narrative of events in the Canal Zone between October 1951 and April 1952, and the second, a long compilation of his period of command in Kenya.[7] His successor in Kenya, Sir Gerald Lathbury, wrote his own report covering his period in command.[8] Commanders in Malaya did likewise. The first, prepared by the Commander-in-Chief FARELF, Sir Neil Ritchie, covered the first year of the Emergency.[9] In July 1950 the minutes of a conference held by the GOC Malaya, Maj.-Gen. Roy Urquhart, to pool the knowledge of senior commanders, were quickly forwarded to the Director-General of Military Training in London. He then circulated them to various army schools and training establishments.[10] The final lessons of Malaya were summarized by the last Director of Operations, Sir Roger Bower, in a report he wrote in

---

[4] TNA WO 261/640. Report on Operation AGATHA, 1 British Infantry Division, 29 June to 2 July 1946; TNA WO 261/640. 1 Infantry Division and North Palestine District, Quarterly Historical Report for the period ending 14 September 1946; TNA WO 261/652. 1 British Inf. Division. Quarterly Historical Report to December 1946; TNA WO 268/117. Quarterly historical report—FARELF Training Centre, 1 January 1950 to 31 March 1950; TNA WO 296/23. Report on the employment of troops in the police role, n.d. but *c.*March 1956.
[5] TNA WO 32/15037. Lt.-Gen. Sir G. H. A. Macmillan, Palestine: final report on evacuation, 26 October 1948.
[6] TNA WO 236/25. COS to all formations in the Canal Zone, 30 October 1951.
[7] TNA WO 236/15. Erskine, Narrative of events in the Canal Zone, October 1951–April 1952; TNA WO 236/18. Erskine to Governor Kenya and other Kenya government officials, CIGS and Military Members Army Council, Colonial Secretary, etc., 25 April 1955.
[8] TNA WO 236/20. Lt.-Gen. Sir G. Lathbury, The Kenya Emergency, 3 May 1955 to 17 November 1956.
[9] WO 106/5884. Gen. Sir N. Ritchie, Report on operations in Malaya, June 1948 to July 1949, 6 September 1949.
[10] TNA WO 231/38. Notes of Conference held by GOC Malay District on 11 July 1950.

September 1957.[11] Cyprus produced no fewer that three reports. Two were written by successive Directors of Operations, Brigadier Baker and Maj.-Gen. Darling, and the third, completed in April 1960, was a History of EOKA with a forward by Darling.[12] Operations in Oman yielded a short General Staff pamphlet on the conduct of operations in arid mountainous areas, and Sir David Luce, the C-in-C Far East, had produced his comments on the lessons to be drawn from the intervention in Brunei by July1963.[13]

Reports by senior officers were supplemented by the work of operational research scientists attached to the Department of the Scientific Adviser to the Army Council. Beginning in 1949 they produced a series of reports on operations in Malaya. Topics they examined included the effectiveness of different patrol and ambush tactics, factors effecting marksmanship, problems of radio communications, the effectiveness of different units in jungle operations, why Chinese squatters joined the insurgents, and why some of them surrendered.[14] Their conclusions were supplemented by a lengthy report, prepared by the Assistant Director of Scientific Research in the Operational Research Section (Malaya), and approved by the military authorities in both Kenya and Malaya, comparing the conduct of the campaigns in Malaya and Kenya.[15] In 1962 a team from the Joint Services Operational Research Branch visited South East Asia to gather possible lessons from on-going operations in South Vietnam that the British might be able to put to use themselves. At the end of the Borneo Confrontation the Operational Requirements and Analysis Branch of FARELF headquarters prepared a report on the lessons of that campaign.[16]

These reports did not remain unread. They were fed into a series of new manuals about the conduct of counter-insurgency operations that the War Office published

[11] TNA WO 106/5990. Director of Operations Malaya, Review of the Emergency in Malaya from June 1948 to August 1957, September 1957.

[12] TNA CO 968/690. Brigadier G. Baker, A Review of the Cyprus Emergency April 1955–March 1958; TNA WO 106/6020. Report on the Cyprus Emergency, 31 July 1959; TNA WO 33/2736. History of EOKA, 1954–1959, 20 April 1960.

[13] TNA WO 279/742. General Staff, *Local Operations in Mountainous Country, 1958* (London: War Office, 1 October 1958); TNA DEFE 6/85/JP.55/63(Final). JPS, Report by the C-in-C Far East on operations in Borneo from December 1962 to February 1963, 5 July 1963.

[14] TNA WO 291/1176. Army Operational Research Group, Some observations on the jungle patrol communication problem in Malaya, 22 December 1949; TNA WO 291/1654. Lt.-Col. J. R. Shirley, Memorandum Number 8. Operational Research in Malaya. Notes for the Chief Scientist, Ministry of Supply, February 1951; TNA WO 291/1734. Dr K. Pennycuick, Memorandum Number 1/54. The assessment of battalion performance in Malaya 1952–1953; TNA WO 291/1764. ORS(PW). Memorandum No. 2/53. A preliminary study of entry behaviour among Chinese communist terrorists in Malaya, 1 June 1953; TNA WO 291/1732. Lt.-Col. R. S. Hawkins, Memorandum Number 7/53. A statistical examination of events in relation to Security Force and CT activities in Malaya (Period September 1952 to July 1953); TNA WO 291/1784. Operational Research Section (Psychological Warfare) Memorandum 12/54. An estimate of the effectiveness of Operation Bison as a means of bringing about group surrenders, 18 August 1954.

[15] TNA WO 291/1670. Operational Research Unit (Far East). Report Number 1/57. A comparison of the emergencies in Malaya and Kenya, 6 June 1957.

[16] TNA WO 291/2482. Report on the visit to the Far East by the Joint Services Operational Research Team, 1 April 1963; TNA WO 291/2407. FARELF. G(Operational Requirements and Analysis) Branch. Report No. 1/69. Lessons learned from Borneo Operations, 17 March 1969.

between 1949 and 1963. Montgomery began the process of revising all of the army's doctrinal publications in 1948.[17] Each manual was to 'be written in good readable English; journalese should be avoided'. The authors who produced the first draft were not to be selected haphazardly from anyone who happened to be available. They were specially selected by the DGMT because they had a special knowledge of the subject and could write well.[18] Theatre commanders showed a similar willingness to tap into the ideas of relatively junior officers who had special knowledge. The most influential manual, *Conduct of Anti-terrorist Operations in Malaya*, commonly known as *ATOM*, was drafted, at Templer's behest, by Walter Walker, then a lieutenant-colonel.[19] In 1954 Erskine ordered each of his brigade commanders to nominate one officer and one NCO to form part of a tactical team at GHQ who were told to produce a draft doctrine for forest operations.[20] His successor, Lathbury, insisted that 'as this is an unconventional type of war, we must use unconventional methods. New ideas must be examined regardless of their degree of originality or the source from which they come.'[21] Because other government departments, most obviously the Colonial Office, were inevitably involved when the army was summoned to assist the civil power, drafts of War Office manuals were habitually submitted to them for comment, correction, and concurrence before they were published. They thus reflected not merely War Office doctrine, but the wider views of interested parties within the machinery of colonial governance.

WRITING DOCTRINE

The task of producing the first draft of a new army-wide internal security pamphlet to replace *Notes on Imperial Policing 1934* and *Duties in Aid of the Civil Power 1937* was given to two comparatively junior officers, Lieutenant-Colonels C. A. Whigham and C. P. Warren. The result was *Internal Security Duties 1947*. However, such was its labyrinthine journey around Whitehall—it was also circulated in draft to the Home Office, Admiralty, Air Ministry, and Scottish Office—that it did not finally appear until 1949, under the title *Imperial Policing and Duties in aid of the Civil Power, 1949*.[22]

---

[17] TNA WO 216/257. Training publications. Notes on a meeting held on 19 April 1948 between the CIGS, VCIGS, and DMT.

[18] TNA WO 216/257. Report by a committee on Army Training Pamphlets, n.d. but *c.*May 1948.

[19] Nagl, *Learning to Eat Soup with a Knife*, 97–8.

[20] TNA WO 276/197. Minutes of the COS's conference of Brigade Commanders at Thika, 10 July 1954.

[21] TNA WO 276/449. Lt.-Col. H. A. Hope to Lt.-Col. H. E. N. Bredin 14 June 1955.

[22] T. Jones, *Postwar Counterinsurgency and the SAS, 1945 to 1952. A Special Type of Warfare* (London: Cass, 2001), 38; TNA WO 216/257. Military Assistant to VCIGS, March 1948; TNA CO 537/1971. Lt.-Col. C. P. Warren to B. D. Edmonds, 12 February 1947; TNA CO 537/1971. Extract of letter from Lt.-Col. Warren, 7 March 1947; TNA CO 537/1971. Undersecretary of State WO to Undersecretary of State CO, 22 August 1947: TNA CO 537/1971. A. B. Acheson to Undersecretary of State War Office, 24 November 1947.

Work on updating the 1949 manual began in 1956. The first draft of what became *Keeping the Peace. Operations in support of the Civil Power*, which was published in 1957, was produced by another junior officer, Major R. C. W. Thomas, who had recent experience of operations in Malaya. In preparing the revision he not only consulted the major War Office publications on counter-insurgency operations going back to *Imperial Policing, 1934*, but also two recent manuals that had been produced in active theatres, *Anti-terrorist Operations in Malaya* and *Handbook of Anti-Mau Mau Operations*.[23] Once again, the author was required to circulate his drafts widely, not just to senior army officers but also to the Colonial Office and to the government's legal advisers in the Treasury Solicitors' Office, and to take account of their suggestions.[24] Further refinements were added to the official doctrine in 1963, with the publication of a new edition of *Keeping the Peace*.[25]

The manuals contained detailed descriptions of how to mount the kinds of operations—such as road blocks, cordon and searches in both rural and urban areas, sweeps, and anti-riot and anti-ambush drills—commonly undertaken by troops operating in aid of the civil power. The 1949 manual, drawing on experiences in Palestine, explained how to establish a controlled area, and how to search villages and houses and to screen their inhabitants.[26] *ATOM* was a milestone in two respects. At the tactical level it described a series of drills that could be employed by units operating in the jungle to establish jungle bases, carry out silent patrols, and mount and avoid ambushes. The same drills were subsequently used, with local modifications, in other theatres, and they were also included in army-wide manuals such as *Keeping the Peace*.[27] But even more significant, *ATOM* codified how through a policy of 'the close control of populated areas such as towns, new villages, kampongs and estate lines', implemented by means of population control measures and food denial operations, it was possible to produce an operational strategy that could be employed to defeat a largely rural insurgency.[28]

With the exception of operations in Palestine and the clearance of Nairobi in 1954, most British operations before the publication of the 1957 edition of *Keeping the Peace* had been directed against rural insurgencies. The 1963 edition embodied the lessons of the 1949 and 1957 manual, but it also reflected the lessons that the

[23] TNA WO 279/241. Director of Operations, Malaya, *Conduct of anti-terrorist operations in Malaya* (Kuala Lumpur: 3rd edn, 1958) (the first edition was published in 1952, and the second in 1954); TNA WO 276/545. *A Handbook of Anti-Mau Mau operations* (Kenya: East Africa Command, n.d. but c.1954).
[24] TNA WO 296/23. Enc. Keeping the Peace. Operations in support of the Civil Power, n.d.; TNA WO 296/23. Minute, Lt.-Col. ?, MT2, 23 January 1957.
[25] TNA WO 279/398. WO, *Keeping the Peace. Part 1. Doctrine* (London: War Office, 7 January 1963); WO 279/399. WO, *Keeping the Peace. Part 2. Tactics and Training* (London: War Office, 16 January 1963).
[26] WO 279/391. WO, *Imperial Policing and Duties in Aid of the Civil Power, 1949* (London: War Office, 13 June 1949), 35–43.
[27] TNA WO 279/241. Director of Operations, Malaya, *Conduct of Anti-terrorist Operations in Malaya* (Kuala Lumpur: 3rd edn, 1958), chs 5–11; WO 296/23. *Keeping the Peace. (Duties in Support of the Civil Power)* (London: War Office, 1957), ch. 8.
[28] TNA WO 279/241. Director of Operations, Malaya, *Conduct of Anti-terrorist Operations in Malaya* (Kuala Lumpur: 3rd edn, 1958), ch. 3, *passim*.

security forces had learnt in Cyprus. EOKA had not only fought a rural insurgency in the mountains and villages, but its cells had also conducted a terrorist campaign in the towns. A cell structure presented the security forces with difficult problems. Each cell was small, and so difficult to penetrate. Even if it were penetrated, the very nature of the cell organization meant that an initial success would not automatically enable the security forces to roll up the entire organization. But the manual did identify three vulnerabilities that might be exploited. The effectiveness of the system depended on its higher commanders. Targeting them should be a priority, because if they were eliminated they would be difficult to replace. The manual recommended emulating the practice in Cyprus, where the security forces had formed combined Special Branch/army snatch teams to seize such people.[29] Couriers were another point of vulnerability. The cells depended on them for communications, but couriers were not only slow, they were liable to be captured by searches at road-blocks. Thirdly, it was difficult for commanders to distribute supplies and arms to their cells and so, just as in a rural insurgency, the security forces needed to establish tight control over supplies of money, arms, food, and medical supplies.[30]

The manual also argued that operations in heavily urbanized areas called for new tactics. These innovations included the need to establish a series of control points to prevent large crowds from forming lest they turn into rioting mobs. The security forces had to dominate the rooftops by deploying standing patrols which could report the movement of crowds and curfew breakers, and direct patrolling helicopters or ground patrols to trouble spots.[31] Patrolling at street level required special techniques. Some patrols operated openly to instil confidence in the population, especially during the hours of daylight. They were supported by mobile patrols, which could move quickly to help them if trouble occurred. But at night units were expected to mount 'soft shoe' patrols. These small parties operated using stealth and guile. They laid-up in concealed locations, moved by unexpected routes, down back alleys and over garden walls. Their role was to impose sudden check-points, to intercept couriers and bomb carriers, and generally take the initiative away from the enemy.[32]

The manuals did not just highlight tactical lessons. Writing in 1966 Thompson explained that one of his purposes in writing *Defeating Communist Insurgencies* was his hope that, 'It may also provide the professional with a framework around which to build a fuller study of all aspects of counter-insurgency, which must inevitably vary according to terrain and the conditions prevailing in a threatened country at any given time.'[33] But an examination of the official doctrinal manuals that the army produced suggests that by 1949 they had already developed their own

---

[29] TNA WO 279/399. WO, *Keeping the Peace. Part 2. Tactics and Training* (London: War Office, 16 January 1963), ch. 4.

[30] TNA WO 279/398. WO, *Keeping the Peace. Part 1. Doctrine* (London: War Office, 7 January 1963), ch. 3.

[31] TNA WO 279/399. WO, *Keeping the Peace. Part 2. Tactics and Training* (London: War Office, 16 January 1963), 41–2.

[32] TNA WO 279/399. WO, *Keeping the Peace. Part 2. Tactics and Training* (London: War Office, 16 January 1963), 42–3.

[33] Sir R. Thompson, *Defeating Communist Insurgency. The Lessons of Malaya and Vietnam* (St Petersburg, FL: Hailer Publishing, 2005; originally published 1966), 9.

understanding of Thompson's model of Communist insurgent strategy, and that by 1957 they had already codified many of the principles that Thompson highlighted a decade later.

Every manual repeated the mantra that troops called upon the assist the civil power were expected to employ no more than the minimum necessary force. Commanders were constantly reminded that, despite the provocation to which they would be subjected, troops had to remain highly disciplined. Being disciplined and polite remained important ideals throughout the 1950s, but by the second half of the decade commanders wanted their men to do more. They wanted them to gain the confidence of the local population by taking part in civic action programmes. The need to ensure a secure base area was a principle of fundamental importance that the army had long recognized as being relevant to all kinds of operations, not just operations in aid of the civil power. The need for timely and accurate intelligence, the fact that the key agency in gathering it was the Special Branch, not the army, were also understood by 1949 and remained a fixed feature of British doctrine thereafter.[34] *ATOM* provided a more detailed gloss on how the Special Branch and military intelligence should co-operate, recommending the establishment of joint operations rooms manned by the police and military intelligence officers.

The biggest shift in the army's written doctrine was the gradual understanding that internal security operations involved far more than troops temporarily replacing policemen in an effort to maintain law and order. Gradually they came to understand that such operations often meant that the army, together with the police and civil administration, had embarked upon a prolonged campaign to restore the legitimacy of the colonial state and that paradoxically doing so might involve granting dependencies self-government. *Keeping the Peace (Duties in Support of the Civil Power)* (1957) embodied for the first time an explicit acknowledgement that, in embarking on operations in support of the civil power, the army was not operating to re-impose the *status quo ante*, but was working within a complex and rapidly changing political environment as part of a dynamic political process. In a forward the Secretary of State for War explained that

> We in Britain have a direct responsibility for many of the peoples affected by the rapid changes—for the peoples of the British Colonies, Protectorates and Trust Territories. Our policy is to help them through all these changes and the stresses and strains to which they give rise, in peace and justice and that they shall arrive at forms of self-government suited to their own circumstances and to modern conditions. This policy has its difficulties and its dangers and, at times, we are faced with disturbances which get beyond the local security resources. These disturbances can be due to many causes, ranging from deliberate communist or other subversion from outside, to internal conflicts between one tribe, race or religious community and another. The causes may be political, social or economic; they may be deliberately fermented by people seeking personal power, or simply to weaken Britain as part of the wider game of power

---

[34] TNA WO 279/391. WO, *Imperial Policing and Duties in Aid of the Civil Power, 1949* (London: War Office, 13 June 1949), 11, 14.

politics, or they may arise from simple confusions and misunderstandings in a world which is changing rapidly in a way unsettling for unsophisticated people.[35]

As early as 1949 the army's manual writers had a clear understanding of the various stages through which a Maoist rural insurgency might develop, and knew that to forestall its advance close co-operation between the army, police, and civil administration was essential.[36] The best way to create and secure good relations was to hold frequent, sometimes daily, conferences, between the military commander, the District Superintendent of Police, the District Commissioner, and the head of the CID.[37] The major innovation in *ATOM*, repeated in *A Handbook of Anti-Mau Mau Operations* published in 1954, and in subsequent army-wide manuals, was to insist that what had begun as an innovation to harmonize day-to-day tactical policies should be employed to harmonize policy at the political and strategic levels. *Keeping the Peace* (1957) called this 'Control by committee'.[38]

A study of the contents of the army's manuals suggests that Thompson did not invent a new counter-insurgency strategy. Rather, he codified, popularized, and brought to a wider audience doctrines that the army had already developed and promulgated in its own manuals some years earlier. But it was one thing to gather and analyse lessons and then to publish them. It was another to ensure that they were effectively disseminated to troops on the ground.

DISSEMINATING DOCTRINE

Both officer cadet and staff college training in Britain were geared heavily towards the conduct of conventional operations in Europe. In the mid-1950s Staff College students spent 390 hours studying how to conduct high-intensity operations, but devoted only 37 hours to the Cold War.[39] In the context of the Cold War, many officers regarded that as right and proper. High-intensity operations in Europe was real warfare, whereas fighting insurgents 'that's hunting for bandits as you might say. Quite a different thing from fighting a proper war.'[40] But the conduct of at least some aspects of counter-insurgency operations was not entirely neglected. In 1950 the army reintroduced compulsory promotion examinations to test whether Captains were fit to become Majors. A year later similar examinations were

---

[35] TNA WO 296/23. 'Forward by the Secretary of State for War', *Keeping the Peace (Duties in Support of the Civil Power)* (London: War Office, 1957).

[36] TNA WO 279/391. WO, *Imperial Policing and Duties in Aid of the Civil Power, 1949* (London: War Office, 13 June 1949).

[37] TNA WO 279/391. WO, *Imperial Policing and Duties in Aid of the Civil Power, 1949* (London: War Office, 13 June 1949), 10–11.

[38] TNA WO 296/23. *Keeping the Peace (Duties in Support of the Civil Power)* (London: War Office, 1957), Part 2, chs 6–7.

[39] TNA WO 231/101. GSO2 Co-ordination, to Assistant Commandant, 18 July 1957.

[40] IWMSA. Accession No. 23225. D. J. Lear, reel 10.

introduced for Lieutenants who wanted to become Captains. Both examinations tested a candidate's knowledge of military law and internal security duties.[41]

Officers who aspired to get to the top of the army had to pass thorough the Staff College, where they were required to study recent practical examples of internal security operations. In 1952 they took part in an exercise based on a detailed consideration of the problems facing the security forces in the Gold Coast. Sir Gerald Lathbury, who was then the commandant, took this part of the syllabus seriously. Shortly before the exercise he invited Sir Cameron Nicholson, who had been GOC West Africa during the 1948 Gold Coast disturbances, to lecture to his students. He also invited Erskine, recently returned from Egypt, to talk to them about his experiences in the Canal Zone.[42] In November 1955 Erskine also lectured about his experiences in Kenya to the Royal United Services Institute, which published his lecture in its journal, and to the Joint Services Staff College on 'Military Aspects of the Cold War'.[43] By 1962 the syllabus at Camberley had grown further. As the army's doctrine had become politicized by the late 1950s, the syllabus now included 'a survey of communism and its dangers, and of guerrilla warfare and how to counter it'.[44]

The *JRUSI* was not the only semi-official publication that carried articles about aspects of counter-insurgency. Articles also appeared in *British Army Journal/Review* and the *Army Quarterly*.[45] By 1959–60, the War Office had also produced three training films that were shown to units about to embark on internal security operations. In 'Keeping the Peace, Part 1' (1959) an infantry battalion called on to give aid to the civil power on an imaginary island was shown guarding vulnerable points, mounting cordons and road blocks, enforcing curfews, and taking part in anti-riot operations. 'Keeping the Peace, Part 2' (1960) showed an infantry company operating against insurgents in open and mountainous country and conducting daylight patrols, anti-ambush drills, and night ambushes. Finally, 'Keeping the Peace, Part 3' (1960) portrayed infantry operating against jungle insurgents, and illustrated how to lay an ambush, conduct anti-ambush drills, make jungle searches,

---

[41] TNA WO 163/107/ECAC/P(48)127. VCIGS, Promotion Examinations, 10 September 1948; TNA WO 163/107/M(48)34. Minutes of the 371 meeting of the ECAC, 17 September 1948.

[42] TNA WO 236/15. Maj.-Gen. G. Lathbury, Commandant Staff College, Camberley, to Lt.-Gen. Sir W. E. J. Erskine, 6 October 1952.

[43] Erskine, 'Kenya—Mau Mau', 11–22; IWMDoD. Gen. Sir G. W. Erskine mss 75/134/3. Erskine, Lecture to the Joint Services Staff College. Military Aspects of the Cold War, n.d. but *c.*1955–56.

[44] TNA WO 32/15665. Commandant, Staff College Camberley, to the DGMT 5 February 1962.

[45] Anon, 'Operation Lowestoft. An account of a successful anti-bandit operation by 1/Suffolk Regiment and Malay police in Negri Sembilan', *British Army Journal*, no. 4 (July. 1950), 16–19; Captain J. M. Carew, 'All this and a medal too', *British Army Journal*, no. 3 (January 1950), 65–71; Lt.-Col. C. A. I. Suther, 'A Malay Battalions' Task', *British Army Journal*, no. 7 (January 1952), 55–60; Maj. J. A. Grover, 'Aid to the civil power, Kenya—1952', *British Army Journal*, no. 10 (July 1953), 30–2; Gen. Sir G. Erskine, 'Kenya—Mau Mau', *JRUSI*, vol. 101 (1956), pp. 11–22; Cooper-Key, 'Some reflections on Cyprus', 40–3; Rifleman C. Maconochie, 'A National Serviceman in Malaya', *Army Quarterly*, vol. 63. 1 (October 1951), 43–50. S. Hutchinson, 'The police role in counter-insurgency operations', *JRUSI*, vol. 114, no. 656 (1969), 56–61; Gen. Sir W. Walker, 'Borneo', *British Army Review*, no. 32 (August 1969), 7–15.

establish a jungle base camps, and assault an enemy hide-out.[46] Units about to be dispatched overseas did what they could to familiarize themselves with local conditions. Officers of the Royal Hampshire Regiment were told to read *Jungle Green*, Major Arthur Campbell's account of his operations as a company commander in the Suffolk Regiment, prior to their arrival in Malaya.[47] Before 1/Royal Northumberland Fusiliers flew to Aden in 1966, they prepared a huge floor map of the city in an RAF hanger at their base in Lincolnshire and made members of the reconnaissance platoon memorize it. It was a wise precaution because the battalion became operational immediately it arrived in Aden.[48]

This represented a considerable effort to disseminate knowledge of counter-insurgency doctrine. But not everyone thought that what they read in the manuals was especially helpful. An officer posted to Cyprus in 1957 recalled that 'We received no indoctrination as to the reason for our presence on the island, a British possession since 1878. There was no talk of preparing the Cypriot people for Independence. We were there "in support of the Civil Power" and, although I had studied the appropriate manual carefully before leaving England, it made little sense in the circumstances.'[49] Furthermore, some gaps remained in what was taught. Looking back on the Brunei operation, Sir David Luce thought that the staff colleges and service schools still paid too little attention to the conduct of joint operations, and that even if they did more to fill this gap 'training in such establishments will not ensure that joint operations are smoothly executed unless joint training in the particular conditions of the theatre concerned is regularly undertaken at all levels.'[50]

The army understood the need for in-theatre training. Troops in Palestine were given some training in conventional internal security techniques involving how to mount cordon and search operations, and internal security problems were discussed at the Haifa Staff College.[51] On arrival in Malaya, Kenya, Cyprus, and Borneo new units sent cadres to theatre training schools who then returned to their unit to pass on what they had learnt.[52] An officer who went through the FARELF Training

[46] TNA WO 279/399. WO, *Keeping the Peace. Part 2. Tactics and Training* (London: War Office, 16 January 1963), 98. A brief description of the story line of each film can be found in the IWM catalogue.
[47] IWMSA. Accession No. 10106. Col. J. B. Buckmaster, reel 2.
[48] IWMSA. Accession No. 13145. Col. J. P. Baxter, reel 3.
[49] Redgrave, *Balkan Blue*, 150.
[50] TNA DEFE 6/85/JP.55/63(Final). JPS, Report by the C-in-C Far East on operations in Borneo from December 1962 to February 1963, 5 July 1963.
[51] Jones, *Postwar Counterinsurgency and the SAS*, 21, 24; Lt.-Col. C. Mitchell, *Having Been a Soldier* (London: Hamish Hamilton, 1969), 55.
[52] TNA WO 106/5884. Gen. Sir N. Ritchie, Report on operations in Malaya, June 1948 to July 1949, 6 September 1949; Miers, *Shoot to Kill*, 30–3; TNA WO 268/117. Quarterly historical report—FARELF Training Centre, 1 January 1950 to 31 March 1950; TNA WO 291/1670. Operational Research Unit (Far East). Report Number 1/57. A comparison of the emergencies in Malaya and Kenya, 6 June 1957; IWMDoD. Gen. Sir G. W. Erskine mss 75/134/4. Notes for British Units coming to Kenya, n.d. but *c.*August 1954; Wilson, *Tempting the Fates* 184–5; TNA WO 276/454. *A Handbook of Anti-Mau Mau Operations* (Kenya: East Africa Command, n.d. but *c.*1954); Col. P. Hall, *Jungle Jim* (Privately Published, 1995), 148–9.

Centre in 1951 thought that the course was 'invaluable' preparation.[53] The Malaya and Cyprus schools also ran refresher courses for army units after they had been in the theatre for about 18 months, and trained some police cadres.[54] The instructors in Cyprus calculated that 'If a unit has had no previous training nor experience in the type of Internal Security duties it is required to perform in a particular territory, it will take about two months before full efficiency is developed. If, however, it is preceded by a strong tactical advance party and has carried out some Internal Security training in its previous station, this period can be reduced by about half.'[55]

But effective learning was impeded by several factors. In Palestine and the early years of Malaya, units suffered from the fact that the rapid demobilization of the wartime army, and in the case of Malaya the disintegration of the Indian army in 1947, meant that units were full of wartime soldiers counting the days until their release and young soldiers who had only recently enlisted.[56] In Palestine troops could not focus solely on learning how to wage counter-insurgency operations. The army was in Palestine to protect the Middle East from a Soviet attack. Units and formations therefore used some time that might have been spent on training to fight the insurgents learning to wage operations against Soviet conventional forces.[57] A more pervasive problem that faced the army wherever it served and until National Service was abandoned, was the high turn-over of personnel. In 1951 the overseas tour of infantry units was fixed at three years, and even regular personnel were not required to spend more than three years overseas before they were due for a home posting.[58] But many subalterns and rank and file soldiers were National Servicemen. They spent only two years in the army before being released, and might spend at most 18 months in an active theatre.[59] There were usually two complete turn-overs of National Service personnel during a battalion's three-year overseas.[60] In July 1954 Sir Geoffrey Bourne complained that one of his battalions, 1/East Yorkshire, would lose 500 men, including 50 experienced NCOs in September, and would have to train 300 replacements. 'They cannot', he lamented,

[53] IWMSA. Accession No. 17571. N. Dobson, reel 1.

[54] Hall, *Jungle Jim*, 69; R. Follows, *The Jungle Beat. Fighting Terrorists in Malaya* (Bridnorth, Shrops.: Travellers Eye Ltd, 1999), 32; TNA WO 279/241. Director of Operations, Malaya, *Conduct of Anti-terrorist Operations in Malaya* (Kuala Lumpur, 3rd edn, 1958), ch. 15.

[55] TNA CO 926/1077. Report on the Cyprus Emergency, 31 July 1959.

[56] TNA WO 261/640. 1 Infantry Division and North Palestine District, Quarterly Historical Report for the period ending 14 September 1946; D. Wilson, *The Sum of Things* (Staplehurst, Kent: Spellmount, 2001), 142; TNA WO 106/5884. Gen. Sir N. Ritchie, Report on operations in Malaya, June 1948 to July 1949, 6 September 1949.

[57] TNA WO 261/640. 1. British Infantry Division. Officers' study days, Palestine, 7 July 1946; TNA WO 261/652. 1 British Infantry Division. Quarterly Historical Report to December 1946.

[58] TNA WO 163/116/ECAC/P(51)80. DCIGS, Length of tour of infantry battalions at home and overseas, 2 October 1951; TNA WO 163/116/ECAC/P(51)24. Minutes of the 486 meeting of the ECAC, 5 October 1951.

[59] T. Royle, *The Best Years of their Lives. The National Service Experience 1945–63* (London: Michael Joseph, 1986), 168, 171.

[60] Lt.-Col. A. J. D'Arcy Mander, 'Reluctant Heroes. Our National Servicemen in Malaya', *The Newsletter of the Green Howards Regimental Museum*, no. 5 (April 1998), 8.

'hope to maintain their jungle efficiency.'[61] National Servicemen were called-up in batches every two weeks, a system he thought

> unable to provide a full strength operational unit at any one time. The system of fortnightly enlistment automatically produces frequent small drafts arriving in an overseas theatre, and this in turn forces a British (but not a Gurkha or Malay) Battalion to keep a training company continuously in being. If we had yearly, or even six monthly drafts the men would become a really good fighting team and be able to stay together in overseas Battalions about a year. Battalions would thus be far better fighting units, but of course it would increase the trooping commitment and what would suit Malaya might not suit other commands.[62]

The fighting potential of units was also degraded by the administrative burdens of the National Service system. The CIGS was horrified to learn in 1954 that every time a company went into the jungle it had to leave behind about 15 men to perform administrative duties. The reasons, according to Sir Charles Lowen, the C-in-C FARELF, were that 'the burden of accounting and paperwork of British units out here is heavy. This is partly due to the turn-over from National Service; partly due to the fact that expensive equipment must be accounted for and its maintenance cannot be done without some paperwork; and partly to various other reasons which you know well.'[63] Consequently, just when soldiers had reached a point where they had become experienced jungle fighters, they were likely to be returned to Britain and demobilized. Their replacements were young and inexperienced soldiers with much to learn, and experienced personnel had to be held back to administer and train them. One reason why Gurkha units were reckoned to be more efficient jungle fighters was because they did not suffer from the same personnel turn-over, and so could build up a greater store of expertise.[64] In Borneo Walker was struck by how quickly the army seemed to have forgotten the tactics of the Malaya campaign.[65]

Like all British army doctrine, how it was applied at unit level was deliberately devolved downwards to battalion commanders and sometimes even to company commanders. They adapted what they read in the manuals and what they were taught in theatre schools according to local conditions.[66] In Malaya and Kenya,

[61] TNA WO 216/874. Lt.-Gen. Sir G. Bourne, Personal estimate, 17 July 1954.
[62] TNA WO 216/874. Lt.-Gen. Sir G Bourne to CIGS, 23 December 1954.
[63] TNA WO 216/874. Gen. Sir C. Lowen to CIGS, 29 September 1954; TNA WO 276/460. Lt.-Col. H. A. Hope to COS, 25 November 1954; TNA WO 276/449. Appreciation by the C-in-C of the operational situation in Kenya in June 1955, 11 June 1955; TNA WO 236/20. Lt.-Gen. Sir G. Lathbury, The Kenya Emergency, 3 May 1955 to 17 November 1956.
[64] IWMSA. Accession No. 10727. Col. A. S. Harvey, reel 3.
[65] TNA WO 305/2525. Minutes of a meeting of the Borneo Operations Committee held at HQ COMBRITBOR, 15 August 1963; TNA WO 305/2530. Minutes of the 10 meeting of Borneo Territories Security Executive Committee (Operations Sub-committee), 7 January 1964; TNA WO 305/1771. Minutes of the 17 meeting of Borneo Territories Security Executive Committee, (Operations Sub-committee), 18 March 1964.
[66] TNA WO 231/38. Notes of Conference held by GOC Malay District on 11 July 1950; WO, *Queen's Regulations for the Army 1955* (London: HMSO, 1955), 7–8, 21; IWMSA. Accession No. 11162. Anon., reel 2.

battalions established their own training wing, and the power that commanding officers could wield led to considerable variations in what happened in practice, and may explain why some units achieved more successes than others.[67] 1/Suffolks, who arrived in Malaya in July 1949, developed a high reputation for tactical effectiveness. This owed a great deal to their commanding officer, Lieutenant-Colonel Ian Wight. He personally interrogated every patrol commander who had a clash with the enemy to find out why they had failed or succeeded, and then passed the lessons on to the rest of his battalion. Wight also knew from his own experience of fighting the Japanese in Burma that good marksmanship was of paramount importance because patrols could only make fleeting contact with the enemy. He therefore improvised training ranges so that everyone in the battalion practised regularly.[68] The battalion also practised immediate action drills for a variety of common situations. This paid dividends when a patrol advancing in single file along a jungle track bumped into a sentry guarding an insurgent camp. The platoon commander immediately shot the sentry and his men, without orders, fanned out to left and right as they had been taught and practised, and engaged the other insurgents in their camp.[69] Similarly, the growing success of 1/Green Howards in ambushing insurgents owed much to the arrival of a new commanding officer in May 1950. He abandoned the previous practice of mounting large, company-sized patrols, in favour of sending small, specially selected 'hunter' squads into the jungle to ambush insurgents on information provided by their surrendered comrades.[70] In Cyprus in early 1956, 2/Parachute Regiment had considerable success in killing and arresting insurgents in the Troodos mountains because its CO devised his own tactics involving the deployment of small, standing patrols required to lie low in the mountains for days at a time to intercept parties of insurgents.[71]

But other commanders remained wedded to large-scale operations. In September 1951, after a police jungle company was ambushed near the Siam border, 1/Manchesters mounted an operation 'on the now classical Malayan pattern. Troops went deep in after the terrorists, other platoons scoured the jungle's farther fringes, 25-pounders shell the area, and Vampire jets blasted it with rockets. Police "stops" waited to catch the scattering terrorists on the outer tracks. 3—out of at least 60—were shot dead by the police on their way out.'[72] Three kills out of a possible 60 was not a good return for the effort expended. This failure showed that there was little guarantee that best practices would necessarily be passed to, or adopted by,

[67] WO 291/1734. Dr K. Pennycuick, Operational Research Section (Malaya) Memorandum Number 1/54. The assessment of Battalion performance in Malaya 1952–1953.
[68] IWMSA. Accession No. 18047/4. Brigadier W. C. Deller, reel 1; Suffolk Record Office GB 554/Y1/304a. Brigadier I. L. Wight, 'Reflections of a Battalion Commander in Malaya, n.d.
[69] J. Starling, *Soldier On! The Testament of a Tom* (Tunbridge Wells: Spellmount, 1992), 18.
[70] Lt. C. Artley, 'A change of tactics', *The Newsletter of the Green Howards Regimental Museum*, no. 5 (April 1998), 16; Anon., 'Malaya: terrorist casualties for the period September 1949 to September 1952', *The Newsletter of the Green Howards Regimental Museum*, no. 5 (April 1998), 20; IWMSA. Accession No. 9141. J. M. Patrick, reel 3.
[71] IWMSA. Accession No. 11147. Col. P. Field, reel 1.
[72] *Manchester Guardian*, 25 September 1951.

other units and formations. Thus, although by 1953 it was widely understood that in Malaya the insurgents only operated in very small parties, and that large numbers of small patrols or ambushes had far more chance of making a successful contact than did a smaller number of larger patrols or ambushes, some unit commanders still persisted in mounting operations in platoon or even occasionally in company strength.[73]

The army did try hard to gather, analyse, and disseminate operational and tactical lessons. The establishment of training schools, the willingness of senior officers to learn from their juniors, and the publication of doctrinal pamphlets, were part of a concerted effort to ensure that the army moved along a learning curve. But these efforts should not blind us to the fact that there were powerful countervailing forces that impeded collective learning, not least the constant turn-over of experienced personnel caused by the National Service system, and the latitude given to battalion commanders to run their units as they saw fit. Although the army attempted to be a learning organization, its structure meant that some units learned more than others, and that the army as a whole was also good at forgetting.[74]

THE COLONIAL OFFICE AND THE GURNEY DOCTRINE

The Colonial Office did more than comment on drafts of War Office manuals. It also tried to gather, assess, and disseminate its own doctrine for dealing with emergencies. The near co-incidence of the Gold Coast riots and the declaration of a state of emergency in Malaya persuaded the Cabinet's Overseas Defence Committee and the Colonial Office that it was time that they began to take stock systematically of how colonial administrations should respond to such crises. They therefore asked their most experienced crisis manager, Sir Henry Gurney, to summarize the lessons he had learnt in Palestine and Malaya.[75] Gurney's response, produced at the end of May 1949, took the form of a dispatch addressed to the Secretary of State. It highlighted that the threat was new. 'Terrorism equipped with modern automatic weapons and political aspirations is a new development in the British Commonwealth. It is a method of warfare to which the training and traditions of police and military forces have not yet been adapted.' International Communism was the most potent danger to the empire, and future insurgencies would follow much the same pattern as the MCP's insurgency in Malaya. Initially

[73] TNA WO 291/1684. Operational Research Unit Far East. Memorandum No. Q13/53. Army patrol contacts in Malaya with particular reference to weapons, 1 September 1952 to 31 August 1953, October 1953; TNA WO 291/1682. Dr K. Pennycuick, Operational Research Unit Far East, Memorandum Number Q11/53. Army Ambushes in Malaya with particular reference to weapons, 1 September 1952 to 30 June 1953, September 1953.
[74] L. Argote and D. Epple, 'Learning curves in manufacturing', *Science*, vol. 247 (1990), 920–4; L. Argote, S. L. Beckman, and D. Epple, 'The persistence and transfer of learning in industrial settings', *Management Science*, vol. 36 (1990), 140–54.
[75] TNA CO 537/5068. Note. Preparation by Malayan government of a paper setting out experience gained in Malayan operations as affecting internal security arrangements, 7 February 1949.

the insurgents would try to dominate the trades union movement. Then they would mount a campaign of terrorism, developing into guerrilla warfare, with the aim of establishing liberated areas. Finally, operating from these safe havens, they would attack and overthrow the government. Only swift, early and ruthless action would stop them in their tracks. The government had to arm itself with a wide range of emergency regulations at the outset of the crisis, and not wait until it had developed. As soon as insurgents' efforts to dominate the trades union movement became apparent, the state should proscribe the local Communist party and arrest its leaders. The population had to be registered and effective frontier controls put in place. The police, not the army, must be the lead agency for they were the only force that had the information and intelligence needed to conduct an underground war in which the insurgents 'aimed at the destruction of economic resources, the organisation of strikes and the paralysis of the civil power'.[76] But most colonial police forces were small, badly equipped, and inadequately trained. Steps should therefore be taken even before an emergency to remedy these defects. Soldiers might be needed to hold the ring until these measures had become effective, but that did not mean that the state should be militarized. The army had to remain subordinate not only to the civil power, but also to local police commanders.[77]

The Cabinet's Overseas Defence committee quickly circulated Gurney's dispatch to other colonial governments, the Ministry of Defence, the Imperial Defence College, the Joint Services Staff College, and the service staff colleges.[78] It was not received with universal approbation. The War Office refused to agree that the army should be subordinated to the police. The Colonial Office's own Police Adviser, W. J. Johnson, deprecated what 'he considers to be an undue emphasis on military functions and training in Colonial police forces',[79] But the biggest obstacle to the implementation of the Gurney doctrine was its potential cost. Gurney had argued that colonial police forces should be expanded and modernized in order to pre-empt an emergency. As one Colonial Office official minuted, he

> states in uncompromising terms what may fairly be described as a 'new policy' for Colonial administration in the conditions of the present 'cold war'. It is that the strengths, efficiency, and morale of the Colonial Police Force are paramount; that they are to be organised if necessary in preference to troops; within the civil budget of the Colony they are to be given precedence; and all this is to be done not upon the onset of an emergency but well in advance on the principle that 'prevention is better than cure'.[80]

---

[76] TNA CO 537/5068. Gurney to Colonial Secretary, 30 May 1949.
[77] Ibid.
[78] TNA CO 537/5068. CO to Governors of Jamaica, and British Honduras, British Guiana, Trinidad, Barbados, Windward Islands, Leeward Islands, Sierra Leone, Gambia, Gold Coast, Nigeria, Nyasaland, Northern Rhodesia, Kenya, Tanganyika, Zanzibar, Uganda, Somaliland, Cyprus, Fiji, Mauritius, Aden, 18 July 1949; TNA CO 537/5068. Gurney to CO, 6 July 1949.
[79] TNA CO 537/5068. Sir T. Lloyd to Gurney, 17 March 1950.
[80] TNA CO 537/5068. Minute by J. C. Morgan, 23 June 1949.

The obvious question was who would pay for the expanded and modernized police? In the absence of a subvention from the home government, the only way most colonies would be able to find the money would be by transferring funds already earmarked to pay for their own locally raised troops. That solution was hardly likely to be welcomed by the War Office, which regarded forces such as the RWAFF and the KAR not merely as forces able to conduct internal security operations, but as a potential imperial reserve that could be employed outside their own colonies if the cold war turned hot.[81] In an apologetic letter to Gurney written in March 1950, Sir Thomas Lloyd, the PUS of the Colonial Office, rang the death knell for any hope that his recommendations would be implemented across the colonial empire. In a phrase that damned them he explained that 'The fact that your views have been challenged in some quarters here as not entirely orthodox is the main reason for the long delay in completing our examination of your dispatch.'[82]

THE COLONIAL OFFICE AS A FORGETTING ORGANIZATION

The dispatch remained the cornerstone of such guidance as the Colonial Office issued, but as Gurney's recommendations were 'not entirely orthodox', colonial governments were left to assimilate as much or as little of his doctrine as they wanted, or could afford to do. In the early 1950s the Colonial Office did little to gather, collate, analyse, or disseminate the lessons of insurgencies while they were in progress, or even when they had ended.[83] Nothing more was done in London until January 1957, when an official in Cyprus with a particular interest in history, K. J. Neale, asked colleagues in London if they thought it would be worthwhile from either a historical or an official point of view to produce an account of the origins and course of the Cyprus Emergency. (Neale was later to become a notable local historian in Essex.) 'In dealing with the Cyprus emergency problems', he remarked, 'we have from time to time felt a need for information regarding what had been done in Palestine but we usually drew [a] blank or had to rely on failing memories. As far as I know the emergencies in Malaya and Kenya were never written up in this way, but it is significant that the general course of events from the point of view of counter-terrorist operations has followed a remarkably similar pattern in Cyprus.'[84] Neale's proposal was taken up avidly by A. M. Macdonald, the Colonial Office's Security and Intelligence Adviser. 'I think that in the past', he wrote in a quick response to Neale,

we have failed to make proper use of previous experience. When the emergency was declared in Kenya, that Government set about its problems of detention, propaganda, rehabilitation, etc as if they were new and strange phenomenons. Cyprus in turn did

[81] Ibid.
[82] TNA CO 537/5068. Sir T. Lloyd to Gurney, 17 March 1950.
[83] TNA CO 1030/16. Mr R. L. Baxter to Sir J. Martin, 8 February 1955.
[84] TNA CO 926/1076. K. J. Neale to Witney, MacDonald, et al, 3 January 1957.

much the same thing. I do not think that this was the fault of either Government. It was merely that the experience gained in Malaya was nowhere summarised in a form available for reference. Cyprus, in turn, suffered from a lack of any systematic collation of experience gained in Kenya.[85]

He contrasted the Colonial Office's attitude towards using the past to inform policy unfavourably with that of the armed services. 'What I would really like to see', he concluded, 'would be a distillation of the experience gained in Malaya, Kenya and Cyprus on such matters as intelligence organisation, information machinery, internment and rehabilitation problems. I think that in this type of work we fall down badly in comparison with the Armed Services; they always analyse their experience and digest it for future use in similar situations. We allow it to become buried in dormant files and attack "de novo" problems which should be old and familiar. It is true that the Colonial Office can draw on previous experience, but we seldom have the whole story and it is not in a readily available form.'[86]

In Cyprus, George Sinclair, the Deputy Governor, agreed that the outgoing Director of Operations, Brigadier Baker, should prepare an outline of the main measures taken during the campaign.[87] But it was not until the autumn of 1957 that the suggestion received some badly needed political impetus. Lord Perth, the Parliamentary Under Secretary at the Colonial Office, wrote to Harding in Cyprus and Baring in Kenya explaining that he thought it was high time that the Colonial Office issued updated advice to colonial governments on how to prepare for and conduct an emergency. He therefore asked them to transmit their reflections so that officials in London could analyse them, although he was careful to concede that, given the varying circumstances of different colonies, it might not be possible to draw conclusions that were universally applicable.[88] However, even with Perth's support, the project ran into the sand. The War Office was slow to grant Baker a temporary release from his duties in West Germany so that he could return to Cyprus to write his reflections, although once there he worked quickly and had completed a draft by March 1958.[89] The War Office liked what he had written.[90] The Colonial Office did not. Baker had not stinted in his criticisms of men and measures, and the Colonial Office civil servant given the task of vetting the paper prior to its circulation decided that, as it contained a number of criticisms of government departments and personnel, it might raise embarrassing difficulties.[91] In view of the criticisms of the Cyprus government, the Colonial Office thought it was only fair to allow the regime on the island to comment on

[85] TNA CO 926/1076. Macdonald to Neale, 4 January 1957.
[86] Ibid.
[87] TNA CO 926/1076. Sinclair to Morris, 13 February 1957.
[88] TNA CO 968/690. Lord Perth to Harding, 24 October 1957; TNA CO 926/532. O. E. B. Hughes to Major D. Colville, 25 November 1957.
[89] TNA CO 968/690. G. E. Sinclair to Sir J. Martin, 6 November 1957; TNA CO 968/690. Baker to Aldridge, 4 March 1958.
[90] TNA CO 968/690. Col. J. A. Hunter to A. Campbell, 13 November 1958.
[91] TNA CO 968/690. Fairclough to Campbell, 16 October 1958. Baker summarized his lessons in TNA CO 968/690. Brigadier G. Baker, A Review of the Cyprus Emergency April 1955–March 1958. Part IV. Lessons of Emergency.

the report before it was circulated more widely.[92] That served only to add to the delay. Governor Foot was dilatory in his response, claiming that pressure of current business meant that he did not have time to devote to it and that as the Baker Report dealt only with the situation up to early 1958 it needed revision in the light of subsequent events.[93]

The Kenya government was even more dilatory and obstructive. The task of preparing its report was given to a government official, F. D. Corfield, who had recently completed a report on the origins of Mau Mau that was intended to justify the government's policies.[94] But he then became the secretary of the Game Policy Committee, something deemed to be more important than writing a report on the conduct of the emergency. Only in May 1958 did the government in Nairobi agree that Corfield could begin work, but warned that it would take him six months to complete the task.[95] When the six months were up, the Colonial Office asked for a progress report, but received no reply. They still had not received one in January 1959.[96] It is difficult to escape the conclusion that the Kenya government's main concern was not to learn the lessons of the emergency, but to ensure that the darker aspects of its conduct remained hidden.

The result was that the Colonial Office abandoned its plan to produce a comparative analysis of the lessons of the Malaya, Kenya, and Cyprus emergencies. Instead, in August 1959 they circulated the Baker Report by itself for clearance by the Colonial Defence Committee. It was finally distributed to colonial governors and the Director of Colonial Studies at the Police College at Ryton in June 1960, while the War Office sent copies to commanders overseas and to the service staff colleges in Britain.[97] Macdonald's earlier criticism of the Colonial Office, that it tended to 'attack "de novo" problems which should be old and familiar', remained justified. One former colonial policeman who served in Malaysia during the Confrontation complained that although after each campaign a report was usually produced for the Colonial Office embodying lessons, it was then classified as secret and no one took any notice of it. 'I cannot remember', he wrote,

> any of these reports being put to any practical use although once, during the Borneo campaign, I was allowed a quick glance at a highly classified booklet on the emergency in Cyprus. Whatever lessons were learned there were not to be divulged to anyone actually engaged in counter-insurgency.
>
> This secrecy and a traditional British distrust of general principles has caused much unnecessary trouble in the past. Lessons painfully learned in one campaign are either

---

[92] TNA CO 968/680. Colonial Secretary to OAG Nyasaland, 16 March 1959.
[93] TNA CO 968/690. Foot to Martin, 22 April 1959.
[94] TNA CO 822/2104 & TNA CO 822/2105. Historical Survey of the Origins and Growth of Mau Mau, 24 August 1959.
[95] TNA CO 968/692. OAG Kenya to Colonial Secretary, 13 May 1958.
[96] TNA CO 968/692. A. Campbell to Kenya Government, 4 November 1958 & 7 January 1959.
[97] IWMDoD Field Marshal Lord Harding mss AFH 10. Colonial Secretary to Harding, 13 June 1960; TNA CO 968/690. J. A. Sankey to Lt.-Col. A. D. Heskett, 4 August 1959; TNA CO 968/690. Aldridge to Baker, 10 August 1959.

forgotten, so that they must be learned again, or rigidly enforced in a different situation where they no longer apply.[98]

CONCLUSION

The British had a chequered history in gathering, analysing, and disseminating the lessons of their campaigns. In part this was because of the very intractability of the problem. In 1952 Lathbury, then Commandant of the Staff College, wondered 'if there is such a thing as a normal IS operation!'[99] The army did its best to formulate usable doctrines by gathering and analysing lessons. It then disseminated them through a series of channels, compulsory promotion exams, the Staff College, and theatre-specific training schools. But they had to work hard at this. Unit commanders were given wide latitude to pick and choose what lessons they taught their men. The nature of the National Service system meant that many of the key personnel who had to put the doctrine into practice on the ground—National Service subalterns and corporals—barely had time to learn their jobs before they left the army. The Colonial Office did not have that excuse. It simply afforded the whole process a low priority, with the result that much valuable experience was lost. Far from travelling along a learning curve, the Colonial Office was all too ready to forget 'lessons painfully learned'.

[98]Hutchinson, 'The police role in counter-insurgency operations', 56. The report he referred to may have been TNA CO 926/1077. Report on the Cyprus Emergency, 31 July 1959.
[99] TNA WO 236/15. Maj.-Gen. G. Lathbury, Commandant Staff College, Camberley, to Lt.-Gen. Sir W. E. J. Erskine, 6 October 1952.

8
The Problems of Sustainability

One lesson that British governments did learn after 1945 was that there were few quick and easy solutions in counter-insurgency campaigns. Sustainability, that is the ability to maintain the effort of the security forces and the civil government over a time-frame measured in years not months, was a prerequisite for success. Counter-insurgency campaigns were attritional. The insurgents were too weak to inflict a military defeat on the security forces. But they could win if they eroded the political will of the colonial state and its masters in London. Victory for the British required them to be able to muster both men and money, and their ability to do that depended on their political determination. That in turn could be undermined if either domestic or international critics raised their voices sufficiently loudly so as to persuade the government that the costs of a continued commitment to an active counter-insurgency policy outweighed any future benefits.

Before the Second World War, the British empire was sustained by a concatenation of fortuitous circumstances. It was a valuable economic asset that contributed significantly to Britain's prosperity, yet the British government was not required to invest expensive resources in maintaining it beyond some military garrisons and the Royal Navy. Occasionally domestic critics raised their voices against particular pieces of imperial mismanagement, but such scandals were infrequent. Governance of the empire neither outraged the electorate's moral sensibilities, nor did its costs tear a hole in their pockets. Abroad, the British had been able to strike a series of accommodations with their Great Power rivals to maintain a hands-off attitude to each other's colonies. Before 1914 this had led them to sign an alliance with Japan in 1902, and Ententes with France in 1904, and Russia in 1907. Without such agreements the British would have found the cost of defending their empire insupportable. The First World War so radically redrew the international map that for two decades afterwards the empire had no serious international rivals.[1] Many of these favourable circumstances persisted for about a decade after 1945. Where they did so, and for as long as they did so, the British were able to mount successful counter-insurgency campaigns. There was no linear progression from a situation in which it was wholly possible for the British to conduct a successful counter-insurgency campaign to one in which circumstances

---

[1] Wm. Roger Louis and R. Robinson, 'The imperialism on decolonisation', *JICH*, vol. 22 (1994), 463–4; J. Darwin, *Britain and Decolonisation. The Retreat from Empire in the Post-war World* (London: Macmillan, 1988), 167; A. G. Hopkins, 'Rethinking decolonization', *Past and Present*, vol. 200 (2008), 211–47.

had so turned against them that doing so had become impossible. Contingent circumstances made it impossible for the British to win in Palestine in the late 1940s, just as they permitted them to win in Malaysia in the mid-1960s. But what is clear is that, from about the mid-1950s, changes in the domestic, international, and economic environments increasingly moved against British interests. The British reacted by trying to find cheaper and politically more acceptable ways of waging counter-insurgencies. But, as the Nyasaland emergency and the Devlin and Hola camp reports demonstrated, they failed. The contrasting outcomes of the campaigns in Aden and Borneo showed that it was not impossible for the British to conduct successful campaigns by the mid-1960s. However, it had become so expensive, not only in terms of money but also in terms of political capital, that the effort no longer seemed worthwhile.

IMPERIAL AMBITIONS

The end of the Indian empire and the Palestine Mandate did not mean the end of Britain's determination to remain an imperial power. On the contrary, the geo-political and economic crisis facing the British, a product of the onset of the Cold War and the parlous state of the national economy in 1945, determined them to create a Fourth British Empire from what remained of the Third. Doing so would provide them with both the power base they needed to resist Soviet pressure in Europe, and the prosperity and full employment needed to recover from the economic impact of the Second World War. Most Labour politicians who thought about colonial affairs in the late 1940s hoped to promote peace and international harmony, but these aspirations were tempered by an instinctive patriotism that had been hardened by participation in the wartime government. A few radicals regarded colonial independence as a basic principle, but most Labour politicians shared assumptions common to many liberal imperialists, including most of the British Colonial Service personnel in the colonies. They could blend high-minded imperial idealism with the less elevated pursuit of cheap foodstuffs and raw materials. They believed that the colonies needed a period of intense social development before they would be ready to become independent states. They were quite willing to subordi-nate the goal of immediate self-government to longer-term social and economic development programmes and local government reform.[2] Returning to Kenya after the war Anthony Swann, a District and later Provincial Commissioner, remem-bered that he and most of his colleagues thought that independence was probably 40 or 50 years away and their priority was 'to get things right on the ground, getting the districts on their feet again after war rather than thinking too far ahead'.[3] Thus, after 1947 the British were trying to bring about the closer integration of the main members of the Sterling Area, expand the output of their Middle Eastern oil

---

[2] J. D. Hargreaves, *Decolonization in Africa* (London: Longman, 1996), 91.
[3] IWMSA. Accession No. 10224. Sir A. Swann, Transcript, 3.

concessions, and develop the economies of their most valuable colonies such as Malaya and the Gold Coast.[4]

All this had to be done in ways that would strengthen, not weaken, Britain's position in the Cold War. As a meeting of senior civil servants involved in formulating colonial policy agreed in June 1948, the public image of the empire 'should be two-fold. On the constructive side we must convince the world that our conduct has been and is progressive and the best in the world. On the destructive side we must give the world a true picture of Russia's conduct in Eastern Europe and in its own territories.'[5] Thus, in the Middle East they hoped to spread prosperity and shift the basis of Britain's informal empire from military bases and autocracies to more broadly based popular regimes.[6] Or, as Bevin put it, they would throw their support behind peasants not pashas, maintaining their military presence, but not attempting to dominate or coerce local regimes.[7] In Kenya they hoped to combine policies to promote African prosperity with the development of modern institutions such as trades unions that would give Africans a training in the ways of western governance and lead to the development of a multi-racial constitution in which no one racial group would be dominant.[8] These were the broad outlines of bipartisan policies that Labour's Conservative successors continued to follow in the 1950s.[9] The ultimate goal that the British promised they were working towards was self-government. But that did not mean separation. Both Labour and Conservative politicians were agreed that the colonies would still be bound to Britain by shared economic interests, by membership of the Commonwealth, and by Britain's moral example.

In the early 1950s this was not a foolish policy. Many underdeveloped countries sought the patronage of a developed power, but were wary of being dominated by the USA. When trying to build independent states in their colonies the British hoped that their creations would one day act as the political and economic partners which British trade and political strategy required. By giving their colonies formal independence they could plausibly pose as the western power that was most prepared to play a benign role in Africa and Asia. Their chosen path to this goal was to bring together existing colonies in federations, such as Nigeria, the CAF, the SAF, and the Federation of Malaysia, in the belief that only large federal states would be able to

[4] J. Darwin, *The Empire Project. The Rise and Fall of the British World-System 1830–1970* (Cambridge: Cambridge University Press, 2009), 541–5; W. Reynolds, 'Whatever happened to the Fourth British Empire? The Cold War, Empire defence and the USA, 1943–57', in M. F. Hopkins, M. D. Kandiah, and G. Staerck (eds), *Cold War Britain, 1945–1964* (London: Palgrave, 2003), 127–42; Roger Louis and Robinson, 'The imperialism on decolonisation', 462–511.
[5] TNA CAB 130/31/GEN 231/4. N. Brook, Anti-Communist propaganda. Anti-Soviet and pro-British propaganda, 16 June 1948.
[6] TNA CAB 128/1/CM(45)38. Cabinet meeting 4 October 1945.
[7] M. T. Thornhill, *Road to Suez. The Battle of the Canal Zone* (Stroud, Gloucs.: Sutton Publishing, 2006), 16.
[8] P. Kelemen, 'Modernizing colonialism: the British Labour movement and Africa', *JICH*, vol. 34 (2006), 223–44; P. W. T. Kingston, *Britain and the Politics of Modernization in the Middle East 1945–1958* (Cambridge: Cambridge University Press, 1996); Darwin, *Britain and Decolonisation*, 186.
[9] Darwin, *The Empire Project*, 566–7, 572, 579. For Conservative thinking see, for example, TNA CAB 129/48/C(51)59. Colonial Secretary, 21 December 1951.

maintain their independence as non-Communist states in the post-colonial world. Thus, far from simply clinging to the remnants of imperial power, the British were actively seeking to shape the post-imperial world to their own advantage.[10]

NATIONAL AND INTERNATIONAL OPINION

In the decade after 1945, there was little indication that the British public objected to the fact that in some circumstances colonial governments were using force to sustain British rule. Few British people knew much about their empire, and they did not see it as one big single issue. A survey conducted by the Central Office of Information for the Colonial Office in 1951 showed that, although they thought the empire was valuable—nearly three-quarters of respondents thought that Britain would be worse off without colonies—only 4 out of 10 could even name a single colony. Nor did they feel much responsibility for improving their welfare. When asked if Britain should give its colonies more help, only 1 in 5 answered in the affirmative. Typical of the remainder were those who answered, 'We are all taxed so high now—how can we help them?'[11] A Colonial Office official sadly concluded that, in all probability, 'the popular press, radio and cinemas will only continue to reflect public indifference and ignorance and Colonial affairs will continue to be a dim side issue in the minds of all but a tiny minority of the British public.'[12] This was perhaps fortunate for, as a Royal Marine who served in Malaya and Cyprus noted, the kinds of low-key misbehaviour by members of the security forces that would attract a flood of adverse publicity at the end of the twentieth century went unreported in the 1950s.[13]

Few voices were raised against the British imperial project in the 1950s beyond that of fringe groups such as the Communist Party of Great Britain. Its mouthpiece, the *Daily Worker*, presented the Malayan emergency as an unwarranted attack by British imperialists on Malayan nationalists and trades unionists and argued that they were being crushed to keep Malaya safe for big business. It also condemned the security forces in Kenya for employing 'Gestapo' methods.[14] Elsewhere, when colonial matters impinged on the public's consciousness, they did so in an incoherent and inconsistent fashion. Rather than focus on the general idea that it was morally wrong to maintain an empire by coercion, critics directed their fire at particular objectionable aspects of the conduct of emergencies: the imposition of laws that seemed to go beyond the bounds of what was morally permissible such as unjust collective punishments, the use of excessive force, and the ill-treatment of

---

[10] R. F. Holland, 'The imperial factor in British strategies from Attlee to Macmillan, 1945–1963', *JICH*, vol. 12 (1984), 173–4.

[11] TNA CO 875/72/3. B. Osborne to C. Y. Carstairs, 18 January 1952.

[12] TNA CO 875/72/3. Minute, P. R. Noakes, 25 January 1952.

[13] IWMSA. Accession No. 18021. F. G. Green, reel 3.

[14] C. L. Carruthers, *Winning Hearts and Minds. British Governments, the Media and Colonial Counter-Insurgency 1944–1960* (Leicester: Leicester University Press, 1995), 96; TNA CO 822/489. 'Gestapo way in Kenya', *Daily Worker*, 18 March 1953.

prisoners by the security forces. From 1952 onwards the Malayan government stopped imposing punishment curfews because they were aware of the criticism that they attracted in the British press.[15] Through their missionary activities some Christian Churches were able to voice concerns about particular issues during the campaigns in Kenya and Nyasaland.[16] In January 1955 the Reverend David Steel, the Moderator of the Church of Scotland in East Africa, gave a sermon in Nairobi in which he said 'a judicial commission of experts in constitutional law is called for to pronounce on the legality of much of our emergency legislation and the multitude of Orders in Council, many of which may be without the framework of constitutional law, and giving the appearance of legality to practices not only unjust in the eyes of God but illegal by the accepted law of man.'[17] The TUC sometimes raised concerns if colonial trades unionists were detained by the security forces.[18] In January 1952 even the *Times*, a paper normally sympathetic to the Tory government's cause, was critical of the degree of force used by the army against the Egyptian auxiliary police at Ismalia, insisting that 'the time has clearly arrived to ask how far the spreading measures of self-defence against terrorism can, or should, be allowed to go.'[19] During the Mau Mau emergency Labour MPs, left-wing newspapers, such as the *Daily Mirror* and *Daily Herald*, and Churchmen raised their concerns about the ill-treatment of detainees, the propensity of the security forces to shoot on sight, and the seemingly excessive numbers of prisoners executed having been found in possession of arms.[20]

Governments rarely found it difficult to brush aside such sporadic and isolated criticisms, particularly when they came from their political opponents. It was more difficult for them to ignore the political fall-out when the army suffered casualties. In 1953 Eden received a letter from a mother whose son was serving in the Canal Zone asking him to hasten the withdrawal of the garrison because 'Our sons are too precious to be thrown to a mob of irresponsible murderers.'[21] Even so, the only campaign in which casualties became a significant political factor was Palestine. Until the destruction of the King David Hotel the Labour government and the Tory

[15] IWMSA. Accession No. 10175. R. J. W. Craig, Transcript, 18–19.

[16] TNA CO 822/796. 'Kenya Government Criticised. Indiscriminate Action', *Times*, 10 January 1955; TNA CO 822/471. Canon T. F. C. Bewes, to Baring, 28 January 1953; TNA CO 822/471 Colonial Secretary to Baring, 12 February 1953; TNA CO 822/471. Extract of a letter from Reverend Neville Langford-Smith to Canon T. F. C. Bewes, 9 February 1953;TNA CO 1015/1789. Reverend Michael Scott to Lennox-Boyd, 14 May 1959.

[17] TNA CO 822/796. 'Kenya Government Criticised. Indiscriminate Action', *Times*, 10 January 1955.

[18] TNA CO 926/396. Colonial Secretary to Miss M. Nicholson, 12 September 1955; TNA CO 926/399. Sir V. Teweson to Lennox-Boyd, 15 March 1956; TNA CO 926/399. Harding to Colonial Secretary, 27 July 1956.

[19] *Times*, 26 January 1952; WO 216/802. CIGS to Robertson, 28 January 1952.

[20] TNA CO 822/471. Canon T. F. C. Bewes to Baring, 28 January 1953; TNA CO 822/471. Baring to Colonial Secretary, 11 February 1953; TNA CO 822/469. Colonial Secretary to Baring, 28 February 1953; TNA CO 822/489. Brockway to Lyttelton, 30 April 1953; TNA WO 236/17. Lt.-Col. Billet, Assistant Director Public Relations, 17 February 1955; *Hansard* HC Deb 24 February 1954 vol. 524 cols 383–5; *Hansard*, HC Deb 21 June 1955 vol. 542 col. 1154; *Manchester Guardian*, 29 September 1955.

[21] TNA FO 371/102868/JE1201/1. Mrs O. Dibden to Eden, 1 January 1953.

party in Parliament had pursued a bipartisan policy. That consensus began to break down when Churchill started to argue that the time had come for the British to withdraw in the face of the base ingratitude of both Jews and Arabs. His suggestion was badly received in the summer of 1946, but a year later, following further insurgent attacks, growing security force casualties, and little indication that the situation might soon improve, withdrawal was widely regarded as inevitable.[22] The final turning point came following the hanging of two sergeants by the Irgun in July 1947. Anti-Semitic riots occurred in several British cities, families of soldiers demanded that their men folk should be brought home, and the cabinet was confirmed in the correctness of its decision to pass the problem back to the United Nations.[23]

There was another important facet of public attitudes towards the conduct of counter-insurgency operations that should not be overlooked. Britain may have been a liberal democracy in which violence was widely regarded as a policy of last resort, but not every member of the public was outraged when they learnt of alleged abuses by the security forces in some distant colony. Some people believed that counter-insurgencies were wars, wars were brutal, and soldiers could not always be expected to behave impeccably. In December 1953 a letter-writer to the *Times* asked, in connection with the Griffiths case, 'Are you not unduly censorious of the men fighting in Kenya? Admittedly the recent court martial revealed certain crudities, but war is crude, and our men there are fighting gangs who indulge in unbelievable brutalities.'[24] Others thought that the security forces were sometimes placed in impossible positions by their political masters, and were justified if on occasions they took the law into their own hands. In any case many believed that the government should itself take more ruthless action. In 1954 some 28,000 people in Manchester signed a petition calling for the reprieve of a soldier condemned for murdering an Egyptian in the Canal Zone. The defendant's MP added that, 'I feel that with the difficulties through which our men are passing in Egypt, incidents of this kind are thoroughly understandable, much as one regrets them.'[25] In 1953 a motion proposed by the Constructional Engineering Union calling on the government 'to end immediately the present reign of terror and repression' in Kenya was rejected by a large majority at the TUC's annual conference.[26] In November 1958 Julian Amery, the Tory Undersecretary of State at the War Office, thought that criticisms made by the Labour MP Barbara Castle about the allegedly brutal behaviour of British troops in Cyprus had failed to strike a sympathetic note with the public. 'Public opinion here', he wrote from London

---

[22] P. Dixon, 'Britain's "Vietnam syndrome"? Public opinion and British military intervention from Palestine to Yugoslavia', *Review of International Studies*, vol. 26 (2000), 99–104; Carruthers, *Winning Hearts and Minds*, 38–9.
[23] N. Rose, '*A Senseless, Squalid War': Voices from Palestine 1945–1948* (London: Bodley Head, 2009), 166–8.
[24] *Times*, 1 December 1953.
[25] *Times*, 15 June 1954; TNA WO 32/21676. C. J. Hopkins to WO, 9 March & 14 April 1954.
[26] *Times*, 12 September 1953.

to the Director of Operations in Cyprus, 'could not be sounder about Cyprus. Mrs Castle must have been worth a million votes to us already!'[27]

Some issues could inflame some sections of public opinion. But the government believed that, with careful management, they could avoid any major political pitfalls. They had to avoid being seen to surrender to political violence in the colonies, for if they did so Britain's image as a major power would evaporate. But they were also reluctant to stand accused of employing excessive or arbitrary force, for then they could no longer claim that they were fulfilling their duty to protect their colonial subjects.[28] Collective punishments and detention without trial became particularly sensitive issues. In February 1951 the *Manchester Guardian* compared the detention of a whole village in South Selangor in Malaya to the Nazis' destruction of the Czechslovak town of Lidice in 1942.[29] Labour MPs and peers condemned collective punishments because they punished the innocent as well as the guilty.[30] Such measures, according to one Labour peer, shamed Britain. 'I remember the same arguments being used when we burned the farms of the Boers in South Africa. I remember the same arguments being used when the Black and Tans were in Ireland. It was always: "We must be firm." We did not sympathise with these people. What we said was that it is not a bad idea to introduce an element of morality when you are trying to govern a country.'[31] The Churchill government reacted by quietly withdrawing regulations permitting the Malayan government to impose collective fines and detain the inhabitants of whole villages.[32] But that did not preclude the use of collective fines in Kenya or Cyprus.[33] When the *Daily Express* denounced proposals by the Kenyan government to introduce draconian coercive laws as 'legislation which will turn these people into citizens of a dictatorship as severe as anything set up by the late Mr Hitler,' Churchill was so concerned at the possible potential political repercussions in the House of Commons that he raised the matter in the Cabinet, where he was reassured that the government could defend the measures by claiming that they were less drastic than some of those approved by Attlee's government.[34]

The government also usually found it possible to fend off international critics. Palestine, however, was an exception, where the Labour government was caught in an impossible position. In October 1945 Bevin 'stressed the importance of seeking a solution of the problem of Palestine as part of the policy of His Majesty's Government for the Middle East as a whole. At the same time, it was essential to

[27] IWMDoD. Gen. Sir K. Darling mss 01/41/1/file 5. Darling to Amery, 21 November 1958 (quoting an earlier letter by Amery).

[28] J. Darwin, *The End of the British Empire* (Blackwell: Oxford, 1991), 18–20.

[29] Anon., 'The strong arm?', *Manchester Guardian*, 20 February 1951; TNA CO 537/7280. Gurney to Colonial Secretary, 25 February 1951.

[30] TNA CO 822/501. 'No human rights', *Daily Worker*, 29 May 1952.

[31] *Hansard* HL Deb 7 April 1952 vol. 176, c. 26.

[32] TNA CO 926/561. Cahill to Neale, 21 November 1955.

[33] TNA CO 822/469. Colonial Secretary to Baring, 28 February 1953; *Hansard*, HC Deb 27 June 1956 vol. 555 col. 464; *Hansard*, HC Deb 17 June 1958 vol. 589 cols 866–7.

[34] TNA PREM 11/472. 'Double danger in Kenya', *Daily Express*, 26 September 1952; TNA CAB 128/25/CC(52)81. Cabinet Conclusions, 26 September 1952.

lay to rest the agitation in the United States which was poisoning our relations with the United States government in other fields.'[35] These goals were incompatible, and the need to maintain cordial relations with the USA in view of Britain's dependence on US loans played a major part in the Attlee government's decision to quit Palestine. But, in the decade after 1945, Palestine was the only counter-insurgency in which a foreign power was able to exercise significant influence over the development of British policy. Elsewhere, foreign powers might protest at British actions, but they rarely had much real effect on British policy. The Americans, who had once wanted to dismantle the British empire, realized after 1948 that its continued existence was a valuable asset in their quest to contain the spread of Communism. In any case the Cold War had hardly yet touched tropical Africa, and the US cared little about what the British did in that part of the world.[36] In Kenya the Mau Mau suffered from the fact that there were no contiguous friendly states that might offer them help, and British propaganda isolated them in the international community by successfully portraying the insurgency as a small, unpopular, but savage tribal rising.[37] British actions in British Guiana were criticized by some Latin American, Soviet bloc, and independent states such as India. But, with the support of the USA, the majority of anti-Communist Latin American governments, and some local politicians in the British West Indies, the British could stifle any critical comments at the UN and ignore those made elsewhere.[38] The British were in general so confident of their international good standing that on the same day that British troops landed in Kenya, Henry Hopkinson, the Minister of State at the Colonial Office, told the UN Trusteeship Committee in unmistakable terms that they had no right of interference in any British colony or protectorate.[39]

THE TEMPLER REPORT

The Churchill government was, therefore, not under any overwhelming domestic political or international pressure to quit fighting to retain its colonies. But the question was whether they could afford to do so in the same old way. When it entered office in October 1951, the government inherited an enormously expensive

---

[35] TNA WO 32/10260. Extracts from the conclusions of 40(45) meeting of the Cabinet, 11 October 1945.
[36] Roger Louis and Robinson, 'The imperialism of decolonisation', 466–9.
[37] A. S. Cleary, 'The myth of Mau Mau in its international context', *African Affairs*, vol. 89 (1990), 227–45.
[38] TNA CO 1031/1189. Foreign Office to British embassy Brazil, 7 October 1953; TNA CO 1031/1189. Foreign Office to British embassies in all Latin American countries, 9 October 1953; TNA CO 1031/1189. British embassy Hungary to Foreign Office, 12 October 1953; TNA CO 1031/1189. British delegation UN to Foreign Office, 13 October 1953; TNA CO 1031/1189. British embassy Washington to Foreign Office, 14 October 1953; TNA CO 1031/1429. Governor Windward Islands to Colonial Secretary, 13 January 1954; TNA CO 1031/1429. K. J. Wilson to M. C. Cahill, 26 March 1954; TNA CO 1031/1429. Jamaica Federation of Trades Unions to Lennox-Boyd, 12 February 1955.
[39] *Times*, 22 October 1952.

rearmament programme from its Labour predecessors, and a series of economic and financial crises. With only a narrow majority, Churchill decided that his government's policy must be 'Houses and meat and not being scuppered'.[40] A decade later nothing had changed. When one minister insisted that 'we can't continue to meet all our oversea[s] commitments unless B[ritish]. people are ready to accept red[uctio]n in current consumption'; none of his Cabinet colleagues dissented.[41]

Trimming government spending to liberate resources for more houses and meat, and not reducing the living standards of the British people, was the way to survive, and that meant cutting defence spending and looking hard at ways to reduce the cost of colonial emergencies.[42]

One way to do this was to shift the cost of counter-insurgency operations onto the shoulders of the colonies themselves. In 1949 Gurney had suggested that spending money on creating colonial police forces able to detect or deter subversive movements before they had got into their stride would be cheaper than summoning troops from the metropolis once an emergency had begun. The COS welcomed the idea, provided it did not mean less spending on British forces.[43] But it was the invention of the hydrogen bomb, a weapon many times more powerful than even the biggest atomic bomb, that gave the idea real purchase. The H-bomb would render large conventional forces obsolete. Better to rely, as the COS recommended in June 1954, on a 'New Strategic Concept', build British hydrogen bombs as a deterrent to global war, save money by cutting the size of conventional forces, and insist that the colonies build up their own security forces so they were less likely to have to call on the British army for assistance.[44] Ministers agreed and Churchill established a Cabinet committee to review the organization of the armed forces, police and security services in the colonies.[45]

The committee asked Templer to carry out the review, and by April 1955 his recommendations were ready. Essentially what he did was to put flesh on the bones of Gurney's formula. The Colonial Office had to become more intelligence-minded. It needed its own Intelligence Department, which should operate in

---

[40] J. Colville, *The Fringes of Power. Downing Street Diaries 1939–1955* (London: Hodder and Stoughton, 1985), 644.

[41] TNA CAB 195/19/CC 38(60). Cabinet meeting, 30 June 1960.

[42] TNA CAB 128/23/CC(51)1. Cabinet Conclusions, 30 October 1951; TNA CAB 128/23/CC(51)2. Cabinet Conclusions, 1 November 1951; TNA AIR 20/11154. Note by the Chief of Air Staff, Global Strategy reconsidered in the light of economic realities, 31 March 1952; TNA CAB 129/52/C(52)166, Butler, Economic policy 17 May 1952; TNA CAB 129/54/C(52)253, MOD, The defence programme, 22 July 1952.

[43] TNA CAB 131/7/DO(49)24. Memorandum by COS, Colonial Forces, 22 March 1949; TNA CAB 131/8/DO(49)9 meeting Cabinet Defence Committee, 23 March 1949; TNA DEFE 6/8/JP(49) 24(Final). Report by the JPS, Colonial forces, 13 April 1949; TNA CAB 134/808/DP(54)6. COS, Memorandum by the COS, United Kingdom Defence Policy, 1 June 1954.

[44] TNA CAB 134/808/DP(54)6. COS, Memorandum by the COS, United Kingdom Defence Policy, 1 June 1954.

[45] TNA CAB 134/811/DR(54)12. Cabinet Committee on Defence Review, 24 September 1954; TNA CAB 128/27/CC(54)73 meeting. Cabinet Conclusions, 5 November 1954; TNA CAB 195/12/CC73(54). Cabinet meeting, 5 November 1954; TNA CAB 21/2999. Sir N. Brook to PM, 31 December 1954; TNA CAB 21/2999/GEN 485/1. Note by Cabinet Secretary, Committee on Security in the Colonies. Terms of reference and composition, 13 January 1955.

tandem with the existing Defence, Police, and General departments, as well as the JIC, the Security Service, and MI6. The whole intelligence machine had to be overhauled to ensure that colonial governments could nip trouble in the bud. Colonial Special Branches had to be expanded and their officers trained in a series of new regional police training schools. Every colony must have an LIC chaired by a full-time official. Second only in importance to an effective domestic intelligence service was an efficient police force. The Colonial Office had to adjust its machinery to improve the quality of its inspectorate by establishing a separate Police Department. Colonial police officers recruited in Britain who would fill the middle and senior leadership posts in the colonial forces needed more training. This too, could be provided by the regional training colleges. In the colonies themselves the locally recruited rank and file often suffered from low pay and poor housing, both of which had to be improved if the service was to attract sufficient recruits of good quality. As colonial military forces would no longer have to prepare to take part in a global war, they could be reduced to a size that each colony could fund from its own revenues. As a back-up if the new and more efficient police and intelligence services did not forestall trouble, the army should organize a specially trained and equipped brigade that, being air-portable, could fly to an emergency quickly and arrive before the situation had got completely out of hand.[46]

The COS supported his recommendations on the grounds that a small sum of money spent on prevention would, in the long run, be far cheaper than the present policy of dispatching troops after an emergency had begun.[47] The War Office was able to fund the creation of an air-portable strategic reserve out of the savings accruing from ending National Service. The Colonial Office did establish a separate Police and Security Department, did secure closer co-operation with the JIC, and did add to the colonial police inspectorate.[48] But thereafter matters stalled. Templer was asking the government to fund new expenditure in the short term in the hope of making speculative savings in the future. He estimated that his recommendations would cost about £250,000 in capital expenditure, and £75,000 per annum in recurrent spending. But colonial governments refused to find the money to establish the regional police training colleges, and the Colonial Office refused to force them to do so. The Treasury, for its part, remained adamant that it would not fund improvements in the pay, conditions of service or housing conditions of colonial police forces.[49] In any case, according to E. E. Bridges, the PUS at the Treasury, it was not lack of funds that was the real problem. It was the Colonial Office, for 'hitherto the Colonial Office had not shown nearly as much energy and

[46] TNA CAB 129/76/CP(54)89. Sir G. Templer, Report on Colonial Security, 23 April 1955.
[47] TNA DEFE 32/4/COS(55)262. Memorandum by the COS, Cold War—countering covert aggression, 12 October 1955.
[48] TNA CAB 129/76/CP(55)89. Lord Chancellor, Security in the colonies, 22 July 1955; TNA CAB 128/29/CM(55)26 meeting. Cabinet Conclusions, 26 July 1955; TNA T 220/1395. A. E. Drake to Sir A. Johnston et al., 25 July 1955.
[49] TNA T 220/1395/GEN 485/13. H. Brooke, Meeting the cost of security in the colonies, 16 March 1955; TNA CAB 21/2999. Airey to Hunt, 15 February 1957 & Hunt to Airey, 15 February 1957; TNA CAB 129/92/C(58)92. Note by the Lord Chancellor, Security in the Colonies, 1 May 1958; TNA CO 968/680. Minute by Carstairs on Baker Report, 22 April 1959.

drive in tackling this problem as they ought to have done. I cannot quote my evidence for this—it is of the under-counter variety.'[50]

But Templer's recommendations were flawed in an even more fundamental way. They were based on a clear principle: that colonies should take more responsibility for the funding and organization of their own emergency preparations and measures. British troops should only be summoned as a last, not as a first, resort. That promised to save the British taxpayer money. But it also threatened to cede control of the conduct of future emergencies to colonial governments, while leaving to ministers in London the responsibility for explaining and justifying the measures that they took. The latter might thus find themselves in the awkward position of having responsibility without power.

'LAWFARE'

The mid-1950s were a dangerous time to be ceding a larger measure of control over the conduct of emergencies to colonial governments. Even in the early 1950s, the British had been aware that international law was making it more difficult for them to conduct counter-insurgency campaigns as they chose. They wanted to be seen to be on the side of the angels, if only because in the Cold War respect for human rights was supposed to be one of the things that distinguished western powers from their opponents.[51] In 1948 ministers had agreed that, in order to limit the appeal of Communism in Africa and Asia, they 'must convince the world that our conduct has been and is progressive and the best in the world.'[52] But they were also reluctant to see their freedom to do what they thought necessary to suppress insurgencies constrained by international agreements. They recognized that 'lawfare' might be used against them many years before the word was coined.[53] In July 1950 James Griffiths was determined to deny British colonial subjects the right to make direct appeals to the European Commission of Human Rights because it would

> be exploited by extremist politicians in the Colonies in order to undermine the authority of the Colonial Government concerned. Loyalty would be shaken: administration would be made more difficult and agitation more easy. Indeed individual petitions might become as much a weapon of political warfare as a method of ventilating the genuine grievances of individuals. Even although it may be assumed that such petitions would in most cases be rejected by the Commission of Human Rights as inadmissible, they would nevertheless in the meantime have achieved their

---

[50] TNA T 220/1395. E. E. Bridges to Couzens, 18 January 1955.

[51] TNA CAB 129/23/CP(48)6. Bevin, The first aim of British foreign policy, 4 January 1948.

[52] TNA CAB 130/31/GEN 231/4. N. Brook, Anti-Communist propaganda. Anti-Soviet and pro-British propaganda, 16 June 1948.

[53] Maj.-Gen. Charles J. Dunlap Jr, 'Lawfare: a decisive element of 21st Century conflicts?', *Joint Forces Quarterly*, no. 54 (2009), 34–9; *idem.*, 'Lawfare today: a perspective', *Yale Journal of International Affairs* (Winter 2008), 146–54. Dunlap, who coined the word, variously defined lawfare as 'the use of law as a weapon of war', or 'a method of warfare where law is used as a means of realizing a military objective', or 'the strategy of using—or misusing—law as a substitute for traditional military means to achieve an operational objective'.

primary purpose by serving as local propaganda against the Colonial Government. It is important that no such unnecessary handle should be offered to trouble-makers within or without Colonial territories in the present delicate stage of constitutional development in some (such as the West African Colonies), or in the incipient difficulties of race relations in others, or in more serious situations such as the struggle against terrorists in Malaya.[54]

His Conservative successors shared his concerns. Faced by the possibility that in 1957 the 19th International Conference of the ICRC might recommend that Article 3 of the Prisoner of War Convention, which prohibited the imposition of collective punishments, should be held to apply in the case of internal disorders, the Colonial Secretary and his officials set their face resolutely against permitting an international body to interfere in what they insisted was a matter of domestic jurisdiction.[55]

The British adopted a three-pronged strategy to avoid such difficulties. They tried to prolong international discussions and raise as many legal and practical difficulties as possible in order to delay the signing and ratification of any agreement that might subsequently embarrass them.[56] Thus, although the British government signed the 1949 Geneva Convention in 1949, they avoided ratifying it until 1957, fearing that it would limit their freedom of action to treat insurgent armed forces and their civilian supporters as rebels.[57] If they could not delay matters indefinitely, their second option was to exploit every available legal loophole they could find. Thus when the British government signed the 1949 Geneva Convention in 1949, it entered the formal reservation that it did not accept Article 68 of the Convention which forbade the execution of civilians by military courts.[58] When the Kenya government wanted to incarcerate over 70,000 KEM in work-camps where they could pursue a policy of 'redemption through work', the Colonial Office warned that they might be in breech of the 1930 ILO Convention against Forced Labour and the ECHR. But a sharp-eyed lawyer spotted two legal loop-holes. Article 2 of the ILO Convention and Article 4 of the ECHR permitted governments to extract forced labour from its citizens in cases of emergency.[59] Finally, if that did not work,

---

[54] TNA CAB 129/49/C(50)189. Colonial Secretary, Council of Europe. Convention on Human Rights. Right of Individual Petition, 28 July 1950.
[55] TNA CO 936/391. Minutes by D. Smith, 2 May 1956, E. Burr, 23 May 1956, and H. T. Bourdillon to Undersecretary of State Foreign Office, 5 June 1956.
[56] TNA CAB 128/19/CM(51)27 meeting, 12 April 1951; TNA CAB 129/46/CP(51)220. Home Secretary and Foreign Secretary, Ratification of the Geneva Convention, 1949, 23 July 1951.
[57] TNA FO 371/61872. Minute by Sir H. R. Satow, Consular Department, Foreign Office, 12 February 1947; TNA WO 32/12526/CRGC/P(47)1. W. H. Gardner, Partisans, 18 August 1947; G. Best, *War and Law since 1945* (Oxford: Oxford University Press, 1994), 168–78; WO, *The Law of War on Land being Part (II) of the Manual of Military Law* (London: HMSO, 1958). Appendix XIV: Geneva Convention relative to the Protection of Civilian Persons in Time of War.
[58] TNA CO 537/6895. Undersecretary of State for the Colonies to High Commissioner, Federation of Malaya, 6 April 1951.
[59] Convention concerning Forced or Compulsory Labour, 1930. Downloaded 6 September 2009 at: http://www.ilo.org/ilolex/cgi-lex/convde.pl?C029; Convention for the Protection of Human Rights and Fundamental Freedoms as amended by Protocol No. 11. Rome, 4.XI.1950. Article 4(3c). Accessed 4 November 2007 at: http://www.conventions.coe.int/Treaty/en/Treaties/Html/005.htm.

they just brazened it out by implementing only those parts of the agreements that they found acceptable, and entering formal derogations from those that were not. Article 15 of the ECHR permitted derogation from the obligations accepted under the Convention during a public emergency, provided the government concerned gave formal written notice of Derogation to the Secretary General of the Council of Europe. The British took advantage of this during almost every major colonial emergency so that they could arrest and detain suspects without trial.[60]

The British had little difficulty in repulsing the first 'lawfare' offensive mounted against them. In 1951 the Egyptian government tried to turn the ILO Forced Labour Convention against the British military administration in the Canal Zone by insisting that they were extracting forced labour from Egyptians they employed. The British refuted the allegations by some deft diplomacy. In January 1952 they permitted a representative from the ILO to visit the Canal Zone to see conditions for himself, and he dismissed the Egyptian's allegations.[61] But that proved to be but an opening skirmish. In 1953 the British extended the ECHR to most of their colonies.[62] They were not obliged to do so, but they probably deemed the risk of future international complications as small. They were wrong. Although their own citizens could not petition against the actions of British or any British colonial administration, other governments could do so on their behalf. In 1956 that was exactly what the Greek government did in its efforts to assist EOKA.

The Greeks complained that not only was the situation on the island insufficiently serious to warrant the British entering a derogation under Article 15, but that they were also torturing, detaining, and deporting prisoners illegally. By caning adolescents they were employing cruel punishments, and by imposing collective punishments they were denying their victims a fair trial.[63] The British, convinced that the troubles on the island could all be traced back to the Greek government, were incensed, but reluctantly allowed the Council of Europe to send a sub-commission to Cyprus to investigate the allegations. To have blocked an investigation would have been tantamount to an admission of guilt, as well as being deeply embarrassing to the British at the UN. The Cyprus question became a regular topic of debate at the UN in the late 1950s, and after the Suez crisis, the British did not

---

[60] K. Vask, 'The European Convention of Human Rights beyond the frontiers of Europe', *The International and Comparative Law Quarterly*, vol. 12, no. 4 (October, 1963), 1206–31, 1212.

[61] TNA FO 371/97071/E2181/42. International Labour Office, Report on the enquiry by the representative of the Director-General into conditions in the Suez Canal Area, 25 January 1952.

[62] Convention for the Protection of Human Rights and Fundamental Freedoms as amended by Protocol No. 11. Rome, 4.XI.1950. Article 63. Accessed 4 November 2007 at http://www.conventions. coe.int/Treaty/en/Treaties/Html/005.htm; Vask, 'The European Convention of Human Rights', 1210. Those that were omitted included the New Hebrides, probably because they were under joint Franco-British jurisdiction, and several of the smaller West Indian islands such as the Cayman Islands, Turks and Caicos Islands, and the Virgin Isles, probably due to their size. But the same reasons probably did not apply to the exclusion of Hong Kong and the Brunei protectorate, nor to the protectorates of the Arabian peninsula, including Kuwait, Bahrain, and Oman.

[63] TNA CAB 129/82/CP(56)152. Secretary of State for Foreign Affairs, Cyprus, 25 June 1956; Sellars, 'Human rights and the colonies', 710–12; TNA CO 926/1082. Colonial Secretary to Deputy Governor, 17 July 1957; TNA CAB 129/90/C(57)258. Foreign Secretary and Minister of State for the Colonies, Cyprus, 4 November 1957.

welcome further embarrassment there.[64] For the next two years, the British exploited every legal loophole and delaying tactic they could muster to delay the work of the investigation.[65] In the short term, their strategy worked. The Greeks dropped their complaints in 1959 as part of the Zurich Agreement that brought a temporary peace to the island and the investigators never published their report.[66]

But the Greek 'lawfare' offensive was not a failure. In the short term it embarrassed the British into curtailing the canning of adolescents and their use of collective punishments. In the longer term it made the British aware that they might not be able to employ many of the methods they had used in the past unless they were prepared to pay a high political price. From the late 1950s onwards one of the leitmotivs of the conduct of counter-insurgencies was the British government's constant efforts to avoid being embarrassed by its obligations under international law. During the Nyasaland emergency, the Colonial Office denied the government permission to cane adolescent prisoners.[67] They did allow Armitage to impose forced labour and collective fines, but only after a public relations exercise that ostensibly redefined their purposes.[68] Lennox-Boyd was not happy with such legal sleights of hand. A collective fine was a punishment no matter what legal gloss was put on it. In April 1959 he hoped that Armitage would not 'indulge very much in this particular form of punitive action'.[69]

HOLA CAMP AND THE DEVLIN REPORT

From the mid-1950s onwards it was not just that the British felt they had to be increasingly careful about *how* they conducted counter-insurgency operations. It was also the case that they had to weigh up the political cost, both international and domestic, of whether it was worthwhile conducting them at all. In the immediate post-war years the perpetuation of empire had been seen as essential to winning the Cold War. By the late 1950s the empire was increasingly viewed as a liability. The Suez crisis robbed Britain of much of the international goodwill it had generated for itself during the Second World War. No longer could it plausibly pose at the UN as a staunch upholder of international right and international law. In July 1957 the Foreign Office counselled against mounting a military operation in Oman to rescue the sultan because 'British intervention would expose both Her

[64] TNA CAB 129/90/C(57)258. Foreign Secretary and Minister of State for the Colonies, Cyprus, 4 November 1957; TNA CAB 128/31/C(57)78 meeting. Cabinet Conclusions, 6 November 1957.
[65] TNA CAB 21/2891. Burk Trend to PM, 21 October 1958; TNA CAB 129/95/C(58)216. Colonial Secretary and Foreign Secretary, Cyprus: human rights, 22 October 1958; TNA CAB 128/32/CC(58)77. Cabinet meeting, 23 October 1958.
[66] IWMDoD. Field Marshal Lord Harding mss AFH 10. FO to Governor Cyprus, 9 July 1959.
[67] TNA CO 936/533. Colonial Secretary to OAG Nyasaland, 20 August 1959 and Governor Nyasaland to Colonial Secretary, 12 October 1959.
[68] TNA CO 1015/1517. Nyasaland Government Gazette, 12 March 1959: The Emergency (Amendment No.6) Regulations, 1959; TNA CO 1015/1521. Henry E. I. Phillips to J. C. Morgan, 25 March 1959.
[69] TNA CO 936/533. W. L. Gorell Barnes to J. C. Morgan, 23 April 1959.

Majesty's Government and the Sultan to the most damaging criticism in hostile propaganda and in the United Nations if Saudi Arabia or any other Arab State chose to bring the matter up there.'[70] A few months later, they recommended against re-imposing the emergency regulations in Cyprus that they had relaxed in the spring for fear that if they did so they would bring down upon Britain's head a torrent of criticism at the UN.[71] Empire, especially if it had to be controlled by coercion, was becoming an international embarrassment.[72]

Criticism of colonial counter-insurgencies was also gathering pace at home. The most successful domestic anti-colonial pressure group in the late 1950s and early 1960s was the Movement for Colonial Freedom, formed in 1954 by the Labour MP Fenner Brockway. As the Tories were in power from 1951 to 1964, the MCF's influence was limited, but, through sympathetic Labour MPs such as Barbara Castle, Jennie Lee, Leslie Hale, Tom Driberg, and Tony Benn, it could raise embarrassing questions in the Commons, and it could sometimes mobilize public outrage against specific excesses and abuses.[73] They could also intensely annoy officials charged with the administration of emergency measures. Robert Wainwright, the Provincial Commissioner for the Rift Valley Province of Kenya, thought that Brockway and Hale 'were terrible thorns in our flesh, they were a perfect nuisance to us, forever criticising us and being tiresome.'[74] When Barbara Castle visited Kenya she did so, as she told Sir Richard Catling, the Commissioner of Police, 'with the declared intention of raking up any material she could with which to beat the government at home. I saw her for a lengthy interview. She came to my headquarters one evening. She stayed there an interminable time. That was her only purpose. She didn't talk to me in an attempt to understand the security situation in Kenya. She didn't attempt to brief herself on matters arising out of the situation there on which the Opposition at home might have helped. She was entirely destructive. She was quite frank. She said, "I am here to gather together as much as I can to form the basis of a sustained attack on the government at home."'[75] Eventually she succeeded. The Nyasaland emergency and subsequent Devlin Report, coinciding as it did with the publication of the report on the Hola camp atrocity, demonstrated the ability of international and domestic critics to render counter-insurgency by coercion, if not impossible, then dangerously costly.

Castle and her colleagues were given their opportunity because the CAF was one part of the empire where the British government had devolved control of the

---

[70] TNA DEFE 7/2415. No. 39 FO to Gault, 16 July 1957; TNA CAB 131/18/D(57)4 meeting. Cabinet Defence Committee, 18 July 1957.
[71] TNA CO 926/1071. UK delegation at UN to Foreign Office, 25 October 1957; TNA CO 926/1071. Note of a meeting on 6 November 1957 to discuss Cyprus propaganda policy; TNA CO 926/1071. Colonial Secretary to Acting Governor Cyprus, 14 November 1957.
[72] Hopkins, 'Rethinking Decolonization', 233–4.
[73] S. Howe, *Anticolonialism in British Politics. The Left and the End of Empire, 1918–1964* (Oxford: Clarendon Press, 1993), 231–67; J. Brownell, 'The taint of communism: the Movement for Colonial Freedom, the Labour Party, and the Communist Party of Great Britain', *Canadian Journal of History*, vol. 42 (2007), 235–58; TNA CO 1031/1425. F. Brockway to J. Jagan, 16 August 1954.
[74] IWMSA. Accession No. 11074. R. E. Wainwright, Transcript, 33.
[75] IWMSA. Accession No. 10392. Sir R. Catling, Transcript, 42.

security forces onto the local government, and thus effectively implemented Templer's recommendation. The Nyasaland government controlled its own police force, but the army was a Federal responsibility. It was controlled by the European settler-dominated government of the Federation, and it was paid for by Federal taxpayers, not by the British government.[76] On the eve of the Nyasaland emergency, which Governor Armitage declared in March 1959, Sir Roy Welensky, the Federal Prime Minister, assured a visiting British general 'that he had sufficient forces to deal with anything that might arise'.[77] The Colonial Office had long recognized that using Federal troops to quell disturbances in Nyasaland would inflame an already difficult situation. Thus as soon as they learnt that Armitage was planning to declare a state of emergency, the Cabinet in London asked the MOD to prepare plans to dispatch a battalion of British troops, either direct from Britain, or from the garrison in Kenya.[78] But Welensky was adamant that he did not want them.[79] British troops would defeat his larger purpose, for he wanted to use the emergency to extend the power of the Federal government so that it controlled all aspects of law and order, including the police, throughout the whole of the Federation.[80]

Without the presence of British troops, the government in London had little control over the behaviour of the Federal security forces. The latter embarked on a policy of wholesale repression, which brought down upon Britain a torrent of international criticism, not only from Radio Moscow and Radio Cairo, but also from members of the Commonwealth.[81] Press reports suggested that the police were responsible for violence, that prison conditions were vile, and that the authorities had resorted to unjust collective punishments. There were awkward questions in the Commons, and a poll published in the *News Chronicle* in May 1959 showed that even amongst Conservative voters, there was a good deal of sympathy for the cause of the Africans, rather than the European settlers, in Africa.[82]

---

[76] TNA WO 163/617/ECAC/M(53)17. Minutes of the 543 meeting of the ECAC, 16 October 1953; TNA CAB 130/114/GEN 520/19(Revise) Commonwealth Relations Office, Colonial Office, and Security Service, The Federation of Rhodesia and Nyasaland, 17 January 1957; TNA CO 1015/1494. Federation of Rhodesia and Nyasaland. Law and Order: Constitutional and General Position, 18 February 1959.

[77] TNA CAB 21/4043. Report on the visit to the Federation of Rhodesia and Nyasaland and the Union of South Africa by the Principle Staff Officer to the Secretary of State for Commonwealth Relations, 1–25 February 1959.

[78] TNA CAB 128/33/CC(59)12 meeting. Cabinet Conclusions, 26 February 1959; TNA CO 1015/1494. Home to Welensky, 26 February 1959; TNA DEFE 6/60/JP(59)Note 9. Directors of Plans, Reinforcement of the Federation of Rhodesia and Nyasaland, 27 February 1959.

[79] TNA CO 1015/1494. Welensky to Home, 1 March 1959; TNA WO 32/14635. Trafford Smith to DMO, 2 February 1953; TNA CAB 128/33/CC(59)14 meeting. Cabinet Conclusions, 4 March 1959.

[80] TNA CO 1015/1494. Armitage to Secretary of State, 13 February 1959; TNA CO 1915/1494. J. C. Morgan to Armitage-Smith, 13 February 1959.

[81] C. Legum, 'Government determined to protect Welensky', *Observer*, 15 March 1959; *Manchester Guardian*, 14 & 17 March 1959; TNA CO 1015/1517. Governor of Eastern Nigeria to Sir J. Macpherson, 24 March 1959.

[82] TNA CO 1015/1515. Colonial Secretary to Armitage, 4 March 1959; TNA CO 1015/1515. Colonial Secretary to Armitage, 5 March 1959; *Manchester Guardian*, 15 March 1959; TNA CO 1015/1789. F. Gough to Lennox-Boyd, 9 April 1959; TNA CO 1015/1789. Reverend M. Scott to Lennox-Boyd, 14 May 1959;TNA CO 1015/2097. Lord Shawcross to Lennox-Boyd, 1 June 1959;

Such was the level of public disquiet that Macmillan felt obliged to establish an inquiry under Lord Justice Devlin into the background and conduct of the emergency. Devlin, to Macmillan's embarrassment and anger, concluded that the Nyasaland administration had run what he labelled a 'police state', a phrase that went far towards discrediting British colonial administration in Africa and elsewhere.[83] That was bad enough, but Devlin's revelations coincided with an equally damning report into the deaths of 11 detainees at the Hola detention camp in Kenya in March 1959. It demonstrated, contrary to an earlier statement by the Kenyan government that the prisoners had died after drinking contaminated water, that they had been beaten to death by their warders, but that there was insufficient evidence to bring anyone to trial.[84]

The reports shook the morale of Macmillan's administration. Lennox-Boyd offered his resignation, which Macmillan refused.[85] The government survived the Commons debate on the Devlin Report with a majority of 63.[86] But, a day earlier, they had come under attack not just from the opposition, but had also been subjected to a stinging rebuke from one of their own senior backbenchers. Enoch Powell, in the course of a speech on the Hola camp deaths which, according to the *Times* correspondent, left the House 'deeply impressed', reminded ministers that British colonial rule could only be justified if they did indeed maintain the principle that equality before the law was a reality, and not a chimera.[87] The British could not

> pick and choose where and in what parts of the world we shall use this or that kind of standard. We cannot say, 'We will have African standards in Africa, Asian standards in Asia and perhaps British standards here at home.' We have not that choice to make. We must be consistent with ourselves everywhere. All Government, all influence of man upon man, rests upon opinion. What we can do in Africa, where we still govern and where we no longer govern, depends upon the opinion which is entertained of the way in which this country acts and the way in which Englishmen act. We cannot, we dare not, in Africa of all places, fall below our own highest standards in the acceptance of responsibility.[88]

TNA CO 1015/1905. Minute by [?]Gorrell-Barnes to J. C. Morgan, 15 June 1959; TNA CO 1015/2098. Secretary of State to Armitage, 16 June 1959; TNA CO 1015/2097. Secretary of State to Armitage, 23 July 1959; C. Legum, 'Policy in Africa under fire', *Observer*, 17 May 1959.

[83] TNA CO 1035/143. Colonial Secretary to Armitage, 10 March 1959; TNA CO 1035/143. Colonial Secretary to Lord Perth, 12 March 1959; TNA CO 1035/143/PM(59)10. Lennox-Boyd to PM, 13 March 1959; TNA CO 1035/143. Lennox-Boyd to Armitage, 15 March 1959; TNA CAB 129/98/C(59)124. Colonial Secretary, Nyasaland Commission of Inquiry, 17 July 1959. Report of the Nyasaland Commission of Inquiry; B. Simpson, 'The Devlin commission (1959): Colonialism, emergencies, and the rule of law', *Oxford Journal of Legal Studies*, vol. 22 (2002), 17–52.

[84] *Manchester Guardian*, 5 March 1959; TNA CAB 129/97/C(59)92. Minister of State for Colonial Affairs, Hola Detention Camp, 2 June 1959; TNA CAB 129/97/C(59)97. Colonial Secretary, Kenya: rehabilitation policy and the use of forced labour, 10 June 1959; CAB 128/33/CC(59)43 meeting. Cabinet Conclusions, 20 July 1959.

[85] TNA CAB 195/18/CC(59)57 meeting. Cabinet Conclusions, 20 July 1959.

[86] *Manchester Guardian*, 29 July 1959.   [87] *Times*, 28 July 1959.

[88] *Hansard*, HC Deb 27 July 1959 vol. 610, col. 237.

Hitherto the Macmillan government had hoped that they might be able to establish multi-racial states in Kenya and the CAF in which Europeans shared power with westernized Africans. The Devlin Report and the deaths at Hola camp rendered such goals impossible. They showed that Britain could no longer remake their colonial polities by force, particularly at the very moment when other European powers in Africa were ending their formal rule.[89] When this was combined with the failure significantly to reduce the financial burden of colonial internal security measures, Macmillan concluded that it was not just the financial cost of colonial counter-insurgencies that was becoming insupportable, but also the moral and political costs.

Besides, by the late 1950s the dependent territories were of much less economic importance to Britain than they had been in the decade after 1945.[90] As Chancellor of the Exchequer Macmillan had been reluctant to see the Treasury invest heavily in colonial development, and one of his first acts as Prime Minister was to order an audit of the economic and strategic benefits of the empire. A year later, he inaugurated a second inquiry into how Britain could best marshal its resources to maintain its overseas interests. The first report, produced by September 1957, suggested that with careful management Britain's overseas financial, commercial and strategic interests would survive the granting of constitutional independence to most of its colonies.[91] The second report, approved in July 1958, insisted that Britain's goal was not to surrender its empire, but to remodel it in such a way that Britain could exert a degree of informal control over its former colonies once they became independent members of the Commonwealth. But success would depend on relinquishing formal power, for 'We shall not maintain our influence if we appear to be clinging obstinately to the shadow of our old Imperial power after its substance has gone.'[92]

These reports were compiled when there was growing international pressure, not just on Britain, but on other European powers, to end their colonial rule.

---

[89] J. Lonsdale, 'Mau Maus of the mind: making Mau Mau and the remaking of Kenya', *Journal of African History*, vol. 31, no. 3 (1990), 393–421; R. Palmer, 'European resistance to African majority rule. The Settlers and Residents Association of Nyasaland, 1960–63', *African Affairs*, vol. 72 (1973), 270; L. J. Butler, 'Britain, the United States and the demise of the Central African Federation', *JICH*, vol. 28 (2001), 131–51.

[90] G. Krozewski, 'Sterling, the "Minor" territories, and the end of formal empire, 1939–1958', *Economic History Review*, vol. 46 (1993), 239–65; C. H. Feinstein, 'The end of empire and the golden age', in P. Clarke and C. Trebilcock (eds), *Understanding Decline. Perceptions and Realities of British Economic Performance* (Cambridge: Cambridge University Press, 1997), 212–33.

[91] T. Hopkins, 'Macmillan's audit of empire, 1957', in P. Clarke and C. Trebilcock (eds), *Understanding Decline. Perceptions and Realities of British Economic Performance* (Cambridge: Cambridge University Press, 1997), 234–59; TNA CAB 134/1555/CPC(57)6. Lord President of the Council, Future constitutional development in the colonies, 25 February 1957; TNA CAB 134/1556/CPC(57)30(Revise). Report by the Chairman of the Official Committee on Colonial policy, Future Constitutional development in the colonies, 6 September 1957.

[92] TNA CAB 130/139/Gen 624/1 meeting. Future Policy. Minutes of a meeting held in Sir Norman Brook's room, Cabinet Office, 6 December 1957; TNA CAB 130/139/Gen 624/10. Future policy. The position of the United Kingdom in world affairs, 9 June 1958; TNA CAB 130/153/Gen 659/1 meeting. The position of the United Kingdom in World Affairs. Minutes of a meeting held at 10 Downing Street, 7 July 1958.

When the UN was established in 1945, it had the whole-hearted endorsement of the British government and public. But fifteen years later, its membership swollen by an influx of former colonies, it was a very different organization. In 1959 the Nyasaland African National Congress leaders threatened to embarrass the British government by asking the Secretary General to visit Nyasaland where, they claimed, 'the British have violated the rights of man'.[93] In December 1960 it was the votes of newly independent Afro-Asian states that ensured that the General Assembly passed Resolution 1514, calling on the colonial powers to lose no time in granting independence to their colonies.[94] Macmillan had no wish to find that France, Belgium, and Portugal had done as they were bidden, and Britain was left in not-so-splendid isolation as the one remaining colonial power.[95] African independence was inevitable, and if, as the Foreign Secretary, Selwyn Lloyd, predicted, 'we are too intransigent in opposing African aspirations or, where European minorities are dominant, are too ready to appease them, we run the risk of being identified with the extreme racial doctrines of the Union of South Africa, of exacerbating African hostility towards the European and of provoking the African States, when they finally achieve independence—as in the end they must—to turn more readily towards the Soviet Union.'[96]

Colonial issues did not figure largely in the October 1959 general election, which was itself symptomatic of the fact that there was little domestic political mileage left in them. Empire was no longer a potent electoral asset for the Tory party. Few Tory candidates risked embarrassing themselves by even mentioning it in their electoral addresses.[97] The Conservatives won a handsome majority, but Macmillan felt that they had enjoyed a lucky escape from the embarrassment that the Devlin and Hola reports might have caused them. The magnitude of his victory, coupled with the election of a group of younger and less imperially committed MPs, gave him the opportunity to ignore his die-hard right wing and to push ahead with his policy of disengagement from Africa.[98] The result was a marked acceleration in the process of decolonization after 1959. It began with the appointment of a new Colonial Secretary, Iain Macleod. Thereafter the speed with which things happened in Africa began to escape from London's control. In East Africa, for example, Macleod discovered in 1960 that, as the colonial legislatures now financed both the police and army, Britain's ability to put a brake on political developments by the threat of

---

[93] TNA FO 371/138399. Conakry to Foreign Office, 31 August 1959; *Times*, 25 August 1959; TNA FO 371/138399. Record of a meeting in room H 340 at the Colonial Office on 9 September 1959. Possible attempt to debate Nyasaland in the General Assembly.

[94] Wm Roger Louis, 'Public enemy Number 1: the British Empire in the dock at the United Nations, 1957–71', in M. Lynn (ed.), *The British Empire in the 1950s* (Basingstoke: Palgrave Macmillan, 2006), 186–213.

[95] F. Heinlein, *British Government Policy and Decolonisation 1945–1963. Scrutinising the Official Mind* (London: Frank Cass, 2002), 166–205.

[96] TNA CAB 128/98/C(59)109. Selwyn Lloyd, Africa: the next ten years, 8 July 1959.

[97] P. Murphy, *Party Politics and Decolonization. The Conservative Party and British Colonial Policy in Tropical Africa, 1951–64* (Oxford: Clarendon Press, 1995), 8, 238; D. Horowitz, 'Attitudes of British Conservatives towards decolonization in Africa', *African Affairs*, vol. 69 (1970), 9–26.

[98] C. Baker, *State of Emergency: Crisis in Central Africa, Nyasaland, 1959–60* (London: I. B. Tauris, 1997), 153–82.

force was evaporating.[99] But a hastening of the speed with which the British were prepared to cede formal political power in their overseas territories did not mean that they had abandoned any hope of continuing to wield influence overseas. The era when the British could exercise power through the machinery of formal rule might be coming to an end. But they had every hope of being able to continue to exercise a degree of control through politically, militarily, and morally less expensive and objectionable means. Their main objective now was to withdraw in haste but with their dignity intact, but also to ensure that they left behind them pro-western nationalist regimes who would work with them in the post-imperial world to resist Soviet incursions.[100]

SUCCESS IN BORNEO, FAILURE IN ADEN

The Conservative administrations of Macmillan and Home, and their Labour successors after the October 1964 general election, fought the final two counter-insurgencies considered in this book, in the SAF and the Federation of Malaysia, in an effort to do just that. After carrying out fact-finding tours of the remaining colonies, Arthur Greenwood, Labour's Colonial Secretary, decided that in order to escape serious criticism at the UN, his policy was 'to liquidate colonialism either by granting independence to a number of territories or by evolving for the others forms of government which secure basic democratic rights for the people but which involve some degree of association with this country without any stigma of colonialism.'[101] But even had the Labour government not been anxious to avoid the stigma of presiding over a colonial empire, economics would have forced their hand. The government had inherited a serious balance of payments deficit, and at the very first meeting of the new Cabinet George Brown, installed as the first Secretary of State for Economic Affairs, told his colleagues that not only must exports be increased and imports decreased, but overseas defence spending also had to be cut.[102] In August 1965 MOD officials had calculated that the required savings could not be achieved unless Britain withdrew from Malaysia and Aden, and by November ministers agreed.[103] In the case of Malaysia they succeeded in leaving behind a pro-western indigenous regime. In the SAF they failed to do so.

---

[99] TNA CAB 129/100/C(60)1. Colonial Secretary, Future of the East African Land Forces, 1 January 1960.

[100] Darwin, *The Empire Project*, 610–48; G. Martel, 'Decolonisation after Suez: retreat or rationalisation?', *Australian Journal of Politics and History*, vol. 46 (2000), 403–17; P. E. Hemming, 'Macmillan and the end of the British empire in Africa', in R. Aldous and S. Lee (eds), *Harold Macmillan and Britain's World Role* (London: Macmillan, 1996), 97–124; Heinlein, *British Government Policy and Decolonisation*, 237–47.

[101] TNA CAB 148/21/OPD(65)89. Colonial Secretary to PM, Future of the remaining British colonial territories, 31 May 1965; TNA CAB 148/18/OPD(65)28 meeting. Defence and Overseas Policy Committee, 2 June 1965.

[102] TNA CAB 128/39/CC(64)1 meeting. Cabinet conclusions, 19 October 1964.

[103] TNA CAB 148/22/OPD(65)122. Note by the Chairman of the Defence and Overseas Policy (Official) Committee, Defence Review, 3 August 1965; TNA CAB 148/18/OPD(65)52 meeting. Defence and Overseas Policy Committee, 24 November 1965.

There were four reasons why the British succeeded in maintaining the Federation of Malaysia and failed to maintain the SAF. The indigenous government of the former enjoyed a wide measure of popular support, whereas the indigenous government of the latter did not. The Malaysian Federation came into being in September 1963, and despite communal tensions between Malays and Chinese, enjoyed wide popular support. Indonesian support for the Brunei revolt had persuaded many people in Sarawak who might otherwise have been at best lukewarm about the Federation, to vote for pro-Federal parties in local elections held between April and June 1963. The alternative, annexation by Indonesia, was even less palatable.[104] A general election in Malaya in April 1964 saw the return of Tunku Abdul Rahman's Alliance Party after a campaign that emphasized the menace from Indonesia and the determination of the Tunku's government to resist it.[105] By contrast, the Federation never enjoyed much popular support in South Arabia. The British suppressed protests in Aden against the latter's forced merger with the protectorates in January 1963 by simply arresting the leader of the main anti-merger political party.[106] Elections were held in Aden State in October 1964. But, of the total population of about 220,000, only about 8,300 people were permitted to vote.[107] Out of fear they would reject the Federation the British had rigged the franchise qualification to exclude the large number of Yemeni and other Arab immigrants who had flocked into the port city.[108] Even so, the candidate who came top of the poll was the same man who had thrown a grenade at Trevaskis in December 1963.[109] The British could rely on neither the police nor the Federal army to offer them effective support. The loyalty of the FRA had been undermined by anti-Federal propaganda from the Yemen and Cairo. '[W]e have strong suspicions,' Governor Turnbull wrote in May 1965, 'suspicions which are not, of course, capable of being proved, that the majority of the police, if witnesses of a grenade or bazooka incident would be inclined to look the other way rather than to take proper action.'[110] In September 1965 he suspended the Aden constitution and introduced direct rule.[111]

In the course of the Aden emergency, Britain found itself under increasing pressure not only from the insurgents' allies in the UAR, but also from parts of

[104] D. Bloodworth, 'Indonesia's arms worry neighbours', *Observer*, 6 January 1963; TNA WO 305/2524. HQ British Forces Borneo. Joint Intsum no. 2, 11 July 1963.

[105] D. Holden, 'Landslide victory for the Tunku: Malaysia's reply to confrontation', *Guardian*, 27 April 1964.

[106] TNA CO 1055/196. Assistant High Commissioner Aden to CO, 21 January 1963.

[107] *Times*, 15 & 17 October 1964.

[108] TNA CAB 195/19/CC 29(61). Cabinet meeting, 30 May 1961.

[109] *Manchester Guardian*, 27 October 1964.

[110] TNA CO 1035/179. Turnbull to Marnham, 25 May 1965; TNA DEFE 13/571. Maj.-Gen J. E. F. Willoughey to Maj.-Gen R.G.V. Fitzgeorge-Balfour, 20 April 1966; TNA CO 1035/181. Note of a meeting between the Minister of Defence and H. E. the High Commissioner for Aden and the South Arabia Federation, 3 January 1964.

[111] TNA CO 1055/208. Turnbull to CO, 17 October 1965; LHCMA Maj.-Gen. Charles Wish Dunbar mss. Dunbar 2/5. Lecture (II), n.d. but *c*.1967; TNA WO 305/4301. Historical Record (1 April 1966 to 1 April 1967) 1/Royal Northumberland Fusiliers; TNA CAB 148/22/OPD(65)129. Colonial Secretary, Aden, 1 October 1965.

the British press and the wider international community at the UN. In part, criticisms were directed at some of the methods the British employed. Cross-border air attacks, the detention of suspects without trial and their alleged torture, and the use of starvation as a tactic in the Radfan were all condemned.[112] Commenting on the outcome of a British cross-border air raid on the Yemeni base at Fort Harib in March 1964, the British head of mission at the UN reported that

> we cannot get away with presenting any action which we have to take merely as an internal security operation. The fact is too that attacks with bombs or cannon fire strike opinion here at any rate as being the methods of the last century and we get no public support from the uncommitted countries, and not much more from our European friends or the Americans. I fully realise the very difficult security situation which has to be faced in the Federation, but violent counter-action, however justifiable or represented, unfortunately now has inevitably hostile repercussions in the United Nations and in our relations throughout the world. Experienced observers here have been surprised at the strength of the opposition aroused by our action at Harib, and unless we can devise alternative methods of protecting our interests, I am afraid that we shall constantly be playing into the hands of our enemies.[113]

It was also the first campaign during which TV news camera had filmed 'British soldiers actually smashing the heads of some of the local natives with rifle butts and kicking them. Now, that was not a done thing. Up to that time, basically, journalism shied away from that. You didn't shine the light on the bad behaviour of your boys.'[114] Soldiers resented such criticisms, believing that they were only doing what the government had told them to do.[115] But criticism went beyond the methods the British employed. It struck at the very fact of Britain's presence in Aden. In December 1963 the UN General Assembly passed resolutions demanding the repeal of all emergency laws, insisting that elections should be held in South Arabia, that the British should withdraw from their base, and should set an early date for independence.[116] Five months later the British mission to the UN reported that 'We have to recognize that the continuance anywhere of a regime which could be stigmatised as "colonial" shifts on to the administering power in the event of trouble, the burden of proving that steady and peaceful progress towards independence is being maintained.'[117]

[112] TNA DEFE 11/498. Sir H. Beeley to Foreign Office, 1 June 1964; Anon, 'Hungry Arabs flee mountains', *Guardian*, 3 June 1964; TNA CO 1055/201. R. Beeston, '"Hunger War" on Radfan tribes', *Sunday Telegraph*, 1 June 1964.
[113] TNA CO 1055/200. Sir Patrick Dean to FO, 7 April 1964; TNA CAB 128/38/CM(64)21 meeting. Cabinet Conclusions, 9 April 1964.
[114] A. Hart, ITN News reporter, *Empire Warriors. Aden—Mad Mitch and his Tribal Law*, BBC, 2004.
[115] IWMSA. Accession No. 13145. J. P. Baxter, reel 3.
[116] TNA CAB 129/109/C(62)73. Foreign Secretary, Colonial Issues at the United Nations, 30 May 1962; Roger Louis, 'Public enemy Number 1', 196–205; TNA DEFE 11/438. Resolutions 1949 & 1972 (XVIII), adopted by the General Assembly on 11 & 16 December 1963.
[117] TNA CO 1055/194. UK Mission UN to Foreign Office, 12 April 1964.

As noted in Chapter 3, some British officials had long entertained private qualms about the morality of some of the measures they felt compelled to employ in the late 1940s and early 1950s. A decade later, when their own doubts were echoed and amplified in the international arena, much of their righteous self-confidence in Britain's imperial mission drained away. By early 1967, the sense that the British were behaving in ways that were morally unacceptable in Aden had become palpable. In February 1967 Turnbull remarked that 'he had, since arriving in London, felt that there was a tiresome air of guilt about our activities in Aden, and that the Services in Aden felt it as well.'[118]

In Malaysia, by contrast, the British were under international pressure not to quit. The USA, Australia, and New Zealand feared that Sukarno was dangerously close to Communist China. They pressed the British to remain, fearing that if they left Malaysia would fall under Communist domination.[119] Even so it was thought prudent to limit the freedom of action of the security forces to ensure they did not provoke international incidents. In January 1964 Walker issued a directive that Indonesian aircraft that drifted into Malaysian airspace were not to be engaged for the same reason that ground forces were not permitted to cross the frontier into Kalimantan. 'Many illwishers [*sic*] are looking for excuses to charge Malaysia with acts of aggression. It is our intention to deny them that excuse.'[120] At the UN they avoided criticism from the Afro-Asian bloc by ensuring that it was the Malaysian government that took the lead in justifying each new military measure, for they could do so on the grounds of national self-defence.[121] In September 1964 only the USSR's veto prevented the Security Council from passing a resolution condemning Indonesian aggression against Malaysia.[122] But they also had a major stroke of good fortune when, in January 1965 Sukharno threw away his best diplomatic card and announced that Indonesia was leaving the UN in protest at the fact that Malaysia had just been elected to the Security Council.[123]

In Aden and the protectorates, the British and their local allies failed to defeat the armed insurgents, who were thus able to undermine the legitimacy of the British-supported administration. British intelligence had learnt of Egyptian plans to assist the NLF to mount an urban terrorist campaign in Aden in the spring of 1964.[124] A British journalist working in Aden was told that the local insurgents intended 'to open an urban campaign of terrorism similar to that mounted by the Jews against

---

[118] TNA DEFE 11/524/COS(67)14 meeting, 2 February 1967.
[119] TNA CAB 148/22/OPD(65)131. Secretary of State for Commonwealth Relations, Repercussions on British policy in South East Asia of the separation of Singapore from Malaysia, 20 September 1965; TNA CAB 148/18/OPD(65)41 meeting. Defence and Overseas Policy Committee, 23 September 1965; Subritzky, 'Britain, Konfrontasi', 222–3; D. Easter, *Britain and the Confrontation with Indonesia, 1960–66* (London: Tauris Academic Studies, 2004), 148–53.
[120] TNA WO 305/2530. Minutes of the 10 meeting of Borneo Territories Security Executive Committee (Operations Sub-committee), 7 January 1964.
[121] TNA DEFE 6/92/DP Note 87/64(Final). Directors of Defence Plans, Operations across the Indonesian Border, 19 August 1964.
[122] *Times*, 18 September 1964; Easter, *Britain and the Confrontation*, 105.
[123] Easter, *Britain and Confrontation*, 122; *Times*, 2, 6–8 January 1965.
[124] TNA CO 1055/194. Trevaskis to Colonial Secretary, 16 April 1964; TNA DEFE 11/497. LIC monthly intelligence summary for April 1964, 5 May 1964.

the British in Palestine and the Muslims against the French in Algeria' because it would be the cheapest and quickest way of bringing their cause to the notice of the world and expelling the British. The campaign began in November 1964.[125] Incidents took a variety of forms, including attacks by a hard-core of gunmen trained by the Egyptian Intelligence Service, grenade attacks, often carried out by less skilful and poorly trained insurgents, and the laying of land mines and booby traps. Targets included service personnel and their families, locally recruited government servants, and pro-Federation politicians.[126] Geography helped the insurgents for after striking it was easy for them to disappear down one of the many crowded city streets.[127]

The British response might have been more effective had they possessed better intelligence. It has been claimed that it was the Labour government's announcement in February 1966 that Britain would leave Aden by January 1968 that caused intelligence to dry up. Informers, it has been alleged, were afraid to place themselves in danger of retaliation from the insurgents to help a government that would soon be gone.[128] In fact, as long ago as July 1964, when the Conservatives were still in power in London, Trevaskis believed that some members of the FRA, civil servants, and even Federal ministers were losing confidence in the British and looking to reinsure themselves with Nasser. It was a trend that accelerated even before the Labour government's announcement, and the flow of intelligence had been reduced to a trickle at least a year before it was made.[129] This was partly because the NLF had systematically and successfully assassinated so many Arab Special Branch officers that the remainder were too frightened to work.[130] But it was also because many people sympathized with the insurgents, even if they did not always like their methods. Henceforth, the British had to depend on routine patrols, cordon and search operations, and the occasional successful interrogation of prisoners to gather intelligence.[131] The failure of the security forces to protect the civilian population from NLF intimidation was such that when, in September 1965, Sir Arthur Charles, the Speaker of the Aden Legislative Council, was assassinated, none of the members of the legislature was willing publicly to condemn the assassination.

---

[125] C. Hollingworth, 'British try to starve out tribesmen', *Guardian*, 16 May 1964; TNA CO 1055/202. Acting High Commissioner to CO, 30 November 1964.

[126] TNA CO 1055/202. Acting High Commissioner to CO, 1 January 1965; TNA CO 1055/63. Acting High Commissioner to CO, 29 & 30 March 1965; TNA CO 1055/63. High Commissioner to Colonial Secretary, 7 April, 4 May, 8 June, 5 October & 7 December 1965; TNA DEFE 11/503. LIC (Aden) Monthly Report for March 1966; TNA DEFE 11/504. C-in-C Mideast to CDS, 4 October 1966; TNA DEFE 11/526. C-in-C Mideast to CDS, 28 March 1967; TNA DEFE 11/526. C-in-C Mideast to CDS, 9 April 1967; TNA DEFE 11/527. C-in-C Mideast to CDS, 2 May 1967.

[127] TNA DEFE 11/506. South Arabia Action Group. Report by Chairman and Deputy Chairman on their visit to South Arabia from 31 October to 12 November 1966, 14 December 1966.

[128] Maj.-Gen. Sir J. Willoughby, 'Problems of counter-insurgency in the Middle East', *JRUSI*, vol. 113 (May 1968), 107.

[129] TNA DEFE 13/570. Trevaskis to CO, 18 July 1964; TNA CAB 148/23/OPD(65)143. A. R. Rushford and A. P. Cumming-Bruce, Report of Security Measures in Aden, 7 October 1965.

[130] TNA CO 1055/63. Turnbull to Colonial Secretary, 18 February 1965.

[131] TNA WO 305/4301. Historical Record (1 April 1966 to 1 April 1967), 1 Royal Northumberland Fusiliers.

As one member asked, who would protect those members who did condemn it from themselves being assassinated?[132] For their part the security forces experienced a growing sense of frustration. They knew that 'The extreme measures which would be necessary to counter such action would also generate increased pressures from a world opinion that is generally hostile to the British position in Southern Arabia as well as to the Federal concept.'[133]

The failure of the security forces' efforts to win Adeni hearts and minds was illustrated by two things, both noted by the diarist of 1/Royal Northumberland Fusiliers, when the battalion operated in the Crater district of Aden in 1966–7. Despite the fact that grenade attacks on the security forces often injured innocent Adeni bystanders, the civil population did not turn against the grenade throwers. The second took place just before Christmas 1966 when a British officer 'present[ed] some equipment supplied by HM Government to a kindergarten in Crater. GSO 1 Civil Affairs who attended the presentation and stage-managed it, had a grenade thrown at him. It was apparent that the terrorists were not going to allow their hearts to be won by presentations of school equipment!'[134]

The British were far more successful in Malaysia, where, by late 1965, they had imposed a military stalemate on the Indonesians. The British military response passed through several phases. In 1963, when the IBTs operated in small and poorly armed gangs, the British employed tactics similar to those used in Malaya. Platoons operated independently from company bases.[135] In 1964 the Indonesians abandoned their ill-planned and haphazard raids in favour of a policy of simultaneous and carefully planned incursions on wide fronts, directed by regular Indonesian army officers, and often involving regular Indonesian troops. Their aim was to link up with the CCO inside Borneo and to mount a prolonged guerrilla campaign.[136] In response the British used SAS and Special Boat Service patrols and locally raised Border Scouts to gather intelligence, and employed conventional infantry units to establish company-sized bases to control likely border-crossing points.[137] Further back from the frontier they maintained larger bases where

---

[132] *Guardian*, 7 September 1965.
[133] TNA CAB 191/12. LIC (Aden), The National Liberation Front for the Liberation of the Occupied South, or the NLF, 25 January 1965.
[134] TNA WO 305/4301. Historical Record (1 April 1966 to 1 April 1967) 1/Royal Northumberland Fusiliers.
[135] TNA WO 305/2522. Assessment of the military situation, 3 Commando Brigade Area, 27 April 1963.
[136] TNA DEFE 11/487. Enclosure 1. Walker to C-in-C Far East, 27 March 1964; TNA DEFE 11/488. C-in-C Far East to CDS, 1 April 1964.
[137] TNA CO 968/873. C-in-C Far East to MOD, 14 February 1963; TNA WO 305/2520. Minutes of a meeting of the Borneo Operations Committee held at HQ COMBRITBOR on 1 March 1963; TNA WO 305/2522. Minutes of a meeting of the Borneo Security Council held at the Office of the High Commissioner for Brunei, 10 May 1963; TNA WO 305/2523. Minutes of a meeting of the Borneo Operations Committee held at HQ COMBRITBOR, 21 June 1963; TNA WO 305/2529. Minutes of the 8 meeting of Borneo Territories Security Executive Committee (Operations sub-committee) 18 December 1963; TNA WO 305/4292. Operation Brand. Patrol report, 13 June 1964; TNA WO 305/2530. Director of Borneo Operations Instruction number 10. Command, roles and employment of the SAS Regiment in Borneo, 10 January 1964; TNA DEFE 11/486. C-in-C Far East to CDS, 8 February 1964.

reinforcements were ready to move by helicopters when an Indonesian penetration was detected, to land behind them, and to ambush them on their way back to Kalimantan.[138]

The Indonesians then further escalated their effort, trebling the strength of their regular forces in Borneo.[139] Walker told London that he had two choices. If he remained committed to his defensive strategy he would need another nine battalions to stabilize the situation. The COS insisted that the army did not have another nine battalions to send to Borneo. But a more aggressive policy that pinned the Indonesians to their own side of the border would actually require fewer men. Aware that if they did not act more decisively the Malaysian government might take matters into their own hands, on 1 July 1964 the Cabinet's defence and overseas policy committee gave Walker permission not only to return fire across the border but also to dispatch SAS patrols up to 3,000 yards inside Kalimantan. In January 1965 ministers extended this to 10,000 yards.[140] The obvious danger was that such operations would be widely publicized by Sukharno, who would use them to rally Indonesian morale and claim they were evidence of British aggression. Fortunately, the British knew that local Indonesian commanders always reported clashes between British and Indonesian forces as a great victory for the latter.[141] Even so it was essential that 'Claret' operations should be deniable. Cross-border patrols were always given 'A cover story for a "Credibly Deniable Op[eration]", with maps marked accordingly, was prepared to misplace the p[a]t[ro]l over the border' and '"Blood Chits" worth $2,000 were carried by each member for use in buying local assistance in an emergency.'[142] 'Claret' patrols were guided by excellent signals intelligence, so they could ambush Indonesian forces and avoid being ambushed by them. They not only allowed the British to win control of the border region, but they also prevented military operations from escalating still further, thus keeping ajar the door to political negotiations.[143]

But imposing a military stalemate on the Indonesians was one thing. Persuading them to abandon Confrontation was another. It is conceivable that Sukarno might have been able to continue the Confrontation beyond the point at which the Labour government could afford to maintain its support at the high level of 1965.

---

[138] Walker, 'Borneo', 9–13; C. Tuck, 'Borneo 1963–66: counter-insurgency operations and war termination', *SW&I*, vol. 15 (2004), 95–6; B. Hall and A. Ross, 'The political and military effectiveness of Commonwealth forces in Confrontation 1963–66', *SW&I*, vol. 19 (2008), 244–5; TNA PREM 11/484. HMS Albion to Admiralty, 3 October 1963; TNA WO 305/2527. HQ British Forces Borneo. Joint Intsum no. 8, 7 October 1963; WO 305/2528. Central Brigade Operations Instruction No. 3, 23 November 1963.

[139] TNA CAB 130/221/Misc30/1 meeting. Indonesia, 4 January 1965.

[140] TNA CAB 130/221/Misc30/1 meeting. Indonesia, 4 January 1965; TNA PREM 13/482. Lord Head to CRO, 9 January 1965; TNA CAB 148/19/OPD(65)2. Secretary of State for Defence, 11 January 1965; TNA WO 305/2544. Director of Borneo Operations, Quarterly Operation Report, 1 January to 31 March 1965, 19 April 1965.

[141] TNA CAB 148/19/OPD(65)8. Secretary of State for Defence, 12 January 1965; TNA CAB 148/18/OPD(65)1 meeting. Defence and Overseas Policy Committee, 13 January 1965.

[142] TNA WO 305/4292. Report on reconnaissance patrol to S. Sembakung south of Lebang by patrol 21, 13–28 August, 30 August 1964.

[143] D. Easter, 'British intelligence and propaganda during the "Confrontation"', 88–9; Tuck, 'Borneo 1963–66', 101; R. Aldrich, *GCHQ. The Uncensored Story of Britain's Most Secret Intelligence Agency* (London: Harper Press, 2010), 165–8.

Fortunately, however, the British were able to take advantage of the instability of Indonesian politics to bring the Confrontation to an end before they felt compelled to reduce that level of support. On 30 September 1965 a group of Indonesian airforce officers attempted a coup during which they assassinated half a dozen army generals. The Indonesian army quickly suppressed the coup. But, suspecting that Sukarno and the PKI had been behind it, they then turned on the PKI and massacred thousands of its supporters and also challenged Sukarno's grip on power.[144] The British carefully desisted from increasing the tempo of their operations on Borneo so as not to 'distract the army from their attempts, which appear to be having some success, to discredit the communist party'. But although in public the British, Singapore, and Malaysian governments pursued a policy of studious non-interference, in secret they intensified covert measures to turn the situation to their advantage. They continued 'unattributable propaganda and psychological warfare activities designed to exploit the present confusion, to encourage anti-Communist Indonesians to vigorous action against the PKI, and to prevent or delay the re-emergence of an all-party government under Sukarno.'[145] By April 1966 Sukarno had been reduced to a figurehead and power in Djakarta was effectively wielded by General Suharto, who promptly banned the PKI. Michael Stewart, the Foreign Secretary, suggested that while the British should make it clear that it would continue to defend Malaysia and Singapore, it would also respond positively to any Indonesian attempt to end Confrontation.[146] That happened in August 1966 when Indonesia signed the treaty of Bangkok and recognized the Federation.[147]

They had no such good fortune in Aden. In February 1966, as part of their policy of reducing overseas defence costs, the government announced that it would leave Aden by no later than 1968. Paradoxically, the announcement made a bad situation worse. The insurgents maintained their pressure because they did not believe that the British really meant to leave, and because they were jockeying amongst themselves to determine who would succeed them.[148] The number of insurgent attacks rose from 36 in 1964 to 286 in 1965, and then to 480 in 1966. The security situation became even more difficult after May 1965 when another insurgent group, the Front for the Liberation of Occupied South Yemen (FLOSY), emerged. FLOSY was sponsored by Egypt as a counter-weight to the NLF, which had become increasingly left-wing and seemed to have escaped from Egyptian

---

[144] TNA CAB 148/18/OPD(65)42 meeting. Defence and Overseas Policy Committee, 2 October 1965; TNA WO 305/2550. Director of Borneo Operations weekly assessment of the threat to East Malaysia and Brunei, 2–9 October 1965, 9 October 1965.

[145] TNA DEFE 6/98/DP 70/65(Final). Defence Planning Staff, Measures to counter Indonesian Confrontation, 15 October 1965.

[146] TNA CAB 148/27/OPD(66)46. Foreign Secretary, Indonesia, 4 April 1966; TNA CAB 148/25/OPD(66)19 meeting. Defence and Overseas Policy Committee, 6 April 1966.

[147] Tuck, 'Borneo 1963–66', 103–7.

[148] O. Miles, 'The British withdrawal from Aden. A personal memory', downloaded 3 January 2009 at: http://www.al-bab.com/bys/articles/miles.htm.

control.[149] The two organizations entered into a period of fratricidal war to determine who would govern after the British had left.[150]

CONCLUSION

The last British soldiers left Aden on 29 November. They were flown by helicopter to the fleet offshore where the last High Commissioner held a review, a '"final proud moment displaying the British lion's still formidable strength to the world," according to the naval task force's broadsheet. For others, Operation LIT-UP constituted an unnecessary, almost pathetic futility.'[151]

'Operation LIT-UP' was about trying to put on an outward show of dignity at the end of what was in fact an undignified scuttle. In the late nineteenth and early twentieth centuries the British empire had been sustained by a set of largely fortuitous circumstances. Until the middle of the 1950s it seemed reasonable to suppose that even if those precise circumstances could not be re-created, it might be possible to remodel the empire on new foundations that would still enable the British to maintain their world-wide influence. But one of the problems that they had to solve was how to defeat those groups who were prepared to take up arms against their colonial rule. Beset by continuing economic problems, in the mid-1950s they opted to try the Templer doctrine. Templer thought that prevention would be cheaper than cure, and so, in financial terms, it might have been. But he also advocated devolving responsibility for the conduct of security operations onto local colonial administrations. This gave them the power to do much as they pleased, but it left the government in London with the responsibility for justifying and defending their actions.

Britain's fund of international goodwill, and the Conservative government's moral standing in Britain, were seriously depleted by the Suez crisis. Even so, Suez was not the point at which the British stopped trying to exercise power in Africa and Asia. It was the co-incidence of the Nyasaland emergency, the Devlin Report, and the Hola camp atrocities that marked the point at which an increasing number of ministers began to realize that the political and moral costs of doing so might be too high. In the immediate post-war period the empire had seemed to be an asset in the Cold War. By the end of the 1950s it was increasingly seen as a liability. Henceforth the priority of both Conservative and Labour governments was to divest themselves of what was left of the empire with as much haste as they could, but with their dignity intact, and ensuring that the regimes they left behind were pro-western and anti-Communist. In Malaysia they succeeded, in Aden they failed. The very different outcomes of the two campaigns showed that even in the mid-1960s the British could still conduct a successful counter-insurgency campaign, but only if circumstances largely beyond their own control were especially propitious.

[149] TNA DEFE 11/524/COS(67)14 meeting, 2 February 1967.
[150] TNA DEFE 11/527. Brigadier Gribbon to CDS, 12 May 1967; TNA DEFE 13/572. Trevelyan to Foreign Office, 25 June 1967; TNA DEFE 11/531. Trevelyan to Foreign Office, 21 August 1967.
[151] J. de St Jorre, 'Emergency is over', *Observer*, 26 November 1967; TNA DEFE 11/534. C-in-C Mideast to CDS, 29 November 1967.

Conclusion

This book has addressed the question of the extent to which the ways the British practised counter-insurgency between 1945 and 1967 actually conformed to the 'ideal-type' as defined by Thompson and refined by subsequent analysts. It has demonstrated that there were in fact significant divergences between these theories and British practice. This misreading of the historical record stems from two things. The first is a misuse of Thompson's work. It was not an historical treatise, and it should not be read as such. It was a didactic book in which he tried to emphasize what future counter-insurgent operators should do if they wanted to succeed. The second is the over-use of the phrase 'hearts and minds'. It conjures up a false image of what the British did. It implies that they had discovered a comparatively painless way of conducting counter-insurgency operations. There may be kind and gentle ways of doing so, and there is every reason for today's practitioners to seek them out. But the historical record does not suggest that the British had found them between 1945 and 1967. On the contrary, the main contention of this book is that they commonly employed a wide variety of coercive techniques to intimidate the civilian population into throwing their support behind the government rather than behind the insurgents.

Against the background of the Cold War it is easy to understand why so many British policy-makers believed that every manifestation of colonial unrest was either Communist inspired, or would be exploited by the Soviets for their own ends. But only in Malaya did the British confront an insurgency that was animated by a Communist programme, and only in Malaya were the insurgents trying to pursue a Maoist strategy. Elsewhere, the opponents of the British empire were radical nationalists, none of whom sought to achieve their goals by following Mao Zedong's precepts. This was important because the 'Malayan-model' of counter-insurgency emphasized that the government did not just have to win a military victory over the guerrillas, but it had to win a political victory over subversion. But if the British neither understood nor took seriously their opponents' political objectives, their own counter-insurgency strategy was likely to go awry. Nowhere did the British follow Thompson's precept that their first priority should be to create a free and independent state. They may have had the long-term aspiration of transforming their empire into a Commonwealth of freely associating countries. But, in the short and medium terms, they made political concessions only when the continuation of an insurgency made the political and economic costs of resisting pressures for change too great.

The British were convinced not only of the moral righteousness of their imperial mission, but also of the certainty that anyone who opposed it was criminally inclined. Hence, they could not recognize that their opponents had their own legitimate political programmes. Rather, they believed that the great majority of their subjects were content with their rule, and those who sided with the insurgents did so because they had been intimidated. But that did not lead, as it logically might have done, to counter-insurgency strategies in which coercion was only employed against the 'guilty'. Coercion—meaning measures that ranged from curfews and cordon and search operations at one end of the scale of violence, through collective fines and large-scale detention without trial, and culminated in forced population resettlement and the creation of free fire zones—was the bedrock of British counter-insurgency policies. They used exemplary force to so intimidate the population that they would cease to support the insurgents. If that failed, and where circumstances allowed, as they did in Malaya, Kenya, Oman, the Radfan and parts of Borneo, they employed counter-terrorism to lock down entire ethnic groups. Asked in 1984 if it was right to behave like this, Harding had no doubts. 'Oh yes, I think you can't possibly inflict a defeat on a terrorist organization unless you adopt all these measures as and when you think they're necessary, and unless you conduct your anti-terrorist campaign just as you would conduct a campaign in a sort of set-piece war against a declared enemy—it is a war, anti-terrorist operations between the security forces and the terrorist organizations is war, and war has to be conducted in a ruthless arbitrary way, otherwise you're wasting both lives and time.'[1] Such policies played a central role in British operations and were often the keys to their successes. But that does not alter the fact that each and every one of them would be unacceptable to public opinion in Britain today.

The paucity of intelligence resources at the disposal of most colonial governments, particularly in the early stages of an emergency, made it difficult for them to distinguish between those who were 'guilty' of actively opposing them, and those who were 'innocent' and merely trying to remain uninvolved. Unable to bring their opponents to open battle, the security forces turned instead on the insurgents' civilian supporters, and, because they could not distinguish between them, on civilians generally. A Chinese squatter, a Kikuyu peasant, or a Radfani tribesman whose homes were destroyed by the security forces in the course of operations to resettle the population elsewhere could be forgiven for failing to recognize the difference between an operation designed to 'search and destroy' and one intended to 'clear and hold'. Governments did sometimes try to buy support, to 'court' rather than 'coerce' the population by instituting development programmes to improve their health and welfare. But shortages of money, expert personnel, and a refusal to be bought meant that their efforts usually had little impact.

Most members of the security forces, most of the time, did operate within the law. But it was a law that was deliberately constructed by the colonial authorities to

---

[1] IWMSA. Accession No. 8736. Field Marshal Lord Harding, Transcript, 413.

allow soldiers, policemen, and administrators to apply coercion with little or no discrimination, and across whole populations and ethnic groups. The British never followed the French in giving hegemonic power to the army to control operations, nor, with the exception of Palestine, did they establish military courts to try civilians. But the British did not eschew imposing martial law on rebellious colonies from high principle, but from low expediency. Emergency regulations gave the security forces most of the advantages of martial law, but with few of its political drawbacks. It also allowed them to suspend civil liberties wholesale in ways reminiscent of what the French did in Algeria, a finding that suggests that the assertion that the British were exceptional in the ways in which they conducted their campaigns compared to their international contemporaries, needs to be qualified.

The supposed commitment of the security forces to the doctrine of 'minimum necessary force' has gained a wide purchase in the literature because it has supported a 'whig' interpretation of decolonization', which saw it as a dignified and orderly process of planned withdrawal from empire. But it is misleading. It is based upon a selective range of sources, namely the accounts of senior officers who were intent on sanitizing the experience of fighting wars of decolonization. By focusing on purely military operations, it failed to take account of the other more varied forms of coercion that the British employed. Finally, it overlooked the fact that the meaning of the concept was ill-defined in both theory and practice. It did preclude the British from practising genocide against their opponents, but it did not stop them from employing a great deal of lethal force.

Soldiers and policemen on the ground did not exhibit a single common attitude towards their opponents and the civil population amongst whom they operated, even in the same theatre. Some sympathized with the plight of the civil population and saw themselves as protecting them from insurgent intimidation. Some resented being forced into uniform and sent to a far away place, and took out their resentment on the locals. Some respected the insurgents they were up against as skilful fighters, albeit in a bad cause. Others, who perhaps might have seen their comrades killed or wounded, hated them. Some understood the political context within which they were working; many did not. Perhaps the most widely shared attitude was that they were engaged in a job of work, and they had to obey orders, whether they liked them or not.

Such attitudes help to explain why, with the partial exception of Kenya, where the settler population was infused with a genuine fear and hatred of the insurgents, the British did not wage 'dirty' wars in the same systematic manner and on the same scale as the French did in Algeria. But that should not blind us to the fact that there were instances, and not only in Kenya, where civilians, prisoners, and detainees were mistreated in ways that violated the UN's Universal Declaration of Human Rights and the ECHR of 1950. Some prisoners were roughed-up shortly after capture. Interrogators might use methods requiring patience, foreknowledge and modern technical aids to extract information from prisoners, or they might employ methods that crossed the line and involved physical brutality. Even ministers and Colonial Office officials grew sceptical of some of the stories of prisoners shot while trying to escape. The treatment of detainees varied, from the almost luxurious conditions enjoyed by Archbishop Makarios in the governor's summer residence on the Seychelles, to the appalling physical and psychological conditions endured by Mau Mau detainees in Kenya.

The legal regimes created by the 1939 Order-in-Council and related local legislation gave the security forces wide latitude about how they went about their job. But there were instances in just about every insurgency when members of the security forces still broke even these lax rules. Transgressors were not just found in the locally raised auxiliaries. They included British soldiers and British policemen. The response of the authorities was inconsistent. If they allowed the security forces too much freedom to take unofficial reprisals, they would forfeit the possibility of winning the hearts and minds of the people. Consequently, their public pronouncements made it clear that they expected soldiers and policemen to refrain from private violence and reprisals. The fact that they made such pronouncements, and did sometimes punish offenders with the full rigour of the law, went a long way towards ensuring that they never entirely lost control of the men on the ground. But offenders were equally likely to escape with a largely symbolic punishment, or with no punishment at all, for the authorities feared that if they went too far in imposing discipline on those elements of the security forces where it had broken down, they would lose their hearts and minds.

The preparation and application of a single, overarching plan to defeat the insurgents was made difficult because of the varied objectives and capabilities of the different government agencies involved. This problem was, briefly, overcome in Malaya during Templer's period as High Commissioner, when he sat atop a pyramidal structure of committees that brought together soldiers, policemen, and civil servants, and united both the civil and military power in his own person. But the fully developed 'Malayan model' of counter-insurgency by committee only lasted from 1952 to 1955 in Malaya, and it was applied inconsistently and incompletely elsewhere.

The ability of the security forces and the colonial administration to 'learn lessons' was equally inconsistent. The army was more successful than the Colonial Office at capturing its past experiences on paper and transmitting theoretical lessons to succeeding generations of soldiers. The machinery for doing this within the Colonial Office was, by contrast, woefully inadequate. But even the army was at least as much a 'forgetting organization' as it was a 'learning organization'. The constant turnover of National Servicemen meant that the same lessons had constantly to be repeated as each new cohort of inexperienced junior officers and other ranks arrived in a theatre of operations. The fragmented structure of the British army, based on the regimental system, meant that battalion commanders had wide latitude to interpret doctrine according to their own interpretation of local circumstances, which helped to account for the fact that the level of efficiency between units in the same theatre could vary widely.

To what extent were the British successful counter-insurgents? If we accept that the aim of the insurgents was to overthrow the *de jure* government that ruled their country at the beginning of the insurgency, their success was mixed. In Palestine,

Aden, and the Canal Zone, they scored unequivocal successes. In Cyprus they toppled the British colonial regime, but secured only an independent Cypriot state, and not the enosis with Greece they had sought. In Malaya, Malaysia, Kenya, and Nyasaland they failed and, at the point at which the British declared the emergency over, the colonial government remained in place. In the case of British Guiana, the PPP remained excluded from power. But if the definition of success and failure is looked at from the point of view of the British, a different picture emerges. In broad terms, by 1945 the British had accepted that the days when they could maintain formal rule over many of their colonies were coming to an end. Their objective was, in the fullness of time, to see the reins of government pass to indigenous elites who would be willing to govern in ways that were consonant with British and broader western interests. But the British rarely regarded insurgents as suitable candidates to form successor regimes. Looked at in this light, the British record was also mixed. Malaya and Malaysia were undoubted successes. In the Canal Zone and Aden they failed. In Oman they had to go back and do the job all over again in the early 1970s. In Cyprus they retained control of the Sovereign Base Areas, but at the cost of surrendering control of the rest of the island, and then discovered that maintaining control of the rest of the island did not matter half so much as they had believed it would. The outcome in Kenya, Nyasaland, and British Guiana was more equivocal, but at least none of them fell into the Soviet orbit.

Where the British won they did so not just because the security forces achieved the first objective of any counter-insurgency campaign, dividing the civil population from the insurgents and protecting the civil population from intimidation directed at them by the insurgents; they also won because the civil population came to understand that the security forces and government could intimidate them more effectively than could the insurgents. The British may have talked as though they believed that counter-insurgency was a popularity contest, and that the prize was the 'hearts and minds' of the people. That was good public relations. It helped to disguise the sometimes unpalatable reality from both the British public and the wider international community of what they were really doing on the ground. They were applying heavy-handed policies of coercion to secure control over the civil population. On balance, where they won they did so by being nasty, not nice, to the people. This was aptly summed up by Andy Nicholl, who served as an infantryman in Malay in the mid-1950s. 'In the end, we won, and perhaps it was done by capturing the hearts and minds. But in a dirty little war, when you win their hearts and minds, you also have them by the b***s.'[2]

These issues are of more than just historical interest. At the beginning of the twenty-first century the British army believed that it had a better understanding of counter-insurgency operations than any other western military. In 2001 the MOD's manual on counter-insurgency operations boasted that 'The experience of numerous small wars has provided the British Army with a unique insight into

[2] J. McBeth, 'Britain's Vietnam', *Daily Mail*, 20 June 2009.

this demanding form of conflict'.[3] But much of the doctrine it had derived from this experience was based upon historical analysis that was at best ill-informed and at worst almost the opposite of what really happened. Armies use history as one of the foundations of the doctrines that guide current operations.[4] If they rely on misleading histories it is likely that their doctrines will lead them down some dangerous paths.[5]

A few examples will suffice to demonstrate this point. There is some truth in the contention that colonial governments in the era of decolonization were better placed to wage counter-insurgency operations than are most western governments today, and that the problems they faced were relatively uncomplicated compared to those confronting the Western powers in Iraq and Afghanistan in the early twenty-first century. But the contrast can be exaggerated. In Aden and Borneo the British faced a whole series of problems caused by the fact that they had to work alongside an independent indigenous government. In the Canal Zone they were actually operating in a foreign country whose government actively opposed their presence. Within the formal empire it would be an exaggeration to suggest that colonial regimes were failed states, but they did resemble fragile states. The governments were poor but remained just about viable. However, their ability to govern and protect the civil population was being eroded, insurgents were calling into question their legitimacy, and they no longer enjoyed a monopoly over the use of violence.[6] No colony had more than an exiguous cadre of senior European civil servants, a small, poorly equipped and inadequately trained police force, and a domestic intelligence service that was too small to do what was required of it.

It did not take much unrest to threaten to shake this system to its foundations and persuade governors to summon military assistance. But the size of the force that the British could send was itself limited. Most of the army had to be deployed in a conventional role in Europe. Shortages of money meant that neither the colonial state nor the British government could afford to raise all the indigenous forces that they might have wished to do. In any case political constraints meant that they could not deploy that manpower as freely as they would have liked. Nor were the British always the masters of the human terrain within which they operated. Soldiers and policemen imported into a rebellious colony could rarely speak the local languages and often had only the most exiguous understanding of local politics.

Too much can also be made of the apparently contrasting aims of mid-twentieth-century and early twenty-first-century insurgents. The objectives being pursued by

---

[3] MOD, *Army Field Manual Volume 1 Combined Arms Operations, Part 10 Counter Insurgency Operations: Strategic and Operational Guidelines*, B-2-1 July 2001.

[4] M. Howard, 'The use and abuse of military history', in M. Howard, *The Causes of War and Other Essays* (London: Templer Smith, 1983), 188–90; T. Farrell and S. Gordon, 'COIN machine: the British military in Afghanistan', *JRUSI*, vol. 154 (2009), 18.

[5] A point highlighted by J. K. Wither in his analysis on what went wrong for the British army in Basra between 2003 and 2007. J. K. Wither, 'Basra's not Belfast: the British Army, "Small Wars" and Iraq', *SW&I*, vol. 20 (2009), 611–35.

[6] MOD, *Security and Stabilisation*—Lexicon 9 & 10.

modern insurgents appear to some western observers to be vague and ill-defined. Some insurgents apparently want to re-establish the Caliphate. Others appear content to make Iraq and Afghanistan ungovernable by maintaining a high level of violence in the hope that they can persuade the western powers to leave in despair. The conclusion that some western observers have drawn is that negotiations with opponents whose objectives appear to be nebulous, negative, and opposed to western liberal norms is all but impossible.[7] But there is nothing new here. Maintaining such a level of violence that the colonial power would decide that the cost of remaining in place was too high was a tactic common to most insurgents in the era of decolonization. Those who aspire to restore the Caliphate reject western liberal values. But so did many of the insurgents the British fought in the era of decolonization and that fact did not, eventually, prove an insuperable barrier to negotiations. The British recognized, albeit reluctantly, that to make peace they eventually had to talk to their enemies.

But there are many ways in which the problems confronting western powers in Iraq and Afghanistan are different from those that their fathers and grandfathers faced in Palestine, Malaya, Kenya and elsewhere. Western powers have to come to terms with the consequences of the globalization of insurgency. Several of the insurgencies that the British confronted in the 'classical' period, such as the Mau Mau or the NAC, looked in vain for outside assistance, or such outside assistance as they did receive was limited to moral support, as in the case of the MCP. EOKA received only limited material support from Greece, although it, like the Zionist insurgents in Palestine, received vital moral and political backing from Greece and the USA respectively. Only in Aden and Borneo did the insurgents receive a significant level of both moral and material assistance from foreign powers. Today, in Iraq and Afghanistan, western powers are not so fortunate. Thanks to modern electronic media, the insurgents can generate support networks across the globe able to supply them with money, weapons, and recruits. They can also summon even more tangible assistance in the shape of home grown terrorism to attack their western enemies in their own homelands.[8] A successful counter-insurgency strategy must be able to contain both internal and external opponents.

Counter-insurgencies in the classical period were not conducted in a media vacuum. However, today counter-insurgents have to deal with the consequences of mobile and satellite phones, the internet, and 24-hour news coverage. Allied to these technological developments are the emergence of influential international human rights groups, and the growing power of 'lawfare', both developments which were only just beginning to affect how the British conducted their operations in the second half of the 1950s. But today these two developments make it

---

[7] M. Crawshaw, '"Running a country". The British colonial experience and its relevance to present-day concerns', *The Shrivenham Papers*, no. 3 (2007), 19; D. M. Jones and M. L. R. Smith, 'Whose hearts and whose minds? The curious case of global counter-insurgency', *JSS*, vol. 33 (2010), 110–12, 115–16.

[8] J. A. Nagl and B. M. Burton, 'Thinking globally and acting locally: counterinsurgency lessons from modern war—a reply to Jones and Smith', *JSS*, vol. 33 (2010), 135–6.

impossible for the British to apply many of the coercive techniques that they employed in the two decades after 1945.

Until the 1960s public support in Britain for military operations in the colonies remained fairly constant. Today, however, modern electronic media mean that insurgents can beam images of operations into the homes of western audiences and, by carefully choosing what images they project, can undermine domestic support for those operations amongst their viewers.[9] As Sir Richard Dannatt, a former Chief of the General Staff, wrote in December 2009, 'we need to win the hearts and minds of the people in Helmand. But perhaps more critically, we also need to win the hearts and minds of the people of this country, too. The biggest threat to our success in Afghanistan is not the Taliban, but a loss of will by the people at home to see this vital task through.'[10] In the past, insurgents operated in a fixed geographical area. Now they can operate on a global stage. The media effect of a military action, such as a suicide bomb, has become far more important than its tactical value. Conventional counter-insurgency operations focusing on the need to stabilize the situation on the ground, to secure territory, and to isolate in a physical sense the insurgents, have not become irrelevant. But they have to be coupled with parallel efforts to undermine the insurgents' media operations and eliminate their 'virtual sanctuary'.[11] Fighting and winning in the electronic battle space has become as important as winning in the conventional battle space. Building up a pool of experience to win on the ground has also proved even more difficult than in the past. Whereas National Servicemen spent at least a year in theatre in the 1950s, the professional soldiers and their Territorial Army colleagues fighting in Iraq and Afghanistan spent only six months on the ground before being flown home, taking their hard-won experience with them.

Although the state apparatus with which the British had to work in their colonies was often fragile, they did not usually face the problem of how to wage a counter-insurgency campaign while simultaneously setting about nation-building and state reconstruction. That said, British commanders in Aden did face problems similar to those that confronted their successor in south-eastern Iraq, a corrupt and inefficient FRA government, civil disorders, tribal feuding, and infiltration of the local security forces by their opponents. But nowhere in the classical period did British commanders have to work amongst the often bewildering array of coalition military commanders, civil officials and non-governmental actors that are commonplace in early twenty-first-century operations.

All this points to the fact that policy-makers (and historians) should be wary of trying to extrapolate easy 'lessons from history', particularly if this means examining single case studies, distilling general rules from them, and then trying to apply them

---

[9] Anon., 'After smart weapons, smart soldiers—Fighting insurgents. (Can regular armies beat insurgents?)' *The Economist* [US], 27 October 2007.

[10] Sir R Dannatt, 'Setting a date for withdrawal plays into the enemy's hands', *Sunday Telegraph*, 6 December 2009.

[11] D. Kilcullen, 'Counterinsurgency *redux*', *Survival: Global Politics and Strategy*, vol. 48 (2006), 112–13.

in radically difference circumstances.[12] The most that the study of history can do is to act as a guide to decision-makers' judgement and analysis. The past, in this case the record of British counter-insurgency campaigns in the two decades after the Second World War, was different from the present, although not always to quite the same degree, and in quite the same ways, as some writers have suggested. That was something that soldiers returning from Afghanistan and Iraq complaining that the 'stretched Malayan doctrine' did not work had discovered for themselves. Afghanistan was not Malaya, and the world had moved on since the lessons of Malay were codified. But unnoticed was the fact that the doctrine that had been distilled not only from Malay but also from Britain's other wars of decolonization, was in several respects not an accurate reflection of what the security forces and colonial governments had actually done. Misleading history had contributed to producing a misleading doctrine.

[12] A. Roberts, 'Doctrine and reality in Afghanistan', *Survival*, vol. 51 (2009), 35–7; K. M. Greenhill and P. Staniland, 'Ten ways to lose at counterinsurgency', *Civil Wars*, vol. 9 (2007), 402–6.

Bibliography

UNPUBLISHED PRIMARY SOURCES

National Archives, Public Record Office, Kew
Air Ministry: AIR 2
Cabinet: CAB, 8, 21, 69, 128, 129, 130, 131, 134, 148, 163, 182, 195
Colonial Office: CO 111, 115, 323, 537, 717, 822, 852, 859, 885, 926, 936, 968, 1015, 1022, 1027, 1030, 1031, 1035, 1037, 1055
Ministry of Defence: DEFE 7, 11, 13, 24, 28, 32, 70
Dominion Office: DO 169, 187
Foreign Office: FO 371
Lord Chancellor's Office: LCO 2, 53
Prime Minister's Office: PREM 8, 11, 13
Security Service: KV 4
Treasury: T 220
War Office: WO 32, 71, 106, 162, 163, 169, 191, 208, 216, 231, 236, 261, 268, 275, 276, 279, 291, 296, 305, 386

Imperial War Museum, Department of Documents
Maj.-Gen. T. H. Birkbeck MSS
Lt. Gen Sir Roger Bower MSS
Maj. C. R. Butt MSS
Field Marshal Lord Carver MSS
General Sir K. Darling MSS
General Sir G. W. Erskine MSS
Field Marshal Lord Harding MSS
Field Marshal Viscount Montgomery MSS
Maj.-Gen. Lewis Owain Pugh MSS
Mrs J. Sommerville MSS
J. K. Windeatt MSS

Imperial War Museum, Department of Sound Records
J. A. S. Adolph
'Anon' [Gen. Sir F. Kitson].
N. J. D. Baptiste
Col. J. P. Baxter
Maj.- Gen. H. E. N Bredin
R. J. D. E. Buckland
J. D. Buckmaster
Sir R. Catling
R. J. W. Craig
Lt.-Gen. Sir N. Crookenden
L. O. Crosland
J. L. H. Davis
Maj.-Gen. A. J. Deane-Drummond

Brigadier W. C. Deller
N. Dobson
Maj.-Gen. J. Dye
Col. P. Field
Sir H. M. Foot
M. Gilbert
Colonel J. S S. Gratton
Col. M. Gray
F. G. Green
Field Marshal Lord Harding
Col. A. S. Harvey
N. Harvey
F. C. Hayhurst
D. E. Henderson
T. L. Hewitson
A. H. P. Humphrey
D. Kelly
R. N. Kemp
R. Knutsen
D. J. Lear
A. L. K. Liddle
J. D. Mercer
J. M. Patrick
P. Plowright
J. A. Rymer-Jones
J. Sankey
E. W. Slade
R. A. A. Smith
Sir A. Swann
J. Taylor
Sir R. Thompson
K. Thorley
Gen. Sir D. Thorne
Sir R. G. Turnbull
Col. H. J. Todd
R. E. Wainwright
W. R. Watton
J. J. West
D. J. Wood
Col. J. Woodhouse
Maj.-Gen B. Wyldbore-Smith
Ezra Yakin

Liddell Hart Centre for Military Archives, King's College London
Maj.-Gen. J. B. Churcher
Maj.-Gen. W. A. Dimoline MSS
Maj.-Gen Charles Wish Dunbar MSS
General Sir H. E. Pyman MSS
Gen. Sir Hugh Stockwell MSS

National Army Museum
Gen. Sir Rob Lockhart MSS
Field Marshal Sir Gerald Templer MSS

Suffolk County Record Office
GB 554/Y1/304a. Brigadier I. L. Wight, 'Reflections of a Battalion Commander in Malaya', n.d.

Websites
Anon., 'The Lancs & the Tanks go into Action' Accessed 28 April 2002 at http://www. britains-smallwars.com/Canal/ISMAILIA-RIOTS.htm
Campbell, A., 'A Report from Kenya', *Time Magazine*, 30 March 1953, downloaded 13 March 2009 at http://www.time.com/time/magazine/article/0,9171,818044-1,00.html
Cater, D., 'After the Cutliffe Murder', downloaded 6 August 2009 at http://www. britains-smallwars. com/cyprus/Davidcarter/aftercutliffe/aftercutliffe.html
Convention concerning Forced or Compulsory Labour, 1930, downloaded 6 September 2009 at http://www.ilo.org/ilolex/cgi-lex/convde.pl?C029
The European Convention on Human Rights, downloaded 7 February 2010 at http://www.hri.org/docs/ECHR50.html.
Hunter, B., 'EOKA meets the Parachute Regiment', downloaded 20 April 2009 at http://www.britains-smallwars.com/cyprus/Davidcarter/hunter/arealisticapproach.html
Joint Services Command and Staff College, 'Library bibliography: Research Guide Series. Counterinsurgency (COIN), downloaded 12 July 2009 at http://www.da.mod.uk/colleges/jscsc/jscsc-library/bibliographies/research-guides
Stack-Hawkley, T., 'That Time in Kenya?', downloaded 13 April 2009 at http://www. nsrafa.org/%5CTimesRemembered.aspx
Universal Declaration of Human Rights', downloaded 7 February 2010 at http://www.un. org/en/documents/udhr/
Walker, A., 'The Intelligent Way', downloaded 20 April 2009 at http://www.britains-smallwars.com/cyprus/Davidcarter/Walker/intelcorps.html
Walton, C., 'Torture and intelligence gathering in Western democracies', downloaded 23 March 2010 at http://www.historyandpolicy.org/papers/policy-paper-78.html

TV documentary films
Empire Warriors. Kenya. The Hunt for Kimanthi, BBC, 2004.
Empire Warriors. Malaya 1948. The Intelligence War, BBC, 2004.
Empire Warriors The Jewish War, BBC, 2004.
Empire Warriors Aden—Mad Mitch and his Tribal Law, BBC, 2004.
Who do you think you are? Series 7. No. 9, Alan Cumming, BBC, 13 September 2010.

PUBLISHED PRIMARY SOURCES

Official Publications and Manuals
Callwell, Colonel C. E., *Small Wars. Their Principles and Practice* (London: General Staff, War Office, 1906, reprinted 1914).
[Cmnd 0672]. *Colonial Development and Welfare Acts*, February. 1959.
Hansards Parliamentary Debates
MOD, *Army Doctrine Publication. Vol. 1 Operations* (London: DGD&D/18/34/46, 1994).

—— *Army Field Manual Volume 1 Combined Arms Operations, Part 10 Counter Insurgency Operations: Strategic and Operational Guidelines* (London, Ministry of Defence, 2001).

—— *Joint Warfare Publication (JW3-50). Military Contribution to Peace Support Operations* (London: Ministry of Defence: 2nd edn, 2004).

MOD, *Joint Doctrine Publication 3–40. Security and Stabilization: the Military Contribution* (London: Ministry of Defence, 2009).

Skeen, Gen. Sir A., *Lessons in Imperial Rule. Instructions for British Infantrymen on the Indian Frontier* (London: Frontline Books, 2008).

US Army and Marine Corps's Field Manual, *FM 3-24/*MCWP 3-33.5, Counterinsurgency* (December. 2006).

War Office, *Manual of Military Law, 1929* (London: HMSO, 1929).

—— *King's Regulations for the Army and the Royal Army Reserve 1940* (London: HMSO, 1940).

—— *Manual of Military Law, 1951–59. Part (II). 1951. Section V. Employment of Troops in Aid of the Civil Power* (London: War Office, 1955).

—— *Queen's Regulations for the Army 1955* (London: HMSO, 1955).

—— *Manual of Military Law. Part 1. 1956* (London: HMSO, 1956).

—— *The Law of War on Land being Part (II) of the Manual of Military Law* (London: HMSO, 1958).

Newspapers and Works of Reference

Al-Ahram *Weekly Online*
Daily Mail
Daily Telegraph
Evening Standard
Financial Times
Jerusalem Post
Manchester Guardian and *Guardian*
New Straits Times (Malaysia)
New York Times
Observer
Oxford Dictionary of National Biography
Palestine Post
Sunday Mail and *The Mail on Sunday*
Sunday Telegraph
The Independent on Sunday
Times
Whitaker's Almanac (London: John Whitaker, various dates).

Memoirs and collections of documents

Begin, M., *The Revolt* (London: W. H. Allen, rev. edn., 1979; first published 1952).

Blacker, Gen. Sir C., *Monkey Business. The Memoirs of General Sir Cecil Blacker* (London: Quiller Press, 1993).

Bruton, P., *A Captain's Mandate. Palestine 1946 to 1948* (London: Leo Cooper, 1996).

Campbell, A., *Jungle Green* (London: Allen & Unwin, 1953).

Catterall, P., (ed.), *The Macmillan Diaries. The Cabinet Years, 1950–1957* (London: Macmillan, 2003).

Chynoweth, J., *Hunting Terrorists in the Jungle. The Experiences of a National Service Subaltern in Malaya in the 1950s* (Stroud, Glouc: Tempus, 2005).

Colville, J., *The Fringes of Power. Downing Street Diaries 1939–1955* (London: Hodder and Stoughton, 1985).

Cross, P., *'A Face Like a Chicken's Backside'. An Unconventional Soldier in South East Asia, 1948–1971* (London: Greenhill Books, 1996).

Dover, Maj. V., *The Silken Canopy* (London: Cassell, 1979).

Faulkner, C., *A Two-Year Wonder. The Kenya Police 1953–1955* (Livingston: Librario, 2004).

Foley, C. (ed.), *The Memoirs of General Grivas* (London: Longman, 1964).

Follows, R., *The Jungle Beat. Fighting Terrorists in Malaya* (Bridnorth, Shrops.: Travellers Eye Ltd, 1999).

Frost, Maj.-Gen. J., *Nearly There. The Memoirs of John Frost of Arnhem Bridge* (London: Leo Cooper, 1991).

Hall, Colonel P., *Jungle Jim* (Privately Published, 1995).

Hatton, T., *Tock Tock Birds* (Lewis, Sussex: The Book Guild, 2004).

Hewitt, P., *Kenya Cowboy. A Police Officer's Account of the Mau Mau Emergency* (London: Avon Books, 1999).

Hosmer S., and Crane, S. O. (eds), *Counterinsurgency: A Symposium, 16–20 April 1962* (Santa Monica, CA: Rand Corporation, 1963/2006).

Kitson, Gen. Sir F., *Bunch of Five* (London: Faber & Faber, 1977).

Miers, R., *Shoot to Kill* (London: Faber & Faber, 1959).

Mitchell, Lt.-Col. C., *Having Been a Soldier* (London: Hamish Hamilton, 1969).

Moran, J. W. G., *Spearhead in Malaya* (London: Peter Davis, 1959).

Nelson, Maj.-Gen. Sir J., *Always a Grenadier* (Privately Published, n.d.).

Peng, C., *My Side of History* (Singapore: Media Masters, 2003).

Peter Mills, I. V. B., *The Dawn Stand-to* (Devon: Edward Gaskill, 2000).

Perkins, K., *A Fortunate Soldier* (London: Brassey's, 1988).

Pimlott, B. (ed.), *The Political Diary of Hugh Dalton, 1918–40, 1945–60* (London: Jonathan Cape, 1986).

Redgrave, R., *Balkan Blue. Family and Military Memories* (Barnsley: Leo Cooper, 2000).

Smiley, D., *Arabian Assignment* (London: Leo Cooper, 1975).

Starling, J., *Soldier On! The Testament of a Tom* (Tunbridge Wells: Spellmount, 1992).

Thompson, Sir R., *Make for the Hills. Memories of Far Eastern Wars* (London: Leo Cooper, 1989).

Wilson, D., *The Sum of Things* (Staplehurst, Kent: Spellmount, 2001).

Wilson, Maj.-Gen. D., *Tempting the Fates. A Memoir of Service in the Second World War, Palestine, Korea, Kenya and Aden* (Barnsley: Pen & Sword, 2006).

PUBLISHED SECONDARY SOURCES

Aldrich, R., *The Hidden Hand. Britain, America and Cold War Secret Intelligence* (London: John Murray, 2001).

—— *GCHQ. The Uncensored Story of Britain's Most Secret Intelligence Agency* (London: Harper Press, 2010).

Anderson, D., 'Policing and communal conflict: the Cyprus emergency, 1954–60', in D. M. Anderson and D. Killingray (eds), *Policing and Decolonisation. Politics, nationalism and the police, 1917–1965* (Manchester: Manchester University Press, 1992), 187–217.

—— *Histories of the Hanged. Britain's Dirty War in Kenya and the End of Empire* (London: Weidenfeld & Nicolson, 2005).

Andrew, C., *The Defence of the Realm. The Authorised History of MI5* (London: Allen Lane, 2009).

Anon., 'Operation Lowestoft. An account of a successful anti-bandit operation by 1/Suffolk Regiment and Malay police in Negri Sembilan', *British Army Journal*, no. 4 (July. 1950), 16–19.

——'Malaya Section', *British Army Journal*, no. 5 (January 1951), 50–2.

——'Malaya: terrorist casualties for the period September 1949 to September 1952', *The Newsletter of the Green Howards Regimental Museum*, No. 5 (April 1998), 20.

——'The Lancs & the Tanks go into Action' Accessed 28 April 2002 at http://www.britains-smallwars.com/Canal/ISMAILIA-RIOTS.htm

——'After smart weapons, smart soldiers—Fighting insurgents (Can regular armies beat insurgents?)', *The Economist* [US], 27 October 2007.

Argote, L., and Epple, D., 'Learning curves in manufacturing, *Science*, vol. 247 (1990), 920–4.

Argote, L., Beckman, S. L., and Epple, D., 'The persistence and transfer of learning in industrial settings', *Management Science*, vol. 36 (1990), 140–54.

Artley, Lt. C., 'A change of tactics', *The Newsletter of the Green Howards Regimental Museum*, no. 5 (April 1998), 16.

Avant, D. D., *Political Institutions and Military Change. Lessons from Peripheral Wars* (Ithaca NY: Cornell University Press, 1994).

Baker, C., *State of Emergency: Crisis in Central Africa, Nyasaland, 1959–60* (London: I. B. Tauris, 1997).

Ball, S., 'Bomber bases and British strategy in the Middle East, 1945–49', *JSS*, vol. 14 (1991), 515–33.

Bauer, Y., 'From Cooperation to Resistance: The Haganha 1938–1946', *Middle Eastern Studies*, vol. 2 (1966), 182–210.

Bayer, K., and Ogilvy, G., 'Veterans' fury at "Malay massacre" claim', *Scotland on Sunday*, 14 December 2003, accessed 17 November 2006 at http://scotlandonsunday.scotsman.com/index.cfm?id=1371332003

Beckett, I. F. W., *Modern Insurgencies and Counter-Insurgencies. Guerrillas and their Opponents since 1750* (London: Routledge, 2001).

Bellis, M. A. *The British Army Overseas 1945–1970* (Privately Published, 2001).

Benbow, T., 'Introduction', in T. Benbow and R. Thornton (eds), *Dimensions of Counter-insurgency. Applying Experience to Practice* (London: Routledge, 2008), xiii–xviii.

——'Maritime Forces and Counter-insurgency', in T. Benbow and R. Thornton (eds), *Dimensions of Counter-insurgency. Applying Experience to Practice* (London: Routledge, 2008), 74–89.

Benest, D., 'British Leaders and Irregular Warfare', *The Defence Academy Journal* (December 2007), 1–16.

Bennett, H., 'British Army counterinsurgency and the use of force in Kenya, 1952–56' (Ph.D. dissertation, University of Wales, Aberystwyth, 2007).

——'"A very salutary effect": the counter-terror strategy in the early Malayan emergency, June 1948 to December 1949', *JSS*, vol. 32 (2009), 415–44.

Best, G., *War and Law since 1945* (Oxford: Oxford University Press, 1994).

Berman, B. J., 'Bureaucracy and incumbent violence: colonial administration and the origins of the Mau Mau emergency', *British Journal of Political Science*, vol. 6 (1976), 143–75.

Betz, D., and Cormack, A., 'Iraq, Afghanistan and British Strategy', *Orbis* (Spring 2009), 319–36.

Blacker, J., 'The demography of Mau Mau: fertility and mortality in Kenya in the 1950s: a demographer's viewpoint', *African Affairs*, vol. 106 (2007), 205–27.

Blaxland, G., *The Regiments Depart. A History of the British Army 1945–1970* (London: William Kimber, 1971).

Bonner, D., *Executive Measures, Terrorism and National Security. Have the Rules of the Game Changed?* (London: Ashgate, 2007).

Boyce, D. G., 'From Assaye to Assaye: reflections on British government, force and moral authority in India', *Journal of Military History*, vol. 63 (1999), 643–68.

Branch, D., 'Imprisonment and Colonialism in Kenya, c.1930–1952: Escaping the Carceral Archipelago', *The International Journal of African Historical Studies*, vol. 38, no. 2 (2005), 239–65.

——'The enemy within: loyalists and the war against Mau Mau in Kenya', *Journal of African History*, vol. 48 (2007), 291–315.

——*Defeating Mau Mau, Creating Kenya. Counterinsurgency, Civil War, and Decolonization* (Cambridge: Cambridge University Press. 2009).

——'Footprints in the sand: British colonial counterinsurgency and the war in Iraq', *Politics & Society*, vol. 38 (2010), 15–34.

Brenner, Y. S., 'The "Stern Gang" 1940–48', *Middle Eastern Studies*, vol. 2 (1965), 2–30.

Brownell, J., 'The taint of communism: the Movement for Colonial Freedom, the Labour Party, and the Communist Party of Great Britain', *Canadian Journal of History*, vol. 42 (2007), 235–58.

Brownlie, I., 'Interrogation in Depth: The Compton and Parker Reports,' *The Modern Law Review*, vol. 35 (1972), 501–7.

Butler, D., and Butler, G., *British Political Facts 1900–1985* (London: Macmillan, 1988).

Butler, L. J., 'Britain, the United States and the demise of the Central African Federation', *JICH*, vol. 28 (2001), 131–51.

——*Britain and Empire. Adjusting to a Post-Imperial World* (London: I. B. Taurus, 2002).

Campbell, A., 'A Report from Kenya', *Time Magazine* (30 March 1953), downloaded 13 March 2009 at http://www.time.com/time/magazine/article/0,9171,818044-1,00.html

Cann III, J. P., 'Portuguese Counterinsurgency Campaigning in Africa—1961–1974: A Military Analysis' (Ph.D. dissertation, University of London, 1996).

Carew, Captain J. M. 'All this and a medal too', *British Army Journal*, no. 3 (January 1950), 65–71.

Carruthers, S. L. *Winning Hearts and Minds. British Governments, the Media and Colonial Counter-Insurgency 1944–1960* (Leicester: Leicester University Press, 1995).

——'Being beastly to the Mau Mau', *Twentieth Century British History*, vol. 16 (2005), 489–96.

Cassidy, Lt.-Col. R. M., 'The British army and counter-insurgency: the salience of military culture', *Military Review* (May–June 2005), 53–9.

Cater, D., 'After the Cutliffe Murder', downloaded 6 August 2009 at http://www.britains-smallwars.com/cyprus/Davidcarter/aftercutliffe/aftercutliffe.html

Cell, J. W., 'Colonial rule', in J. M. Brown and Wm. Roger Louis (eds), *The Oxford History of the British Empire* (Oxford: Oxford University Press, 1999), 232–54.

Cesarani, D., *Major Farran's Hat* (London: William Heineman, 2009).

——'The British security forces and the Jews in Palestine, 1945–48', in Claus-Christian W. Szejnmann (ed.), *Rethinking History, Dictatorship and War* (London: Continuum, 2009), 191–210.

Charters, D. A., *The British Army and Jewish Insurgency in Palestine, 1945–47* (London: Macmillan, 1989).

——'Eyes of the underground: Jewish insurgent intelligence in Palestine, 1945 to 1947', *INS*, vol. 13 (1998), 163–77.

Chin, W., 'Examining the Application of British Counterinsurgency Doctrine by the American Army in Iraq', *SW&I*, vol. 18 (2007) 1–26.

Clayton, A., *Counter-insurgency in Kenya 1952–60. A study of military operations against Mau Mau* (Nairobi: Transafrica Publishers, 1976).

Cleary, A. S., 'The myth of Mau Mau in its international context', *African Affairs*, vol. 89 (1990), 227–45.

Cline, L. E., *Pseudo Operations and Counterinsurgency: Lessons From Other Countries* (Carlisle, PA: Strategic Studies Institute, 2005).

Cloake, J., *Templer. Tiger of Malaya* (London: Harrap, 1985).

Comber, L. 'The Malayan Security Service (1945–1948)', *INS*, vol. 18 (2003), 128–53.

——*Malaya's Secret Police 1945–60. The Role of the Special Branch in the Malayan Emergency* (Victoria, Australia: Monash University Press, 2008).

Cooper-Key, Maj. E. A., 'Some reflections on Cyprus', *British Army Review*, no. 5 (September 1957), 40–3.

Corum, J. S.,'Air control. Reassessing the history', *Royal Air Force Air Power Review*, vol. 4 (2001), 15–36.

——'Training indigenous forces in counterinsurgency: a tale of two insurgencies', 26–7. Downloaded 14 December 2009 at http://www.StrategicStudiesInstitute.army.mil/

Cradock, C., and Smith, M. L. R., 'No Fixed Values' A Reinterpretation of the Influence of the Theory of guerre révolutionnaire and the Battle of Algiers, 1956–1957', *Journal of Cold War Studies*, vol. 9, (2007), 68–105.

Crawshaw, M., '"Running a country". The British Colonial experience and its relevance to present-day concerns', *The Shrivenham Papers*, no. 3 (2007), 1–36.

Crawshaw, N., *The Cyprus Revolt* (London: Allen & Unwin, 1978).

Croker, Maj. G. W., 'Mau Mau', *JRUSI*, vol. 100 (1955), 47–53.

Cunninghm, C., 'International Interrogation Techniques', *JRUSI*, vol. 117 (June 1972), 31–4.

Darwin, J., *Britain and Decolonisation. The Retreat from Empire in the Post-War World* (London: Macmillan, 1988).

——*The End of the British Empire* (Oxford: Blackwell, 1991).

——*The Empire Project. The Rise and Fall of the British World-System 1830–1970* (Cambridge: Cambridge University Press, 2009).

Deery, P., 'The terminology of Terrorism: Malaya, 1948–52', *Journal of South East Asian Studies*, vol. 34 (2003), 231–47.

——'Malaya, 1948. Britain's Asian Cold War?', *Journal of Cold War Studies*, vol. 9 (2007), 29–54.

Dewar, Lt.-Col. M., *Brush Fire Wars. Minor Campaigns of the British Army since 1945* (London: Robert Hale, 1984).

Dewhurst, J., 'Complicity', *British Medical Journal*, 22 January 2005.

Dicey, A. V., *Introduction to the Study of the Law of the Constitution* (London: Macmillan, 1914).

Dimitrakis, P., 'British Intelligence and the Cyprus Insurgency, 1955–1959', *International Journal of Intelligence and Counter Intelligence*, vol. 21 (2008), 375–89.

Dixon, P., 'Britain's "Vietnam syndrome"? Public opinion and British military intervention from Palestine to Yugoslavia', *Review of International Studies*, vol. 26 (2000), 99–121.

——'"Hearts and Minds"? British counter-insurgency from Malaya to Iraq', *JSS*, vol. 32 (2009), 353–81.

Dorril, S., *MI6. Fifty Years of Special Operations* (London: Fourth Estate, 2001).

Dunlap Jr, Maj.-Gen. Charles J., 'Lawfare today: a perspective', *Yale Journal of International Affairs* (Winter 2008), 146–54.

——'Lawfare: a decisive element of 21st Century conflicts?', *Joint Forces Quarterly*, no. 54, (2009), 34–9.

Easter, D., 'British intelligence and propaganda during the "Confrontation", 1963–1966', *INS*, vol. 16 (2001), 83–102.

——*Britain and the Confrontation with Indonesia, 1960–66* (London: Tauris Academic Studies, 2004).

Efimova, L., 'Did the Soviet Union instruct Southeast Asian communists to revolt? New Russian evidence on the Calcutta Youth conference of February 1948', *Journal of South East Asian Studies*, vol. 40 (2009), 449–69.

Eickman, D. F., 'From theocracy to monarchy: authority and legitimacy in inner Oman, 1935–57', *International Journal of Middle Eastern Studies*, vol. 17 (1985), 3–24.

Elkins, C., *Britain's Gulag. The Brutal End of Empire in Kenya* (London: Jonathan Cape, 2005).

Elstein, D., 'Tell me where I'm wrong', *London Review of Books*, vol. 27, no. 11, 2 (June 2005).

Erskine, Gen. Sir G., 'Kenya—Mau Mau', *JRUSI*, vol. 101 (1956), 11–22.

Farrell, T., and Gordon, S., 'COIN machine: The British military in Afghanistan', *JRUSI*, vol. 154 (2009), 18–25.

Fedorowich, K., 'Axis prisoners of war as sources for British military intelligence, 1939–42', *INS*, vol. 14 (1999), 156–78.

Feinstein, C. H., 'The end of empire and the golden age', in P. Clarke and C. Trebilcock (eds), *Understanding Decline. Perceptions and Realities of British Economic Performance* (Cambridge: Cambridge University Press, 1997), 212–33.

Fieldhouse, D. K., *Western Imperialism in the Middle East, 1914–1958* (Oxford: Oxford University Press, 2006).

Fitzsimmons, M., 'Hard Hearts and Open Minds? Governance, Identity and the Intellectual Foundations of Counterinsurgency Strategy', *JSS*, vol. 31 (2008), 337–65.

Flint, J., 'Planned decolonisation and its failure in British Africa', *African Affairs*, vol. 82 (1983), 389–411.

Foley, C., and Scobie, W. I. *The Struggle for Cyprus* (Stanford, Calif: Hoover Institution Press, 1975).

French, D., *Military Identities. The Regimental System, the British Army, and the British People c. 1870–2000* (Oxford: Oxford University Press, 2005).

Fui, Lim Hin, and Yong, Fong Tian, *The New Villages in Malaysia—the Journey Ahead* (Kuala Lumpur: Institute of Strategic Analysis and Policy Research, 2005),

Furedi, F., *Colonial Wars and the Politics of Third World Nationalism* (London: I. B. Tauris, 1998).

Gentry, J., 'Intelligence learning and adaptation: lessons from counterinsurgency wars', *INS*, vol. 25 (2010), 50–75.

Gordon Simpson, J., 'Not by bombs alone', *Joint Forces Quarterly* (1999), 91–8.

Greenhill, K. M., and Staniland, P., 'Ten Ways to lose at counterinsurgency', *Civil Wars*, vol. 9 (2007), 402–19.

Gregorian, R., '"Jungle bashing" in Malaya: towards a formal tactical doctrine', *SW&I*, vol. 5 (1994), 338–59.

Grover, Maj. J. A, 'Aid to the civil power, Kenya—1952', *British Army Journal*, no. 10 (July 1953), 30–2.

Gwynn, Maj.-Gen. Sir C. W., *Imperial Policing* (London: Macmillan, 1934).

Hack, K., 'British intelligence and counter-insurgency in the era of decolonisation: the example of Malaya,' *INS*, vol. 14 (1999), 124–55.

—— 'Corpses, prisoners of war and captured documents: British and Communist narratives of the Malayan Emergency, and the dynamics of intelligence transformation', *INS*, vol. 14 (1999), 211–41.

Hahn, P. L., 'Containment and Egyptian nationalism: the unsuccessful effort to establish the Middle East Command, 1950–53', *Diplomatic History*, vol. 11 (1987), 23–40.

Hall, B., and Ross, A., 'The political and military effectiveness of Commonwealth forces in Confrontation 1963–66', *SW&I*, Vol. 19 (2008), 238–55.

Halliday, Maj. P., 'Employment of the Intelligence Corps', *British Army Review*, No 10 (April 1960), 22–3.

Hargreaves, J. D., *Decolonization in Africa* (London: Longman, 1996).

Harper, S., *Last Sunset. What Happened in Aden* (London: Collins, 1978).

Harper, T. N., *The End of Empire and the Making of Malaya* (Cambridge: Cambridge University Press, 1999).

Hart, P., *The IRA and its Enemies. Violence and Community in Cork 1916–1923* (Oxford: Oxford University Press, 1998).

—— *The Heat of Battle: 16th Battalion Durham Light Infantry 1943–45. The Italian Campaign* (London: Leo Cooper, 1999).

Heather, R. W., 'Intelligence and counter-insurgency in Kenya, 1952–56', *INS*, vol. 5 (1990), 57–83.

Heinlein, F., *British Government Policy and Decolonisation 1945–1963. Scrutinising the Official Mind* (London: Frank Cass, 2002).

Hemming, P. E., 'Macmillan and the end of the British empire in Africa', in R. Aldous and S. Lee (eds), *Harold Macmillan and Britain's World Role* (London: Macmillan, 1996), 97–124.

Hoare, O. (ed.), *Camp 020. MI5 and Nazi spies. The Official History of MI5's Wartime Interrogation Centre* (London: Public Record Office, 2000).

Holland, R. F., 'The imperial factor in British strategies from Attlee to Macmillan, 1945–1963', *JICH*, vol. 12 (1984), 165–86.

Holland, R. F., *Britain and the Revolt in Cyprus 1954–1959* (Oxford: Oxford University Press, 1998).

Hopkins, A. G., 'Rethinking Decolonization', *Past and Present*, no. 200 (2008), 211–47.

Hopkins, T., 'Macmillan's audit of empire, 1957', in P. Clarke and C. Trebilcock (eds), *Understanding Decline. Perceptions and Realities of British Economic Performance* (Cambridge: Cambridge University Press, 1997), 234–59.

Horowitz, D., 'Attitudes of British Conservatives towards decolonization in Africa', *African Affairs*, vol. 69 (1970), 9–26.

Howard, M., *The Causes of War and Other Essays* (London: Templer Smith, 1983).

Howe, S., *Anticolonialism in British Politics. The Left and the End of Empire, 1918–1964* (Oxford: Clarendon Press, 1993).

Hughes, G., 'A "Model Campaign Reappraised: The Counter-Insurgency War in Dhofar, Oman, 1965–1975', *JSS*, vol. 32 (2009), 271–305.

—— and Tripodi, C., 'Anatomy of a surrogate: historical precedents and implications for contemporary counter-insurgency and counter-terrorism', *SW&I*, vol. 20 (March 2009), 1–35.

Hughes, M., 'The banality of brutality: British armed forces and the repression of the Arab revolt in Palestine, 1936–39', *EHR*, vol. 124 (2009), 313–54.

Hughes, M., 'The practice and theory of British counterinsurgency: the histories of the atrocities at the Palestinian villages of al-Basa and Halhul, 1938–39', *SW&I*, vol. 20 (2009), 528–50.

Hunt, Wing-Commander B. J., 'Air Power and Psychological Warfare Operations Malaya 1948–1960', *Air Power Review*, vol. 11 (2008), 6–18.

Hunter, B., 'EOKA meets the Parachute Regiment', Downloaded 20 April 2009 at http://www.britains-smallwars.com/cyprus/Davidcarter/hunter/arealisticapproach.html

Hutchinson, S., 'The police role in counter-insurgency operations', *JRUSI*, vol. 114, no. 656 (1969), 56–61.

Hyam, R., 'The geopolitical origins of the Central African Federation: Britain, Rhodesia and South Africa, 1948–63', *Historical Journal*, vol. 30 (1987), 145–72.

Hynd, S., 'Killing the condemned: the practise and process of capital punishment in British Africa, 1900–1950s', *Journal of African History*, 49 (2008), 403–18.

——'Decorum or deterrence? The politics of execution in Malawi, 1915–66', *Cultural and Social History*, vol. 5 (2008), 437–48.

Ibhawoh, B., 'Stronger than the maxim gun. Law, human rights and British colonial hegemony in Nigeria', *Africa*, vol. 72 (2002), 55–81.

Jackson, A., 'British counter-insurgency in history: a useful historical precedent?' *British Army Review*, no. 139 (2006), 12–22.

Jackson, Gen. Sir W., *Withdrawal From Empire. A Military View* (London: Batsford, 1986).

Jeffery, K., 'Intelligence and Counter-Insurgency Operations: some reflections on the British experience', *INS*, vol. 2 (1987), 118–49.

Jones, D. M., and Smith, M. L. R., 'Whose hearts and whose minds? The curious case of global counter-insurgency', *JSS*, vol. 33 (2010), 81–121.

Jones, T., *Postwar Counterinsurgency and the SAS, 1945 to 1952. A Special Type of Warfare* (London: Cass, 2001).

Jordan, D., 'Counter-insurgency from the air: the post-war lessons', in T. Benbow and R. Thornton (eds), *Dimensions of Counter-insurgency. Applying Experience to Practice* (London: Routledge, 2008), 90–105.

Kelemen, P., 'Modernizing colonialism: the British Labour movement and Africa', *JICH*, vol. 34 (2006), 223–44.

Kent, J., 'The Egyptian base and the defence of the Middle East, 1945 to 1954', in R. Holland (ed.), *Emergencies and Disorder in the European Empires after 1945* (London: Cass, 1994), 45–65.

Kerr, R., 'A Force for Good? War, Crime and Legitimacy: The British Army in Iraq', *Defense and Security Analysis*, vol. 24 (2008), 401–19.

Kilcullen, D., 'Counterinsurgency *redux*', *Survival: Global Politics and Strategy*, vol. 48 (2006), 111–30.

Killingray, D., 'The idea of a British Imperial Army', *Journal of African History*, vol. 20 (1979), 421–36.

——'The maintenance of law and order in British colonial Africa', *African Affairs*, vol. 85 (1986), 411–37.

Kingston, P. W. T., *Britain and the Politics of Modernization in the Middle East 1945–1958* (Cambridge: Cambridge University Press, 1996).

Kirk-Greene, A. H. M., 'The Thin White Line: the size of the British Colonial Service in Africa', *African Affairs*, vol. 79 (1980), 25–44.

——*On Crown Service. A History of HM Colonial and Overseas Civil Service, 1837–1997* (London: I. B. Tauris, 1999).

Kitson, F., *Low Intensity Operations. Subversion, Insurgency, Peace-Keeping* (London: Faber & Faber, 1971).

Kizley, J., 'Learning about counter-insurgency', *JRUSI*, vol. 151 (2006), 16–21.

Knox, B. A., 'The British Government and the Governor Eyre Controversy, 1865–1875', *Historical Journal*, vol. 19 (1976), 877–900.

Komer, R. W., *The Malayan Emergency in Retrospect: Organization of a Successful Counter-insurgency Effort* (Santa Monica, CA: Rand Corporation, 1972).

Krozewski, G., 'Sterling, the "Minor" territories, and the end of formal empire, 1939–1958', *Economic History Review*, vol. 46 (1993), 239–65.

Ladwig III, W. C., 'Supporting allies in counterinsurgency: Britain and the Dhofar Rebellion', *SWI*, vol. 19 (2008), 62–88.

Lamb, C., 'What a bloody hopeless war; Interview', *Sunday Times*, 10 September 2006.

Lazreg, L., *Torture and the Twilight of Empire from Algiers to Baghdad* (Princeton, NJ: Princeton University Press, 2008).

Leeson, D., 'Death in the afternoon: the Croke Park massacre, 21 November 1920', *Canadian Journal of History*, vol. 38 (2003), 43–67.

Lonsdale, J., 'Mau Maus of the mind: making Mau Mau and the remaking of Kenya', *Journal of African History*, vol. 31, no. 3 (1990), 393–421.

Macfie, A. L., 'My Orientalism', *Journal of Postcolonial Writing*, vol. 45 (2009), 83–90.

Mackinlay, J., 'Is UK doctrine relevant to global insurgency', *JRUSI*, vol. 152 (2007), 34–8.

Maconochie, Rifleman C., 'A National Serviceman in Malaya', *Army Quarterly*, vol. 63. 1 (October 1951), 43–50.

Majid, H.A., *Rebellion in Brunei. The 1962 Revolt, Imperialism, Confrontation, and Oil* (London: I. B. Tauris, 2007).

Mander, Lt.-Col. A. J. D'Arcy, 'Reluctant Heroes. Our National Servicemen in Malaya', *The Newsletter of the Green Howards Regimental Museum*, no. 5 (April 1998), 8.

Markel, W., 'Draining the Swamp: The British Strategy of Population Control', *Parameters*, Spring 2006, 35–48.

Marshall, A., 'Imperial nostalgia, the liberal lie, and the perils of postmodern counter-insurgency', *SW&I*, vol. 21 (2010), 233–58.

Martel, G., 'Decolonisation after Suez: retreat or rationalisation?', *Australian Journal of Politics and History*, vol. 46 (2000), 403–17.

Mason, T. D., and Krane, D. A.,'The Political Economy of Death Squads: Toward a Theory of the Impact of State-Sanctioned Terror', *International Studies Quarterly*, vol. 33, no. 2 (June, 1989), 175–98.

Mawby, S., 'Britain's Last Imperial Frontier: The Aden Protectorates, 1952–59', *JICH*, vol. 29 (2001), 75–100.

——*British Policy in Aden and the Protectorates 1955 to1967. Last outpost of a Middle East Empire* (London: Routledge, 2005).

——'Orientalism and the failure of British policy in the Middle East: the case of Aden', *History*, vol. 95 (2010), 332–53.

McInnes, C., *Hot War, Cold War. The British Army's Way in Warfare 1945–95* (London: Brassey's, 1996).

McMillan, R., *The British occupation of Indonesia 1945–1946* (London: Routledge, 2005).

McConville, M., 'General Templer's Capitol idea' Downloaded on 30 March 2009 at http://www.themightyorgan.com/features_geese.html

Mcculloch, J., 'Empire and Violence, 1900–1939', in P. Levine (ed.), *Gender and Empire* (Oxford: Oxford University Press, 2004), 220–39.

Miles, O., 'The British withdrawal from Aden. A personal memory', downloaded 3 January 2009 at http://www.al-bab.com/bys/articles/miles.htm

Miller, S. M., 'Duty or Crime? Defining Acceptable Behaviour in the British Army in South Africa, 1899–1902', *Journal of British Studies*, vol. 49 (April 2010), 311–31.

Mockaitis, T. R., *British Counterinsurgency, 1919–60* (London: Macmillan, 1990).

—— 'Winning hearts and minds in the "war on terrorism"', *SW&I*, vol. 14 (2003), 21–38.

Morsy, L., 'The Military Clauses of the Anglo-Egyptian Treaty of Friendship and Alliance, 1936', *International Journal of Middle East Studies*, vol. 16 (1984), 67–97.

Moyar, M., *A Question of Command. Counterinsurgency from the Civil War to Iraq* (New Haven & London: Yale University Press, 2009).

Mumford, A., 'Unnecessary or unsung? The utilisation of airpower in Britain's colonial counterinsurgencies', *SW&I*, vol. 20 (2009), 636–55.

—— 'Sir Robert Thompson's Lessons for Iraq: Bringing the "Basic Principles of Counter-Insurgency" into the 21st Century', *Defence Studies*, vol. 10 (2010), 177–94.

Murphy, P., *Party Politics and Decolonization. The Conservative Party and British colonial policy in tropical Africa, 1951–64* (Oxford: Clarendon Press, 1995).

Nagl, J. A., *Learning to Eat Soup with a Knife. Counterinsurgency Lessons from Malaya and Vietnam* (Chicago: University of Chicago Press, 2002/2005).

—— and Burton, B. M., 'Thinking globally and acting locally: counterinsurgency lessons from modern war—a reply to Jones and Smith', *JSS*, vol. 33 (2010), 123–38.

Newsinger, J., 'Review of T. R. Mockaitis, "British Counterinsurgency 1919–1960"', *Race and Class*, vol. 34 (1992), 96–8.

—— *British Counterinsurgency from Palestine to Northern Ireland* (London: Palgrave, 2002).

Norris, J., 'Repression and Rebellion: Britain's Response to the Arab Revolt in Palestine of 1936–39,' *JICH*, vol. 36 (2008), 25–45.

Ogot, B. A., 'Review Article', *Journal of African History*, vol. 46 (2005), 493–505.

Omissi, D., Air Power and Colonial Control. *The Royal Air Force, 1919–1939* (Manchester: Manchester University Press, 1990).

Ovendale, R., 'The Palestine Policy of the British Labour government, 1945–46', *International Affairs*, vol. 55 (1979), 409–31.

—— 'The Palestine Policy of the British Labour government, 1947', *International Affairs*, vol. 56 (1980), 73–93.

—— 'Egypt and the Suez Base agreement', in J. W. Young (ed.), *The Foreign Policy of Churchill's Peacetime Administration 1951–1955* (Leicester: Leicester University Press, 1988), 135–58.

Paget, J., *Counter-Insurgency Campaigning* (London: Faber & Faber, 1967).

Packwood, Major L. V., 'Popular support as the objective in counter-insurgency. What are we really after', *Military Review* (May–June 2009), 67–77.

Palmer, R., 'European resistance to African majority rule. The Settlers and Residents Association of Nyasaland, 1960–63', *African Affairs*, vol. 72 (1973), 256–72.

Panagiotis, D., 'British Intelligence and the Cyprus Insurgency, 1955–1959', *International Journal of Intelligence and Counter Intelligence*, vol. 21 (2008), 375–89.

Percox, D. A., *Britain, Kenya and the Cold War. Imperial Defence, Colonial Security and Decolonization* (London: Tauris Academic Studies, 2004).

Peterson, J. E., *Oman's Insurgencies. The Sultanate's Struggle for Supremacy* (London: Saqi, 2007).

Phau, K. H., 'The development of health services in Malaya and Singapore 1867 to 1960', (Ph.D. dissertation, London School of Economics, 1987).

Pimlott, J., 'The British Army: the Dhofar campaign, 1970–1975', in I. F. W. Beckett and J. Pimlott (eds), *Armed Forces and Modern Counter-insurgency* (New York: St Martin's Press, 1985), 16–45.

Pound, Captain E. G. D, 'Operations in the Troodos sub-area', *British Army Review*, no. 3 (September 1956), 8–13.

Rahman, H., 'British post-Second World War military planning for the Middle East', *JSS*, vol. 5 (1982), 511–30.

Ramakrishna, K., 'Content, credibility and context: propaganda, government surrender policy and the Malayan Communist mass surrender of 1958', *INS*, vol. 19 (1999), 242–66.

——'Anatomy of a Collapse: Explaining The Malayan Communist Mass Surrenders of 1958', *War and Society*, vol. 21 (2003), 109–33.

Reynolds, W., 'Whatever happened to the Fourth British Empire? The Cold War, Empire defence and the USA, 1943–57', in M. F. Hopkins, M. D. Kandiah, and G. Staerck (eds), *Cold War Britain, 1945–1964* (London: Palgrave, 2003), 127–42.

Rid, T., 'Razzia: a turning point in modern strategy', *Terrorism and Political Violence*, vol. 21 (2009), 617–35.

Rielly, Lt.-Col. R., 'The inclination for war crimes', *Military Review* (May–June 2009), 17–23.

Roberts, A., 'Doctrine and Reality in Afghanistan', *Survival*, vol. 51 (2009), 29–60.

Roger Louis, Wm., *The British Empire in the Middle East 1945–51. Arab Nationalism, the United States, and post-war imperialism* (Oxford: Oxford University Press, 1984).

——'Public enemy Number 1: the British Empire in the dock at the United Nations, 1957–71', in M. Lynn (ed.), *The British Empire in the 1950s* (Basingstoke: Palgrave Macmillan, 2006), 186–213.

——and Robinson, R., 'The Imperialism of Decolonisation', *JICH*, vol. 22 (1994), 462–511.

Rose, J. G., 'British colonial policy and the transfer of power in British Guiana, 1945–1964' (Ph.D. dissertation, University of London, 1992).

Rose, N., *'A Senseless, Squalid War': Voices from Palestine 1945–1948* (London: Bodley Head, 2009).

Royle, T., *The Best Years of their Lives. The National Service Experience 1945–63* (London: Michael Jospeh, 1986).

Schultz, R., 'Force and military strategy: deterrence logic and the cost-benefit model of counterinsurgency warfare', *The Western Political Quarterly*, vol. 32, (1979), 444–60.

Scott Lucas, W., and Morey, A., 'The hidden "Alliance": the CIA and MI6 before and after Suez', *INS*, vol. 15 (2000), 95–120.

Seecharan, C., 'Whose Freedom at Midnight? Machinations towards Guyana's Independence, May 1966', *The Round Table*, vol. 97 (October 2008), 719–36.

Seedorf, M. F., 'The Lloyd George government and the Strickland report on the burning of Cork, 1920', *Albion*, vol. 4 (1972), 59–66.

Sellars, K., 'Human rights and the colonies: deceit, deception and discovery', *The Round Table*, vol. 93 (2004), 709–24.

Shallice, T., 'The Ulster depth interrogation techniques and their relation to sensory deprivation research', *Cognition*, vol. 1 (1973), 385–405.

Shoul, S. B., 'Soldiers, Riots and Aid to the Civil Power, in India, Egypt and Palestine, 1919–1939 (Ph.D. dissertation, London University, 2006).

Simpson, A. W. B., 'Round up the usual suspects: the legacy of British colonialism and the European convention on human rights', *Loyola Law Review*, vol. 41 (1995–96), 629–711.

Simpson, B., 'The Devlin commission (1959): Colonialism, emergencies, and the rule of law', *Oxford Journal of Legal Studies*, vol. 22 (2002), 17–52.

Sinclair, G., *At the End of the Line. Colonial Policing and the Imperial Endgame, 1945–80* (Manchester: Manchester University Press, 2006).

——' "Get into a crack force and earn £20 a month and all found . . .": the influence of the Palestine Police upon Colonial Policing 1922 to 1948', *European Review of History*, vol. 13 (2006), 49–65.

Siver, C., 'The Other Forgotten War: Understanding atrocities during the Malayan Emergency' (Prepared for delivery at the 2009 Annual Meeting of the American Political Science Association, 3–6 September 2009. Copyright by the American Political Science Association).

Smith, C., 'Communal conflict and insurrection in Palestine, 1936–48', in D. M. Anderson and D. Killingray (eds), *Policing and Decolonisation. Politics, Nationalism and the Police, 1917–1965* (Manchester: Manchester University Press, 1992), 62–83.

Smith, M.L.R., 'William of Ockham, Where Are You When We Need You? Reviewing Modern Terrorism Studies', *Journal of Contemporary History*, vol. 44 (2009), 319–34.

——and Roberts, S., 'War in the Gray: Exploring the Concept of Dirty War', *Studies in Conflict & Terrorism*, vol. 31 (2008), 377–98.

Smith, P. (ed.), *Government and the Armed Forces in Britain 1856–1990* (London: Hambledon Press, 1996).

Smith, R., and Zametica, J., 'The Cold Warrior: Clement Attlee reconsidered', *International Affairs*, vol. 61 (1985), 237–52.

Smith, S. C., 'Rulers and residents: British relations with the Aden Protectorate, 1937–1959', *Middle Eastern Studies*, vol. 31 (1995), 509–23.

——'General Templer and counter-insurgency in Malaya: hearts and minds, intelligence, and propaganda,' *INS*, vol. 16 (2001), 60–78.

Spear, T., 'Neo-traditionalism and the limits of invention in British colonial Africa', *Journal of African History*, vol. 44 (2003), 3–27.

Stack-Hawkley, T., 'That Time in Kenya?' Downloaded 13 April 2009 at: http://www. nsrafa.org/%5CTimesRemembered.aspx

Stammers, N., *Civil Liberties in Britain during the Second World War* (London: Croom Helm, 1983).

Stewart, B., 'The interrogation dilemma', *INS*, vol. 24 (2010), 642.

Stockwell, A. J., 'Insurgency and decolonization during the Malayan emergency', *Journal of Commonwealth and Comparative Politics*, vol. 25 (1987), 71–81.

——'Policing during the Malayan emergency, 1948–60: communism, communalism and decolonisation', in D. M. Anderson & D. Killingray (eds), *Policing and Decolonisation. Politics, nationalism and the police, 1917–1965* (Manchester: Manchester University Press, 1992), 105–26.

——'A widespread and long-concocted plot to overthrow government in Malaya? The origins of the Malayan emergency', *Journal of Imperial and Commonwealth History*, 21:3 (1993–4), 66–88.

Strachan, H., 'British counter-insurgency from Malaya to Iraq', *JRUSI*, vol. 152 (2007), 8–11.

Stubbs, R., *Hearts and Minds in Guerrilla Warfare. The Malayan Emergency 1948–60* (Oxford: Oxford University Press, 1989).

Subritzky, J., 'Britain, Konfrontasi, and the end of Empire in South East Asia, 1961–65', *Journal of Imperial and Commonwealth History*, vol. 28 (2000), 209–27.

Suther, Lt.-Col. C. A. I. 'A Malay Battalions' Task', *British Army Journal*, no. 7 (January 1952), 55–60.

Sutherland, R., *Resettlement and Food Control in Malaya* (Santa Monica, CA: Rand Corporation, 1964).

Sutton, K., 'Population Resettlement—Traumatic Upheavals and the Algerian Experience', *Journal of Modern African Studies*, vol. 15, no. 2 (June, 1977), 279–300.

Thomas, M., 'Algeria's violent struggle for independence', in M. Thomas, B. Moore, & L.J. Butler (eds), *Crises of Empire. Decolonization and Europe's Imperial States, 1918–1975* (London: Hodder Education, 2008), 228–51.

Thompson, Sir R., *Defeating Communist Insurgency. The Lessons of Malaya and Vietnam* (St Petersburg, Florida Hailer Publishing, 2005. Originally published 1966).

Thornhill, M. T., *Road to Suez. The Battle of the Canal Zone* (Stroud, Gloucs: Sutton Publishing, 2006).

Thornton, R., '"Minimum Force": a reply to Huw Bennett', *SW&I*, vol. 20 (2009), 215–26.

Throup, D., 'Crime, politics and the police in colonial Kenya, 1939–63', in D. M. Anderson and D. Killingray (eds), *Policing and Decolonisation. Politics, Nationalism and the Police, 1917–1965* (Manchester: Manchester University Press, 1992), 127–57.

Tignor, R. L., 'Colonial Chiefs in Chiefless societies', *Journal of Modern African Studies*, vol. 9 (1971), 339–59.

Townshend, C, 'The defence of Palestine: insurrection and public security, 1936–1939', *EHR*, vol. 103 (1988), 917–49.

Tripodi, C., 'British policy on the North-West Frontier of India 1877–1947: a suitable precedent for the modern day?', downloaded at: http://www.rusi.org/research/military-sciences/history/commentary/ref:C4AB377DACA5CF/, 28 September 2009.

Tuck, C., 'Borneo 1963–66: counter-insurgency operations and war termination', *SW&I*, vol. 15 (2004), 89–111.

——'The Royal Navy and Confrontation, 1963–66', in G. Kennedy (ed.), *British Naval Strategy East of Suez, 1900–2000* (London: Frank Cass, 2005), 199–220.

Ucko, D., 'Countering Insurgents through Distributed Operations: Insights from Malaya 1948–1960', *JSS*, vol. 30 (2007), 48–72.

——'The Malayan Emergency: The Legacy and Relevance of a Counter-Insurgency Success Story', *Defence Studies*, vol. 10 (2010), 13–39.

Utting, K., 'The strategic information campaign: lessons from the British experience in Palestine 1945–1948', in T. Benbow and R. Thornton (eds), *Dimensions of Counterinsurgency. Applying Experience to Practice* (London: Routledge, 2008), 36–56.

Vask, K., 'The European Convention of Human Rights beyond the Frontiers of Europe', *The International and Comparative Law Quarterly*, vol. 12, no. 4 (October, 1963), 1206–31.

Walker, A., 'The Intelligent Way', downloaded 20 April 2009 at http://www.britains-smallwars.com/cyprus/Davidcarter/Walker/intelcorps.html

Walker, J., *Aden Insurgency. The Savage War in South Arabia, 1962–67* (Staplehurst, Kent: Spellmount, 2005).

Walker, Gen. Sir W., 'Borneo', *British Army Review*, No 32 (August 1969), 7–15.

Walton, C., 'Torture and intelligence gathering in Western democracies', downloaded 23 March 2010 at http://www.historyandpolicy.org/papers/policy-paper-78.html

Wang, L. H., 'New Villages Growing Old in Malaysia', *Habitat International*, vol. 12 (1988), 35–42.

Whetham, D., 'Killing Within the Rules', *SW&I*, vol. 18 (2007), 721–33.

Wiener, M. J., *An Empire on Trial. Race, Murder, and Justice under British Rule, 1870–1935* (Cambridge: Cambridge University Press, 2009).

Willoughby, Maj.-Gen. Sir J., 'Problems of counter-insurgency in the Middle East', *JRUSI*, vol. 113 (May 1968), 104–12.

Wilson, Maj. R. D., *Cordon and Search. With 6th Airborne Division in Palestine* (Aldershot: Gale & Polden, 1949).

Wither, J. K., 'Basra's not Belfast: the British Army, "Small Wars" and Iraq', *SW&I*, vol. 20 (2009), 611–35.

Wolfendale, J., 'The myth of "torture lite"', *Ethics and International Affairs*, vol. 23 (2009), 47–61.

Index

Griffiths, Captain G. S. L.
  prosecuted for murder 168
Griffiths, James 13, 42
  counter-insurgency through coercion 66
  European Commission of Human Rights 229
Grivas, Colonel George 24, 25, 32, 48–9
  and enosis 62
Grogan, Colonel E. S. 66
Gruner, Dov 148
'Guerre révolutionnaire' 137
Gurkhas 36, 37, 39, 40
  effective jungle fighters 211
Gurney, Sir Henry
  assassination 93
  civil-military relations 95–6
  coercion as counter-insurgency
    strategy 65–6
  dispatch of May 1949 2, 213–215, 227
  emergency regulations 81, 82
  martial law 75
  reluctant to criticise security forces 171
  shoot to kill policy 85

Haganah 26, 47, 48
Hale, Leslie 233
Haifa 148
Handbook of Anti-Mau Mau Operations, 207
Harding, Field Marshal Lord 22, 91, 101,
    135, 190, 216
  coercion as counter-insurgency strategy
    67, 248
  collective punishments and fines 108
  death penalty 92
  detention without trial 113
  EOKA 64
  minimum force doctrine 82
  misbehaviour by security forces
    forbidden 140
  rough handling of captured insurgents 158–9
Hare, John 143
Harington, Sir Charles 129, 182
Head, Anthony 168, 191
Heath, Air Vice Marshal M. L. 127–8
'hearts and mind' strategy 2- 5, 64–5, 138,
    174–99, 247, 248, 251
Hinde, Maj.-Gen. 'Looney' 103
historiography of British counter-insurgency
    campaigns 2–8
history as a basis for counter-insurgency
    doctrine 252–3
Hola detention camp 163, 195
  Report on deaths of Mau Mau detainees 235
Hollingworth, Clare 199
hooded informers 107, 116
Hopkinson, Henry 190, 226
hydrogen bomb 227

Iban trackers, 152
ICRC 131, 142, 165–6, 230

investigations allegations brutality by security
    forces 145
'Ideal Type' of British counter-insurgency
    4–5, 247
  critics of 5–7
Ikhwan (the Moslem brotherhood) 26
ILO
  Canal Zone 231
  investigations allegations brutality by security
    forces 145
  Kenya 230
Imperial Defence College 214
*Imperial Policing and Duties in Aid of the Civil
    Power* (1949) 127, 203–4
India 39, 40
  North West Frontier 65
  indigenous collaborators 15–16
Indonesia 46, 47
  1965 coup 244–5
Indonesian Confrontation
  see Borneo
insurgency, definition 9
insurgents
  casualties 133
  denied political status by British officials
    59–61, 62–3
  British reluctant to accept their political
    agendas 63–4
Intelligence Corps 147
  interrogation training and techniques 159–62
intelligence systems 19–21, 33, 248
  contribution to security forces' successes 32
  intelligence systems and relations between
    police, army and Special Branch 27–28
  'Malayan model' 28–29
interrogation
  in-depth interrogation, techniques 159–62
  Judges rules 88–9
  tactical interrogation by army and
    police 157–9
  torture, 140, 141, 142, 147, 160–2
Irgun 148, 224
Irish War of Independence (1919–21) 166
Iraq, British campaign in 11, 253–5
  treatment of detainees 162
Ismalia 114, 136, 177
IZL 47

Jackson, Ashley, 5
Jackson, Gen. Sir William 4
Jagan, Cheddi 191
Jebel Akhdar 53
  see also Oman
Jenkin, Sir William 31
Jerusalem 75–76
Jewish Agency 12, 47, 60
Johnson, W. J. 214
Johore 182
Joint Intelligence Committee 20, 228